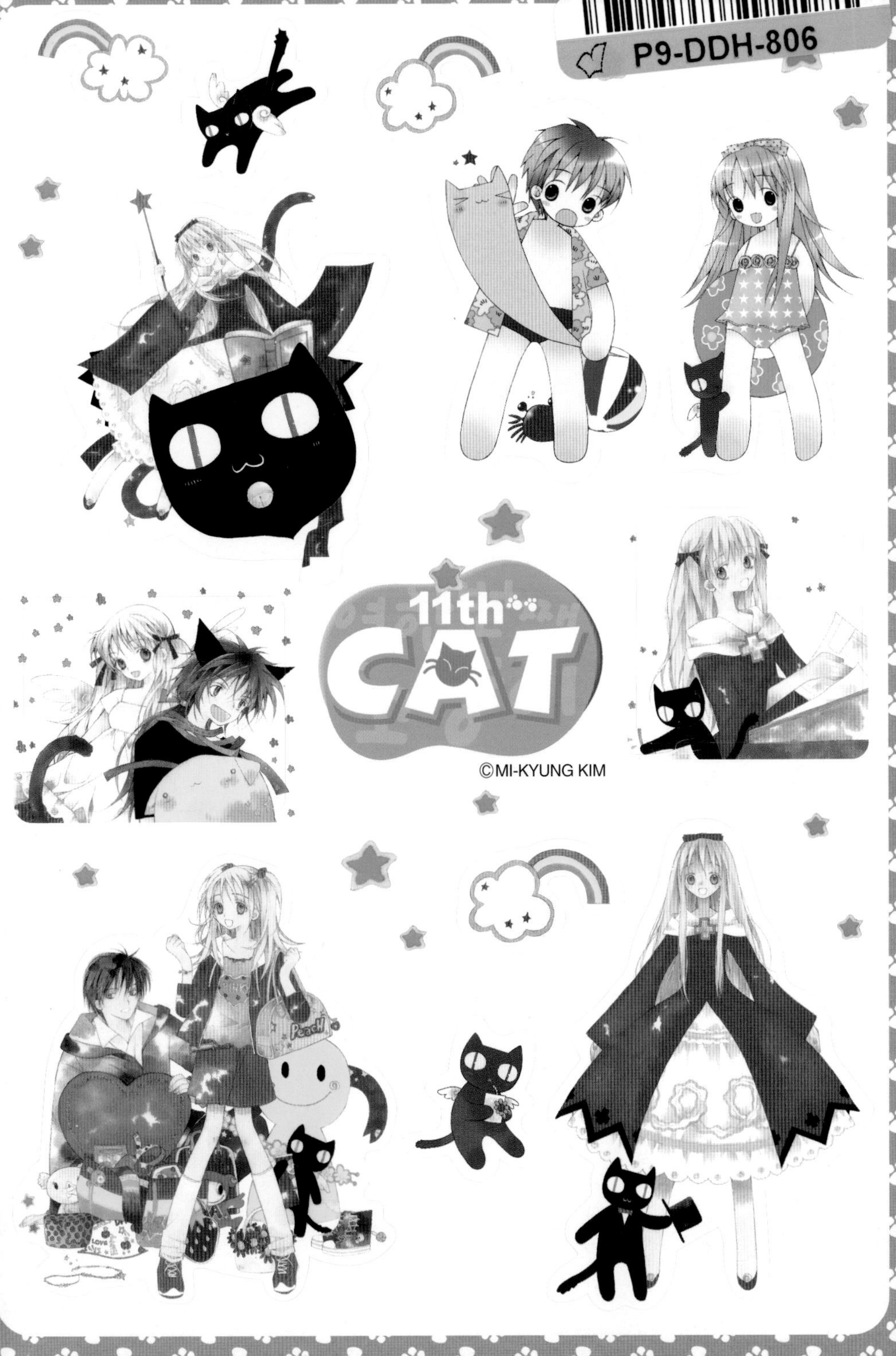
11th
CAT
©MI-KYUNG KIM
Peach

iginal · Danbi Original · Danbi Original · Danbi Original · Danbi Original · Danbi Original · D

11th CAT

vol.1

Kim MiKyung

ice Kunion

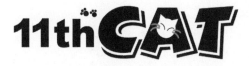

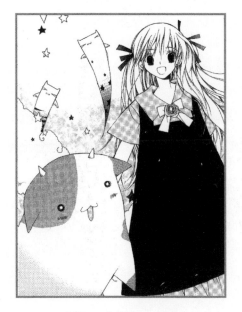

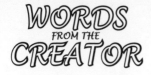

WORDS FROM THE CREATOR

HEY! MY BOOK'S FINALLY OUT! (WELL, NOT REALLY SINCE I'M WRITING THIS NOW...BUT, YOU KNOW WHAT I MEAN).

A BIG THANK'S TO EVERYONE WHO'S ALWAYS BEEN THERE FOR ME. I WANT TO MENTION EVERY ONE OF YOU, BUT THERE ARE SO MANY... *COUGH*

I DIDN'T WANT ANY PETS UNTIL I FINALLY SETTLED DOWN ON MY OWN, BUT MY FIRST CAT, NENE, JUST CRAWLED IN MY WINDOW ONE DAY. HOW COULD I KICK HIM OUT? SO NOW WE LIVE TOGETHER. (ALBEIT HE'S AN ALOOF AND EGOTISTICAL MEANIE! T.T)

THEN CAME MITZ, SHY AND LONELY. AND THE CHARMING PICO, WHOM EVERYONE ADORES. AND FINALLY, MY NEW BABY. HER DELICATE HEALTH MAKES ME A WORRYWART.

OH! AND I ALMOST FORGOT... AGAIN! THE TITLE OF THIS SERIES, "THE 11TH CAT" COMES FROM THE NAME OF AN INTERNET SHOPPING MALL. HTTP://WWW.10THCAT.COM/ THERE ARE SOOO MANY CUTE THINGS THERE!

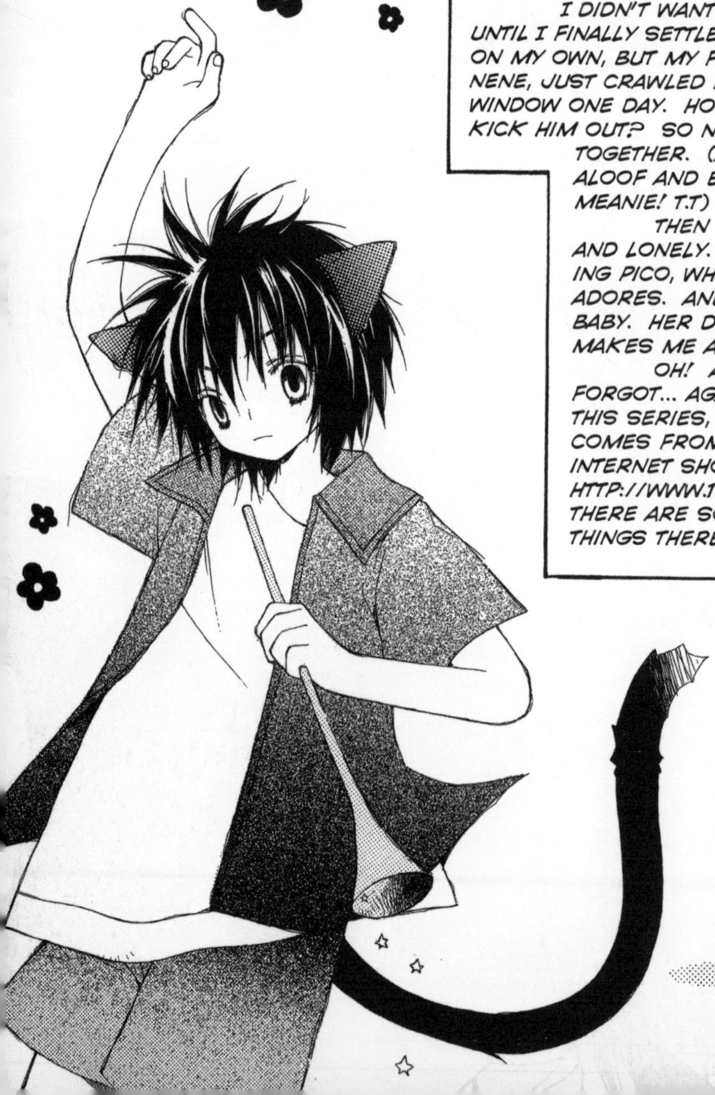

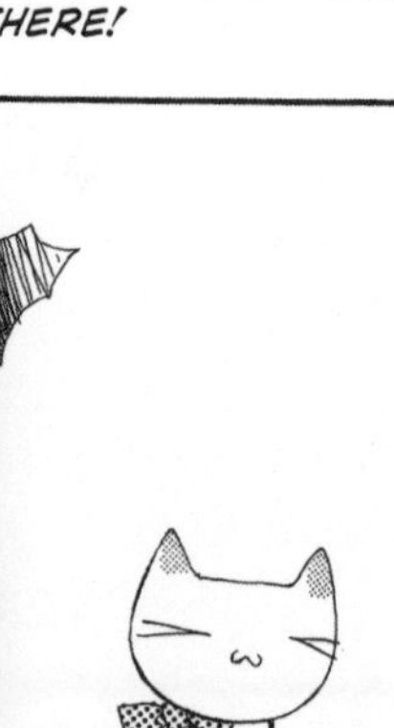

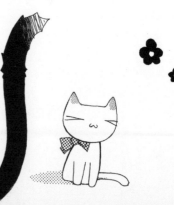

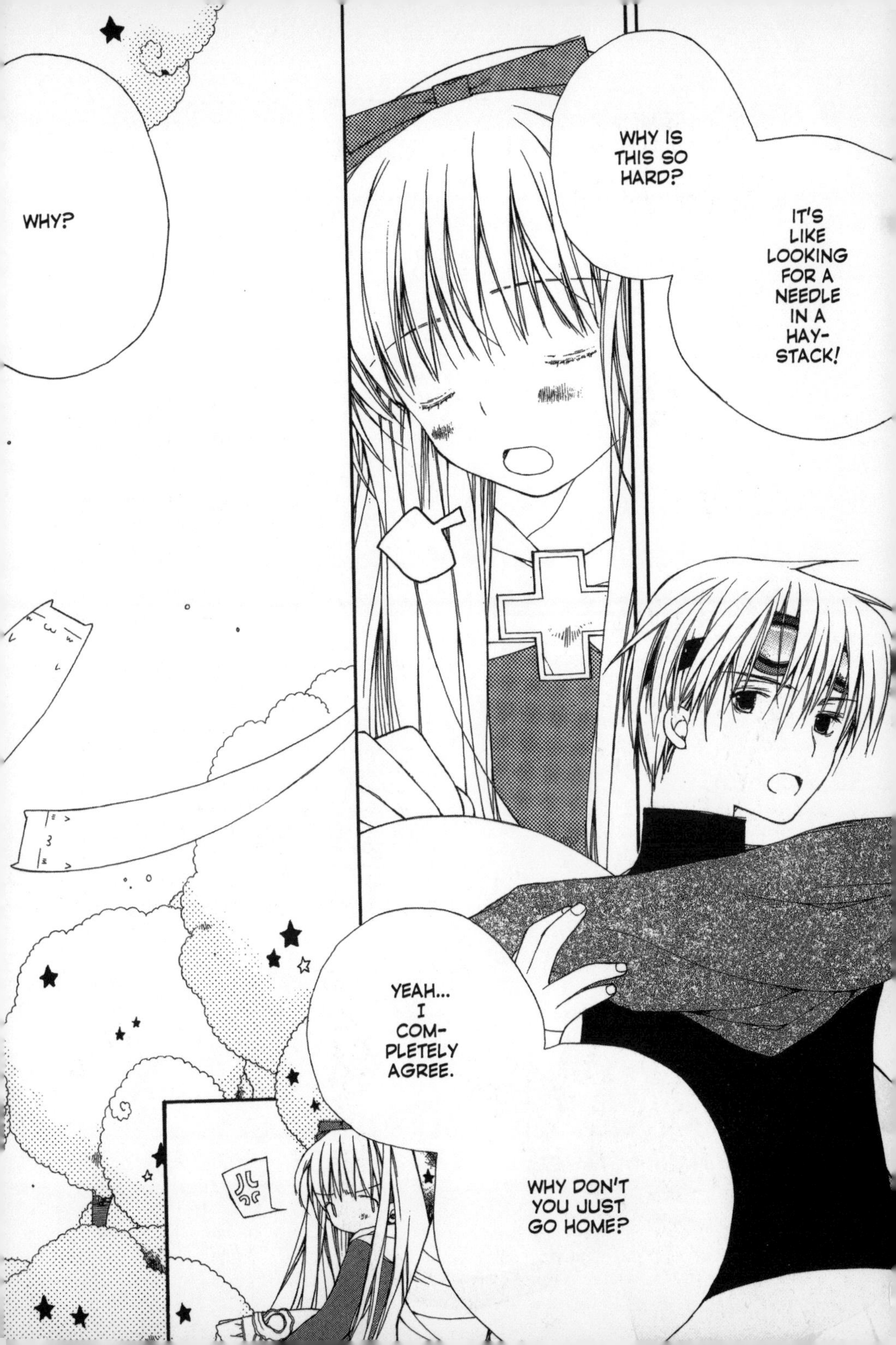
WHY?
WHY IS THIS SO HARD?
IT'S LIKE LOOKING FOR A NEEDLE IN A HAY-STACK!
YEAH... I COM-PLETELY AGREE.
WHY DON'T YOU JUST GO HOME?

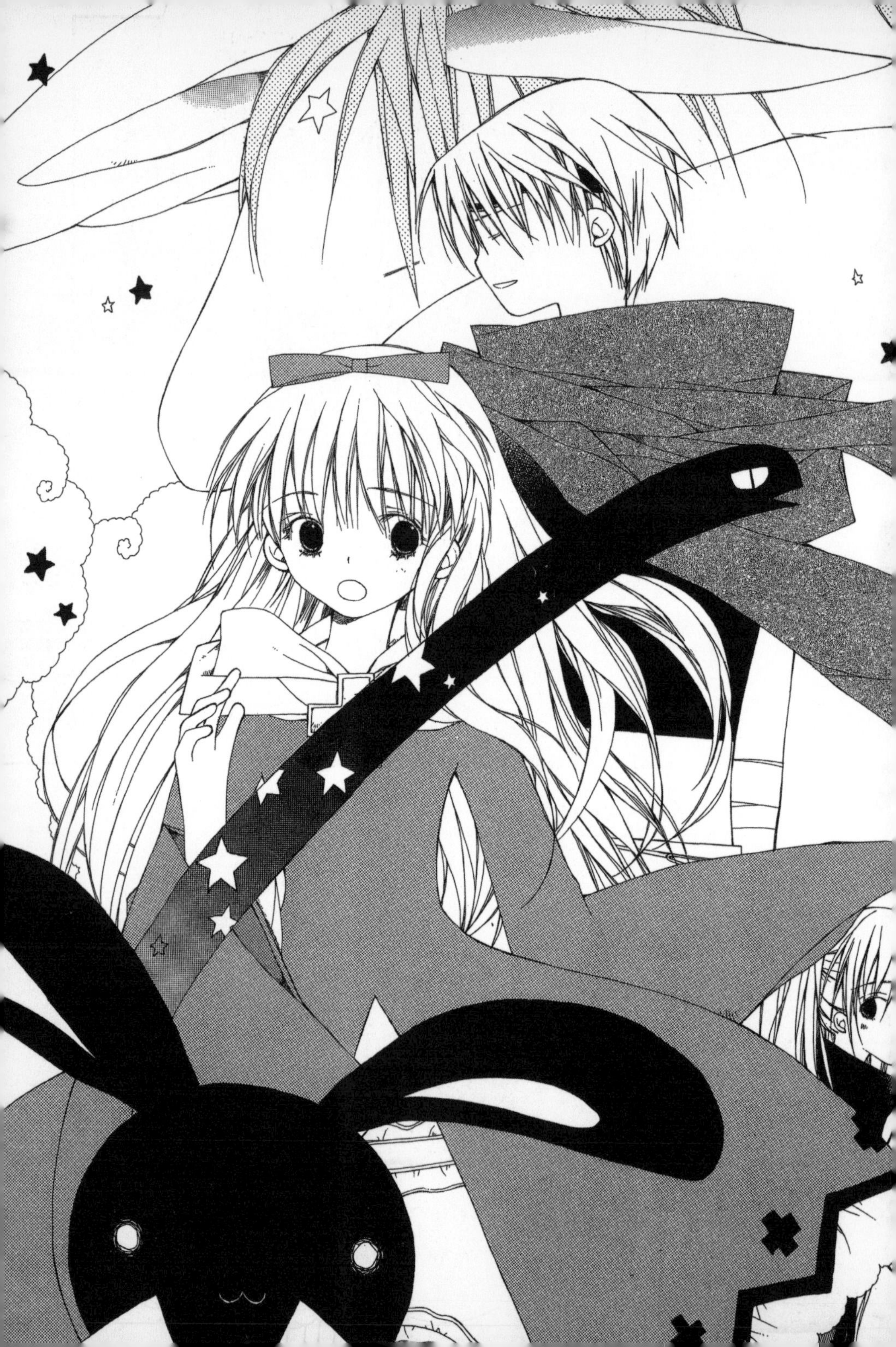

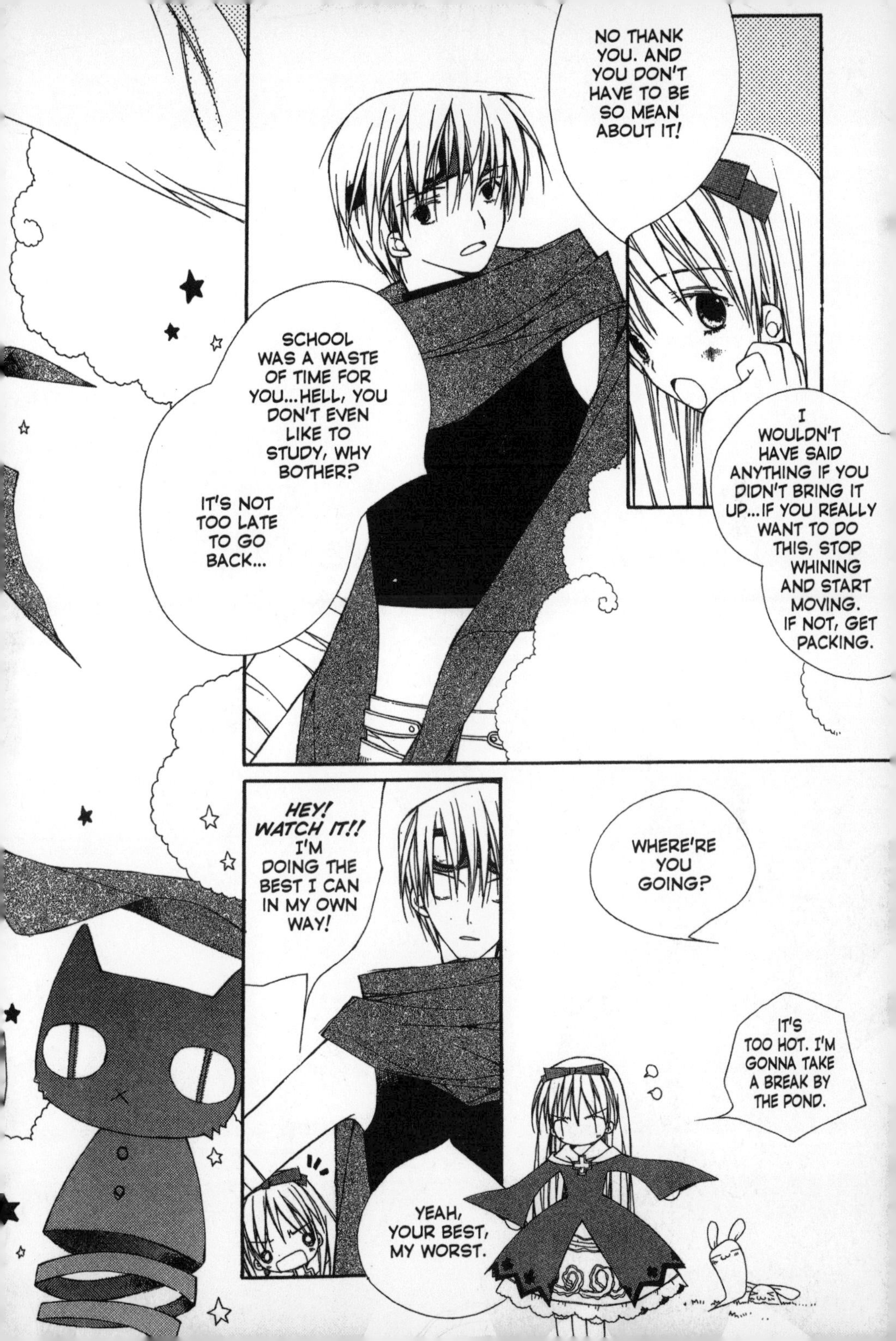
SCHOOL WAS A WASTE OF TIME FOR YOU...HELL, YOU DON'T EVEN LIKE TO STUDY, WHY BOTHER?
IT'S NOT TOO LATE TO GO BACK...
NO THANK YOU. AND YOU DON'T HAVE TO BE SO MEAN ABOUT IT!
I WOULDN'T HAVE SAID ANYTHING IF YOU DIDN'T BRING IT UP...IF YOU REALLY WANT TO DO THIS, STOP WHINING AND START MOVING. IF NOT, GET PACKING.
HEY! WATCH IT!! I'M DOING THE BEST I CAN IN MY OWN WAY!
YEAH, YOUR BEST, MY WORST.
WHERE'RE YOU GOING?
IT'S TOO HOT. I'M GONNA TAKE A BREAK BY THE POND.

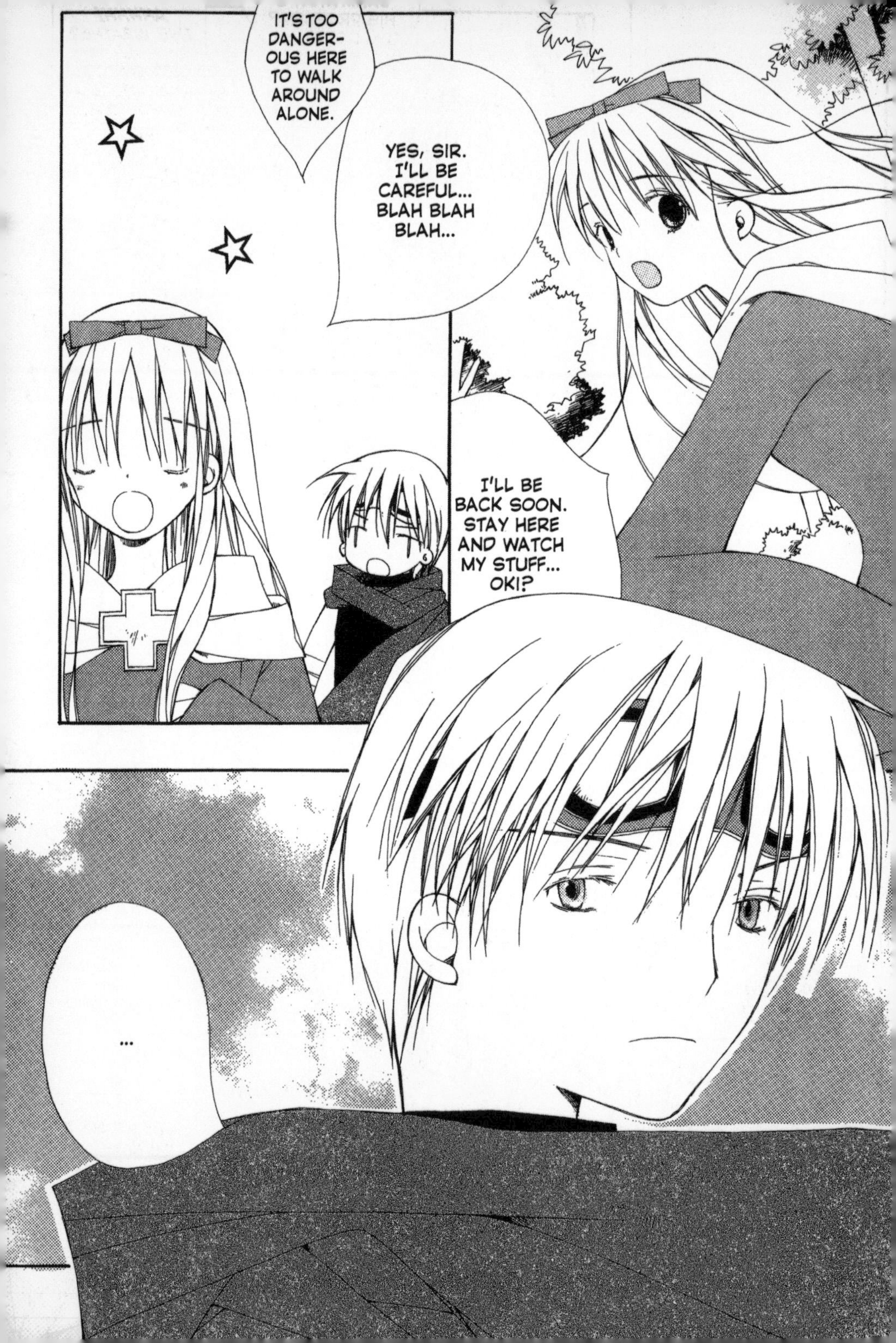
IT'S TOO DANGER-OUS HERE TO WALK AROUND ALONE.
YES, SIR. I'LL BE CAREFUL... BLAH BLAH BLAH...
I'LL BE BACK SOON. STAY HERE AND WATCH MY STUFF... OK!?
...

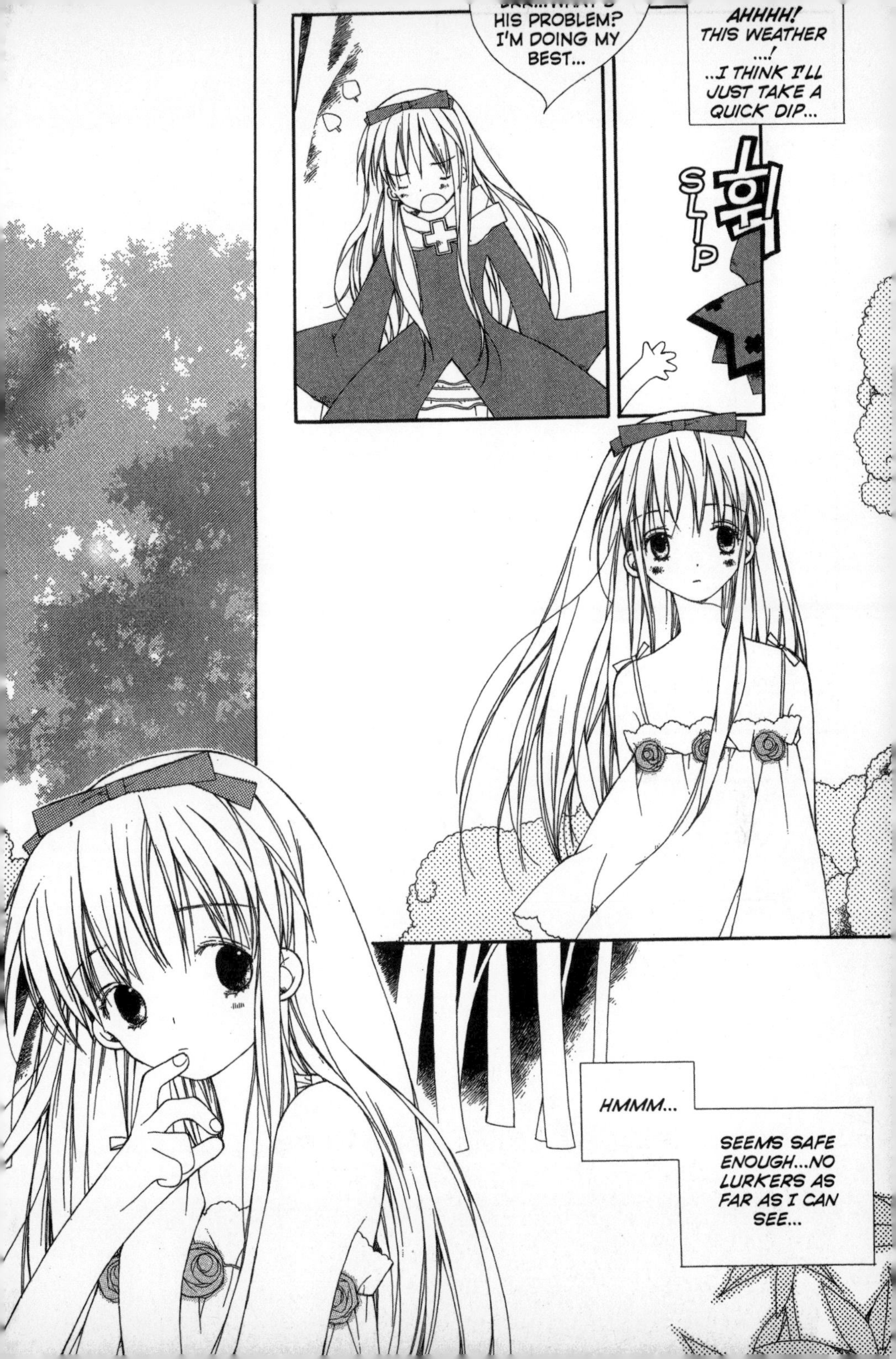
HIS PROBLEM? I'M DOING MY BEST...
AHHHH! THIS WEATHER ...! ...I THINK I'LL JUST TAKE A QUICK DIP...
휘
SLIP
HMMM...
SEEMS SAFE ENOUGH...NO LURKERS AS FAR AS I CAN SEE...

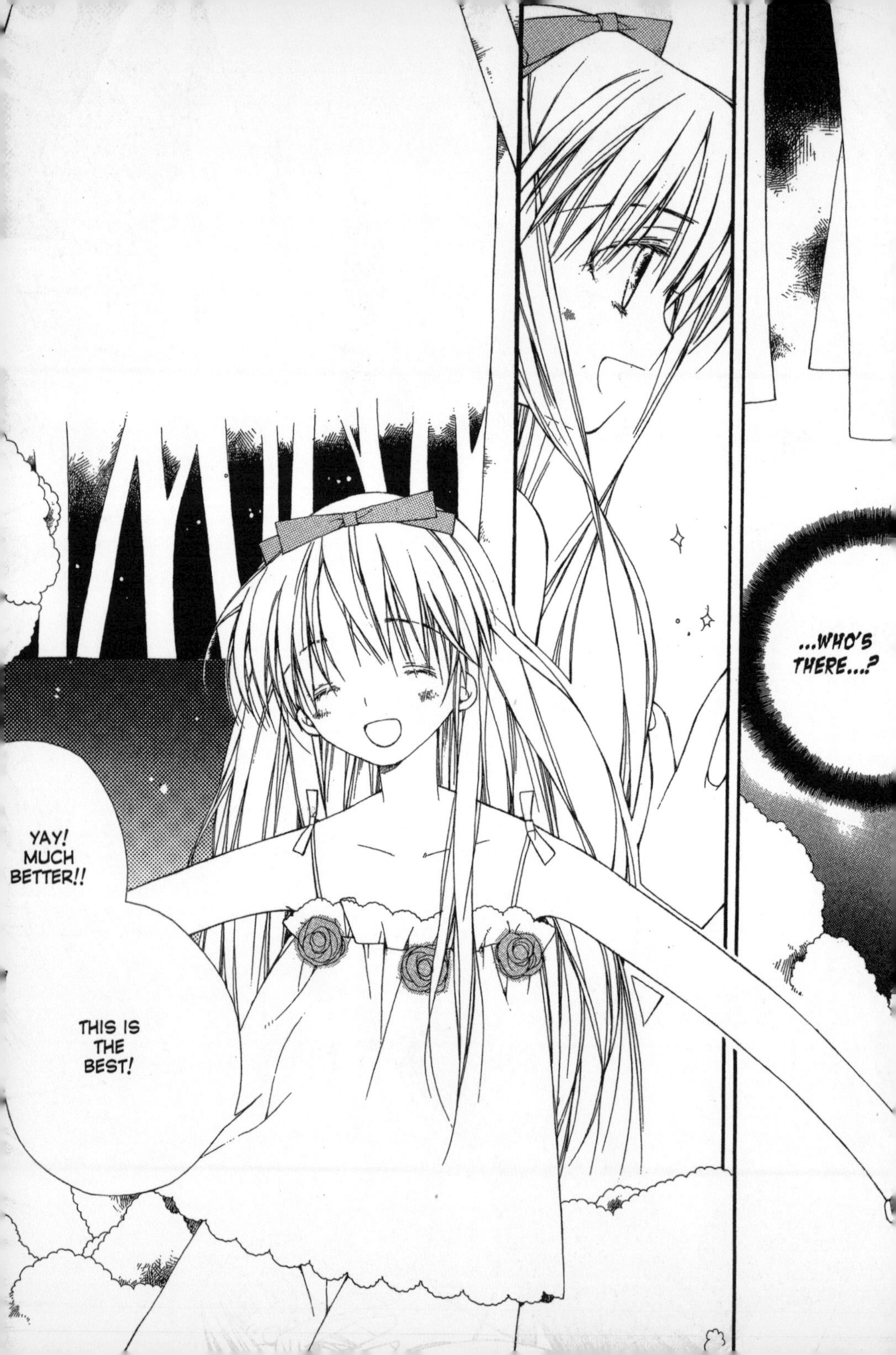
YAY! MUCH BETTER!!
THIS IS THE BEST!
...WHO'S THERE...?

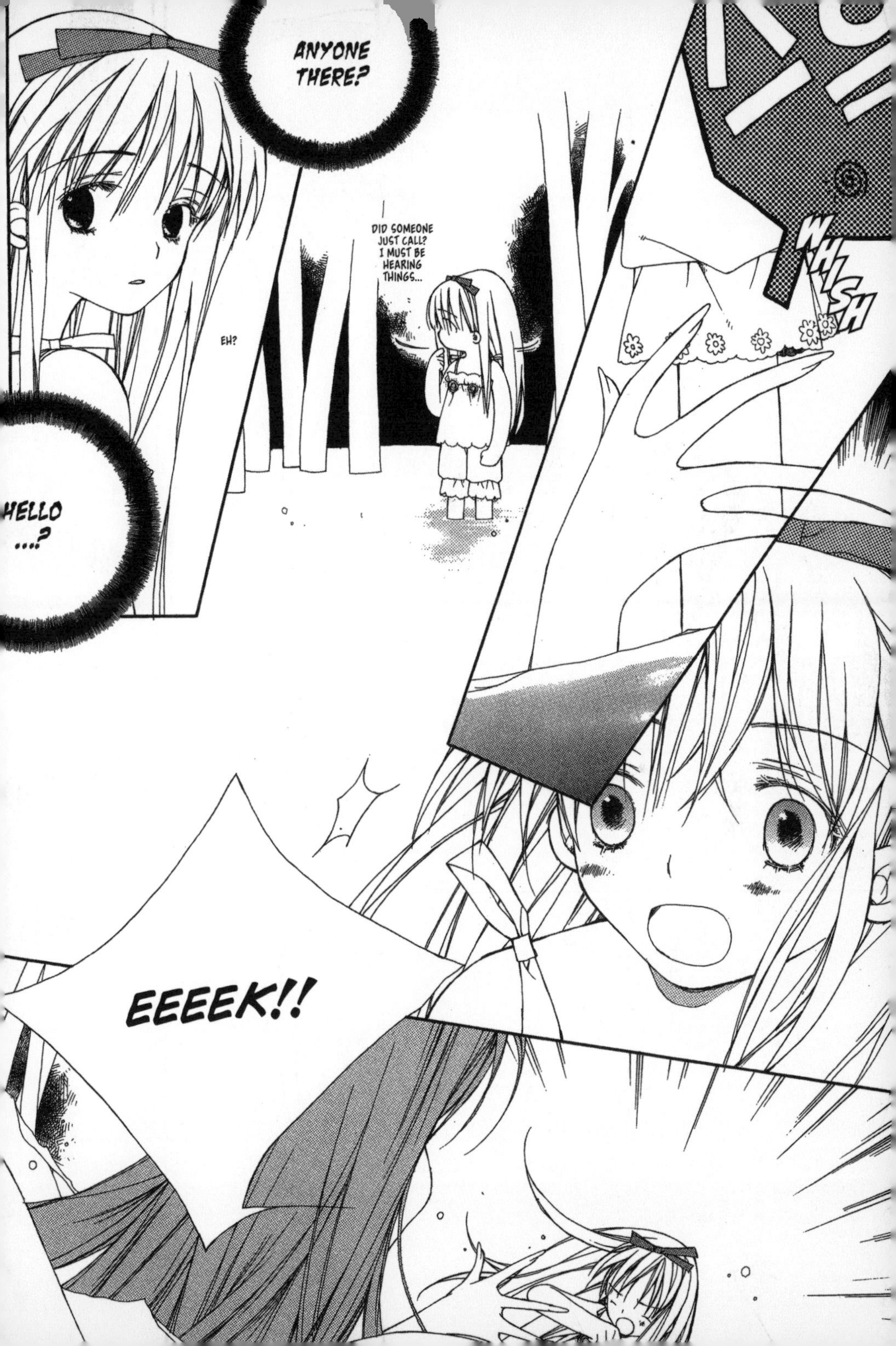
ANYONE THERE?
HELLO ...?
EH?
DID SOMEONE JUST CALL? I MUST BE HEARING THINGS...
WHISH
EEEEK!!

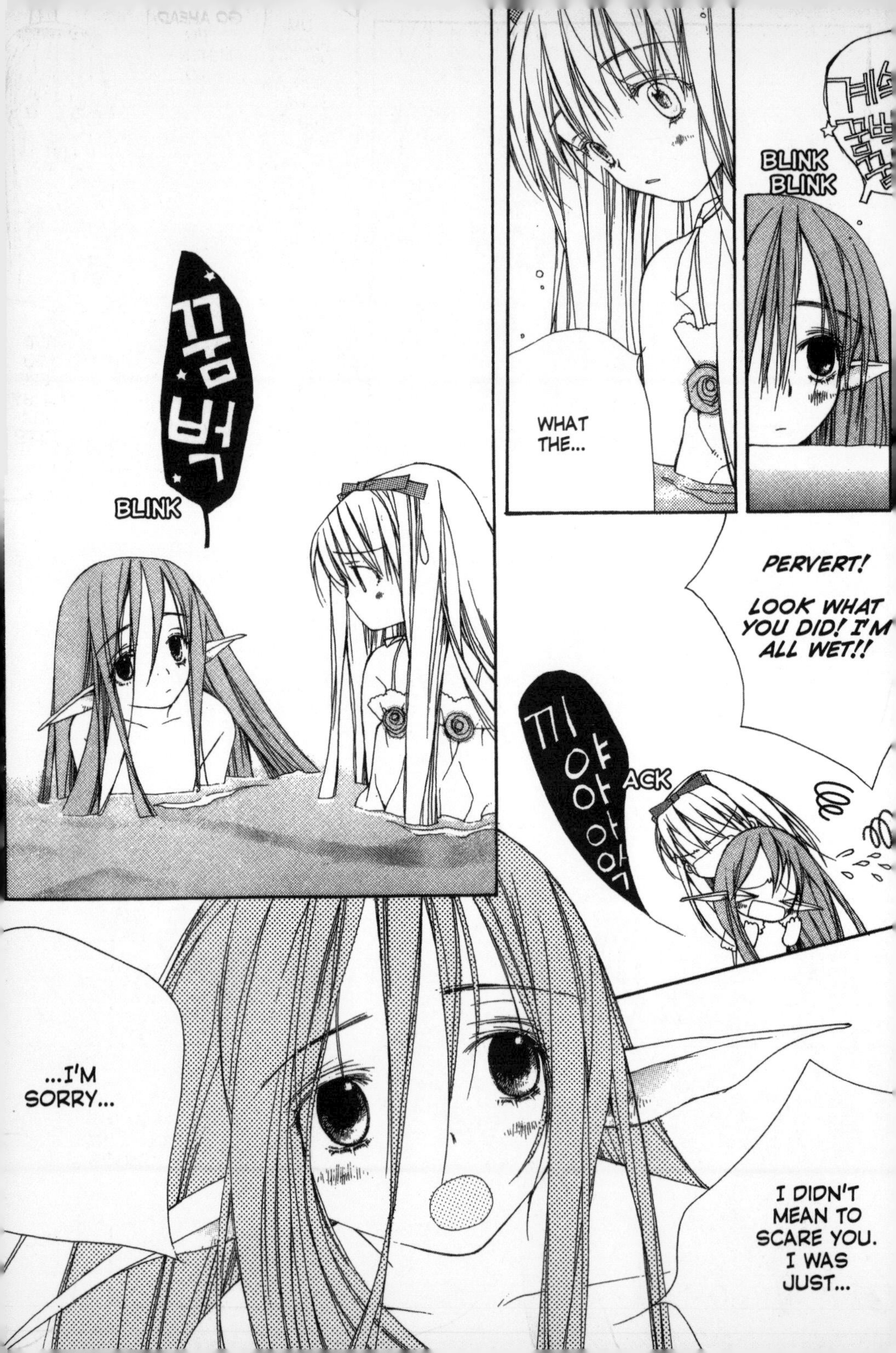

깜박
BLINK
WHAT THE...
깜빡
BLINK BLINK
PERVERT!
LOOK WHAT YOU DID! I'M ALL WET!!
끼야아아악
ACK
...I'M SORRY...
I DIDN'T MEAN TO SCARE YOU. I WAS JUST...

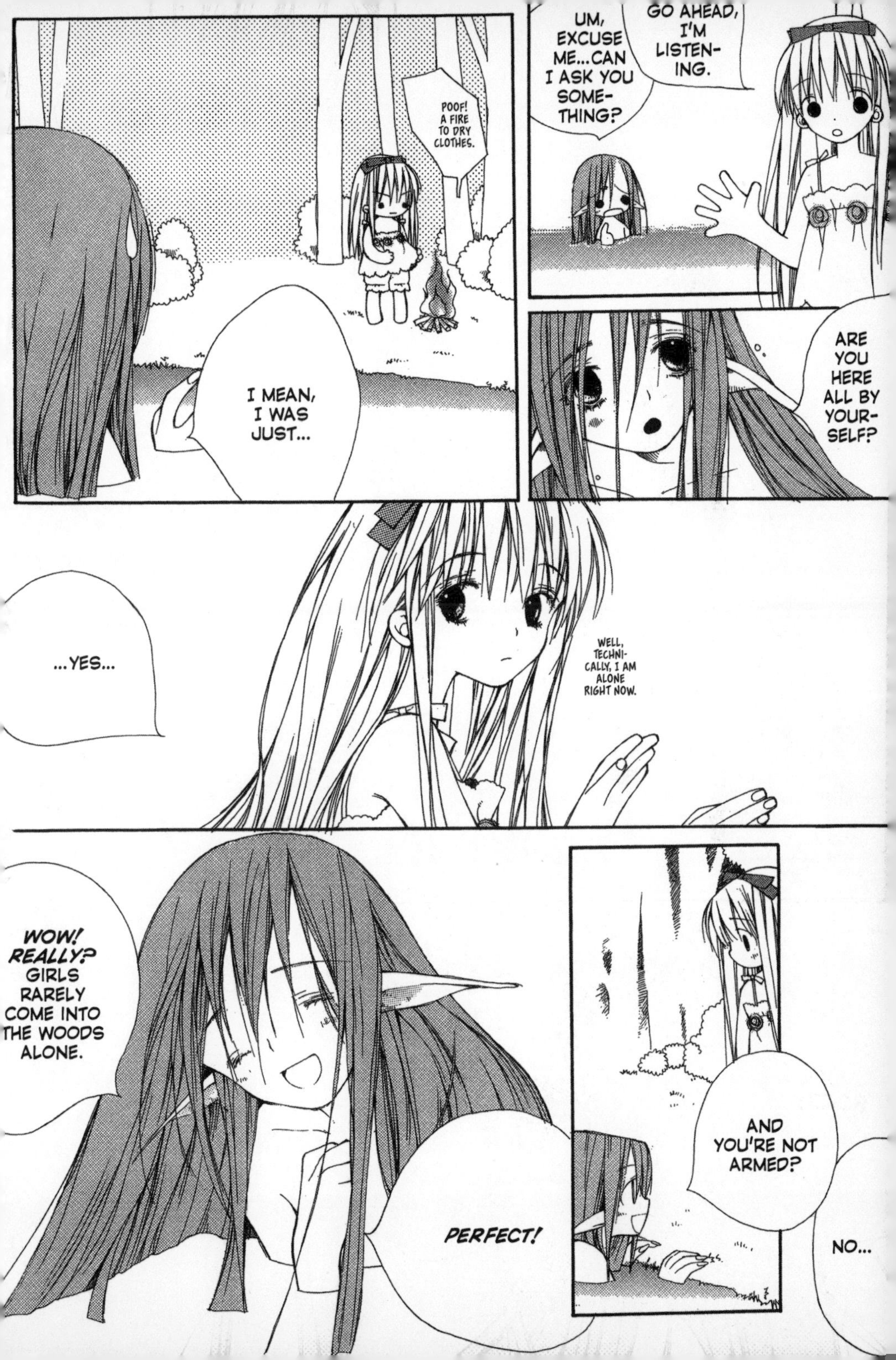
POOF! A FIRE TO DRY CLOTHES.
I MEAN, I WAS JUST...
UM, EXCUSE ME...CAN I ASK YOU SOME-THING?
GO AHEAD, I'M LISTEN-ING.
ARE YOU HERE ALL BY YOUR-SELF?
...YES...
WELL, TECHNI-CALLY, I AM ALONE RIGHT NOW.
WOW! REALLY? GIRLS RARELY COME INTO THE WOODS ALONE.
PERFECT!
AND YOU'RE NOT ARMED?
NO...

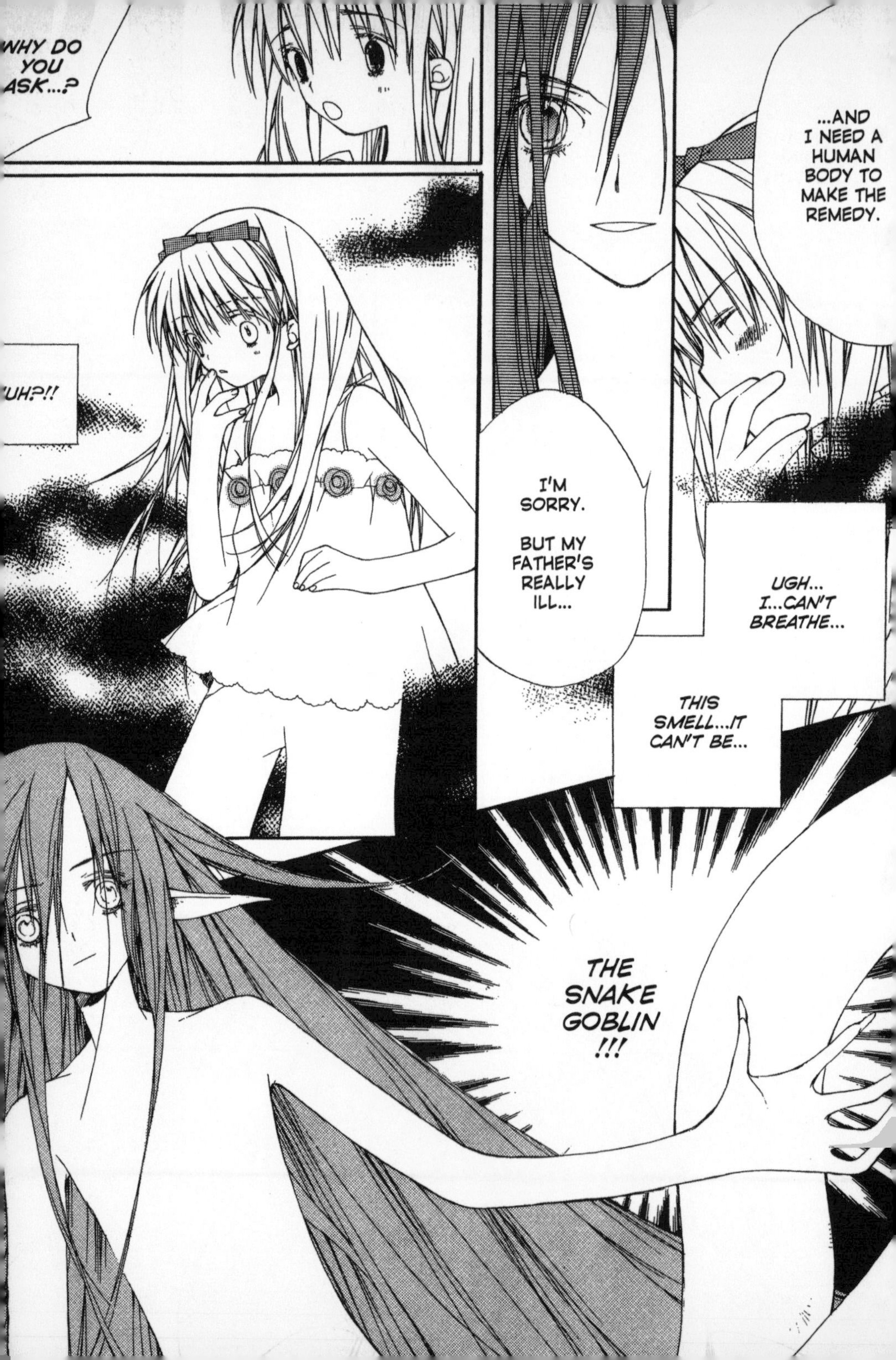

WHY DO YOU ASK...?
...AND I NEED A HUMAN BODY TO MAKE THE REMEDY.
UH?!!
I'M SORRY.
BUT MY FATHER'S REALLY ILL...
UGH... I...CAN'T BREATHE...
THIS SMELL...IT CAN'T BE...
THE SNAKE GOBLIN!!!

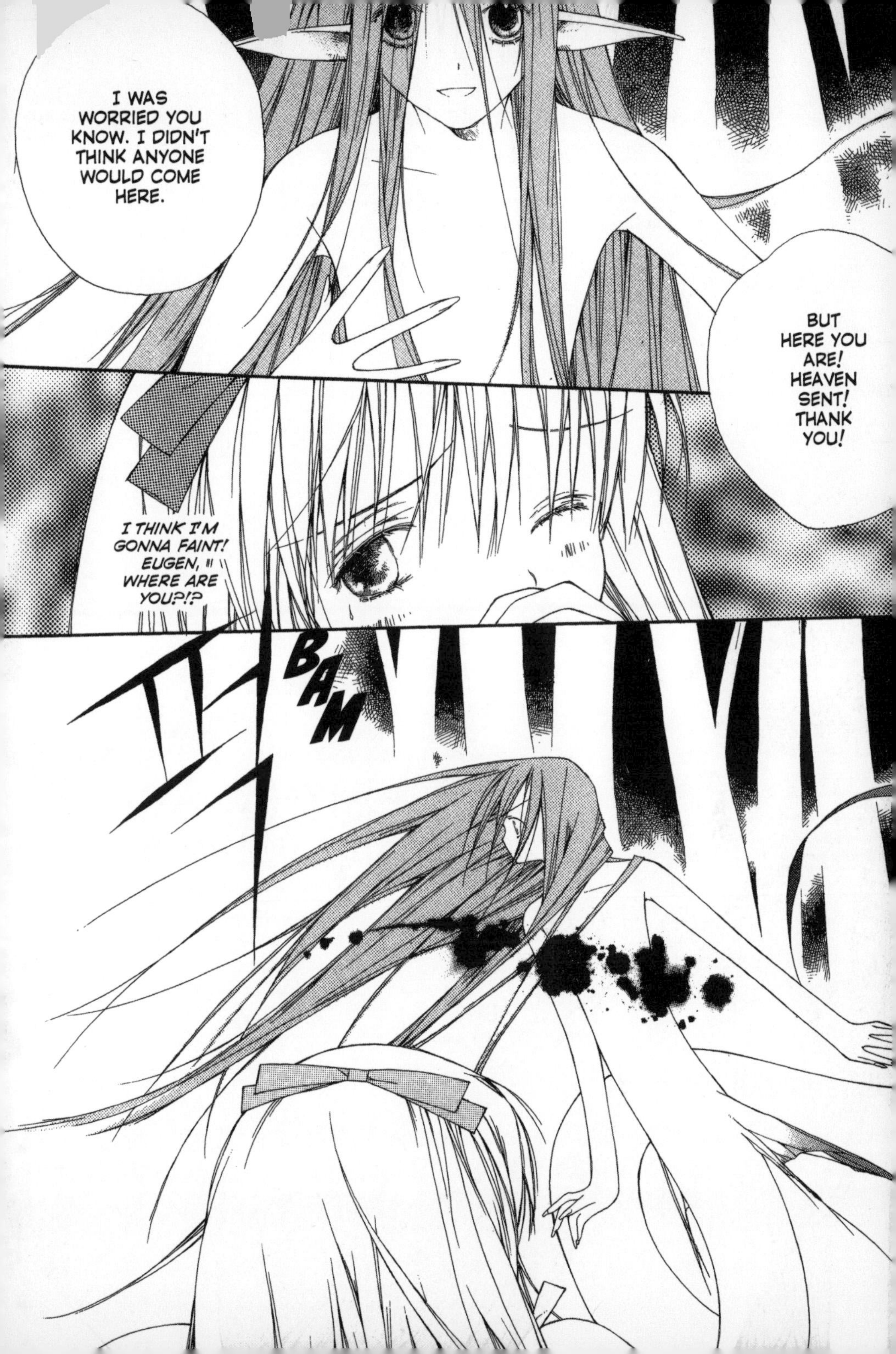
I WAS WORRIED YOU KNOW. I DIDN'T THINK ANYONE WOULD COME HERE.
BUT HERE YOU ARE! HEAVEN SENT! THANK YOU!
I THINK I'M GONNA FAINT! EUGEN, WHERE ARE YOU?!?
BAM

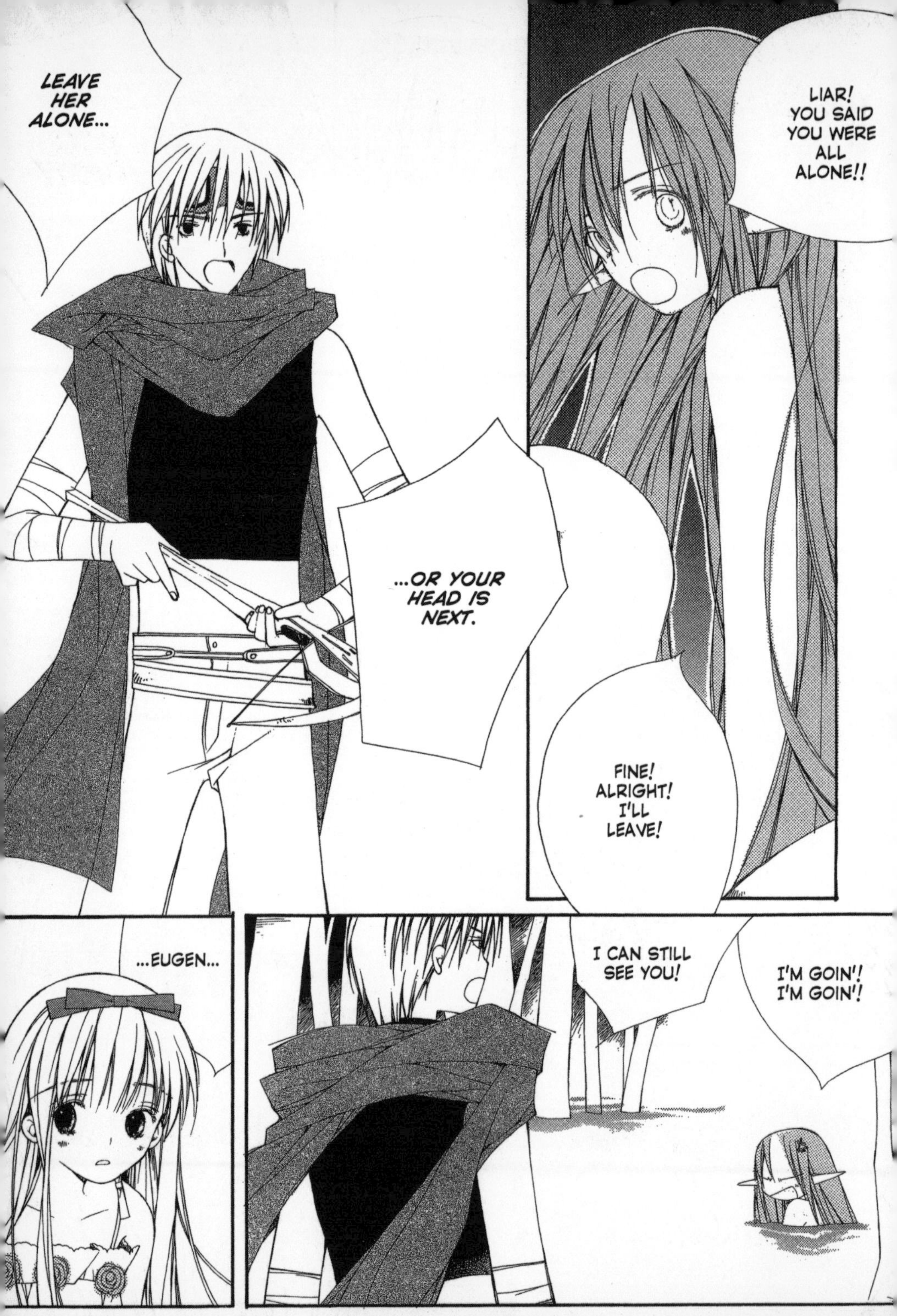
LEAVE HER ALONE...
...OR YOUR HEAD IS NEXT.
LIAR! YOU SAID YOU WERE ALL ALONE!!
FINE! ALRIGHT! I'LL LEAVE!
...EUGEN...
I CAN STILL SEE YOU!
I'M GOIN'! I'M GOIN'!

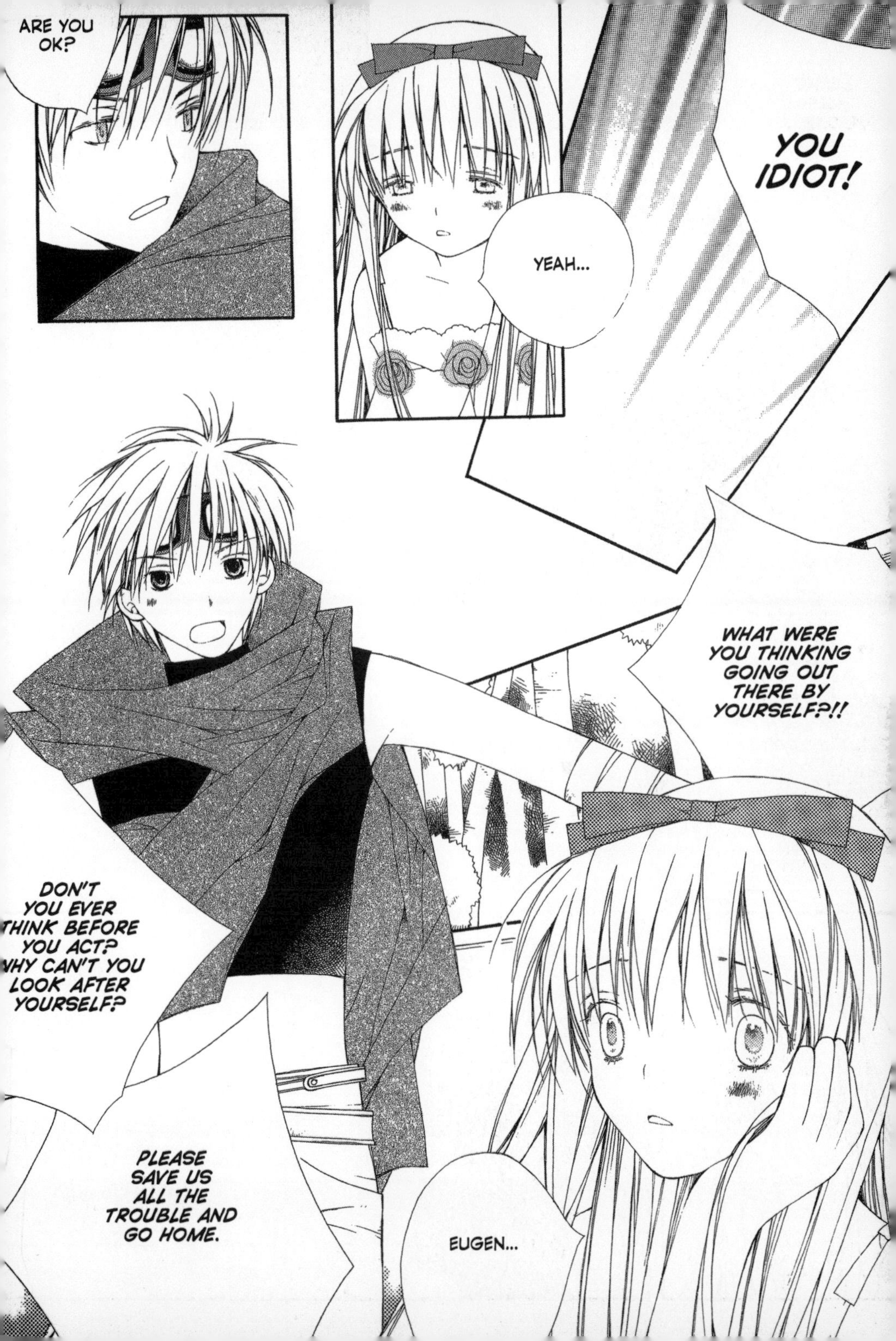

ARE YOU OK?
YEAH...
YOU IDIOT!
WHAT WERE YOU THINKING GOING OUT THERE BY YOURSELF?!!
DON'T YOU EVER THINK BEFORE YOU ACT? WHY CAN'T YOU LOOK AFTER YOURSELF?
PLEASE SAVE US ALL THE TROUBLE AND GO HOME.
EUGEN...

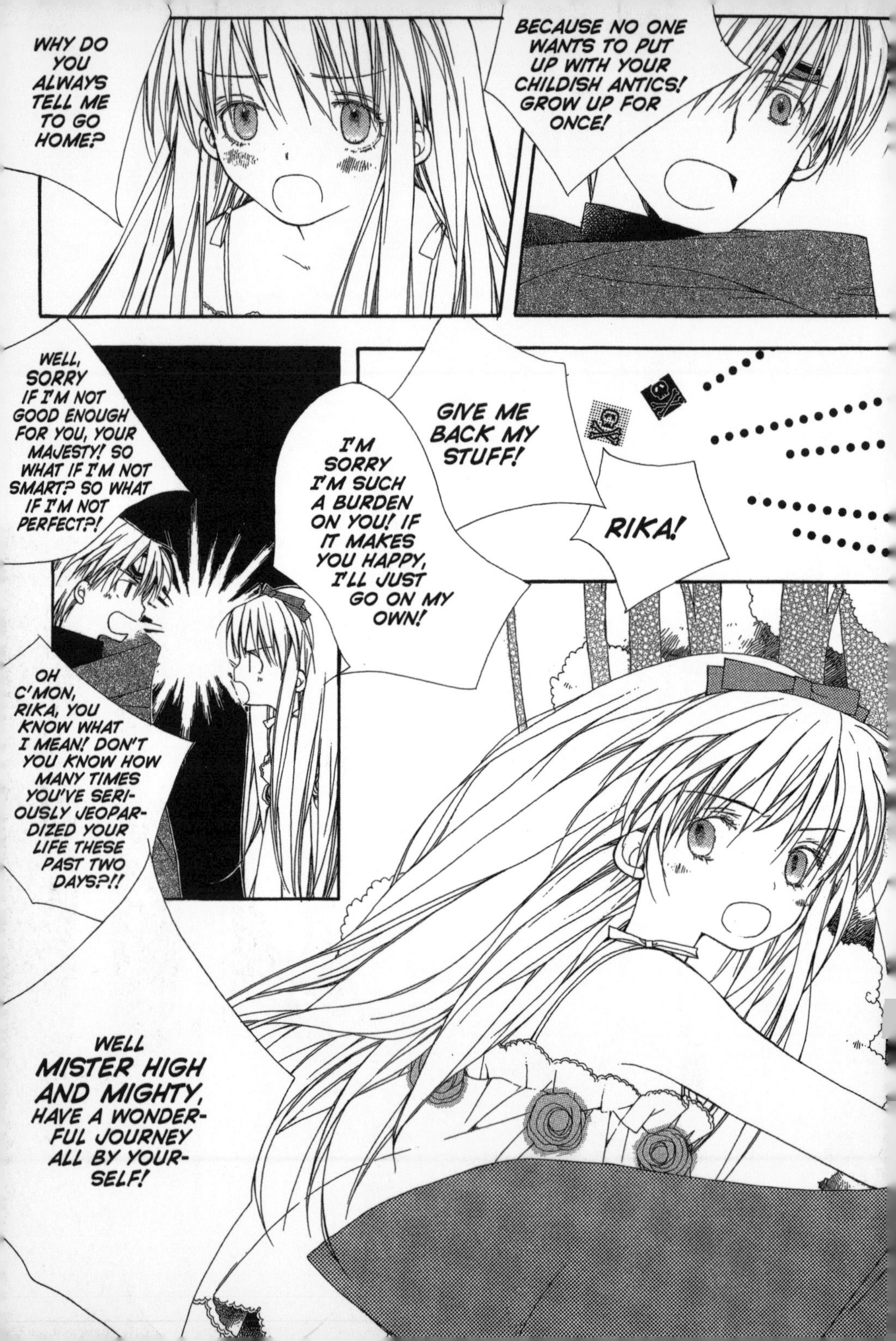
WHY DO YOU ALWAYS TELL ME TO GO HOME?
BECAUSE NO ONE WANTS TO PUT UP WITH YOUR CHILDISH ANTICS! GROW UP FOR ONCE!
WELL, SORRY IF I'M NOT GOOD ENOUGH FOR YOU, YOUR MAJESTY! SO WHAT IF I'M NOT SMART? SO WHAT IF I'M NOT PERFECT?!
I'M SORRY I'M SUCH A BURDEN ON YOU! IF IT MAKES YOU HAPPY, I'LL JUST GO ON MY OWN!
OH C'MON, RIKA, YOU KNOW WHAT I MEAN! DON'T YOU KNOW HOW MANY TIMES YOU'VE SERIOUSLY JEOPARDIZED YOUR LIFE THESE PAST TWO DAYS?!!
GIVE ME BACK MY STUFF!
......
RIKA!
WELL MISTER HIGH AND MIGHTY, HAVE A WONDERFUL JOURNEY ALL BY YOURSELF!

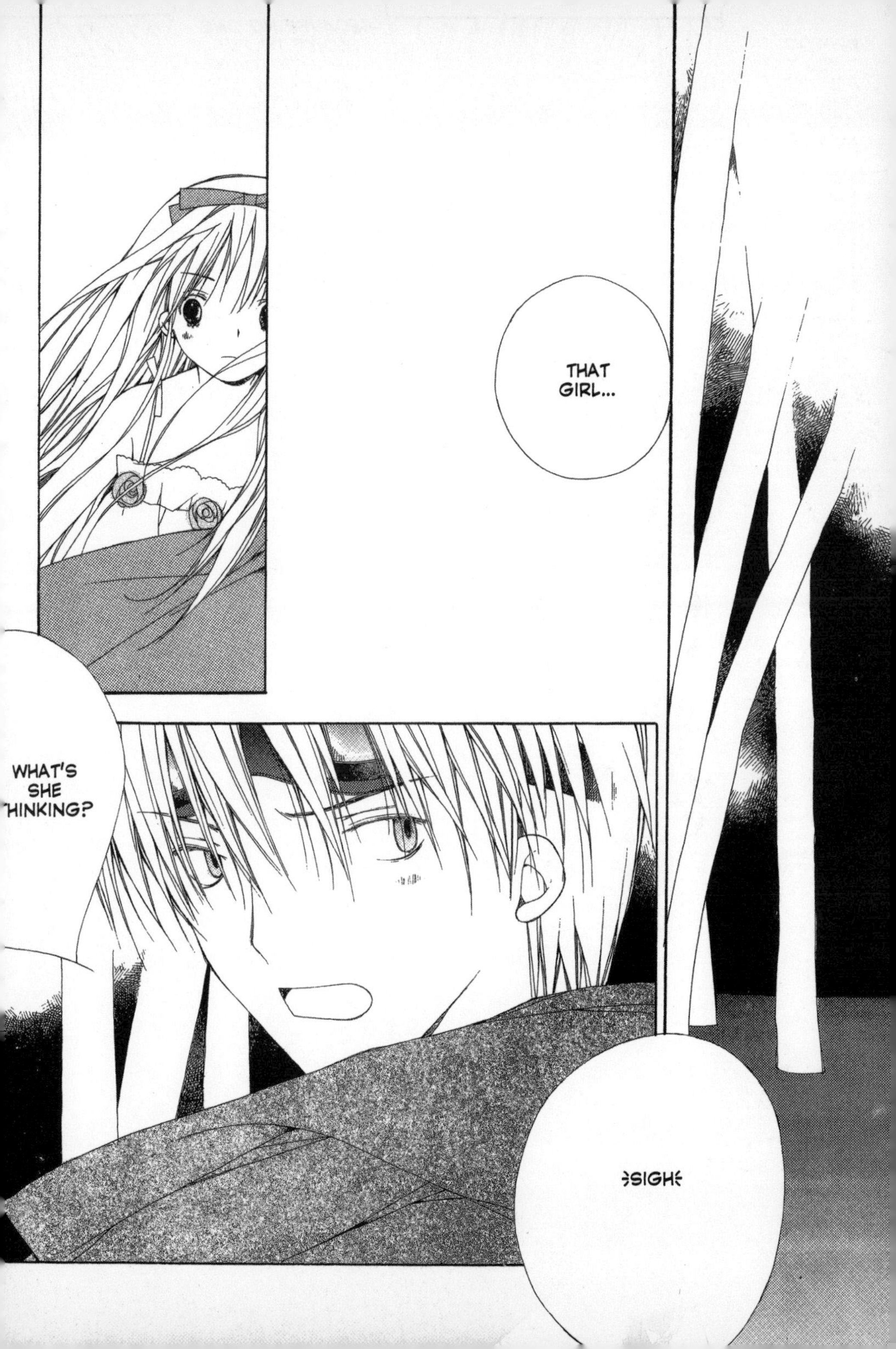

THAT GIRL...
WHAT'S SHE THINKING?
SIGH

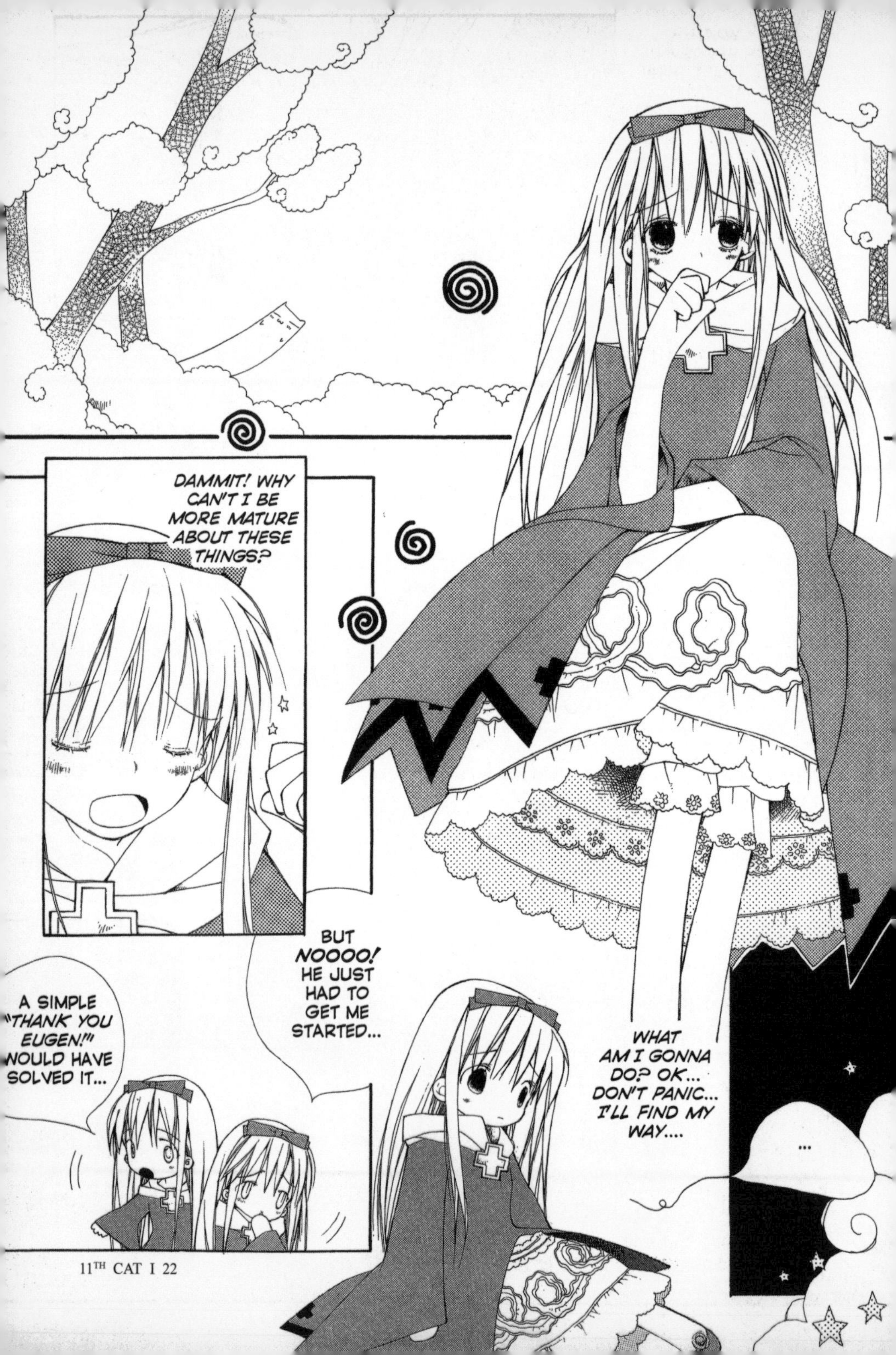
DAMMIT! WHY CAN'T I BE MORE MATURE ABOUT THESE THINGS?
A SIMPLE "THANK YOU EUGEN!" WOULD HAVE SOLVED IT...
BUT NOOOO! HE JUST HAD TO GET ME STARTED...
WHAT AM I GONNA DO? OK... DON'T PANIC... I'LL FIND MY WAY....
...

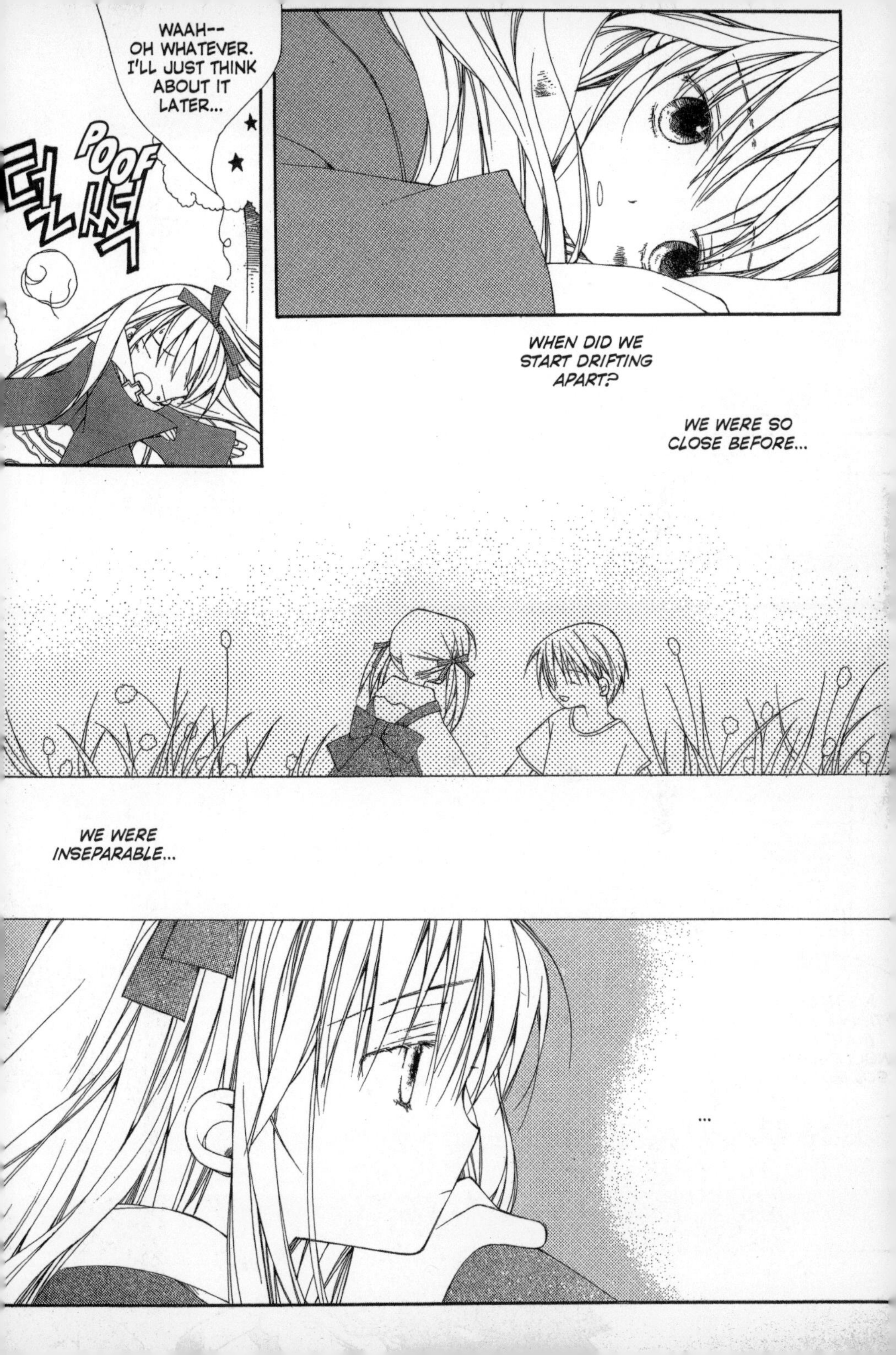
WAAH-- OH WHATEVER. I'LL JUST THINK ABOUT IT LATER...
POOF
WHEN DID WE START DRIFTING APART?
WE WERE SO CLOSE BEFORE...
WE WERE INSEPARABLE...
...

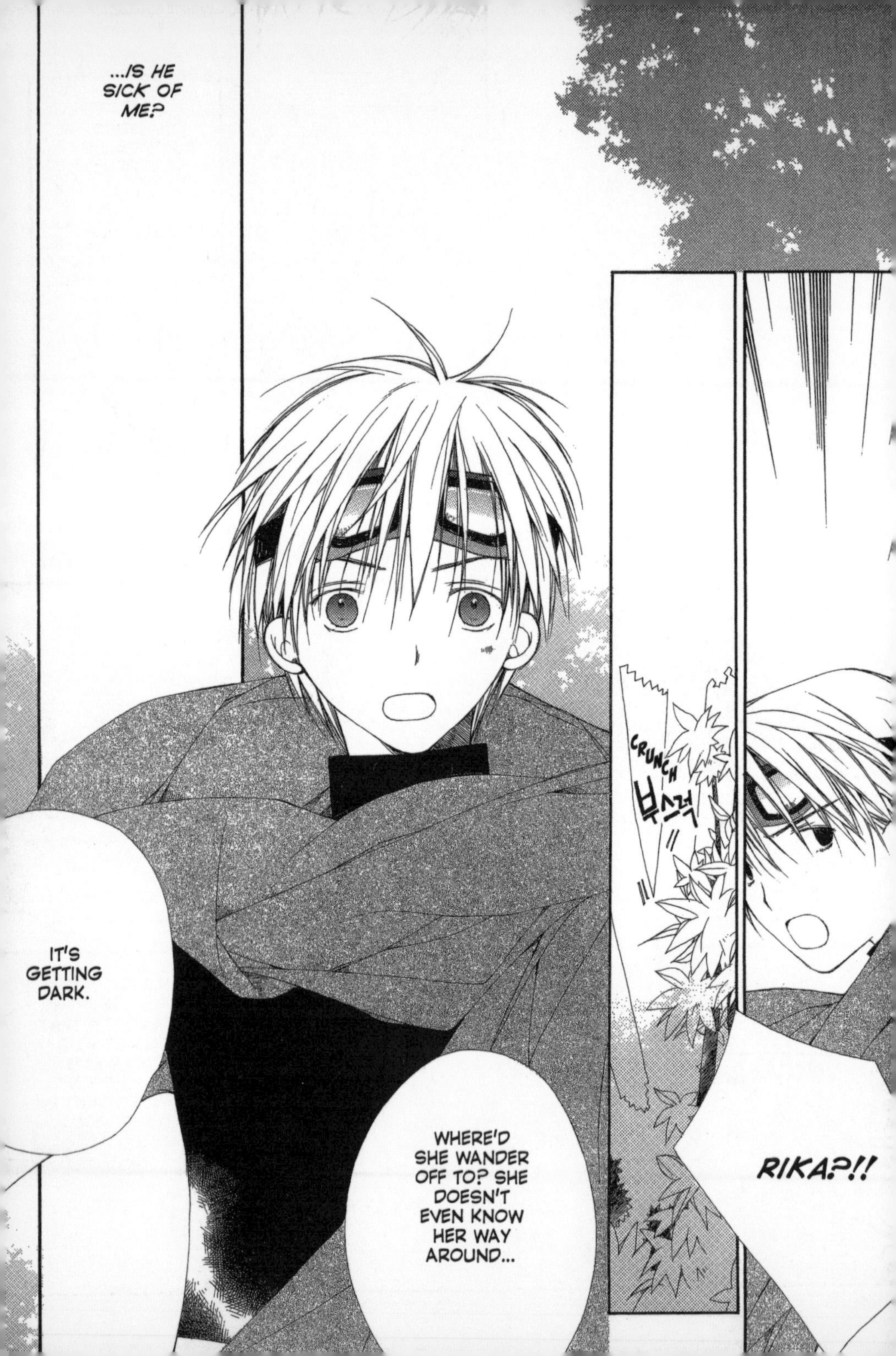
...IS HE SICK OF ME?
IT'S GETTING DARK.
WHERE'D SHE WANDER OFF TO? SHE DOESN'T EVEN KNOW HER WAY AROUND...
CRUNCH
부스럭
RIKA?!!

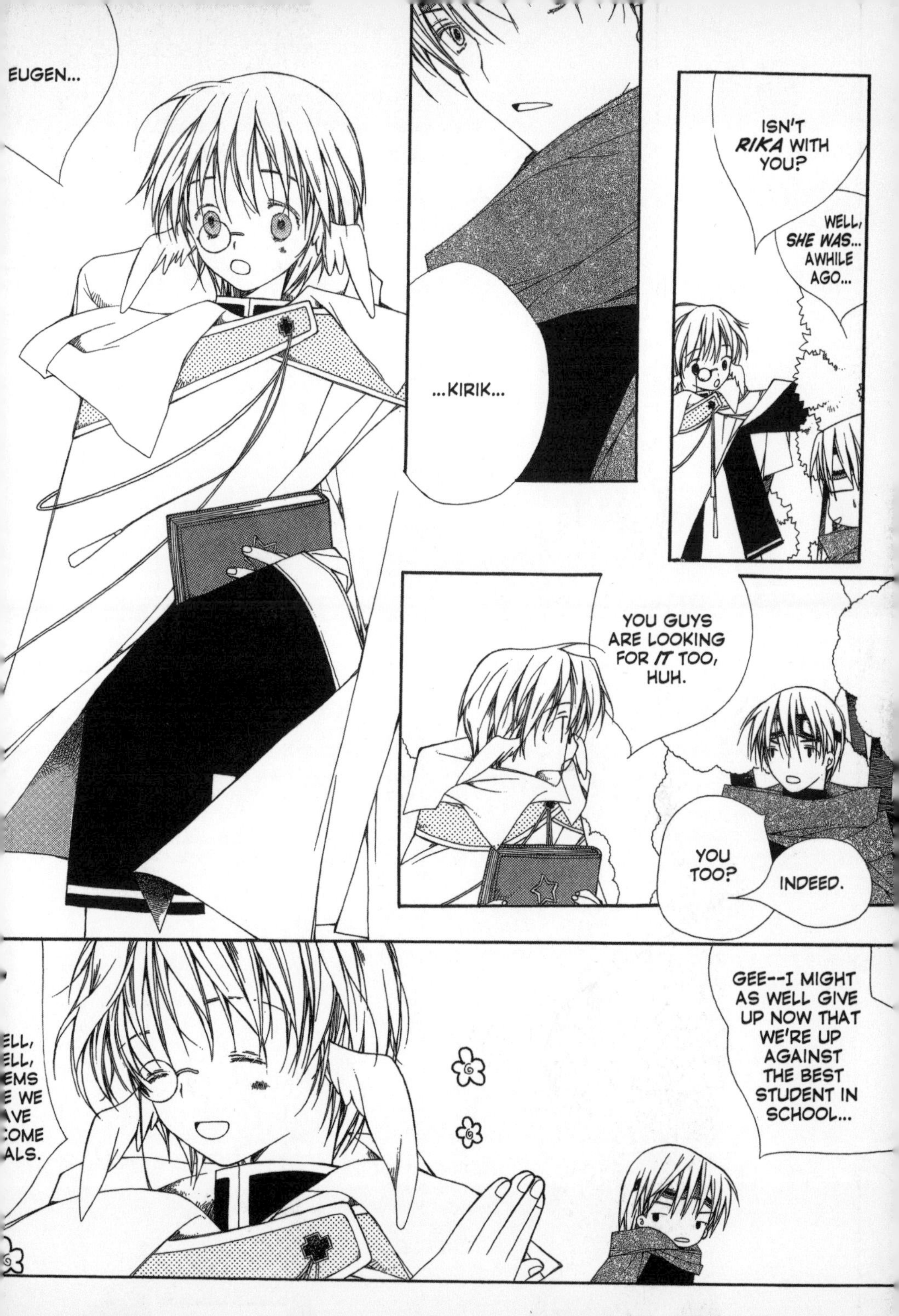
EUGEN...
...KIRIK...
ISN'T *RIKA* WITH YOU?
WELL, *SHE WAS*... AWHILE AGO...
YOU GUYS ARE LOOKING FOR *IT* TOO, HUH.
YOU TOO?
INDEED.
ELL, ELL, EMS E WE AVE COME ALS.
GEE--I MIGHT AS WELL GIVE UP NOW THAT WE'RE UP AGAINST THE BEST STUDENT IN SCHOOL...

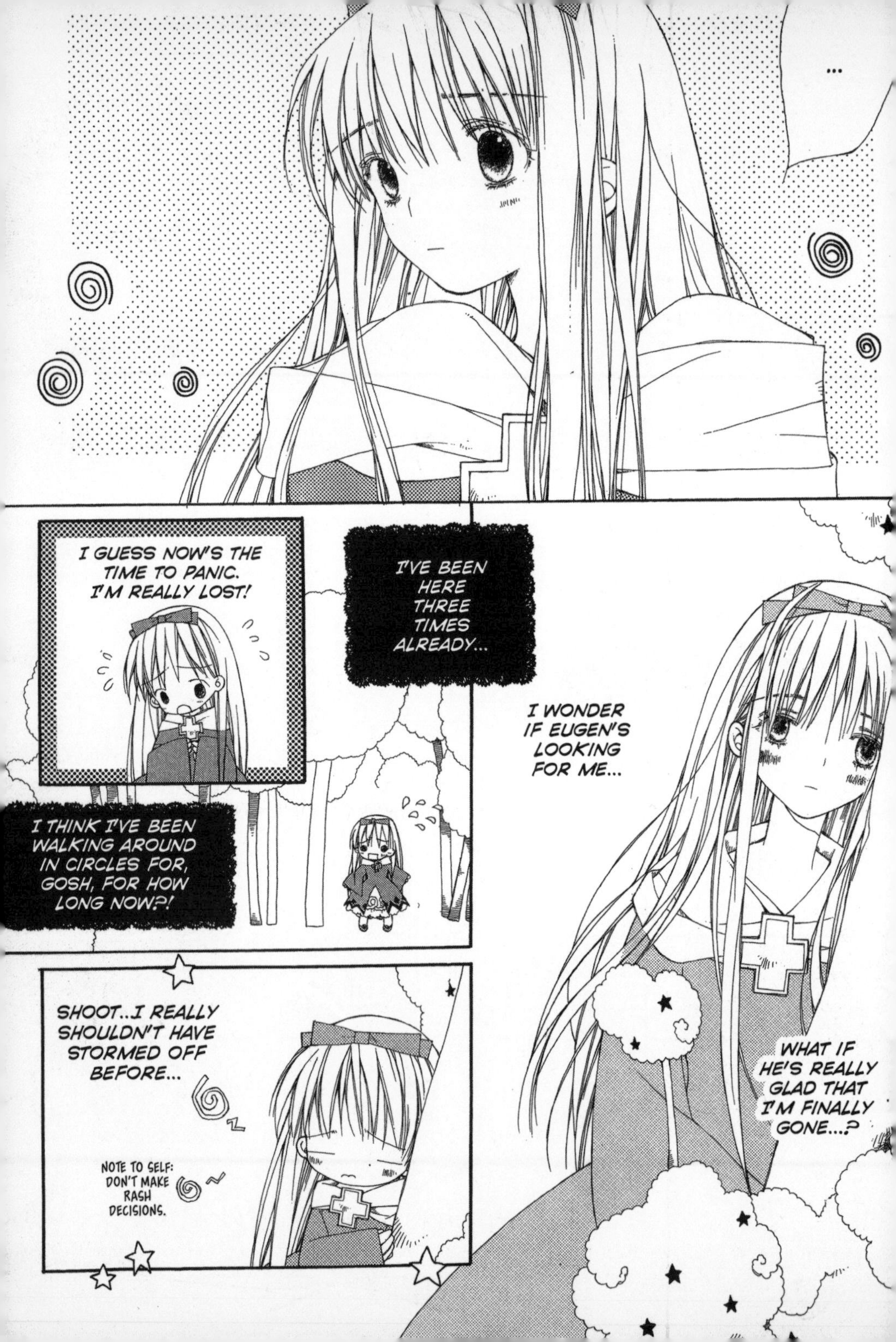
...
I GUESS NOW'S THE TIME TO PANIC. I'M REALLY LOST!
I'VE BEEN HERE THREE TIMES ALREADY...
I THINK I'VE BEEN WALKING AROUND IN CIRCLES FOR, GOSH, FOR HOW LONG NOW?!
SHOOT...I REALLY SHOULDN'T HAVE STORMED OFF BEFORE...
NOTE TO SELF: DON'T MAKE RASH DECISIONS.
I WONDER IF EUGEN'S LOOKING FOR ME...
WHAT IF HE'S REALLY GLAD THAT I'M FINALLY GONE...?

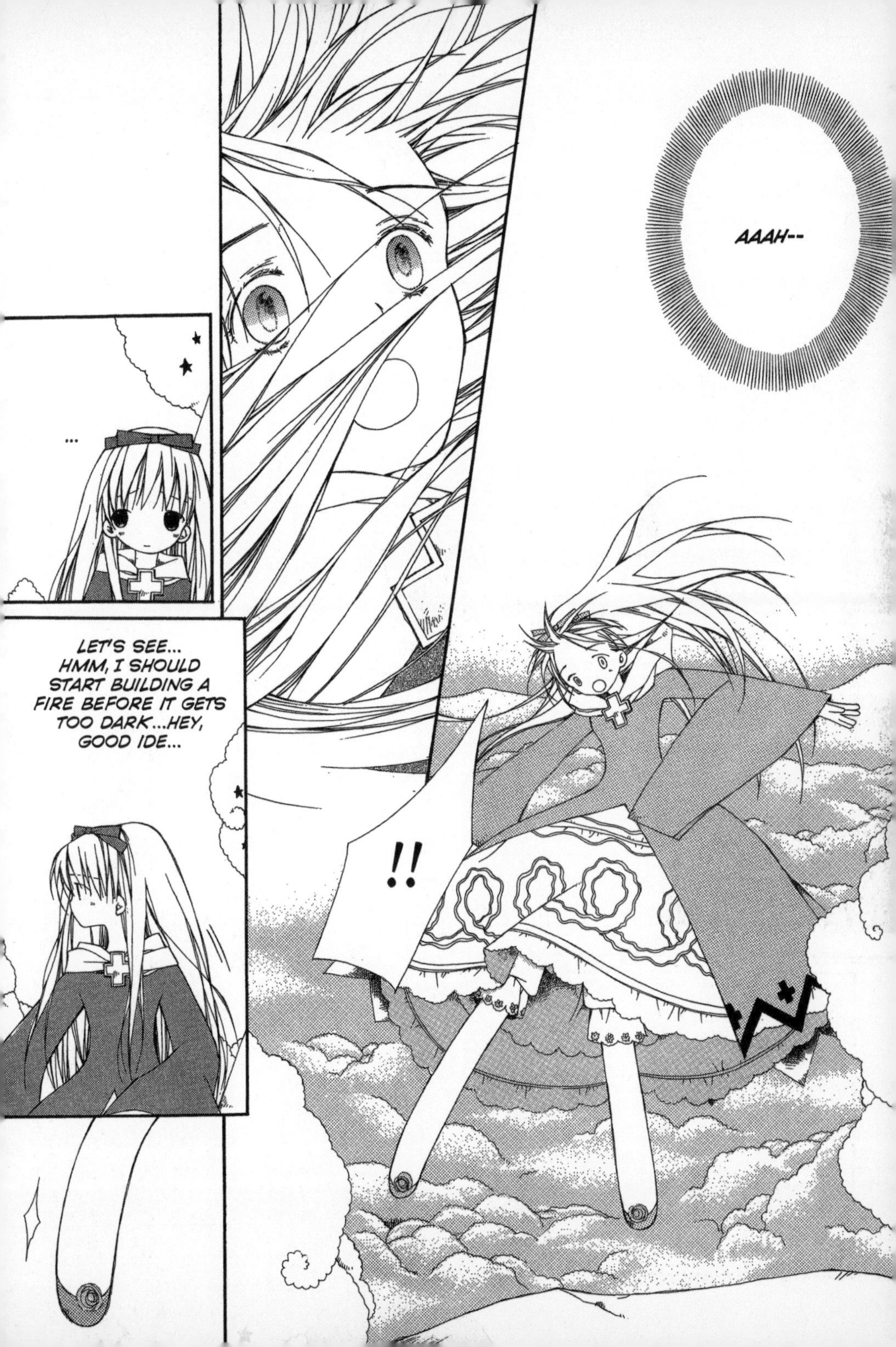
...
LET'S SEE... HMM, I SHOULD START BUILDING A FIRE BEFORE IT GETS TOO DARK...HEY, GOOD IDE...
AAAH--
!!

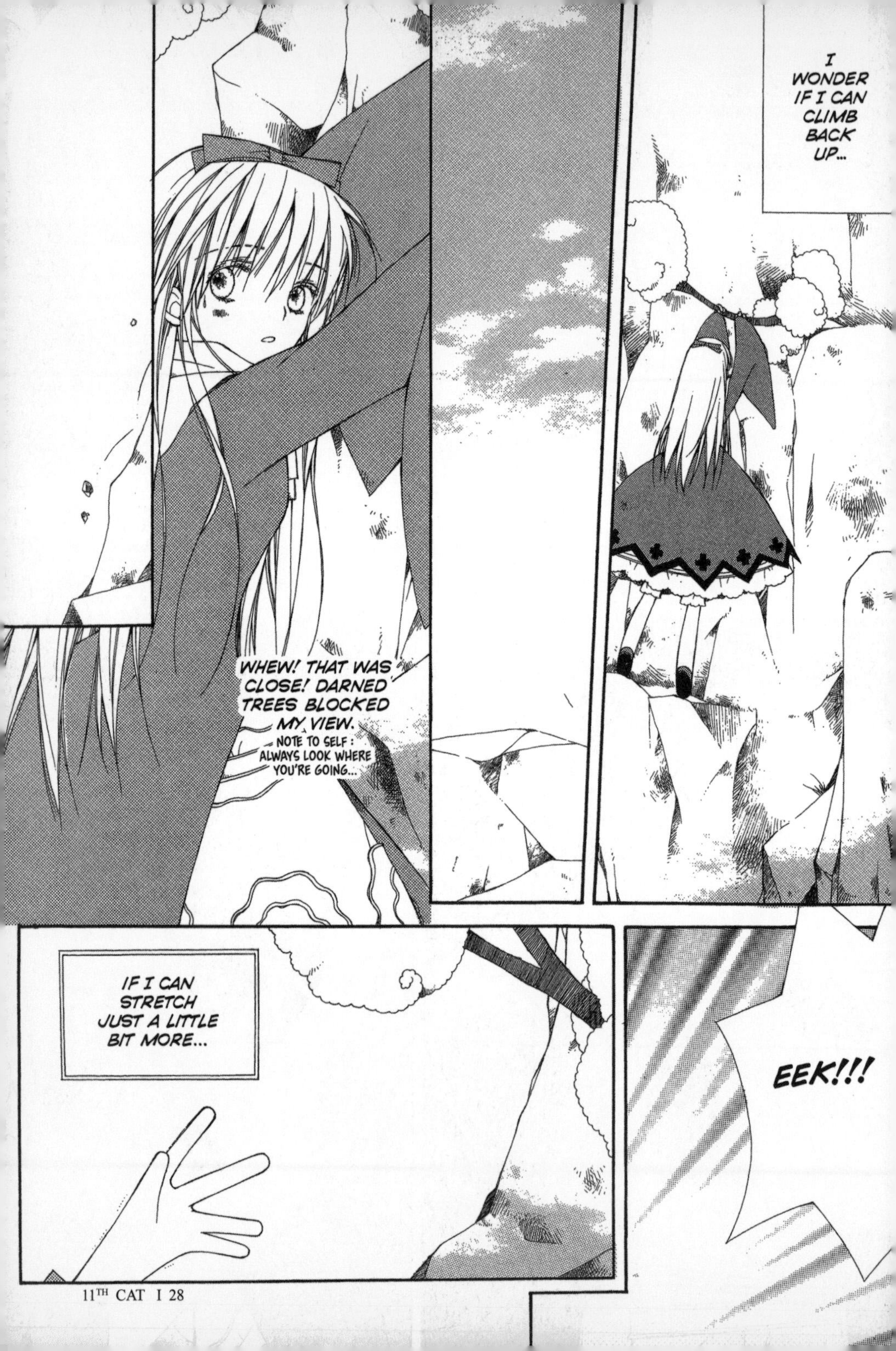
WHEW! THAT WAS CLOSE! DARNED TREES BLOCKED MY VIEW.
NOTE TO SELF: ALWAYS LOOK WHERE YOU'RE GOING...
I WONDER IF I CAN CLIMB BACK UP...
IF I CAN STRETCH JUST A LITTLE BIT MORE...
EEK!!!

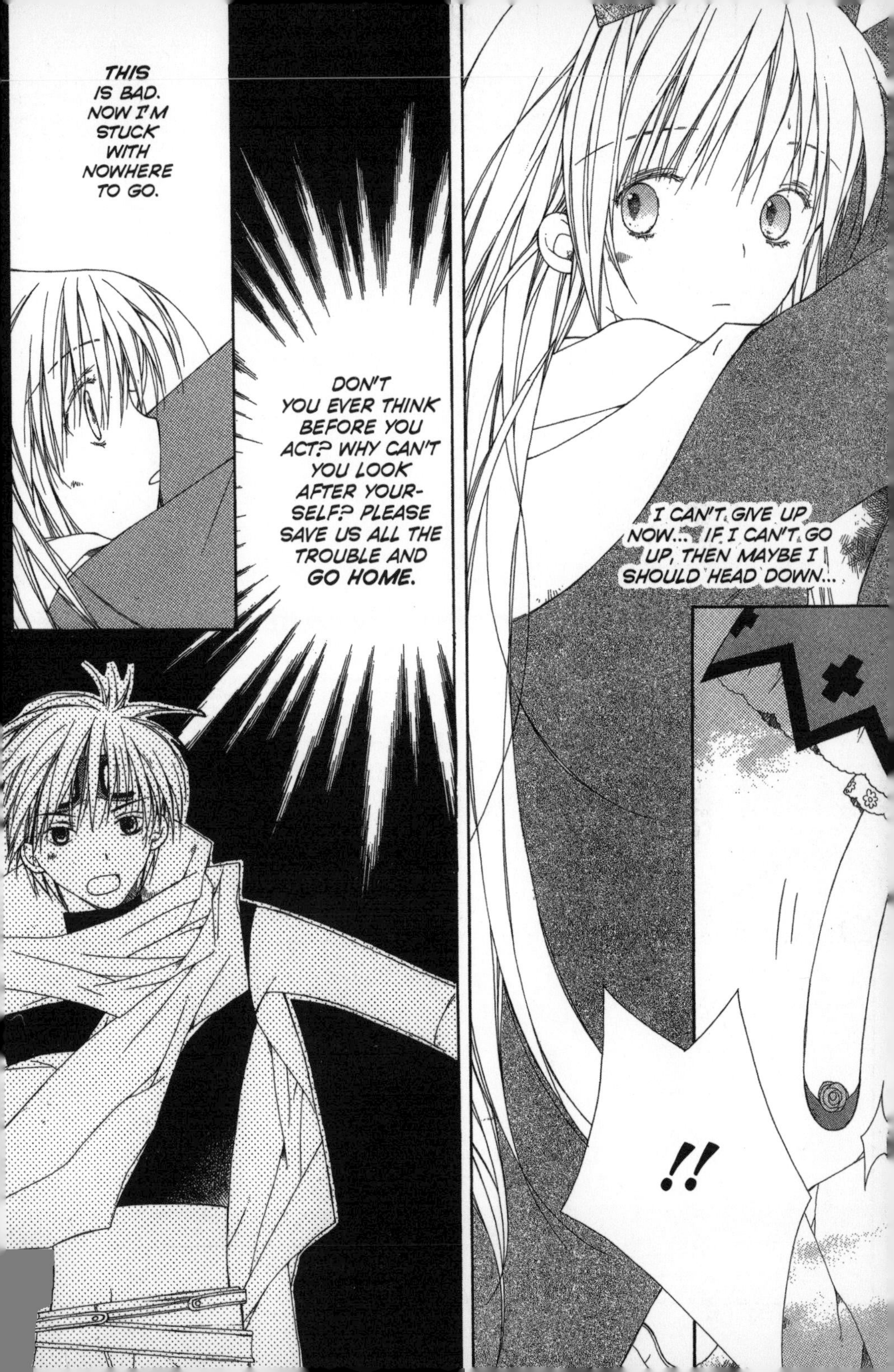
THIS IS BAD. NOW I'M STUCK WITH NOWHERE TO GO.
DON'T YOU EVER THINK BEFORE YOU ACT? WHY CAN'T YOU LOOK AFTER YOURSELF? PLEASE SAVE US ALL THE TROUBLE AND GO HOME.
I CAN'T GIVE UP NOW... IF I CAN'T GO UP, THEN MAYBE I SHOULD HEAD DOWN...
!!

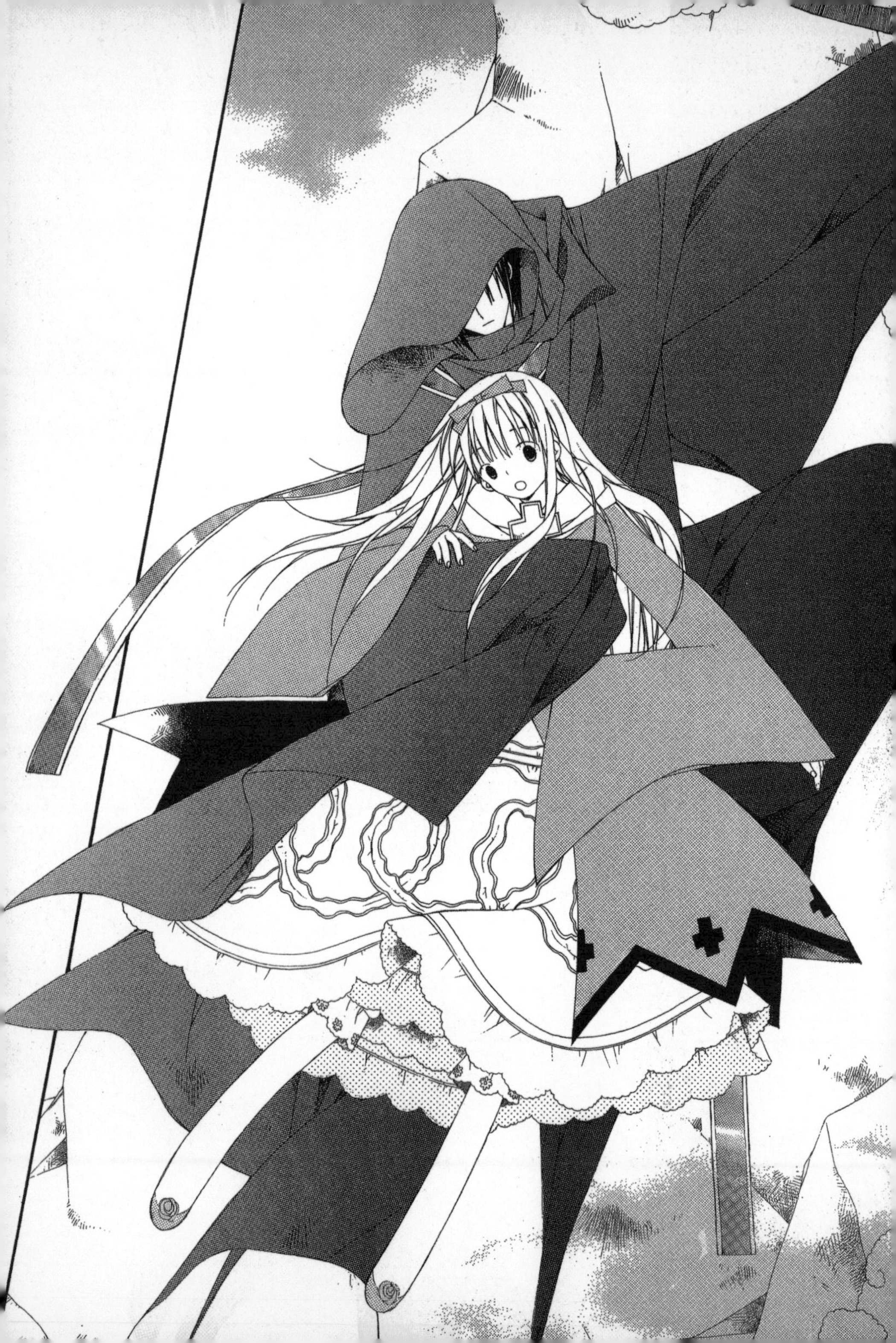

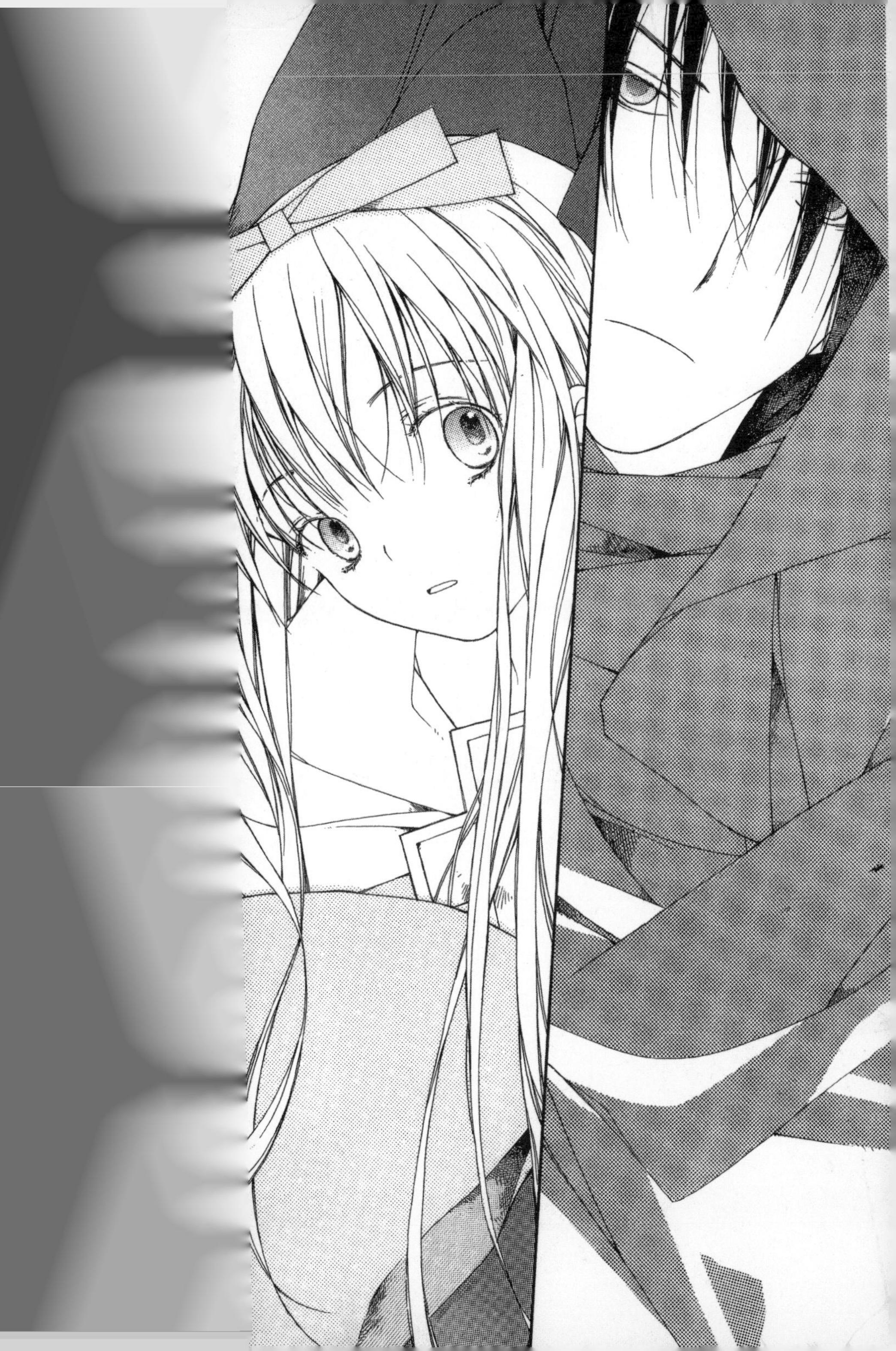

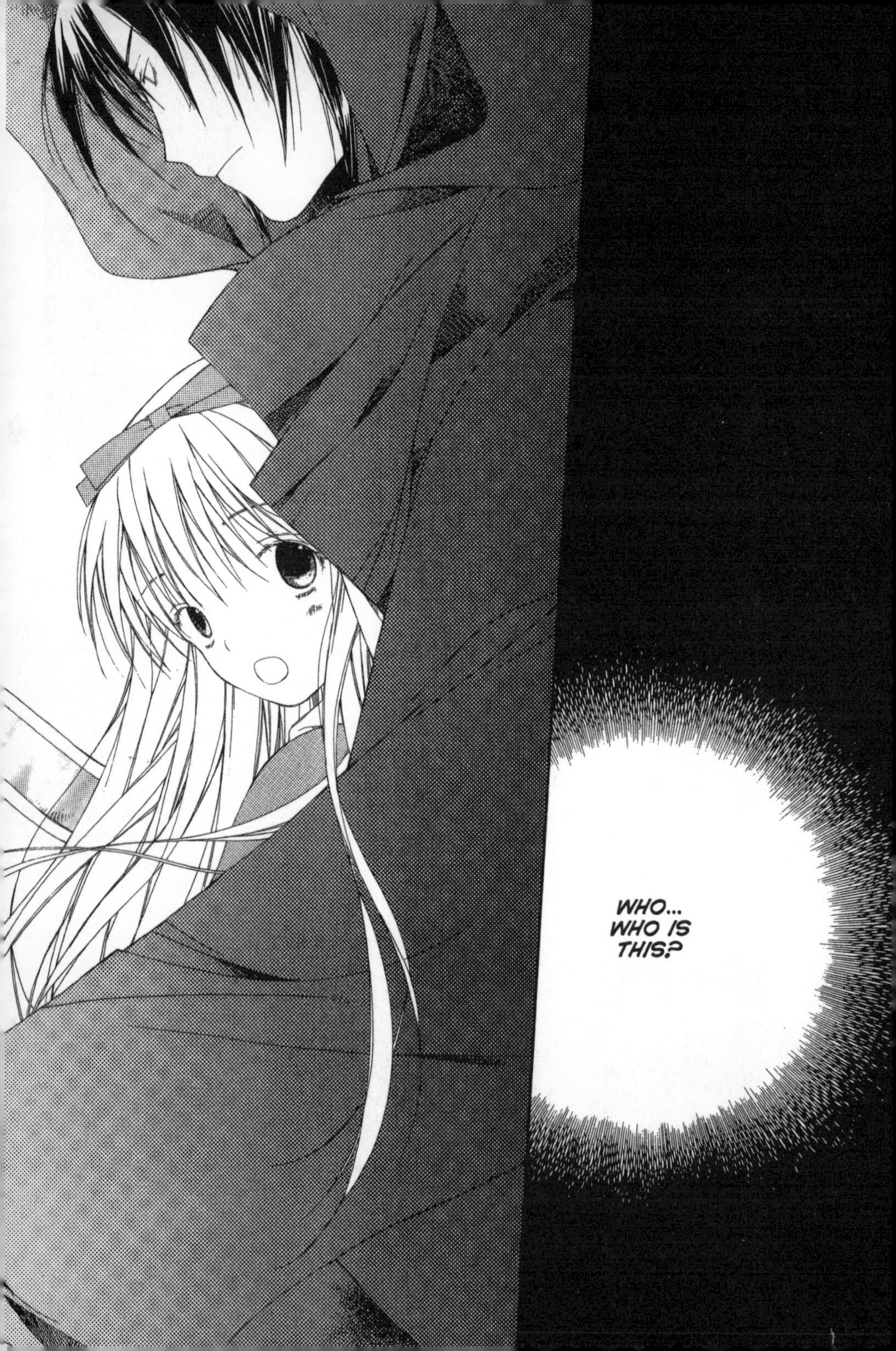
WHO...
WHO IS
THIS?

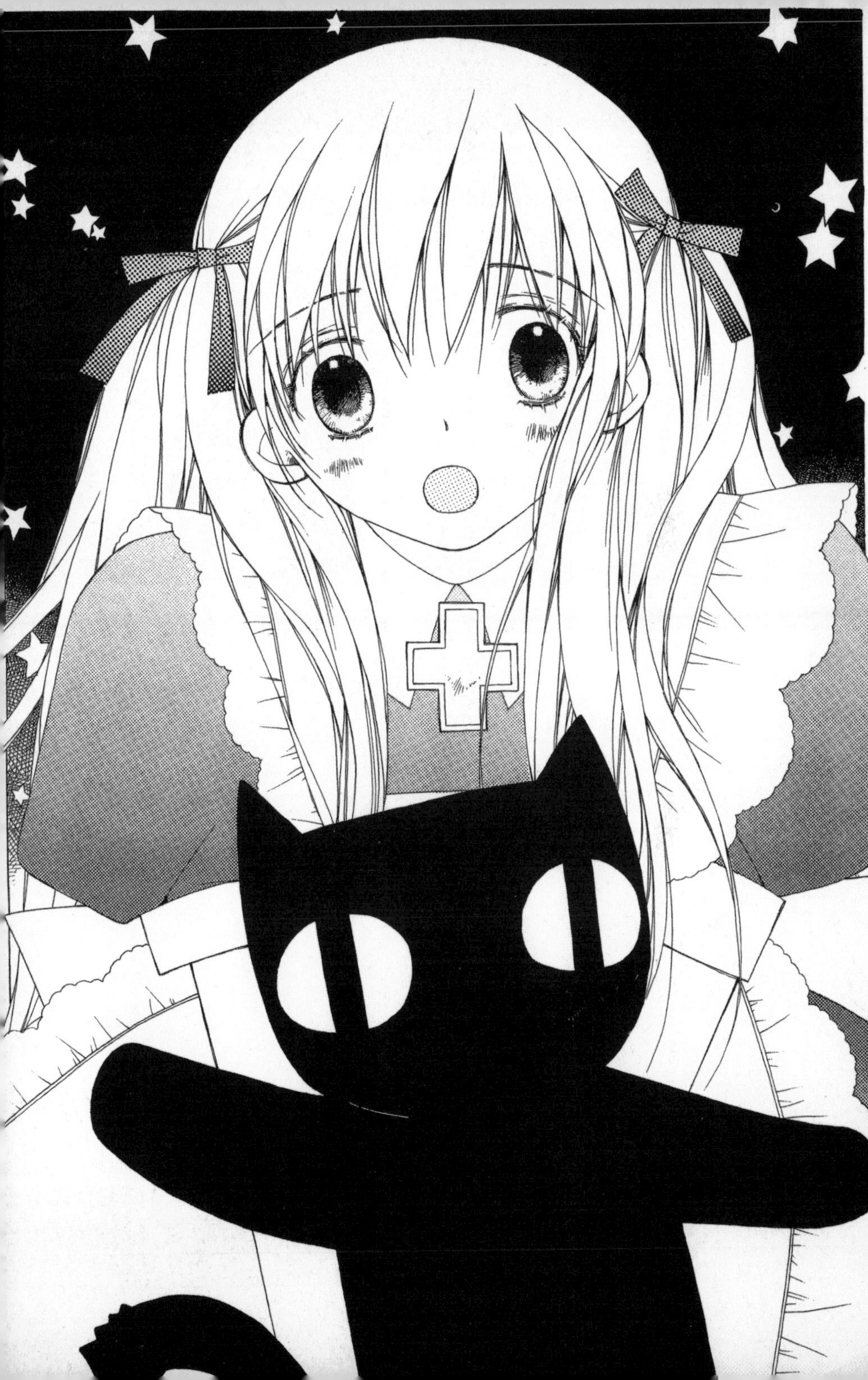

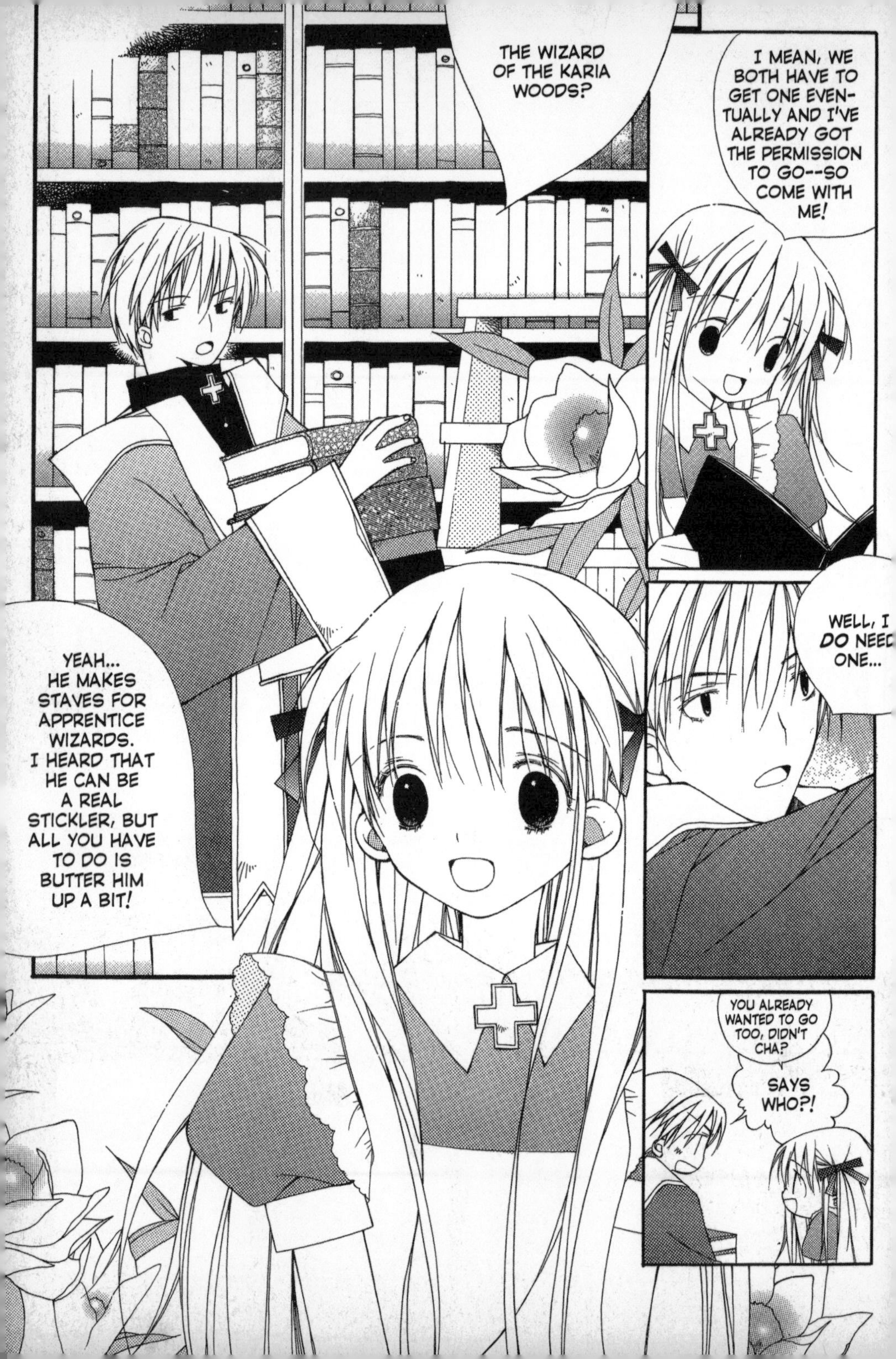
THE WIZARD OF THE KARIA WOODS?
YEAH... HE MAKES STAVES FOR APPRENTICE WIZARDS. I HEARD THAT HE CAN BE A REAL STICKLER, BUT ALL YOU HAVE TO DO IS BUTTER HIM UP A BIT!
I MEAN, WE BOTH HAVE TO GET ONE EVEN-TUALLY AND I'VE ALREADY GOT THE PERMISSION TO GO--SO COME WITH ME!
WELL, I *DO* NEED ONE...
YOU ALREADY WANTED TO GO TOO, DIDN'T CHA?
SAYS WHO?!

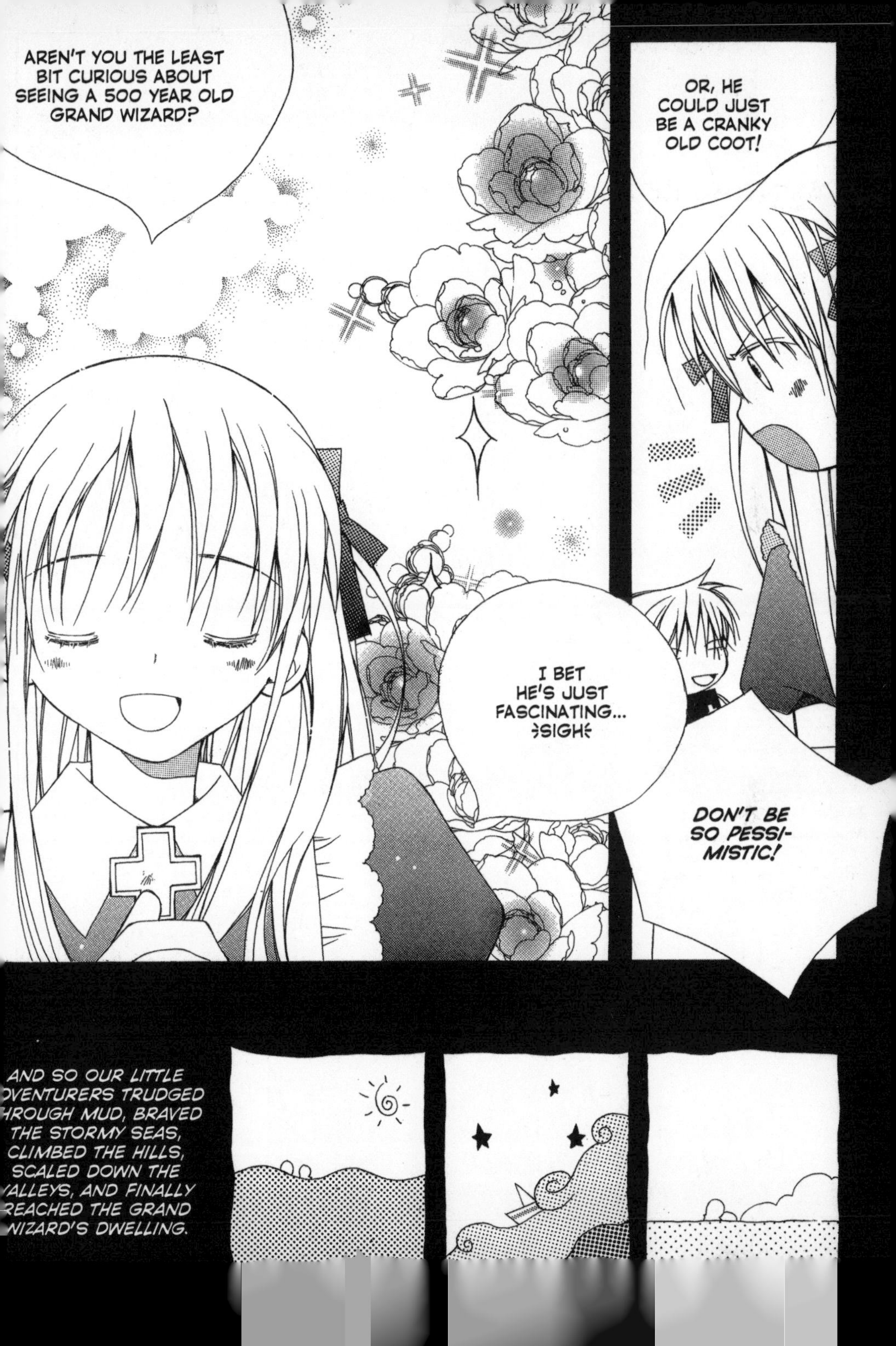
AREN'T YOU THE LEAST BIT CURIOUS ABOUT SEEING A 500 YEAR OLD GRAND WIZARD?
I BET HE'S JUST FASCINATING... SIGH
OR, HE COULD JUST BE A CRANKY OLD COOT!
DON'T BE SO PESSIMISTIC!
AND SO OUR LITTLE
DVENTURERS TRUDGED
HROUGH MUD, BRAVED
THE STORMY SEAS,
CLIMBED THE HILLS,
SCALED DOWN THE
ALLEYS, AND FINALLY
REACHED THE GRAND
WIZARD'S DWELLING.

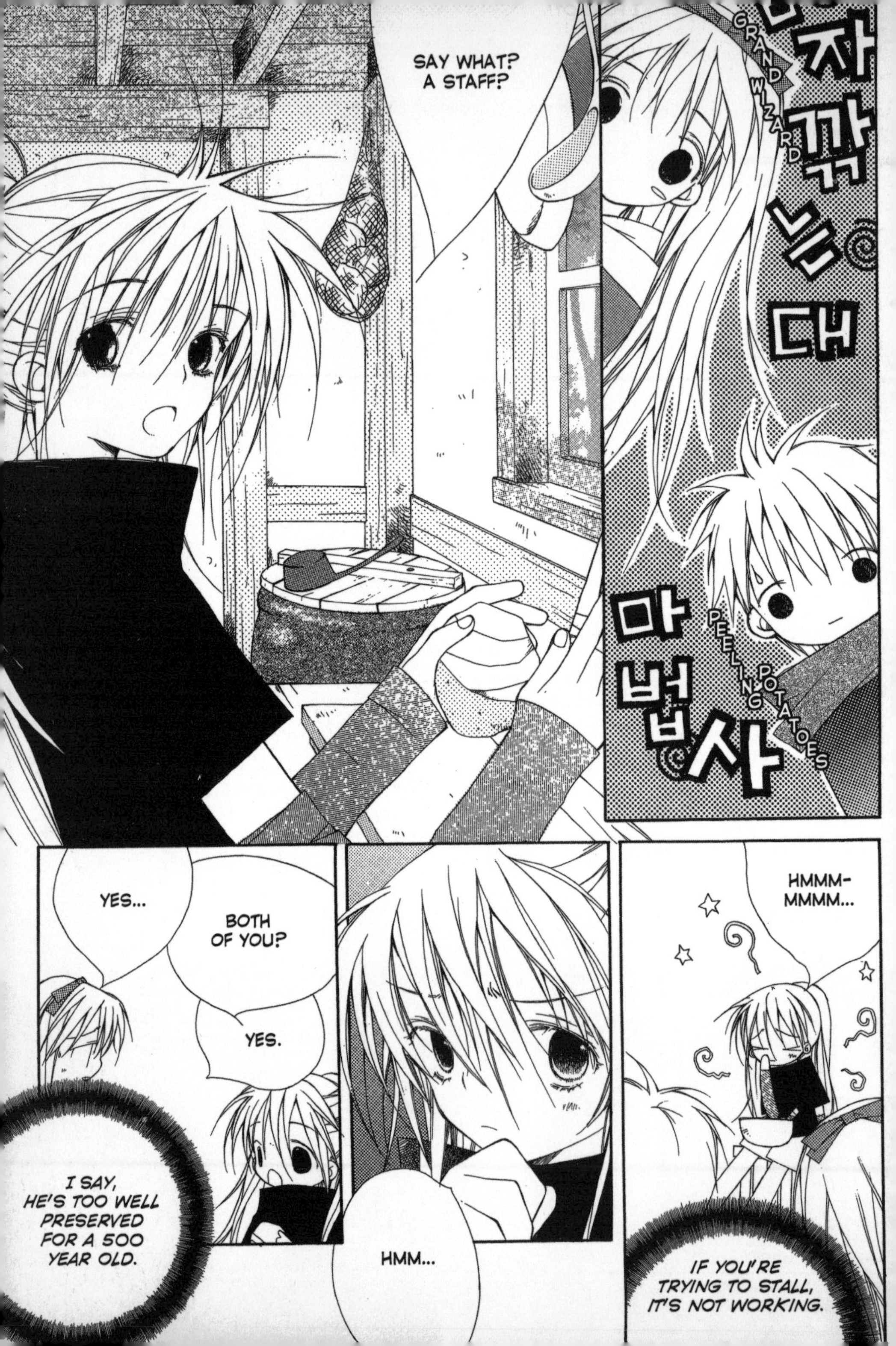
SAY WHAT? A STAFF?
자 깎는 대 마법사
GRAND WIZARD
PEELING POTATOES
YES...
BOTH OF YOU?
YES.
I SAY, HE'S TOO WELL PRESERVED FOR A 500 YEAR OLD.
HMM...
HMMM-MMMM...
IF YOU'RE TRYING TO STALL, IT'S NOT WORKING.

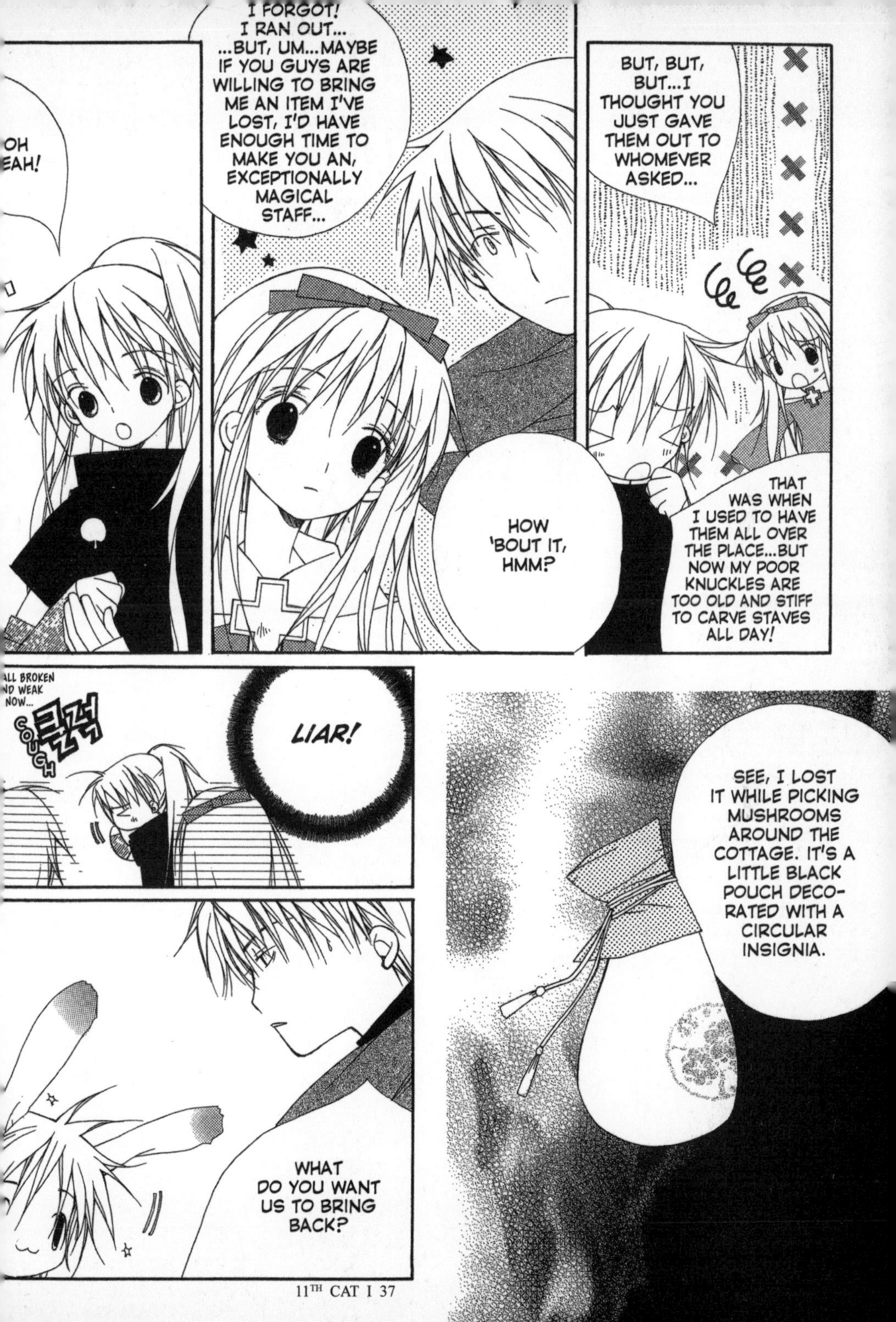
OH
EAH!
I FORGOT! I RAN OUT... ...BUT, UM...MAYBE IF YOU GUYS ARE WILLING TO BRING ME AN ITEM I'VE LOST, I'D HAVE ENOUGH TIME TO MAKE YOU AN, EXCEPTIONALLY MAGICAL STAFF...
HOW 'BOUT IT, HMM?
BUT, BUT, BUT...I THOUGHT YOU JUST GAVE THEM OUT TO WHOMEVER ASKED...
THAT WAS WHEN I USED TO HAVE THEM ALL OVER THE PLACE...BUT NOW MY POOR KNUCKLES ARE TOO OLD AND STIFF TO CARVE STAVES ALL DAY!
ALL BROKEN ND WEAK NOW...
COUGH
LIAR!
WHAT DO YOU WANT US TO BRING BACK?
SEE, I LOST IT WHILE PICKING MUSHROOMS AROUND THE COTTAGE. IT'S A LITTLE BLACK POUCH DECO-RATED WITH A CIRCULAR INSIGNIA.

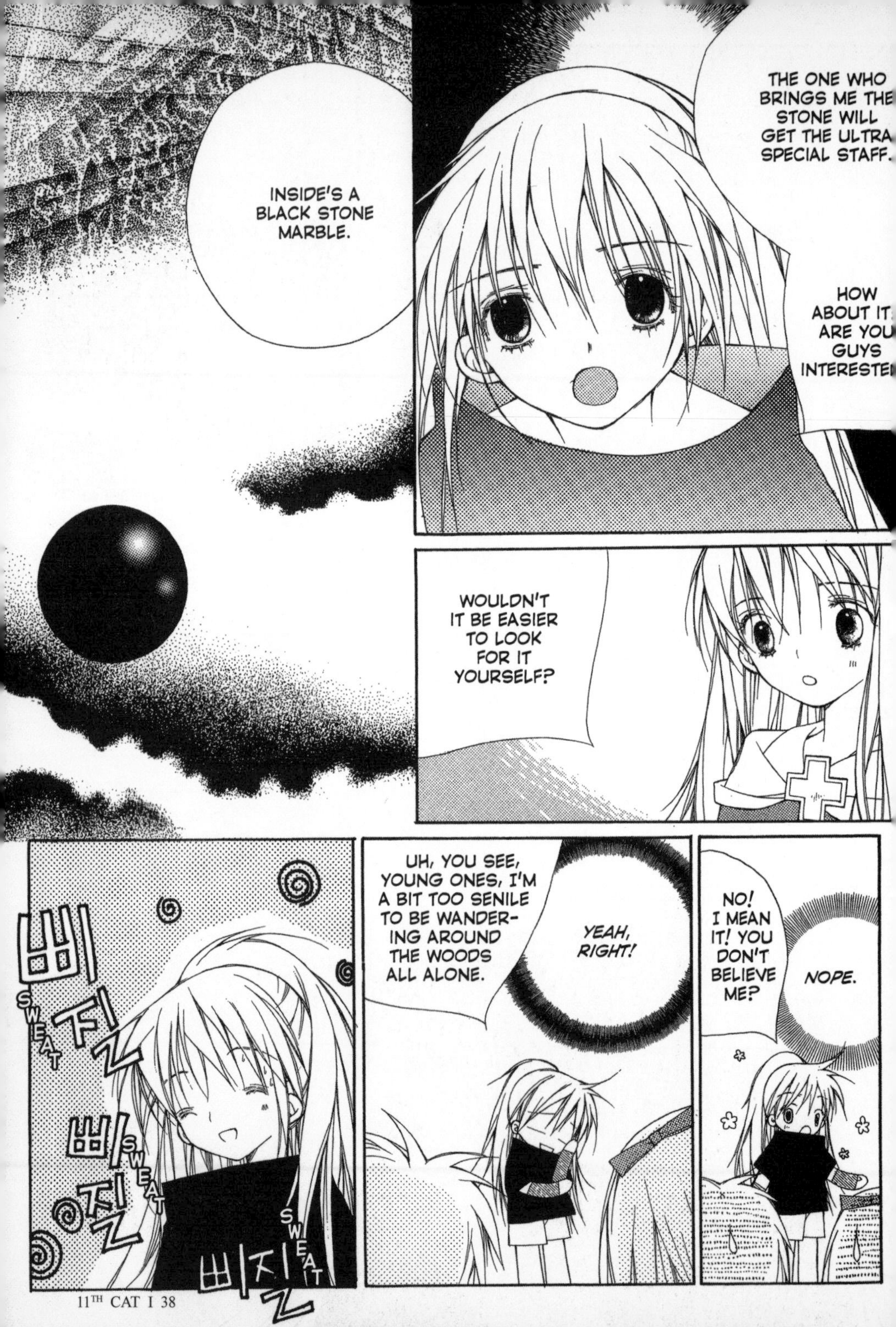
INSIDE'S A BLACK STONE MARBLE.
THE ONE WHO BRINGS ME THE STONE WILL GET THE ULTRA SPECIAL STAFF.
HOW ABOUT IT? ARE YOU GUYS INTERESTE
WOULDN'T IT BE EASIER TO LOOK FOR IT YOURSELF?
삐질 SWEAT
삐질 SWEAT
삐질 SWEAT
UH, YOU SEE, YOUNG ONES, I'M A BIT TOO SENILE TO BE WANDER-ING AROUND THE WOODS ALL ALONE.
YEAH, RIGHT!
NO! I MEAN IT! YOU DON'T BELIEVE ME?
NOPE.

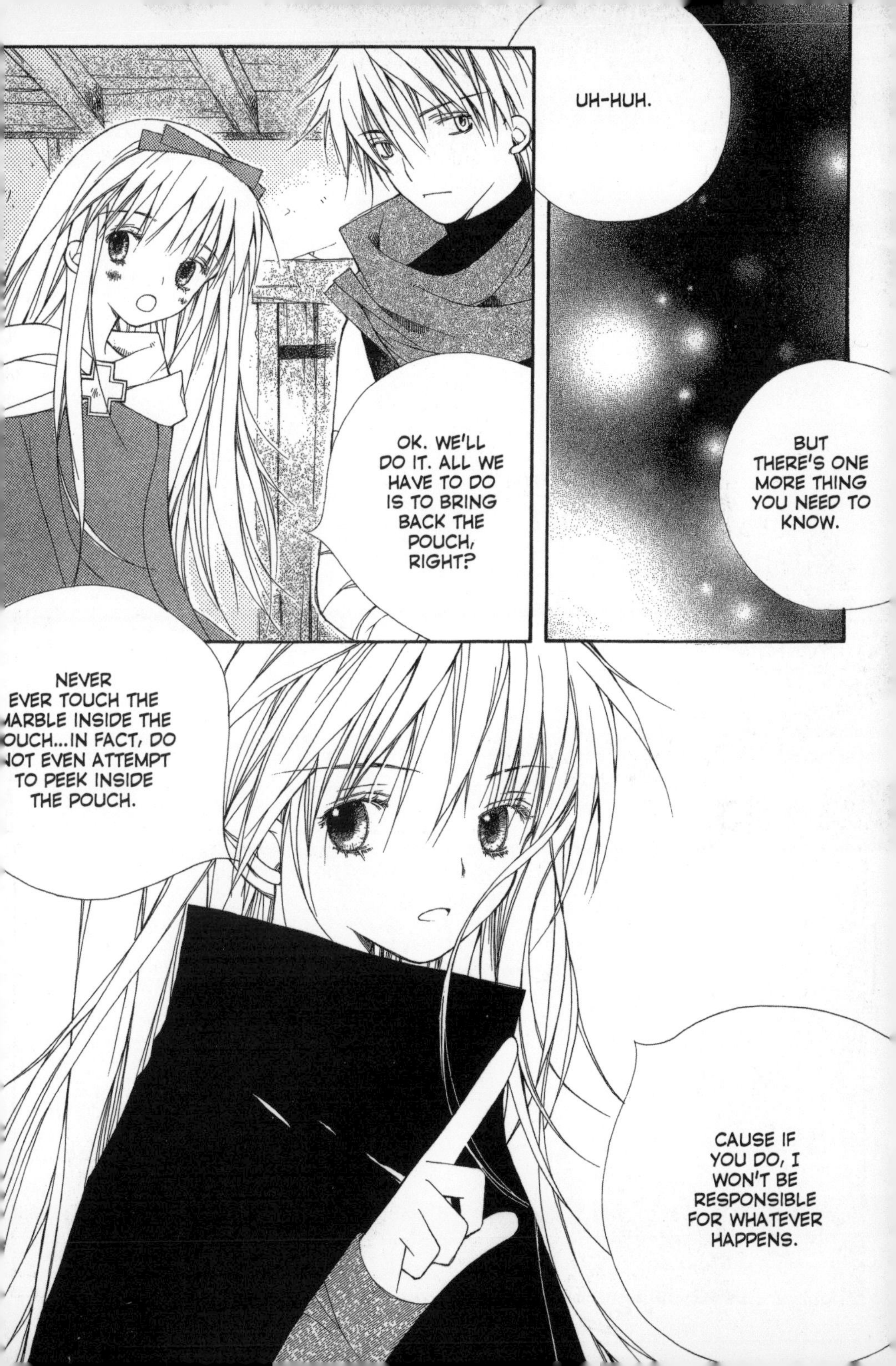
OK. WE'LL DO IT. ALL WE HAVE TO DO IS TO BRING BACK THE POUCH, RIGHT?
UH-HUH.
BUT THERE'S ONE MORE THING YOU NEED TO KNOW.
NEVER EVER TOUCH THE ARBLE INSIDE THE OUCH...IN FACT, DO OT EVEN ATTEMPT TO PEEK INSIDE THE POUCH.
CAUSE IF YOU DO, I WON'T BE RESPONSIBLE FOR WHATEVER HAPPENS.

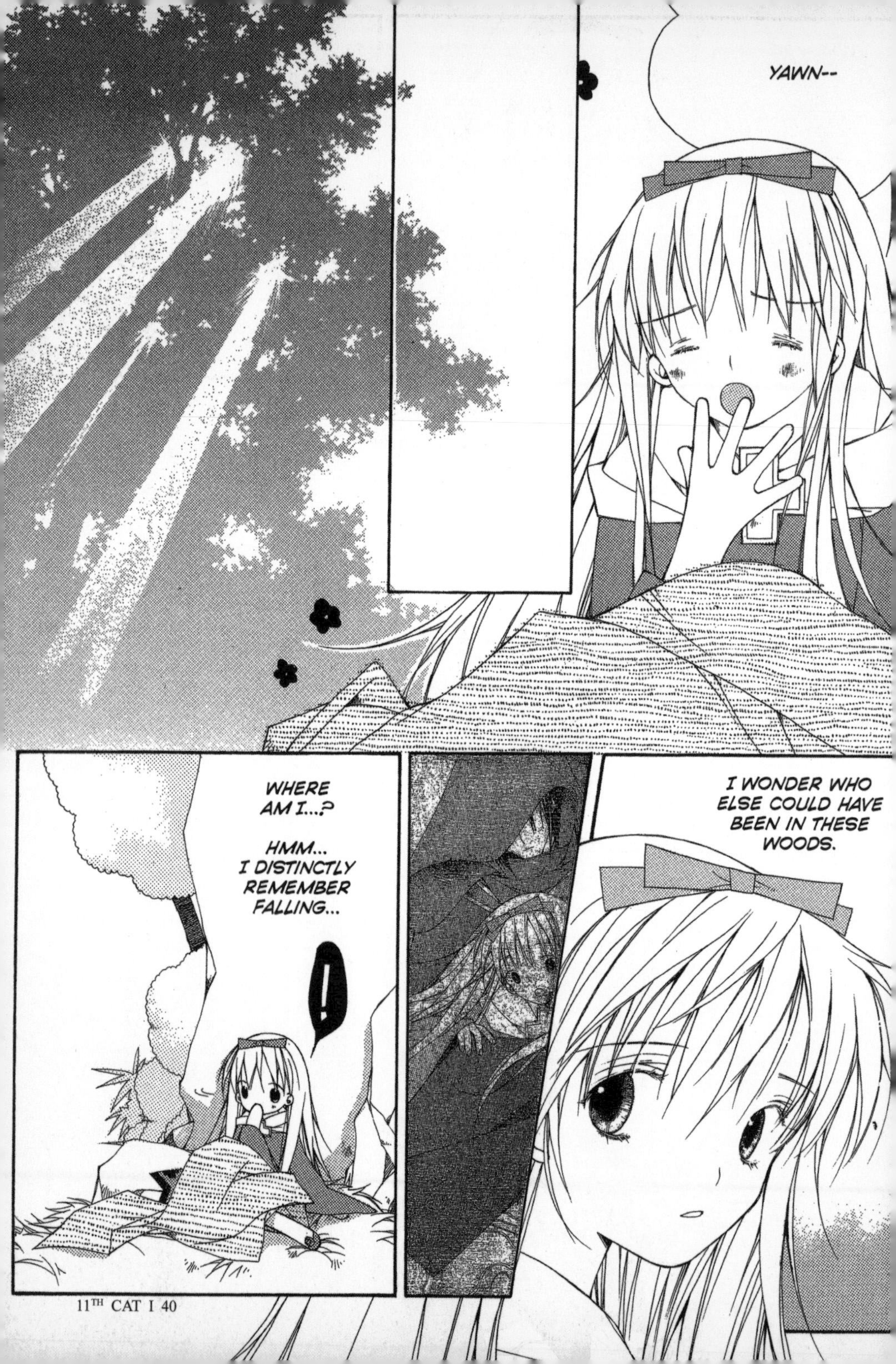
YAWN--
WHERE AM I...?
HMM... I DISTINCTLY REMEMBER FALLING...
!
I WONDER WHO ELSE COULD HAVE BEEN IN THESE WOODS.

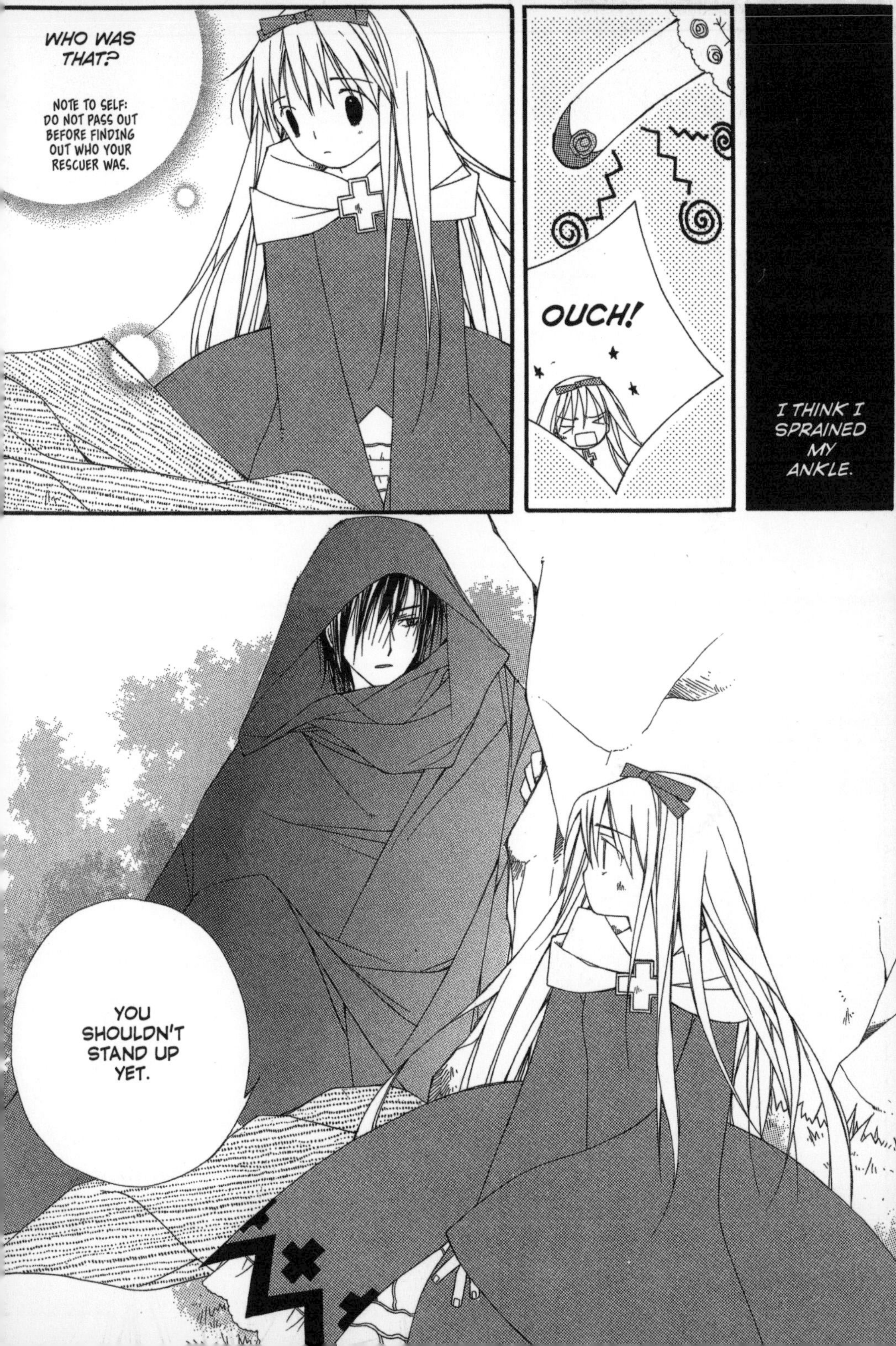
WHO WAS THAT?
NOTE TO SELF: DO NOT PASS OUT BEFORE FINDING OUT WHO YOUR RESCUER WAS.
OUCH!
I THINK I SPRAINED MY ANKLE.
YOU SHOULDN'T STAND UP YET.

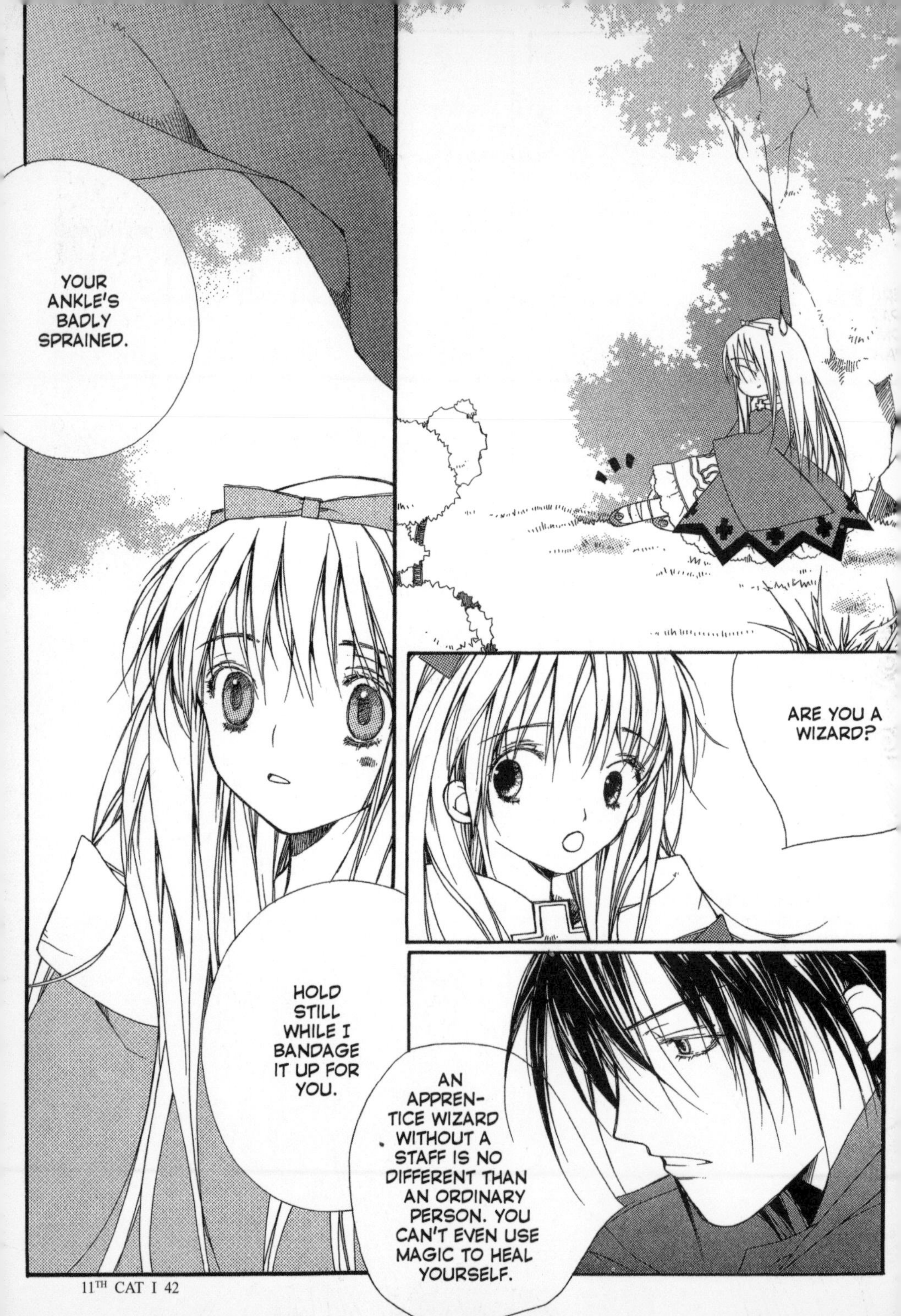
YOUR ANKLE'S BADLY SPRAINED.
HOLD STILL WHILE I BANDAGE IT UP FOR YOU.
ARE YOU A WIZARD?
AN APPREN- TICE WIZARD WITHOUT A STAFF IS NO DIFFERENT THAN AN ORDINARY PERSON. YOU CAN'T EVEN USE MAGIC TO HEAL YOURSELF.

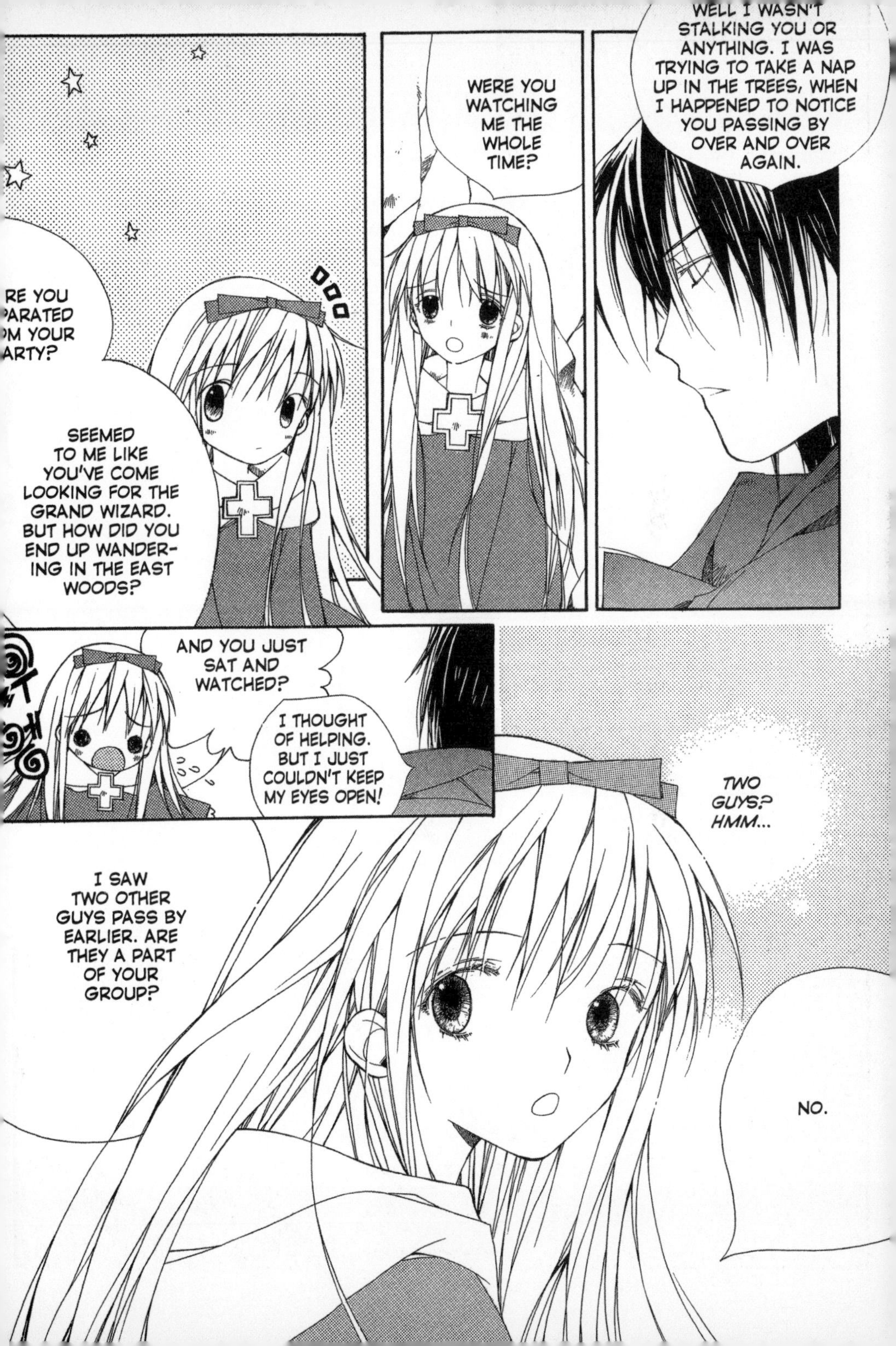
RE YOU PARATED OM YOUR ARTY?
SEEMED TO ME LIKE YOU'VE COME LOOKING FOR THE GRAND WIZARD. BUT HOW DID YOU END UP WANDER-ING IN THE EAST WOODS?
WERE YOU WATCHING ME THE WHOLE TIME?
WELL I WASN'T STALKING YOU OR ANYTHING. I WAS TRYING TO TAKE A NAP UP IN THE TREES, WHEN I HAPPENED TO NOTICE YOU PASSING BY OVER AND OVER AGAIN.
AND YOU JUST SAT AND WATCHED?
I THOUGHT OF HELPING. BUT I JUST COULDN'T KEEP MY EYES OPEN!
I SAW TWO OTHER GUYS PASS BY EARLIER. ARE THEY A PART OF YOUR GROUP?
TWO GUYS? HMM...
NO.

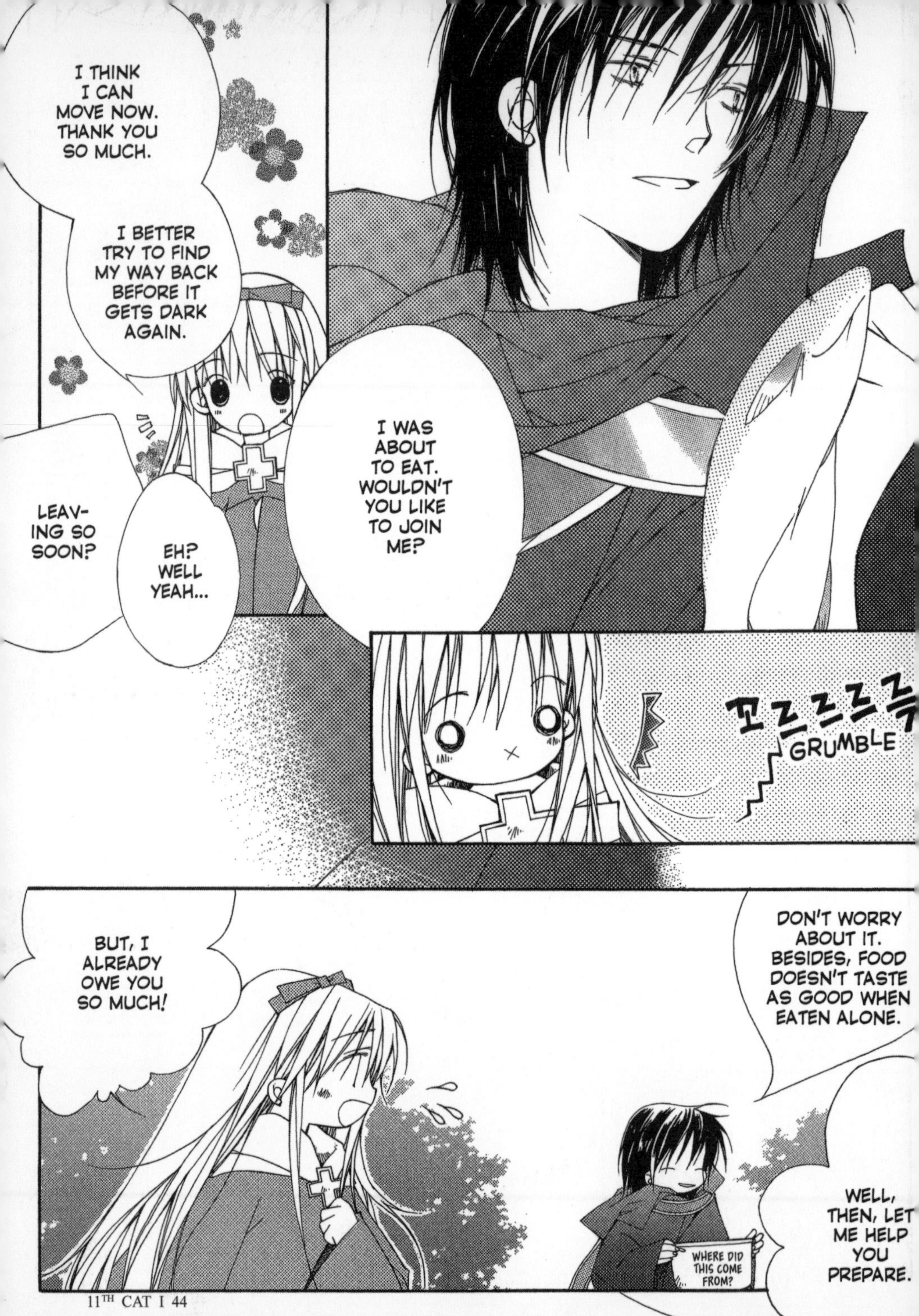
I THINK I CAN MOVE NOW. THANK YOU SO MUCH.
I BETTER TRY TO FIND MY WAY BACK BEFORE IT GETS DARK AGAIN.
LEAV-ING SO SOON?
EH? WELL YEAH...
I WAS ABOUT TO EAT. WOULDN'T YOU LIKE TO JOIN ME?
꼬르르르륵
GRUMBLE
BUT, I ALREADY OWE YOU SO MUCH!
DON'T WORRY ABOUT IT. BESIDES, FOOD DOESN'T TASTE AS GOOD WHEN EATEN ALONE.
WHERE DID THIS COME FROM?
WELL, THEN, LET ME HELP YOU PREPARE.

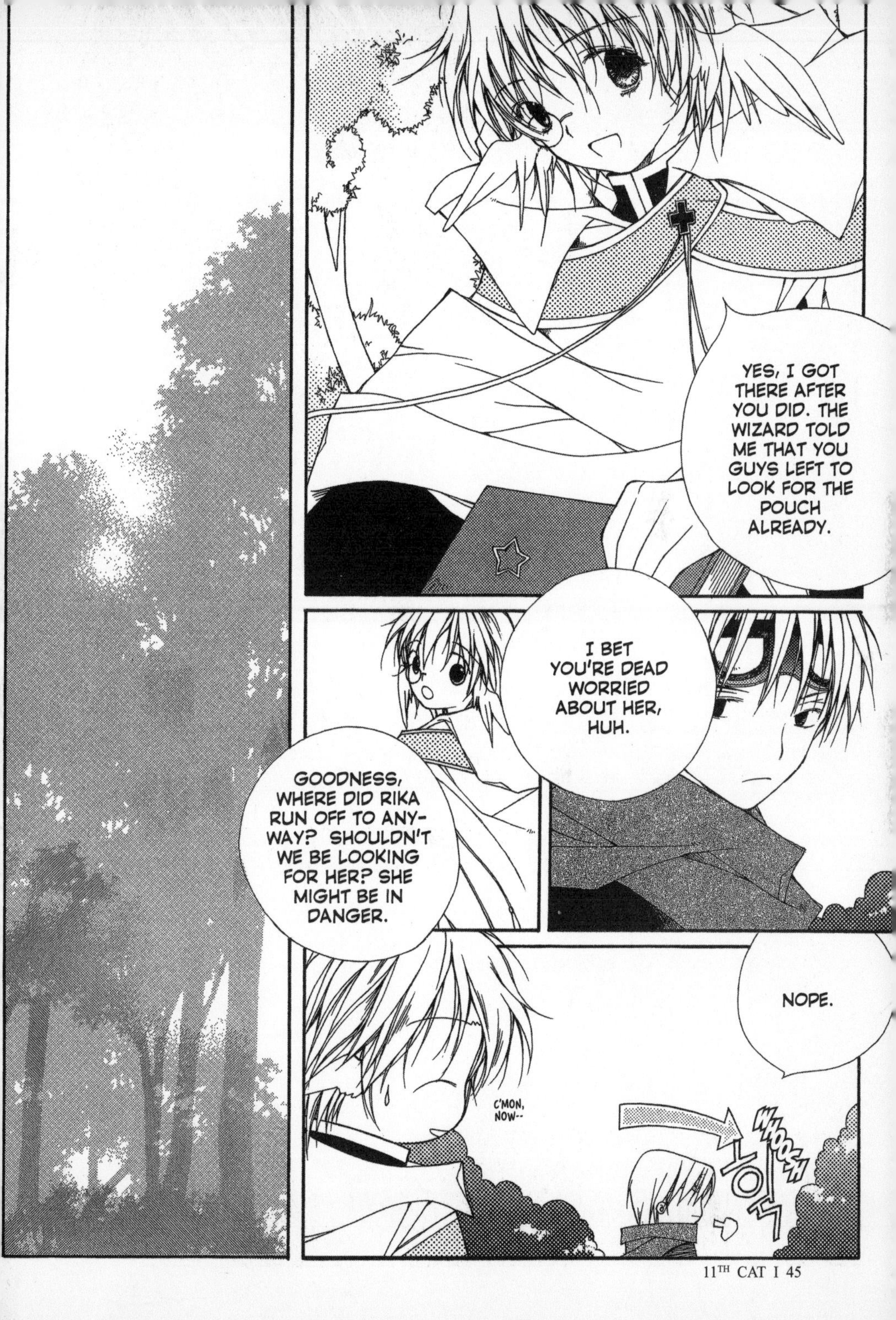
YES, I GOT THERE AFTER YOU DID. THE WIZARD TOLD ME THAT YOU GUYS LEFT TO LOOK FOR THE POUCH ALREADY.
GOODNESS, WHERE DID RIKA RUN OFF TO ANYWAY? SHOULDN'T WE BE LOOKING FOR HER? SHE MIGHT BE IN DANGER.
I BET YOU'RE DEAD WORRIED ABOUT HER, HUH.
NOPE.
C'MON, NOW--
WHOOSH

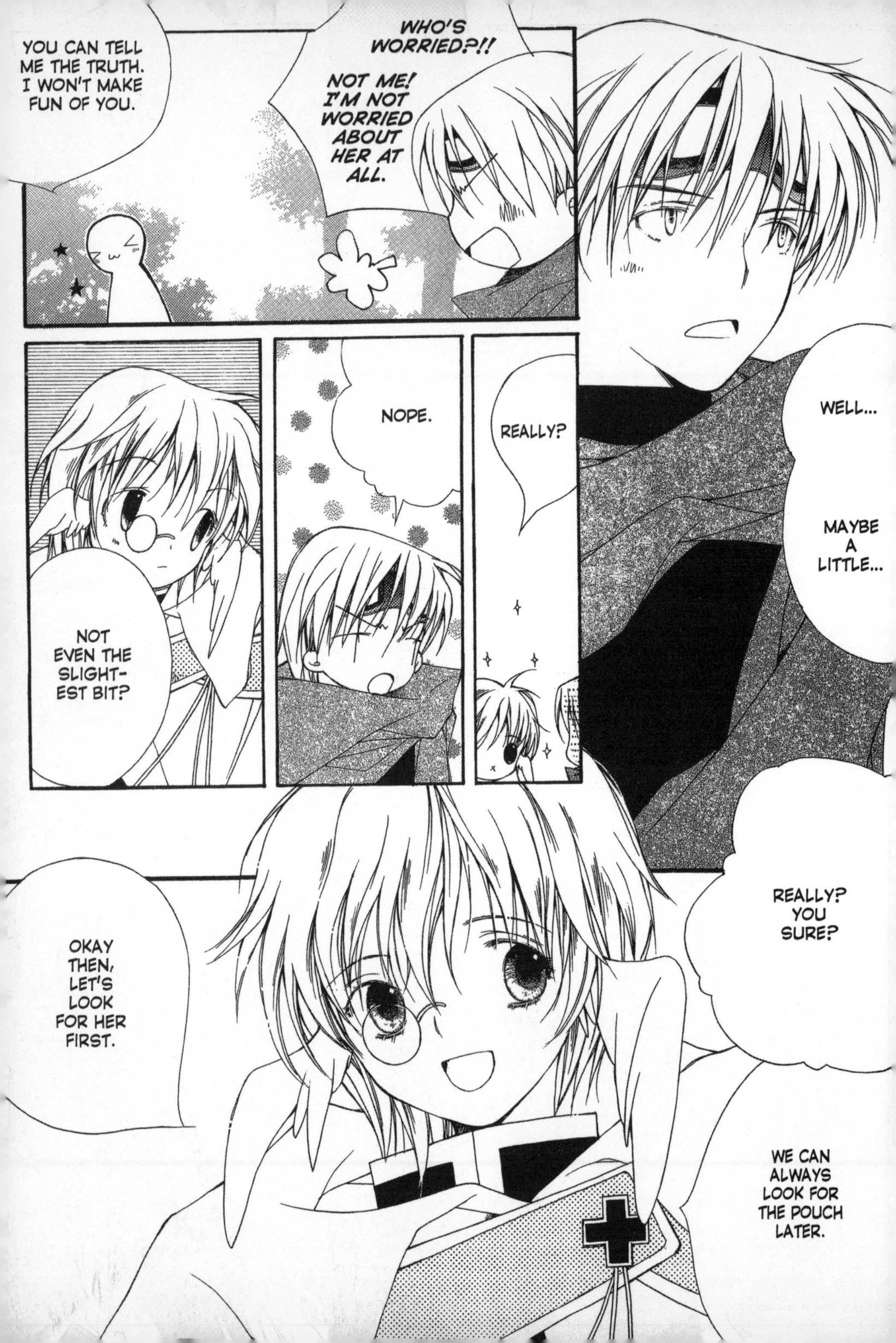
YOU CAN TELL ME THE TRUTH. I WON'T MAKE FUN OF YOU.
WHO'S WORRIED?!!
NOT ME! I'M NOT WORRIED ABOUT HER AT ALL.
NOT EVEN THE SLIGHT-EST BIT?
NOPE.
REALLY?
WELL...
MAYBE A LITTLE...
OKAY THEN, LET'S LOOK FOR HER FIRST.
REALLY? YOU SURE?
WE CAN ALWAYS LOOK FOR THE POUCH LATER.

WHERE THE HELL IS RIKA ANYWAY?

I THINK RIKA WAS PRETTY CLOSE TO HIM THOUGH.

MMM-- THAT WAS SCRUMP- TIOUS!

KIRIK AND I...WE NEVER HAD MUCH IN COMMON...I DOUBT WE'VE EVEN HAD A FRIENDLY CONVER- SATION.

THEN AGAIN, KIRIK WAS NEVER THE TALKATIVE TYPE.

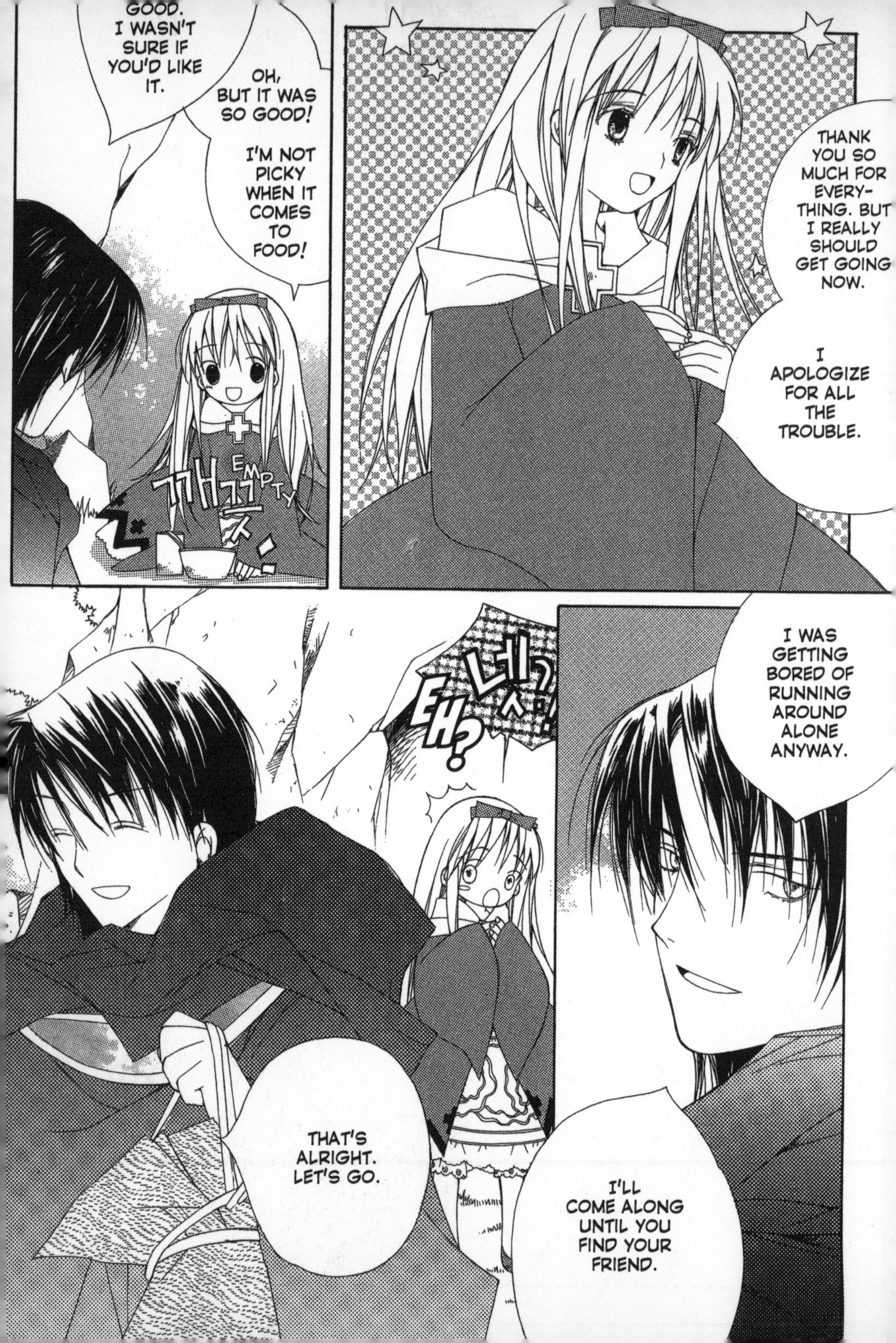
GOOD. I WASN'T SURE IF YOU'D LIKE IT.
OH, BUT IT WAS SO GOOD!
I'M NOT PICKY WHEN IT COMES TO FOOD!
EMPTY
THANK YOU SO MUCH FOR EVERY-THING. BUT I REALLY SHOULD GET GOING NOW.
I APOLOGIZE FOR ALL THE TROUBLE.
EH?
THAT'S ALRIGHT. LET'S GO.
I WAS GETTING BORED OF RUNNING AROUND ALONE ANYWAY.
I'LL COME ALONG UNTIL YOU FIND YOUR FRIEND.

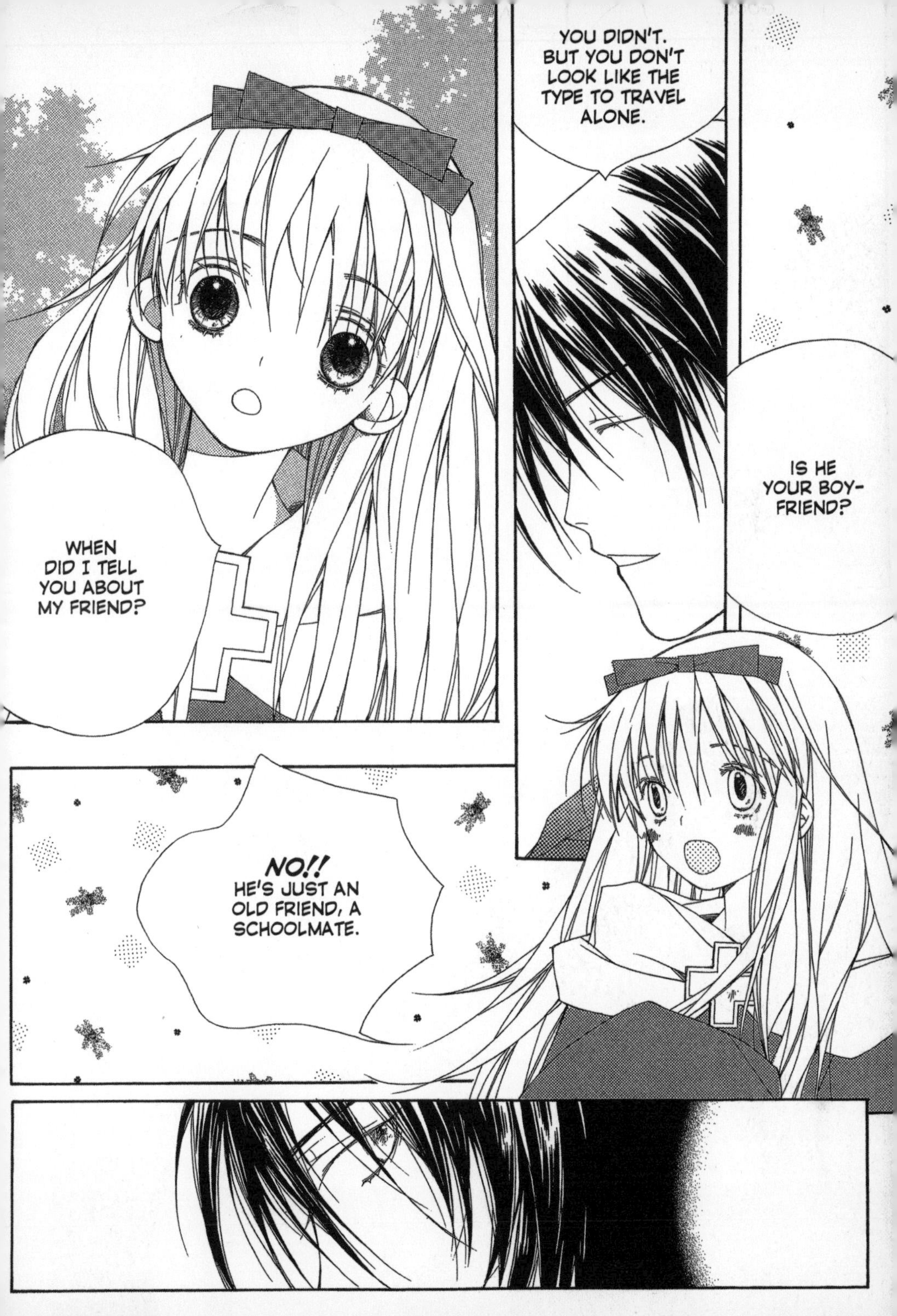
WHEN DID I TELL YOU ABOUT MY FRIEND?
YOU DIDN'T. BUT YOU DON'T LOOK LIKE THE TYPE TO TRAVEL ALONE.
IS HE YOUR BOY-FRIEND?
NO!! HE'S JUST AN OLD FRIEND, A SCHOOLMATE.

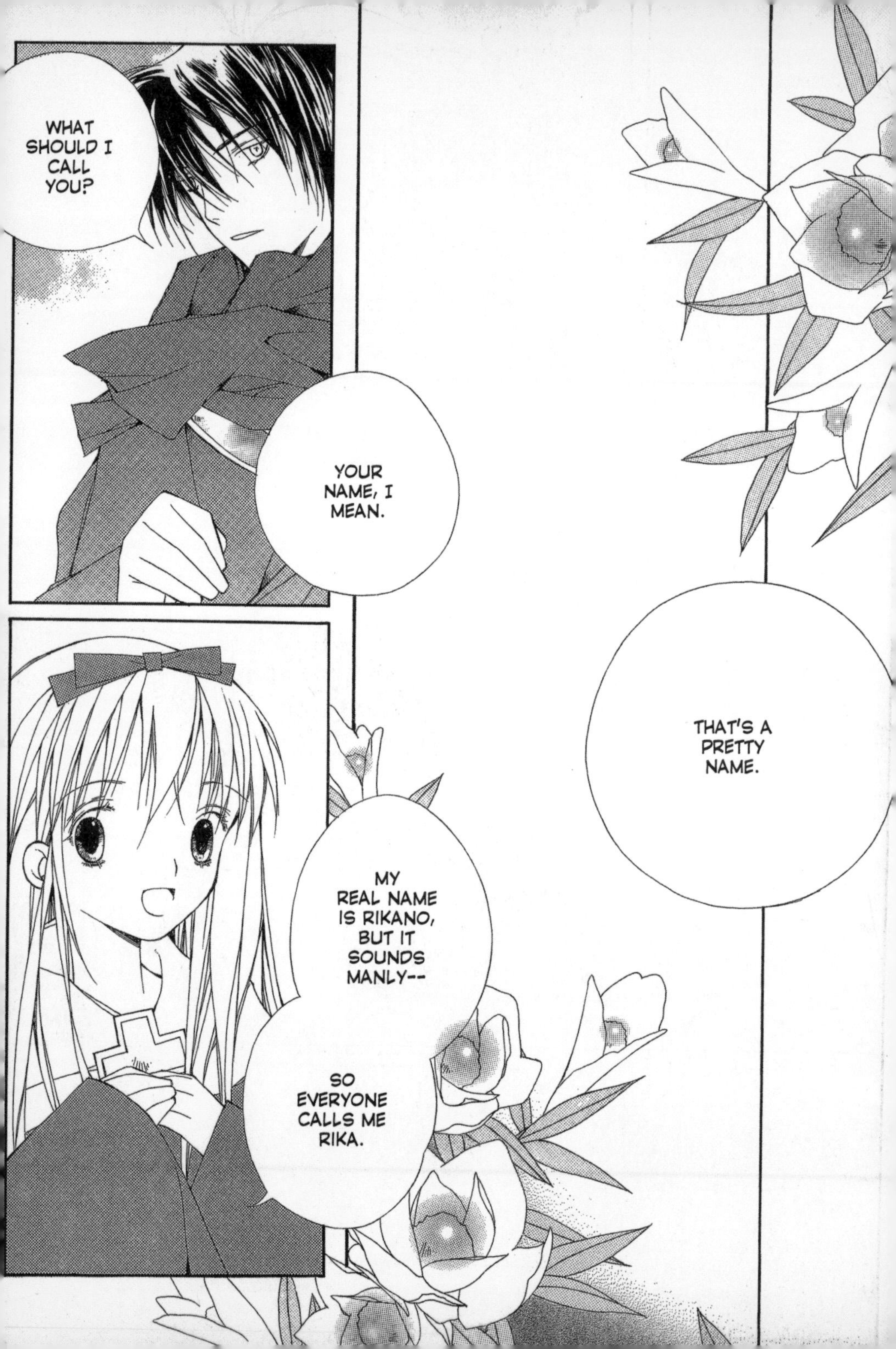
WHAT SHOULD I CALL YOU?
YOUR NAME, I MEAN.
MY REAL NAME IS RIKANO, BUT IT SOUNDS MANLY--
SO EVERYONE CALLS ME RIKA.
THAT'S A PRETTY NAME.

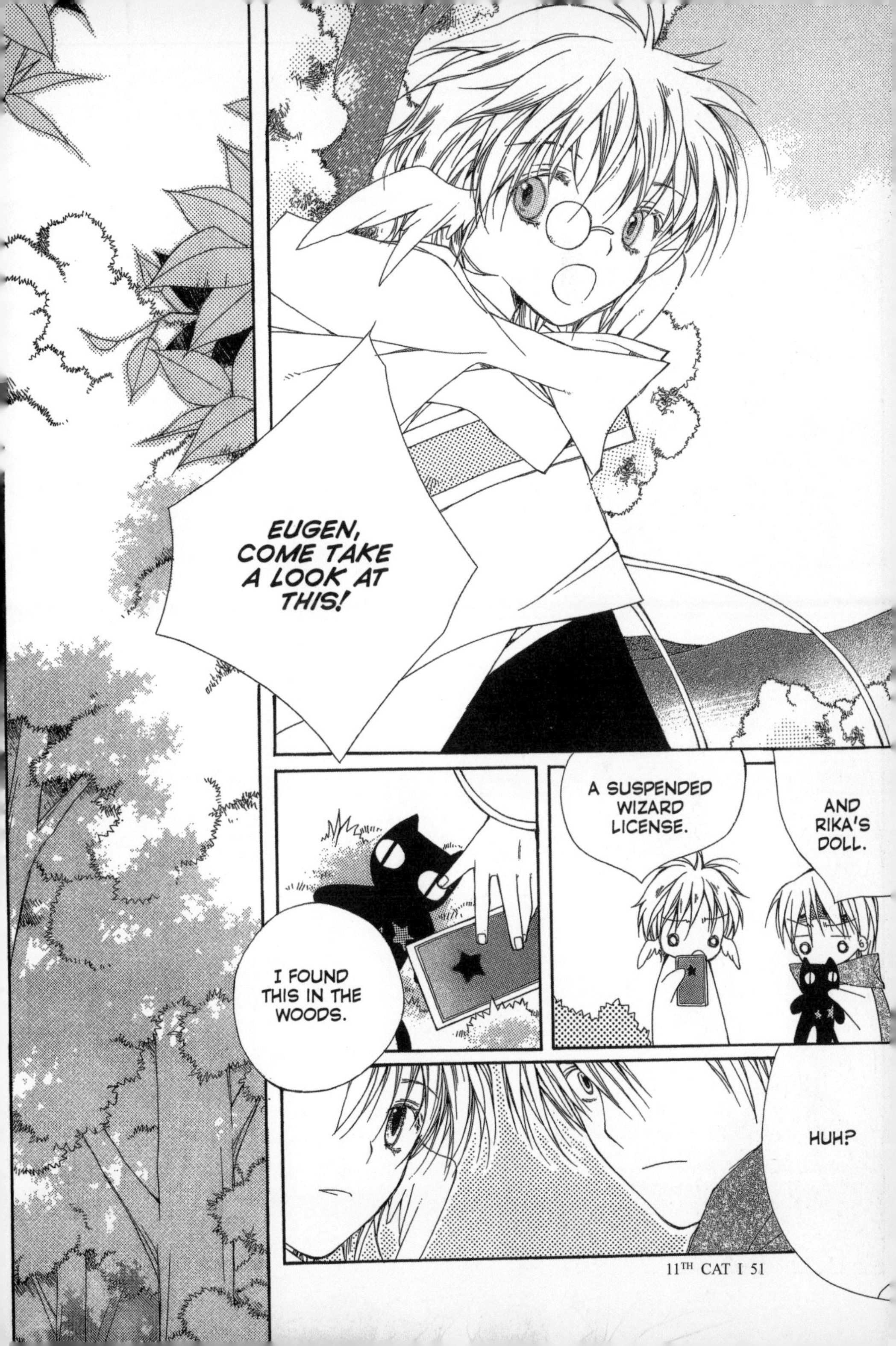
EUGEN, COME TAKE A LOOK AT THIS!
I FOUND THIS IN THE WOODS.
A SUSPENDED WIZARD LICENSE.
AND RIKA'S DOLL.
HUH?

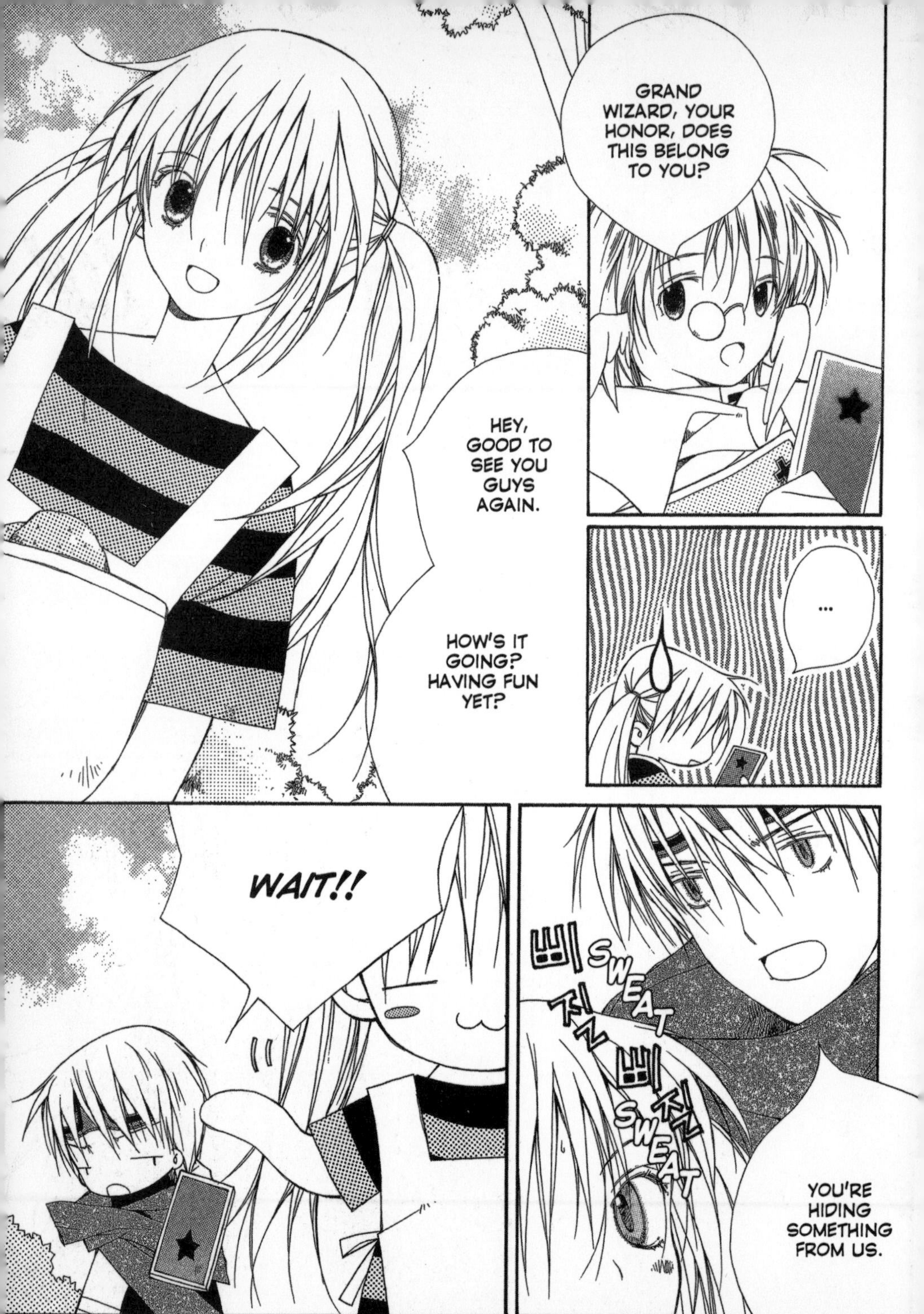
HEY, GOOD TO SEE YOU GUYS AGAIN.
HOW'S IT GOING? HAVING FUN YET?
GRAND WIZARD, YOUR HONOR, DOES THIS BELONG TO YOU?
...
WAIT!!
SWEAT
SWEAT
YOU'RE HIDING SOMETHING FROM US.

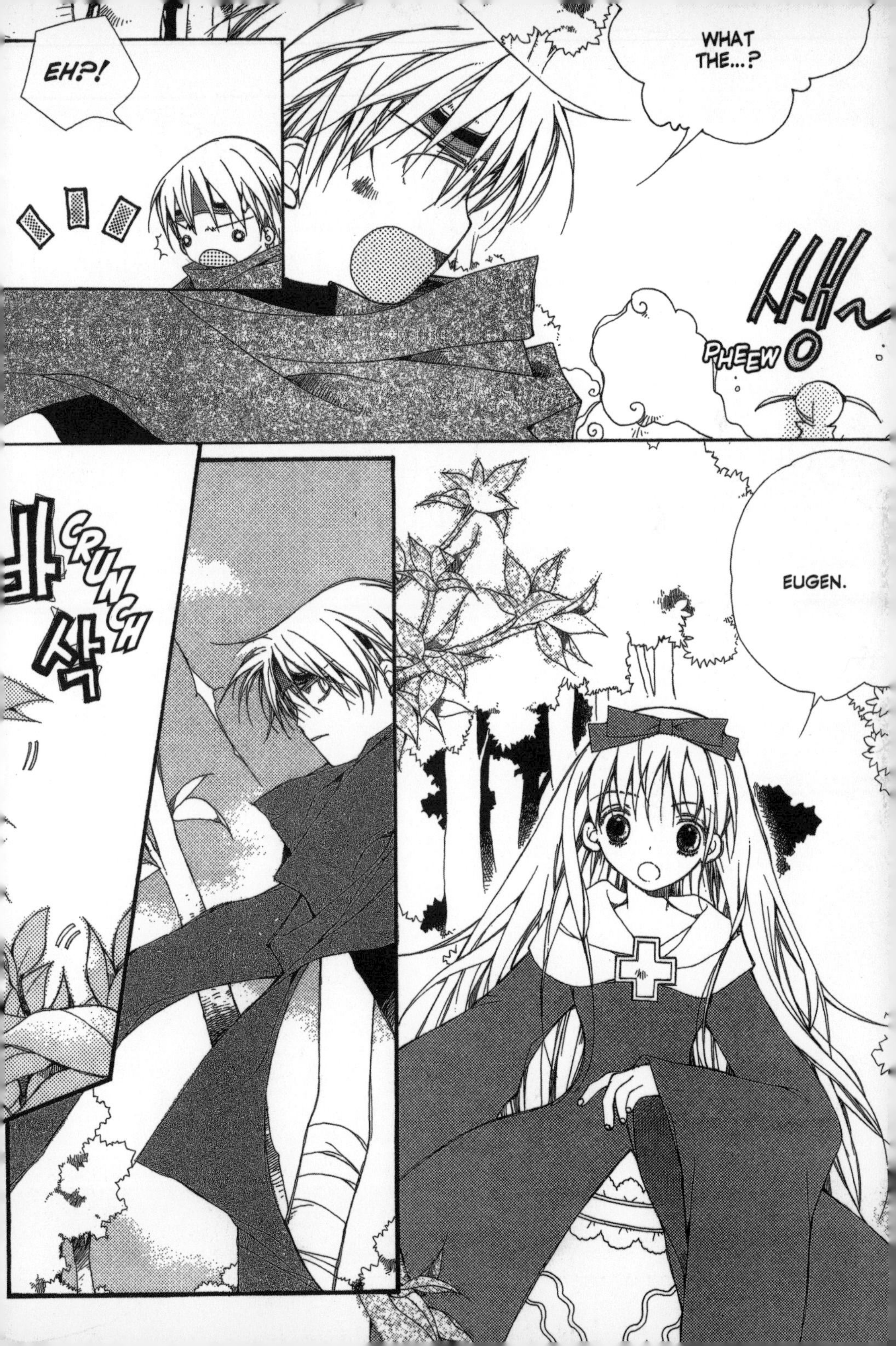
EH?!
WHAT THE...?
PHEEW
CRUNCH
EUGEN.

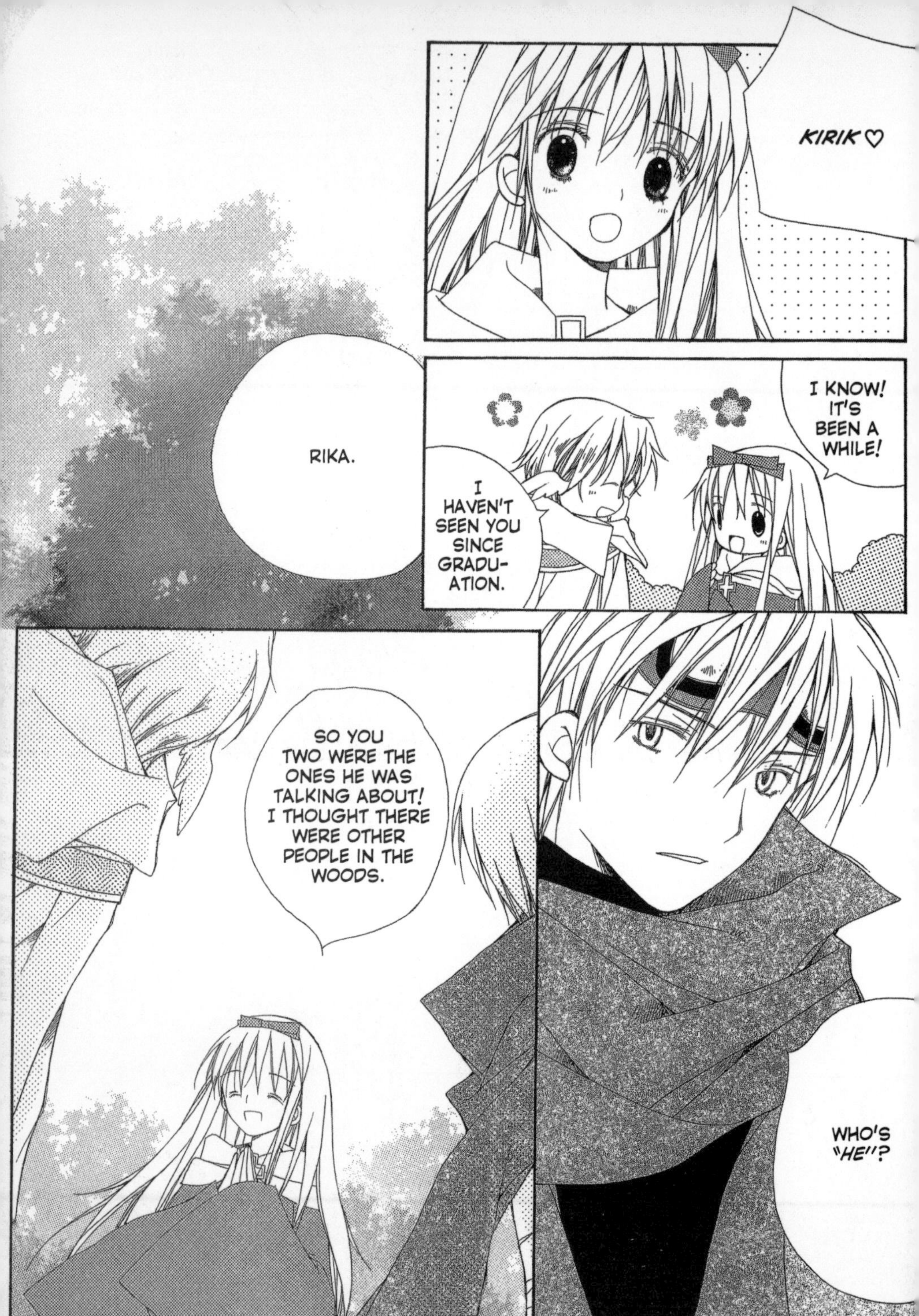
KIRIK♡
RIKA.
I KNOW! IT'S BEEN A WHILE!
I HAVEN'T SEEN YOU SINCE GRADU-ATION.
SO YOU TWO WERE THE ONES HE WAS TALKING ABOUT! I THOUGHT THERE WERE OTHER PEOPLE IN THE WOODS.
WHO'S "HE"?

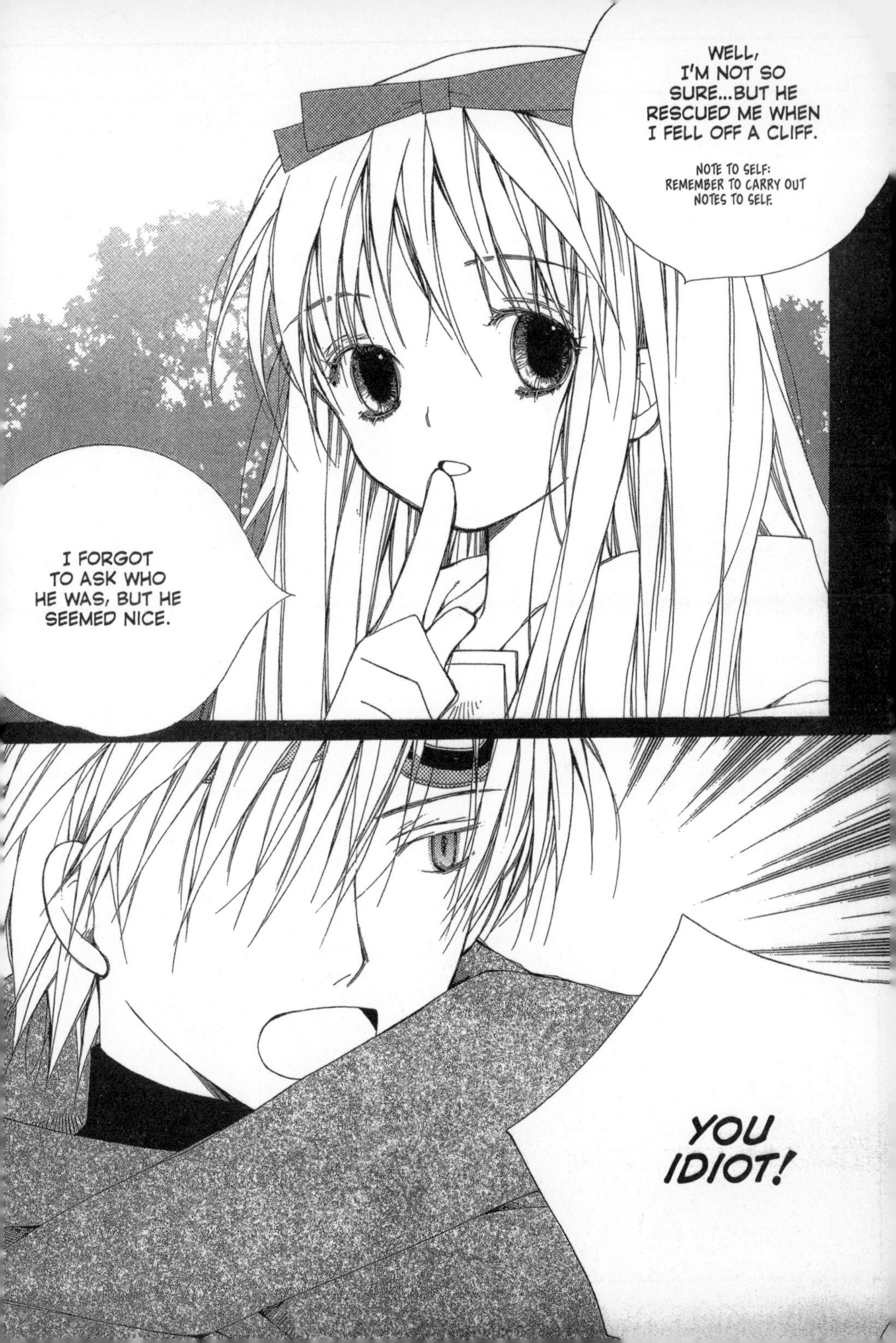
WELL, I'M NOT SO SURE...BUT HE RESCUED ME WHEN I FELL OFF A CLIFF.
NOTE TO SELF: REMEMBER TO CARRY OUT NOTES TO SELF.
I FORGOT TO ASK WHO HE WAS, BUT HE SEEMED NICE.
YOU IDIOT!

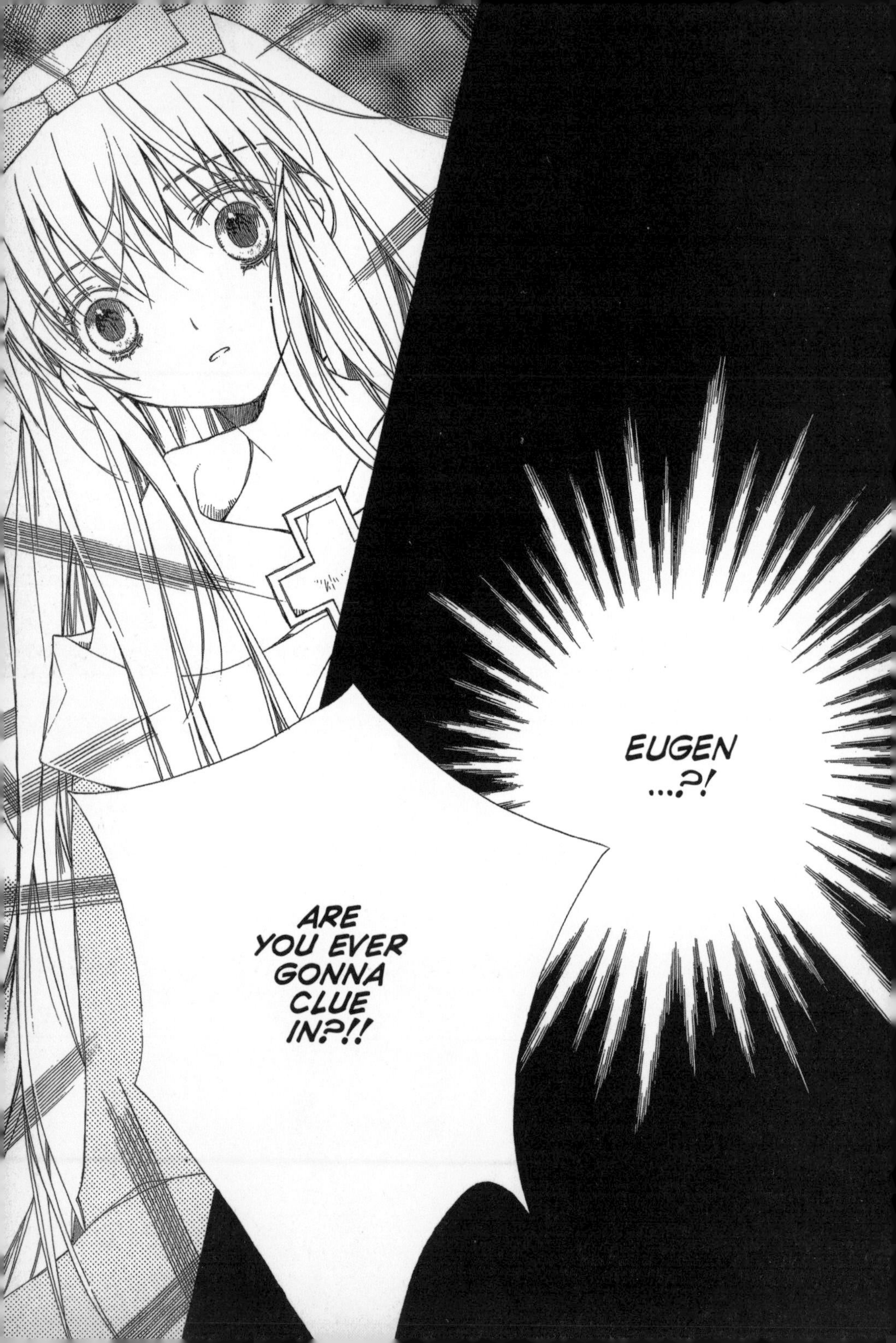
EUGEN ...?!
ARE YOU EVER GONNA CLUE IN?!!

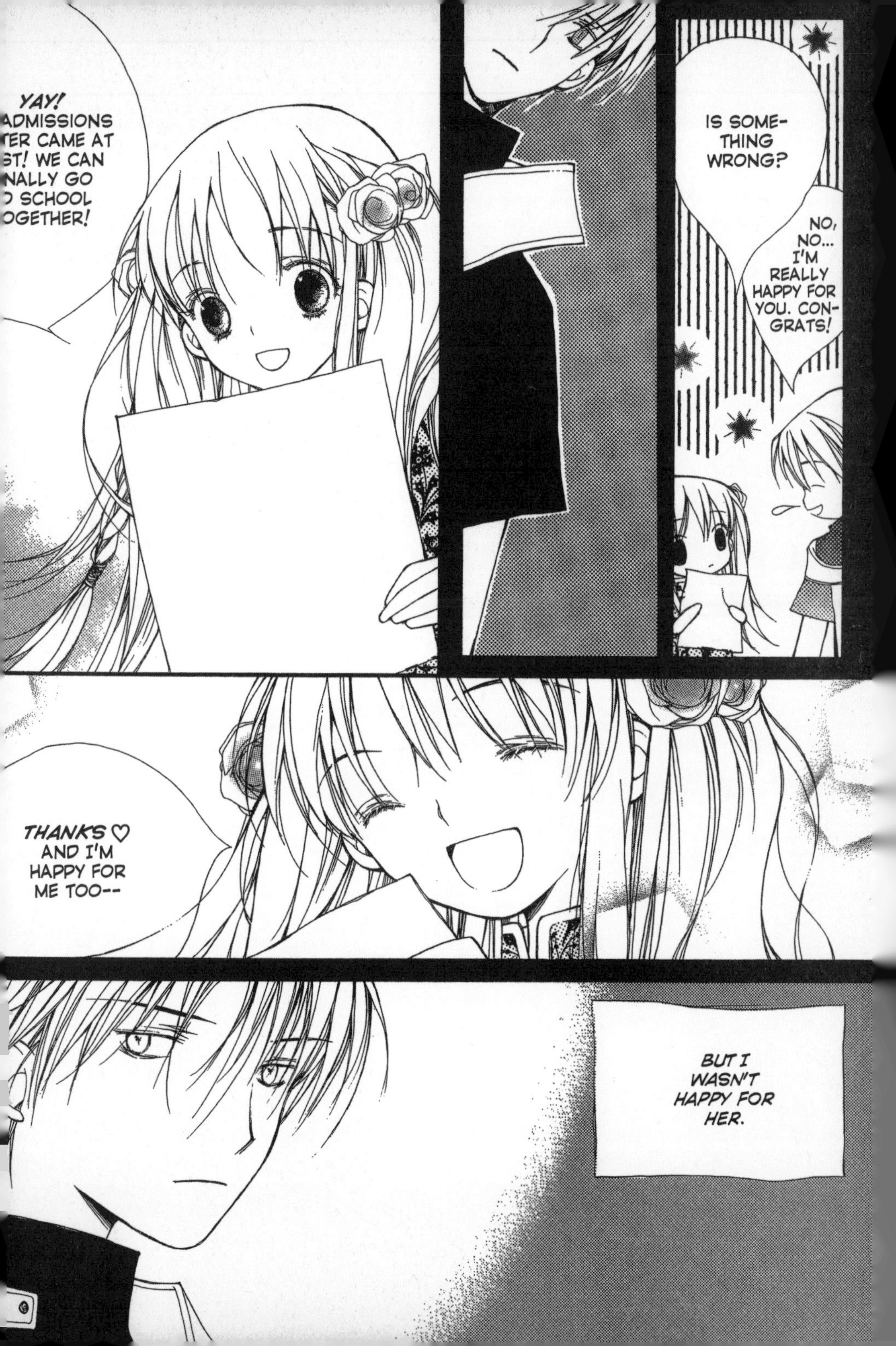
YAY! ADMISSIONS TER CAME AT ST! WE CAN NALLY GO D SCHOOL OGETHER!
IS SOME-THING WRONG?
NO, NO... I'M REALLY HAPPY FOR YOU. CON-GRATS!
THANKS ♡ AND I'M HAPPY FOR ME TOO--
BUT I WASN'T HAPPY FOR HER.

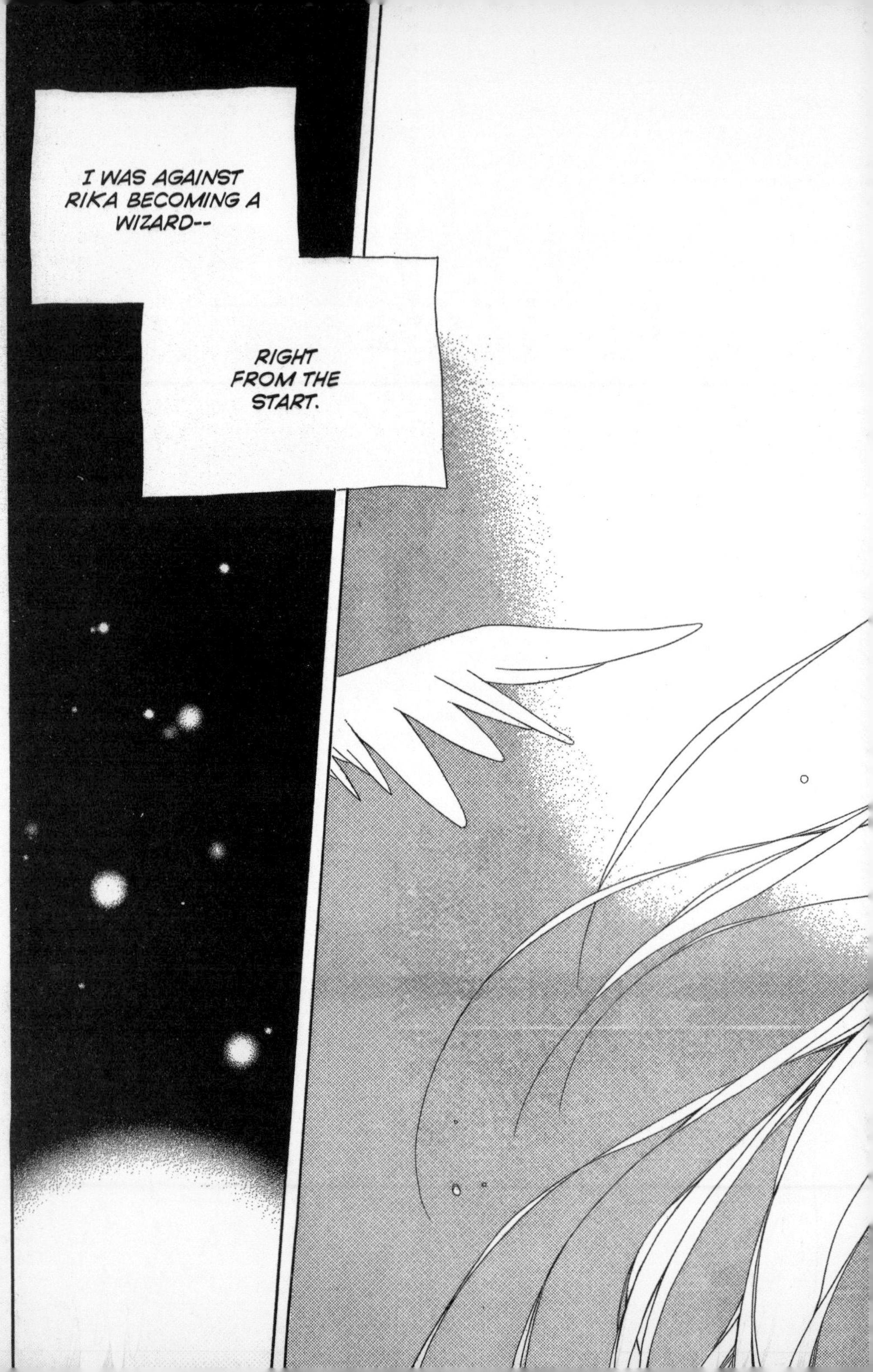
I WAS AGAINST RIKA BECOMING A WIZARD--
RIGHT FROM THE START.

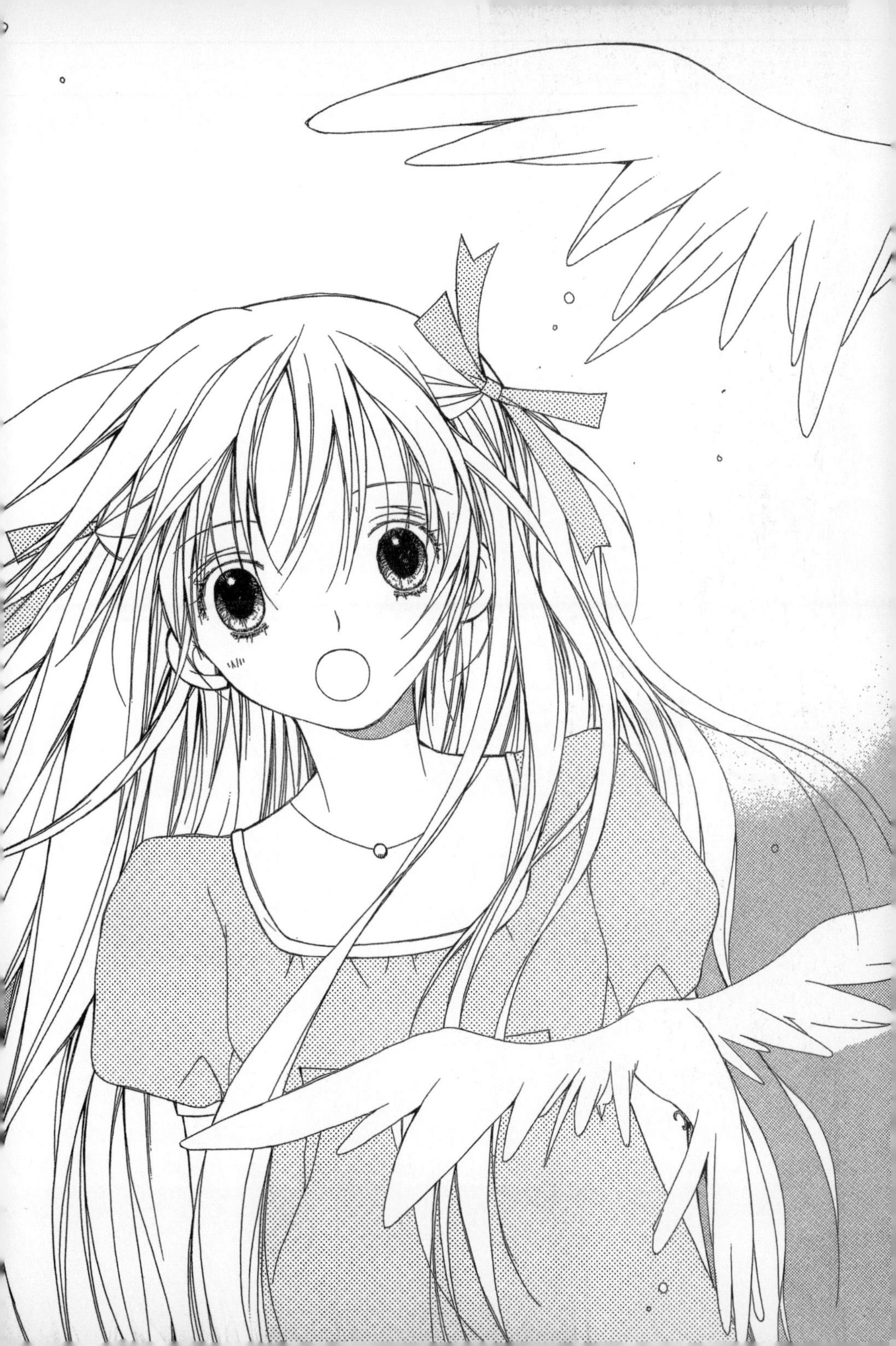

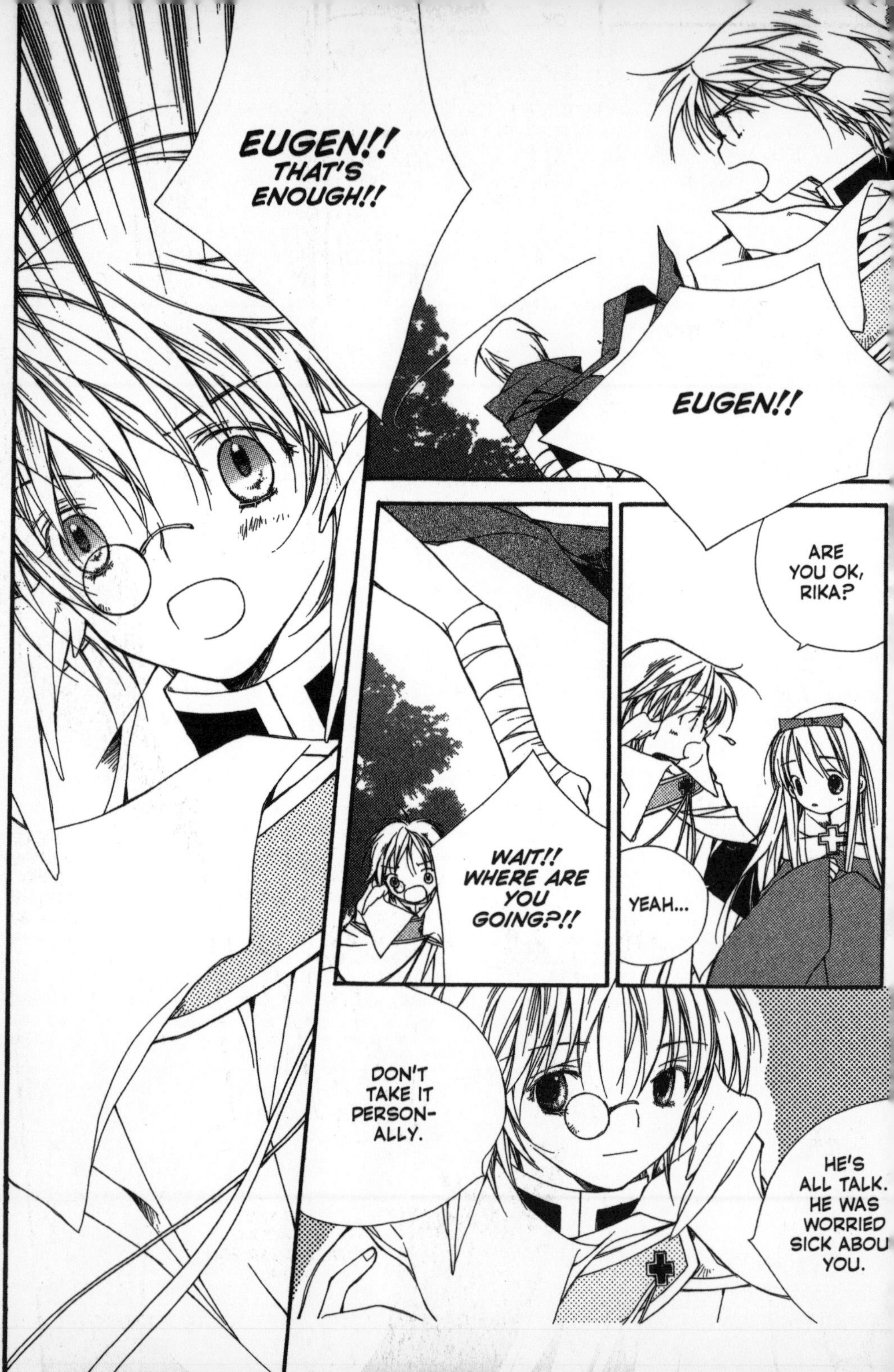
EUGEN!! THAT'S ENOUGH!!
EUGEN!!
WAIT!! WHERE ARE YOU GOING?!!
ARE YOU OK, RIKA?
YEAH...
DON'T TAKE IT PERSON-ALLY.
HE'S ALL TALK. HE WAS WORRIED SICK ABOU YOU.

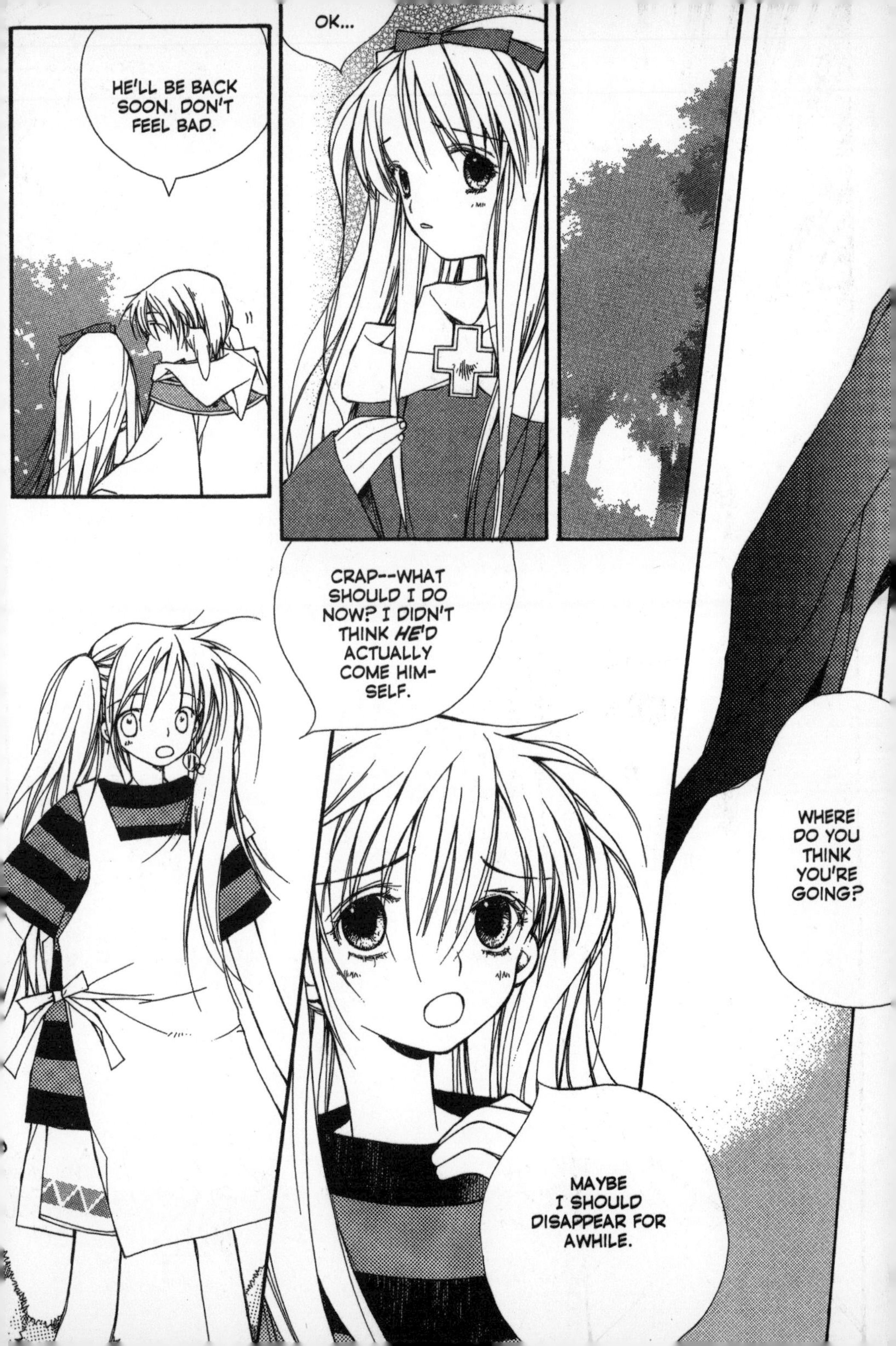
HE'LL BE BACK SOON. DON'T FEEL BAD.
OK...
CRAP--WHAT SHOULD I DO NOW? I DIDN'T THINK *HE*'D ACTUALLY COME HIM-SELF.
MAYBE I SHOULD DISAPPEAR FOR AWHILE.
WHERE DO YOU THINK YOU'RE GOING?

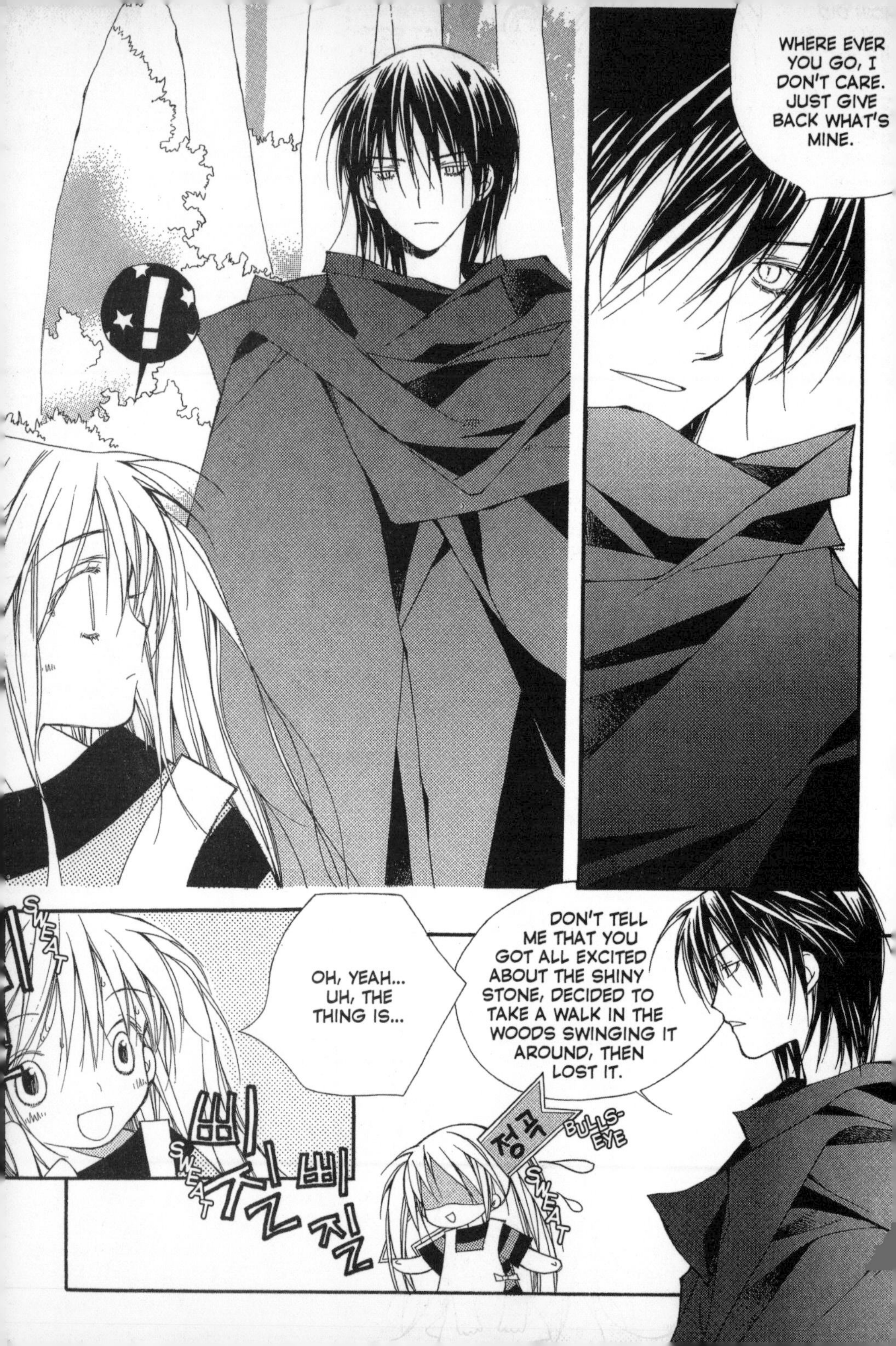
!
WHERE EVER YOU GO, I DON'T CARE. JUST GIVE BACK WHAT'S MINE.
SWEAT
OH, YEAH... UH, THE THING IS...
DON'T TELL ME THAT YOU GOT ALL EXCITED ABOUT THE SHINY STONE, DECIDED TO TAKE A WALK IN THE WOODS SWINGING IT AROUND, THEN LOST IT.
삐질 삐질
SWEAT
정곡
BULLS-EYE
SWEAT

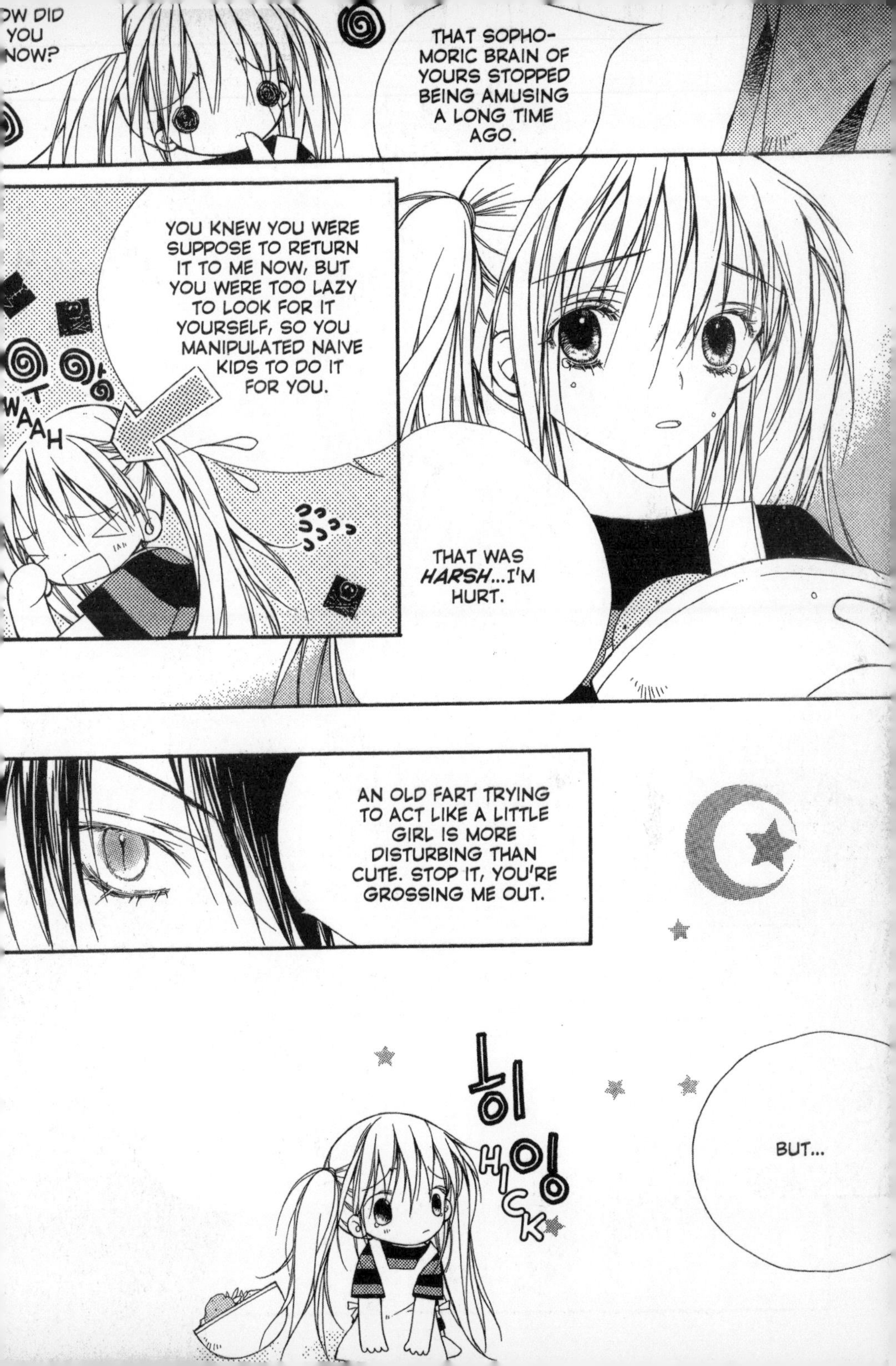

OW DID YOU NOW?
THAT SOPHOMORIC BRAIN OF YOURS STOPPED BEING AMUSING A LONG TIME AGO.
YOU KNEW YOU WERE SUPPOSE TO RETURN IT TO ME NOW, BUT YOU WERE TOO LAZY TO LOOK FOR IT YOURSELF, SO YOU MANIPULATED NAIVE KIDS TO DO IT FOR YOU.
WAAH
THAT WAS *HARSH*...I'M HURT.
AN OLD FART TRYING TO ACT LIKE A LITTLE GIRL IS MORE DISTURBING THAN CUTE. STOP IT, YOU'RE GROSSING ME OUT.
HICK
BUT...

THE STONE IS MUCH TOO DANGEROUS FOR NOVICE WIZARDS.

AL
EUG
DOES
GET
AT M

MAYBE I SHOULD'VE ASKED KIRIK TO COME ALONG INSTEAD.

I HOPE THOSE KIDS DON'T FIND IT.

BLINK

BLINK

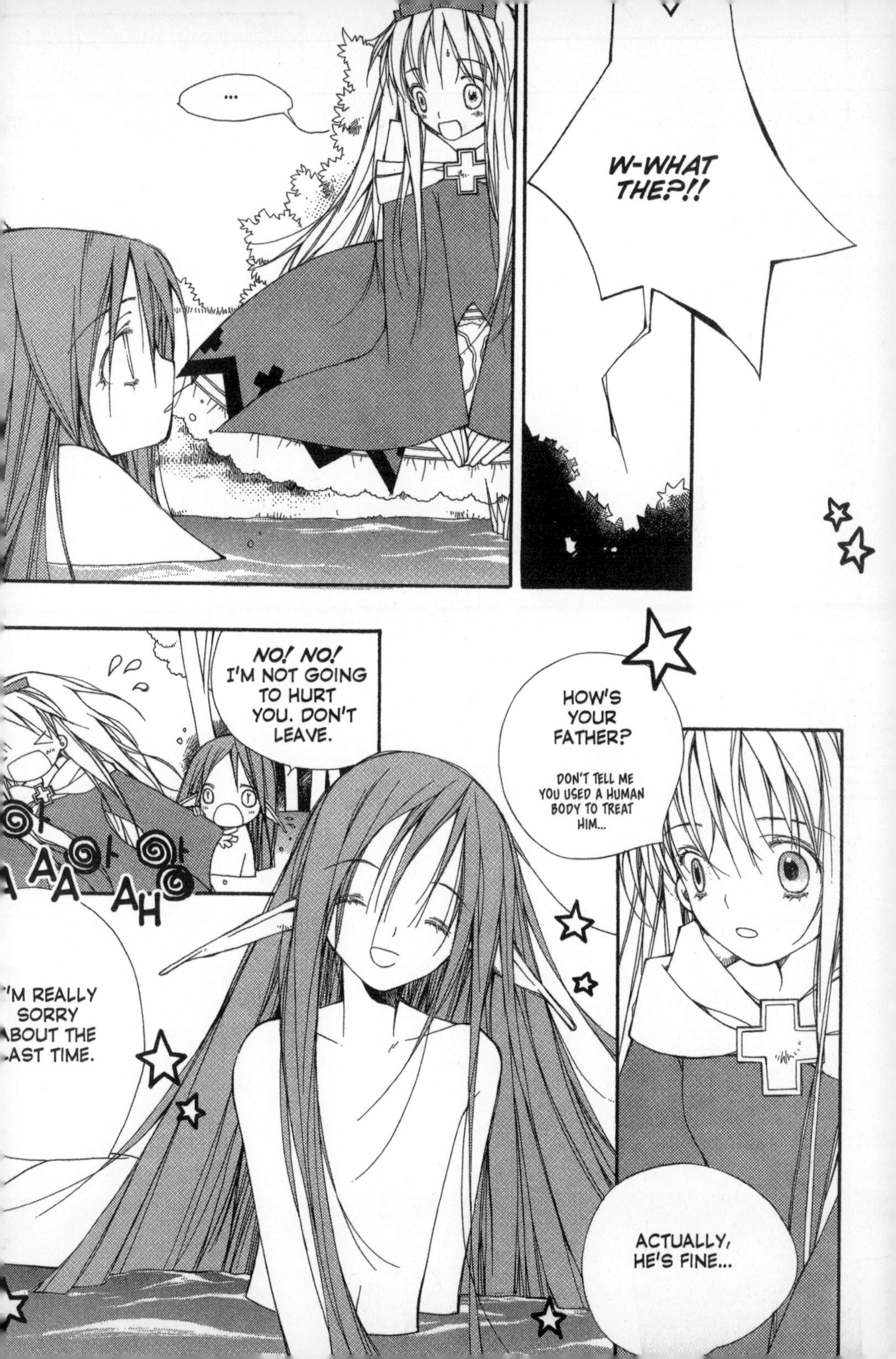
...
W-WHAT THE?!!
NO! NO! I'M NOT GOING TO HURT YOU. DON'T LEAVE.
A A A AH
'M REALLY SORRY BOUT THE AST TIME.
HOW'S YOUR FATHER?
DON'T TELL ME YOU USED A HUMAN BODY TO TREAT HIM...
ACTUALLY, HE'S FINE...

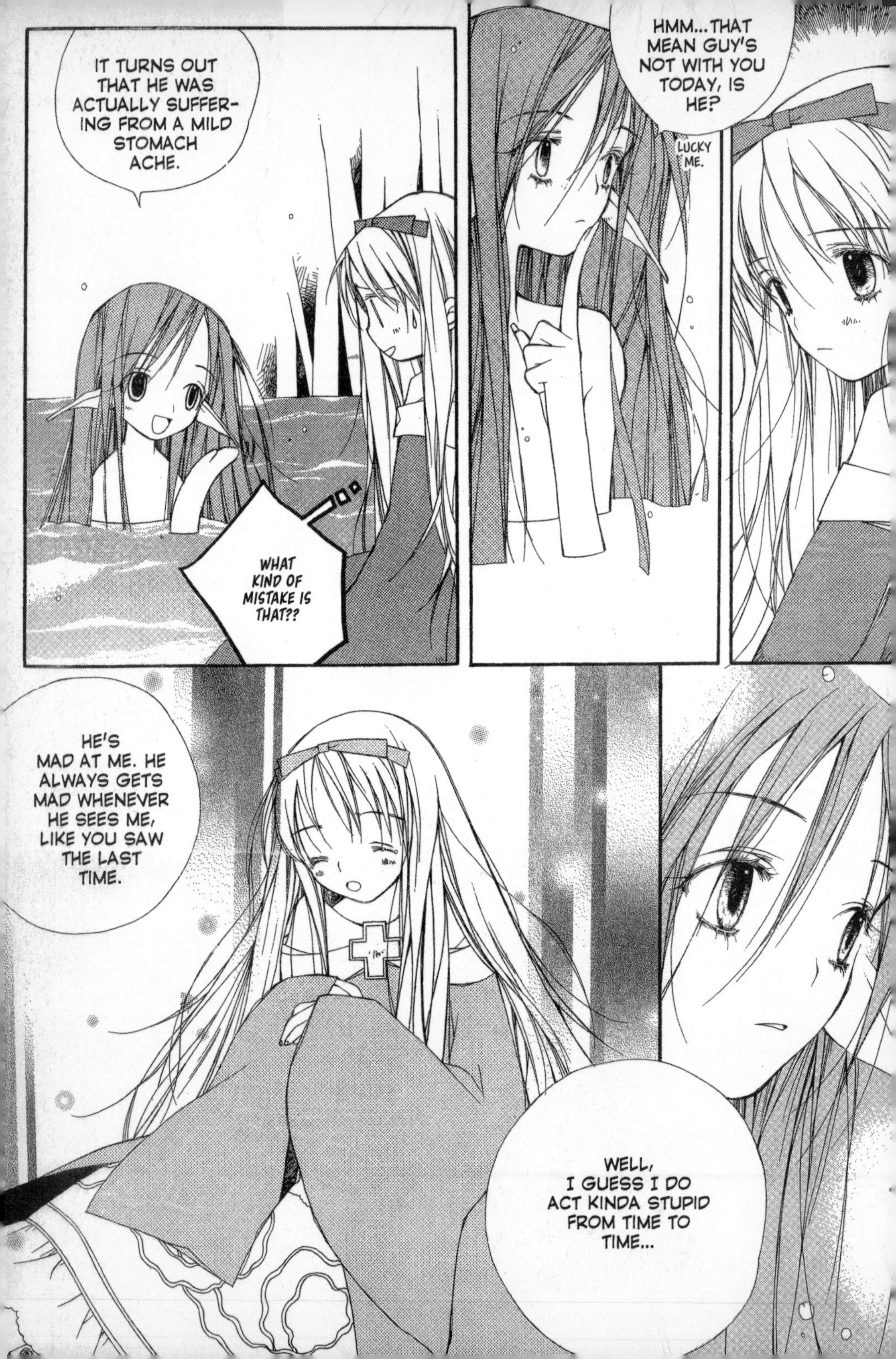
IT TURNS OUT THAT HE WAS ACTUALLY SUFFER-ING FROM A MILD STOMACH ACHE.
WHAT KIND OF MISTAKE IS THAT??
HMM...THAT MEAN GUY'S NOT WITH YOU TODAY, IS HE?
LUCKY ME.
HE'S MAD AT ME. HE ALWAYS GETS MAD WHENEVER HE SEES ME, LIKE YOU SAW THE LAST TIME.
WELL, I GUESS I DO ACT KINDA STUPID FROM TIME TO TIME...

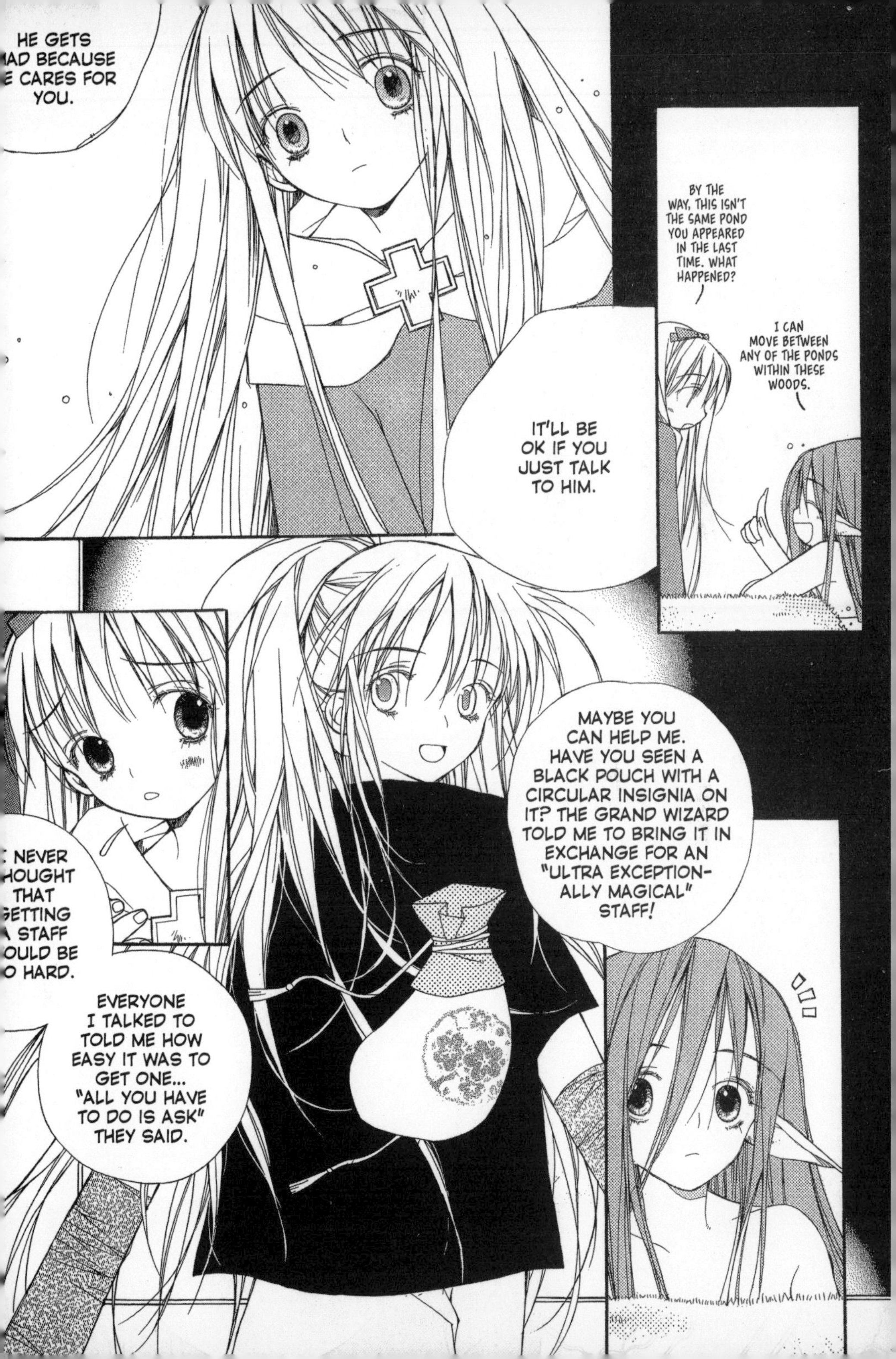
HE GETS MAD BECAUSE E CARES FOR YOU.
IT'LL BE OK IF YOU JUST TALK TO HIM.
BY THE WAY, THIS ISN'T THE SAME POND YOU APPEARED IN THE LAST TIME. WHAT HAPPENED?
I CAN MOVE BETWEEN ANY OF THE PONDS WITHIN THESE WOODS.
NEVER HOUGHT THAT ETTING A STAFF OULD BE O HARD.
EVERYONE I TALKED TO TOLD ME HOW EASY IT WAS TO GET ONE... "ALL YOU HAVE TO DO IS ASK" THEY SAID.
MAYBE YOU CAN HELP ME. HAVE YOU SEEN A BLACK POUCH WITH A CIRCULAR INSIGNIA ON IT? THE GRAND WIZARD TOLD ME TO BRING IT IN EXCHANGE FOR AN "ULTRA EXCEPTION-ALLY MAGICAL" STAFF!

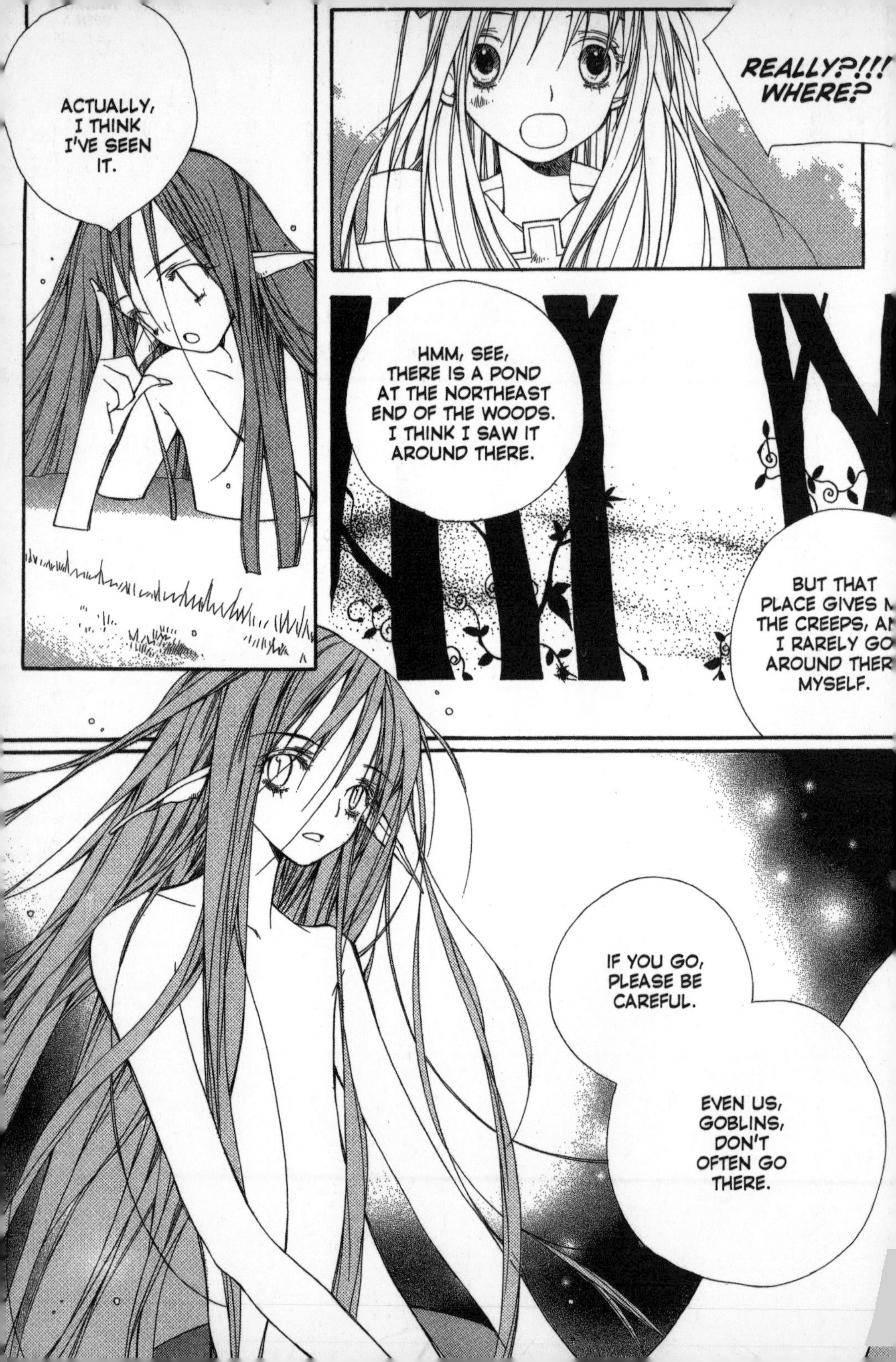
ACTUALLY, I THINK I'VE SEEN IT.
REALLY?!!! WHERE?
HMM, SEE, THERE IS A POND AT THE NORTHEAST END OF THE WOODS. I THINK I SAW IT AROUND THERE.
BUT THAT PLACE GIVES M THE CREEPS, A I RARELY GO AROUND THER MYSELF.
IF YOU GO, PLEASE BE CAREFUL.
EVEN US, GOBLINS, DON'T OFTEN GO THERE.

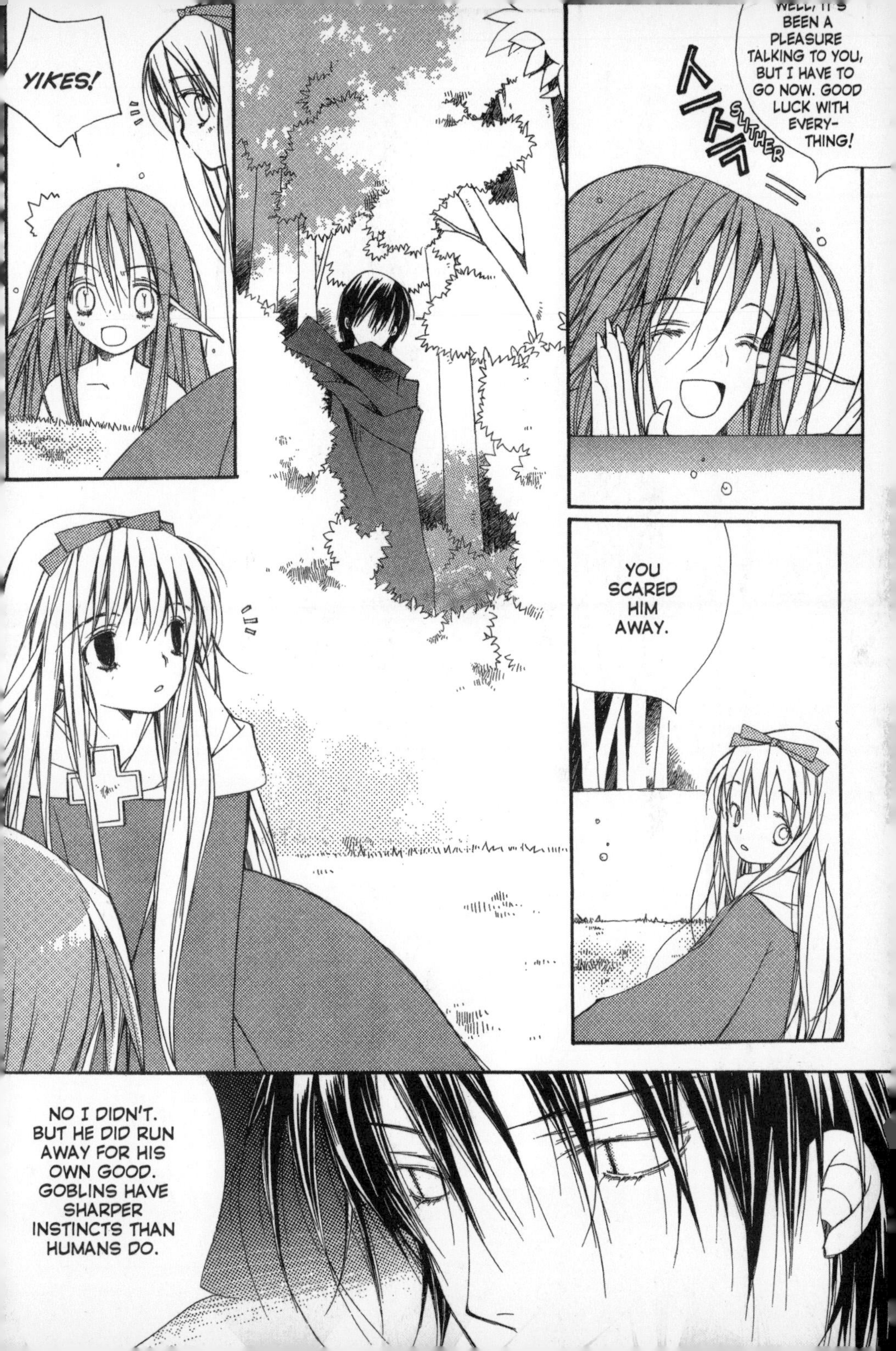
YIKES!
WELL, IT'S BEEN A PLEASURE TALKING TO YOU, BUT I HAVE TO GO NOW. GOOD LUCK WITH EVERY-THING!
SLITHER
YOU SCARED HIM AWAY.
NO I DIDN'T. BUT HE DID RUN AWAY FOR HIS OWN GOOD. GOBLINS HAVE SHARPER INSTINCTS THAN HUMANS DO.

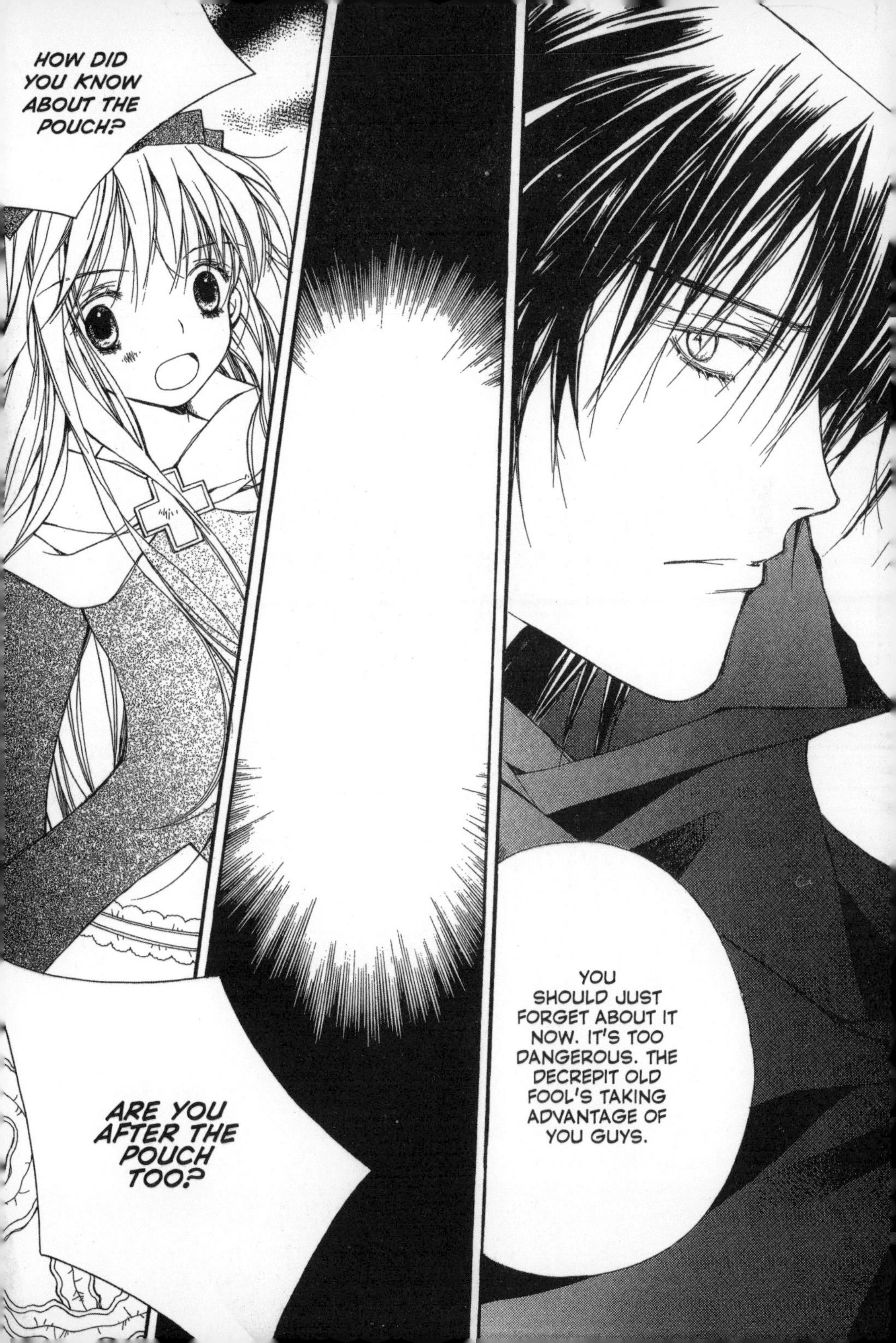
HOW DID YOU KNOW ABOUT THE POUCH?
YOU SHOULD JUST FORGET ABOUT IT NOW. IT'S TOO DANGEROUS. THE DECREPIT OLD FOOL'S TAKING ADVANTAGE OF YOU GUYS.
ARE YOU AFTER THE POUCH TOO?

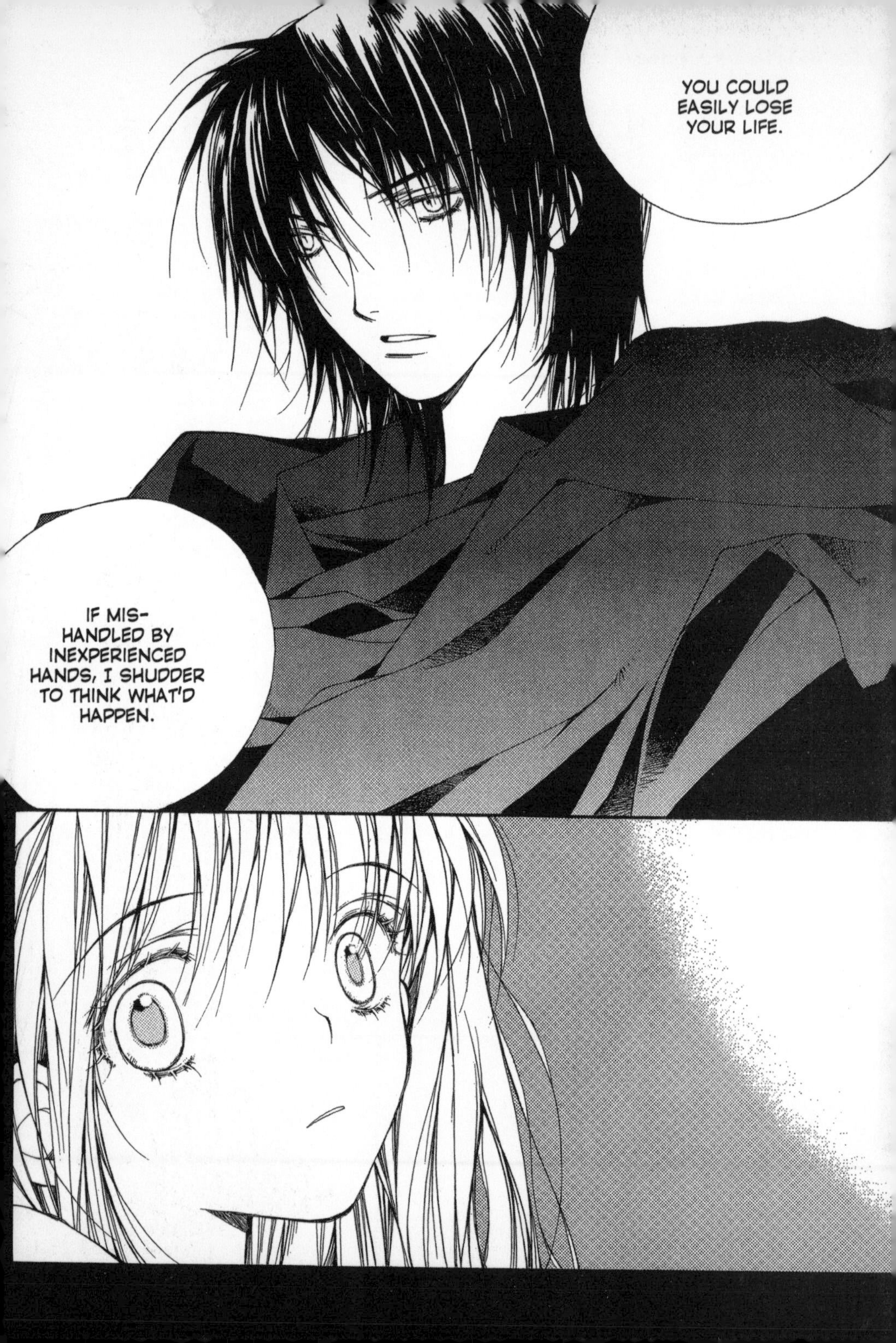
YOU COULD EASILY LOSE YOUR LIFE.
IF MIS-HANDLED BY INEXPERIENCED HANDS, I SHUDDER TO THINK WHAT'D HAPPEN.

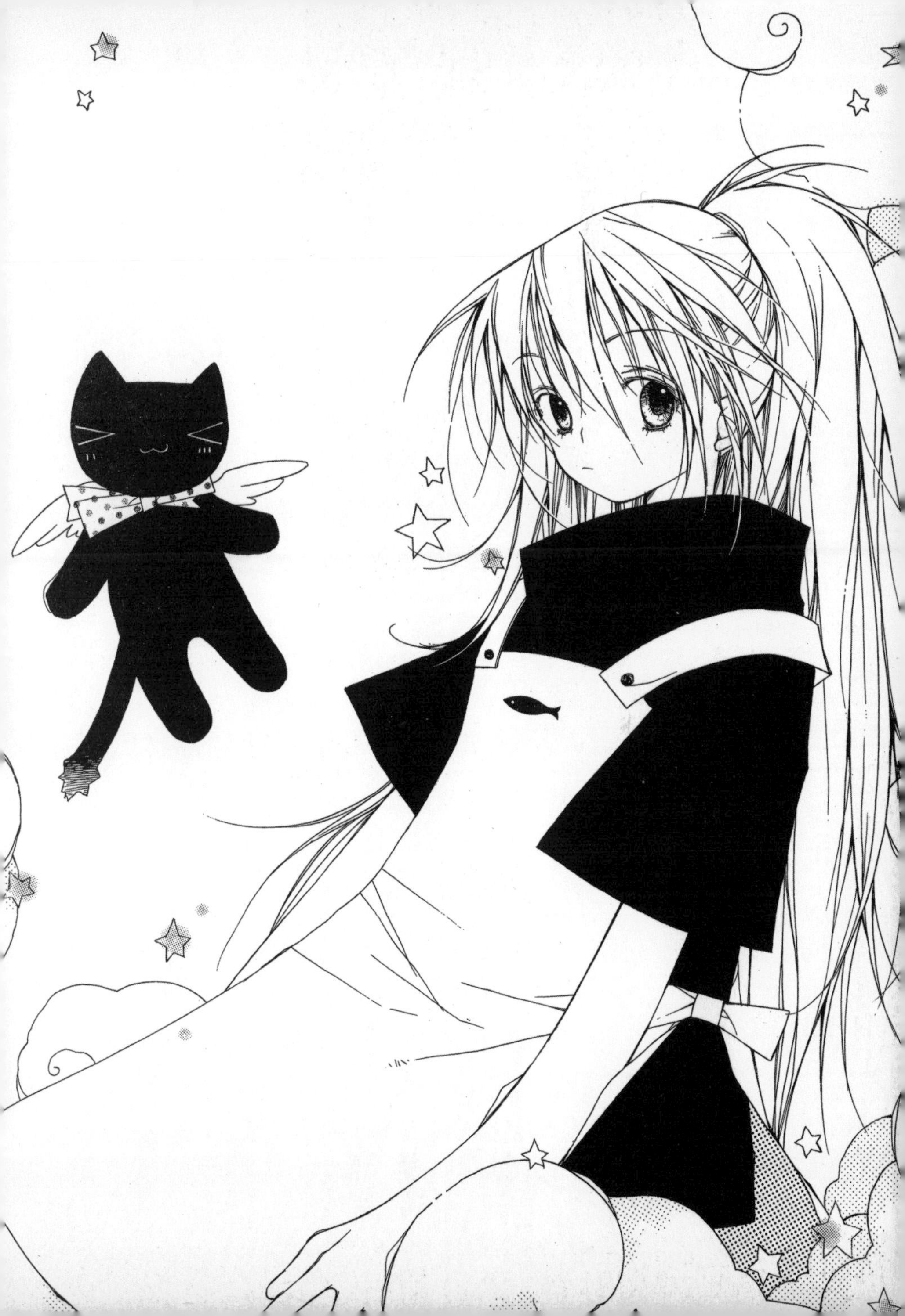

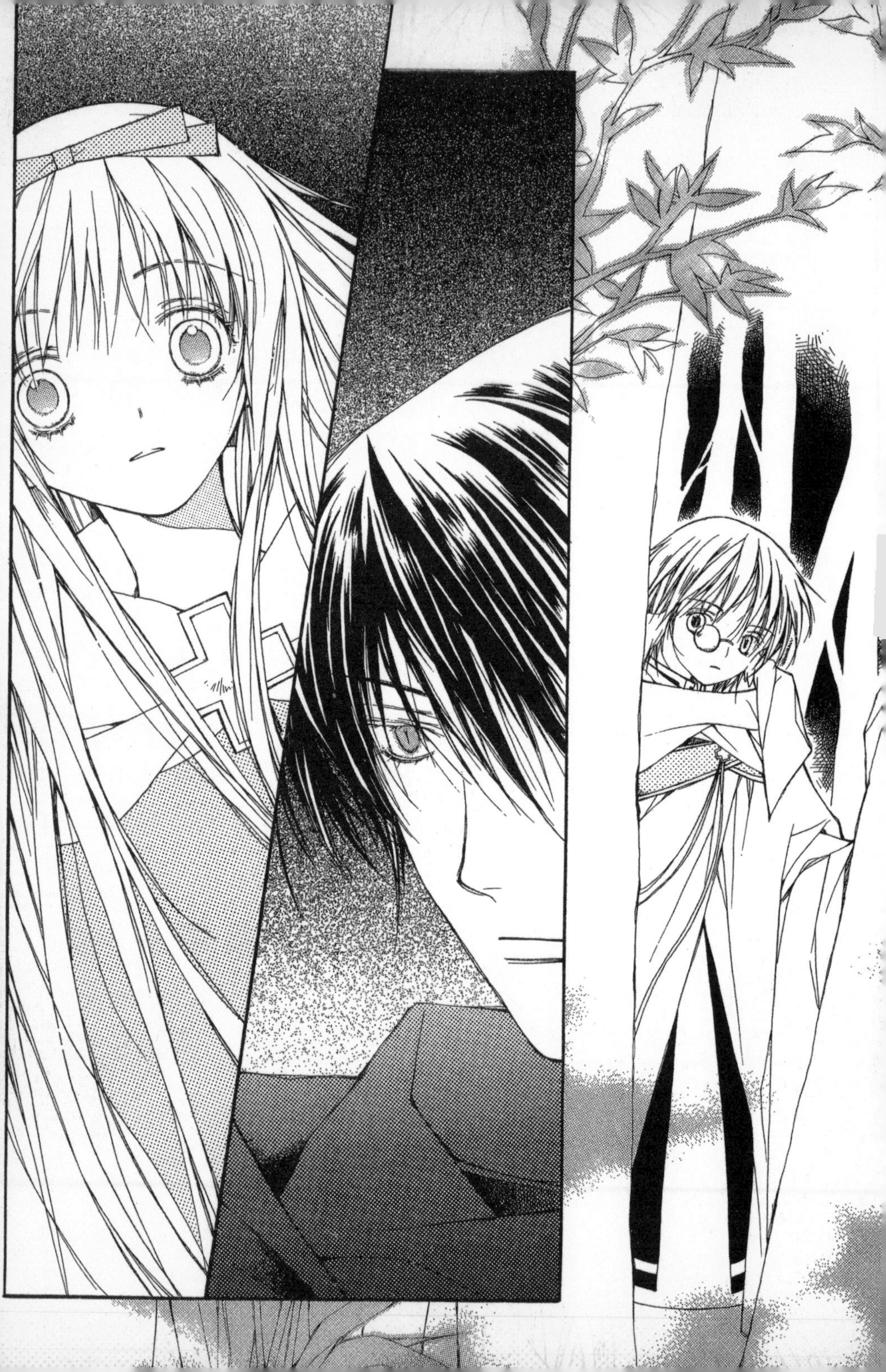

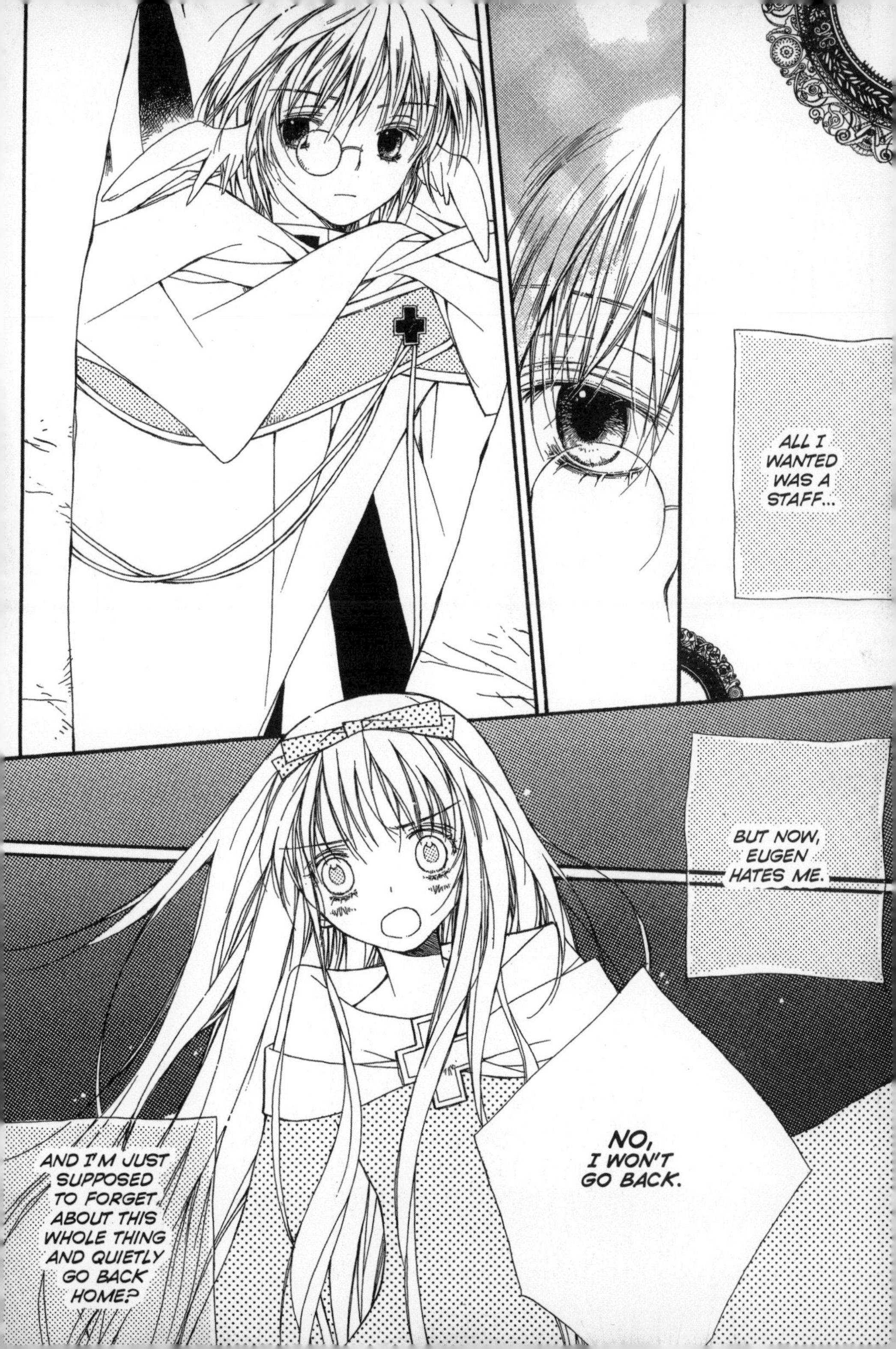
ALL I WANTED WAS A STAFF...
BUT NOW, EUGEN HATES ME.
AND I'M JUST SUPPOSED TO FORGET ABOUT THIS WHOLE THING AND QUIETLY GO BACK HOME?
NO, I WON'T GO BACK.

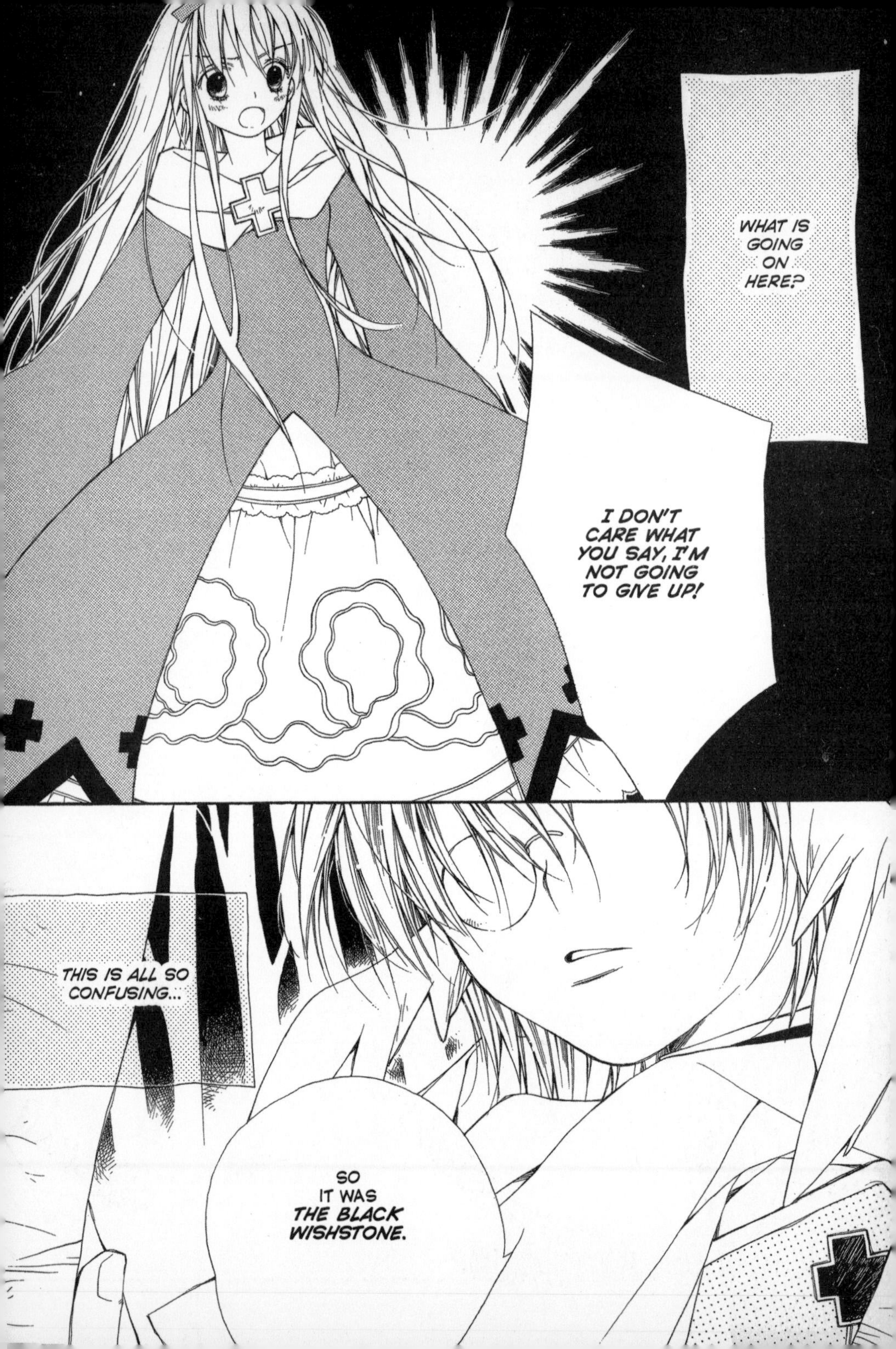
WHAT IS GOING ON HERE?
I DON'T CARE WHAT YOU SAY, I'M NOT GOING TO GIVE UP!
THIS IS ALL SO CONFUSING...
SO IT WAS *THE BLACK WISHSTONE.*

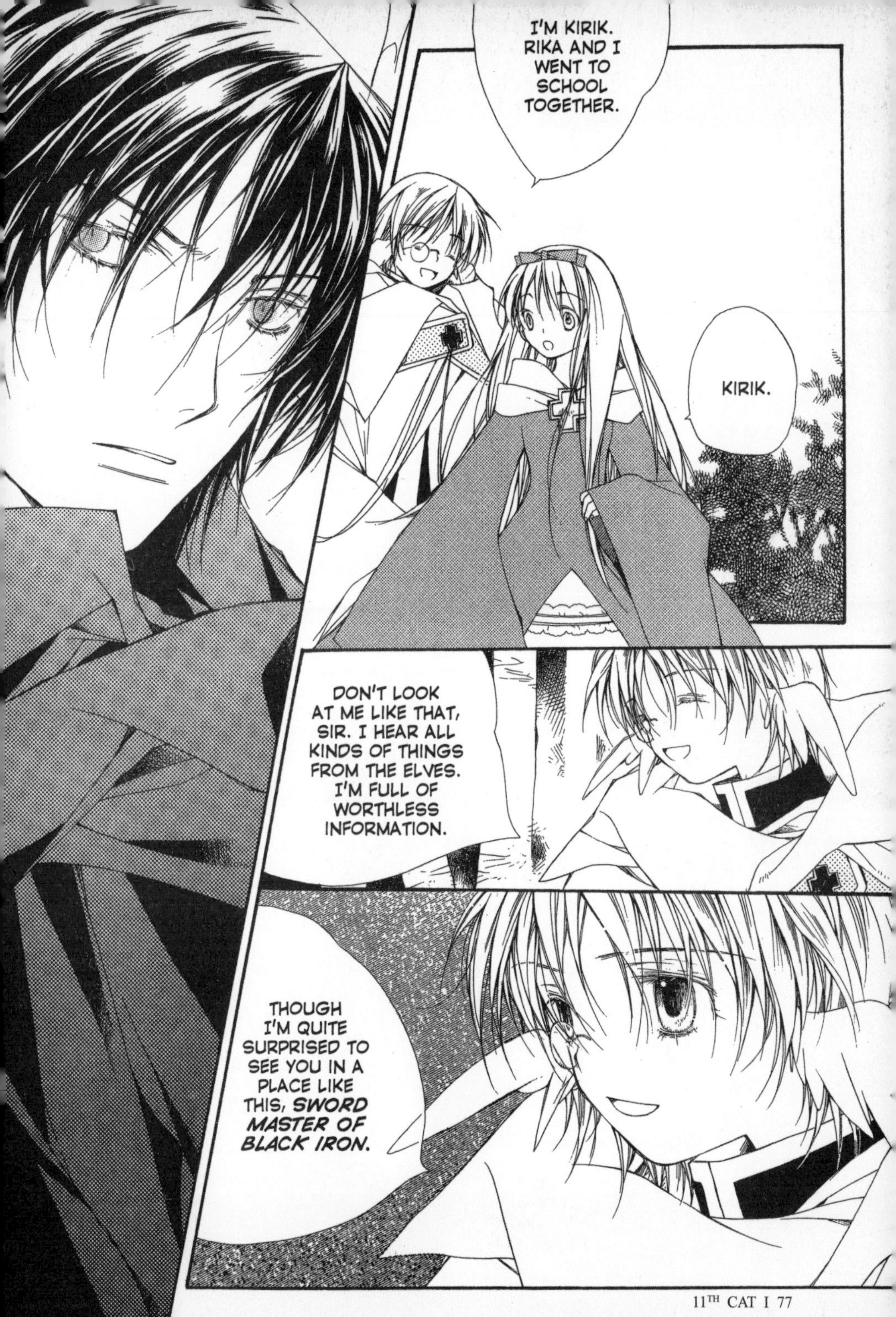
I'M KIRIK. RIKA AND I WENT TO SCHOOL TOGETHER.
KIRIK.
DON'T LOOK AT ME LIKE THAT, SIR. I HEAR ALL KINDS OF THINGS FROM THE ELVES. I'M FULL OF WORTHLESS INFORMATION.
THOUGH I'M QUITE SURPRISED TO SEE YOU IN A PLACE LIKE THIS, *SWORD MASTER OF BLACK IRON*.

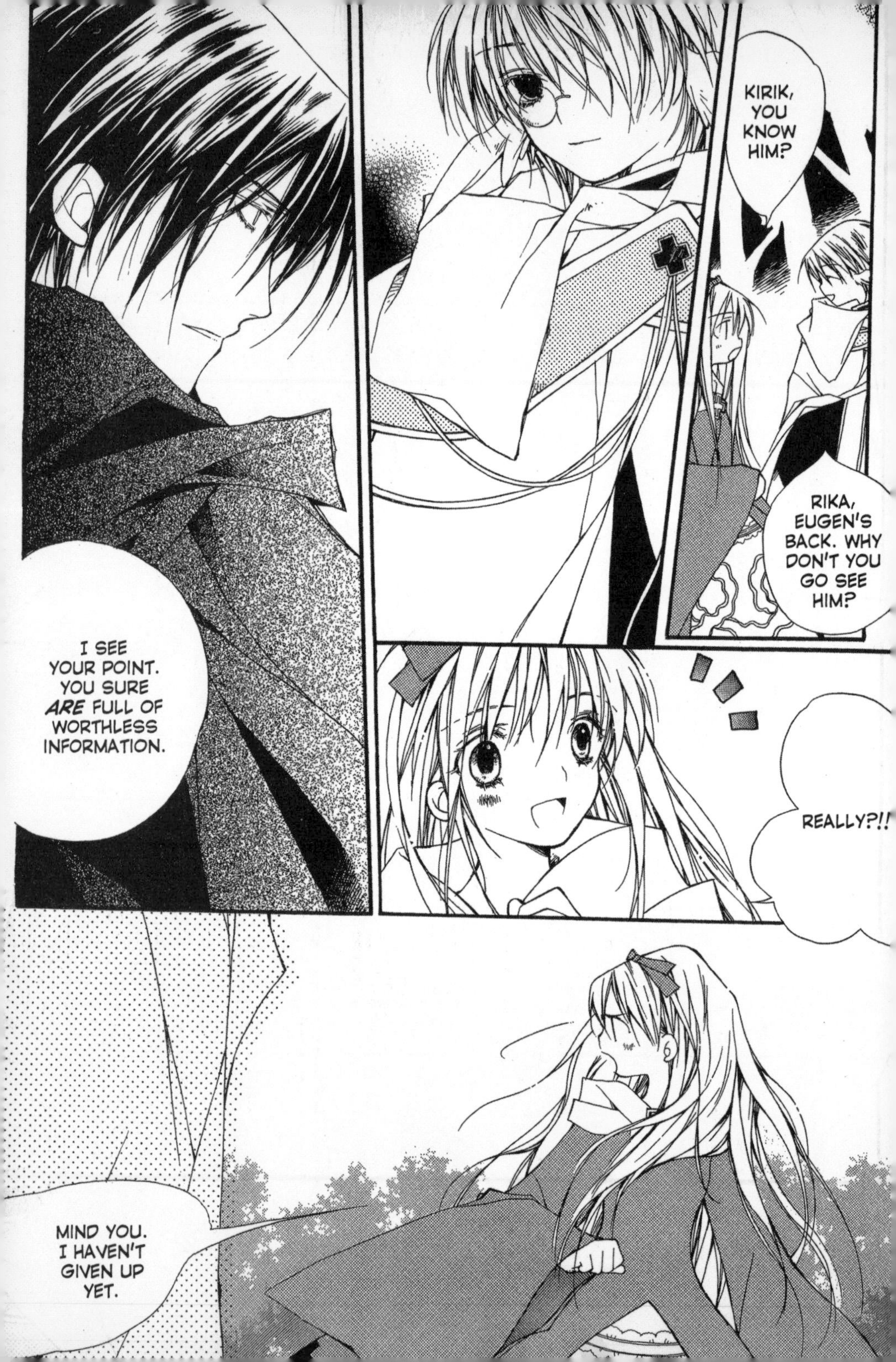
I SEE YOUR POINT. YOU SURE *ARE* FULL OF WORTHLESS INFORMATION.
KIRIK, YOU KNOW HIM?
RIKA, EUGEN'S BACK. WHY DON'T YOU GO SEE HIM?
REALLY?!!
MIND YOU. I HAVEN'T GIVEN UP YET.

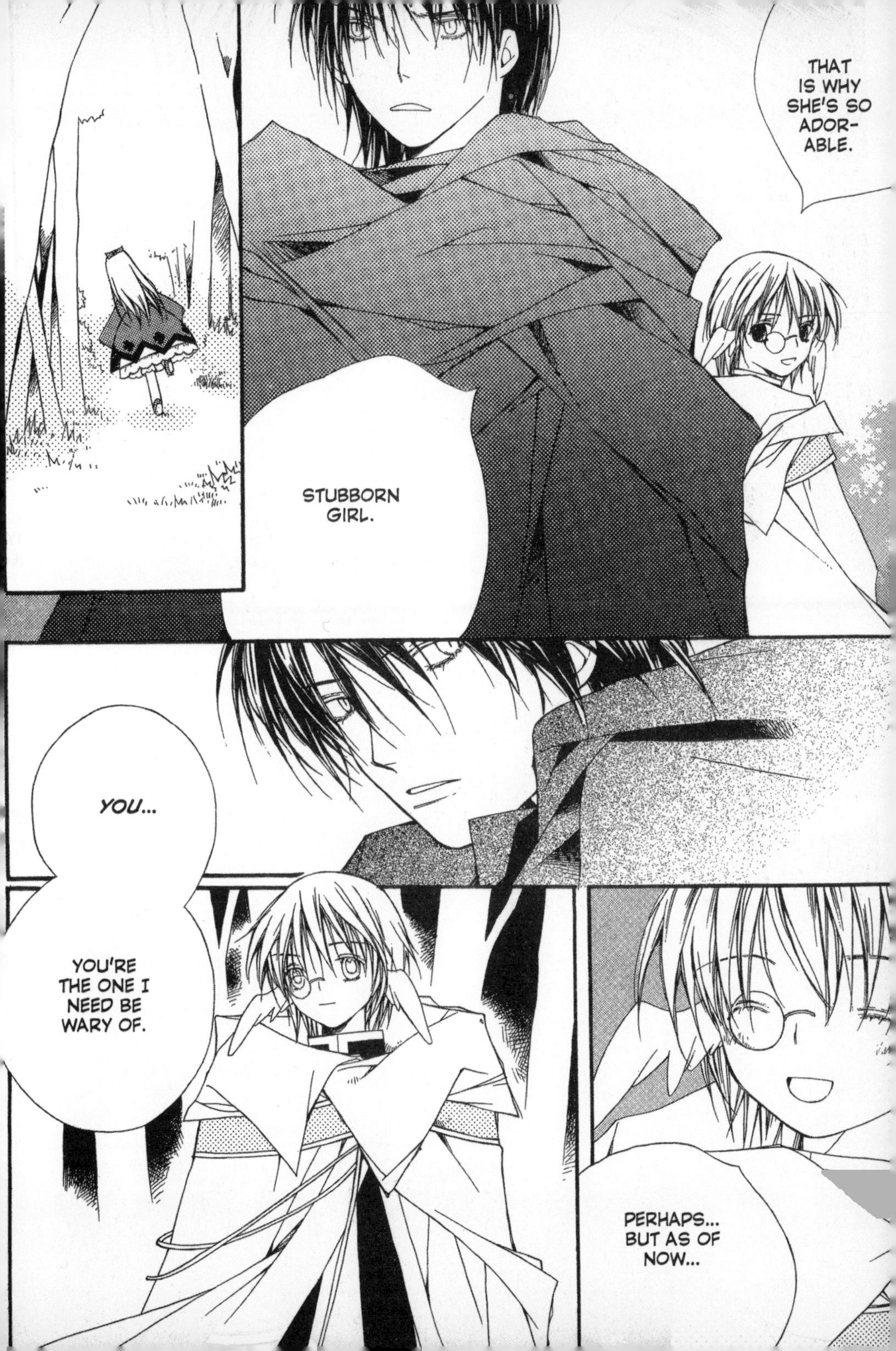
STUBBORN GIRL.
THAT IS WHY SHE'S SO ADOR-ABLE.
YOU...
YOU'RE THE ONE I NEED BE WARY OF.
PERHAPS... BUT AS OF NOW...

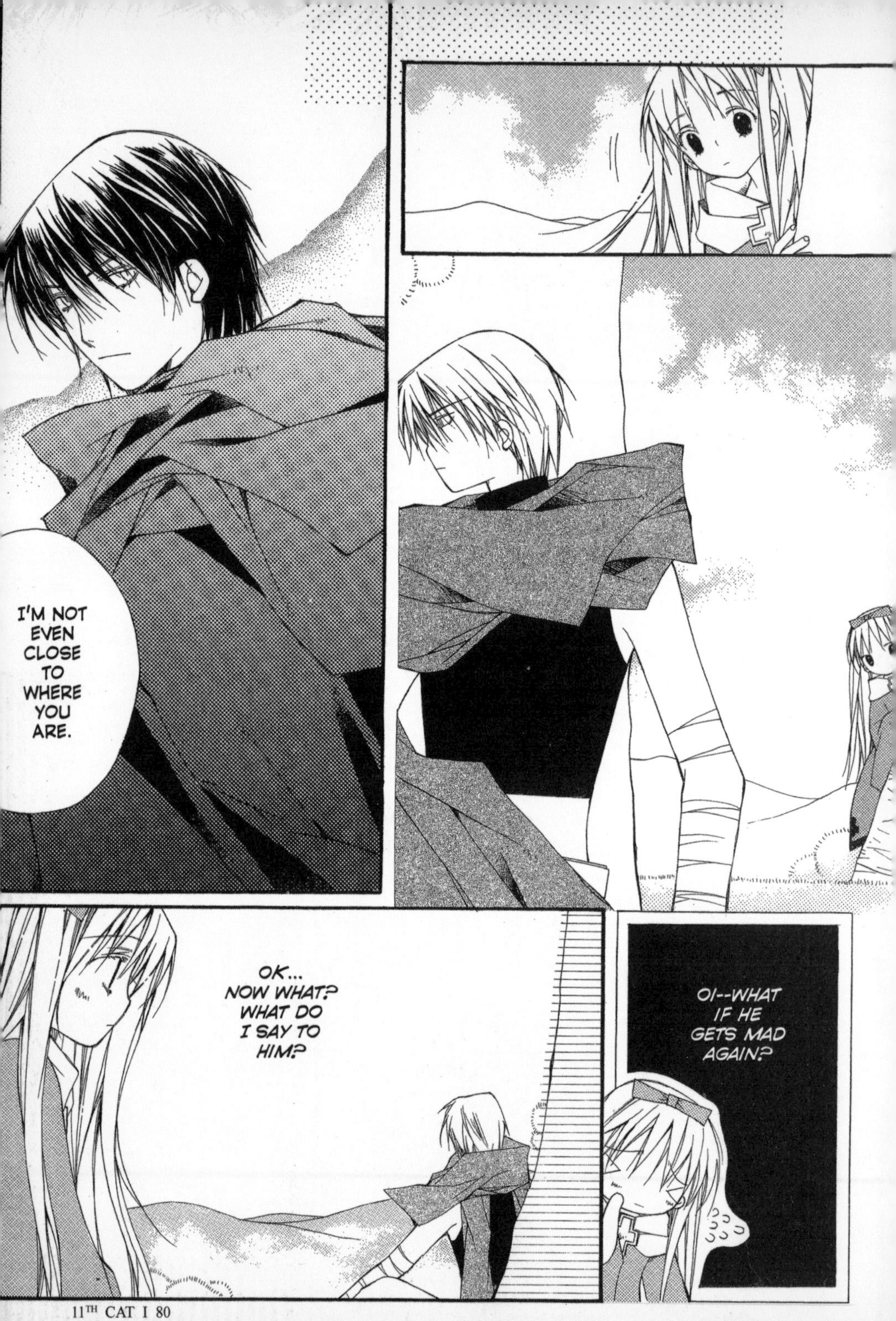
I'M NOT EVEN CLOSE TO WHERE YOU ARE.
OK... NOW WHAT? WHAT DO I SAY TO HIM?
OI--WHAT IF HE GETS MAD AGAIN?

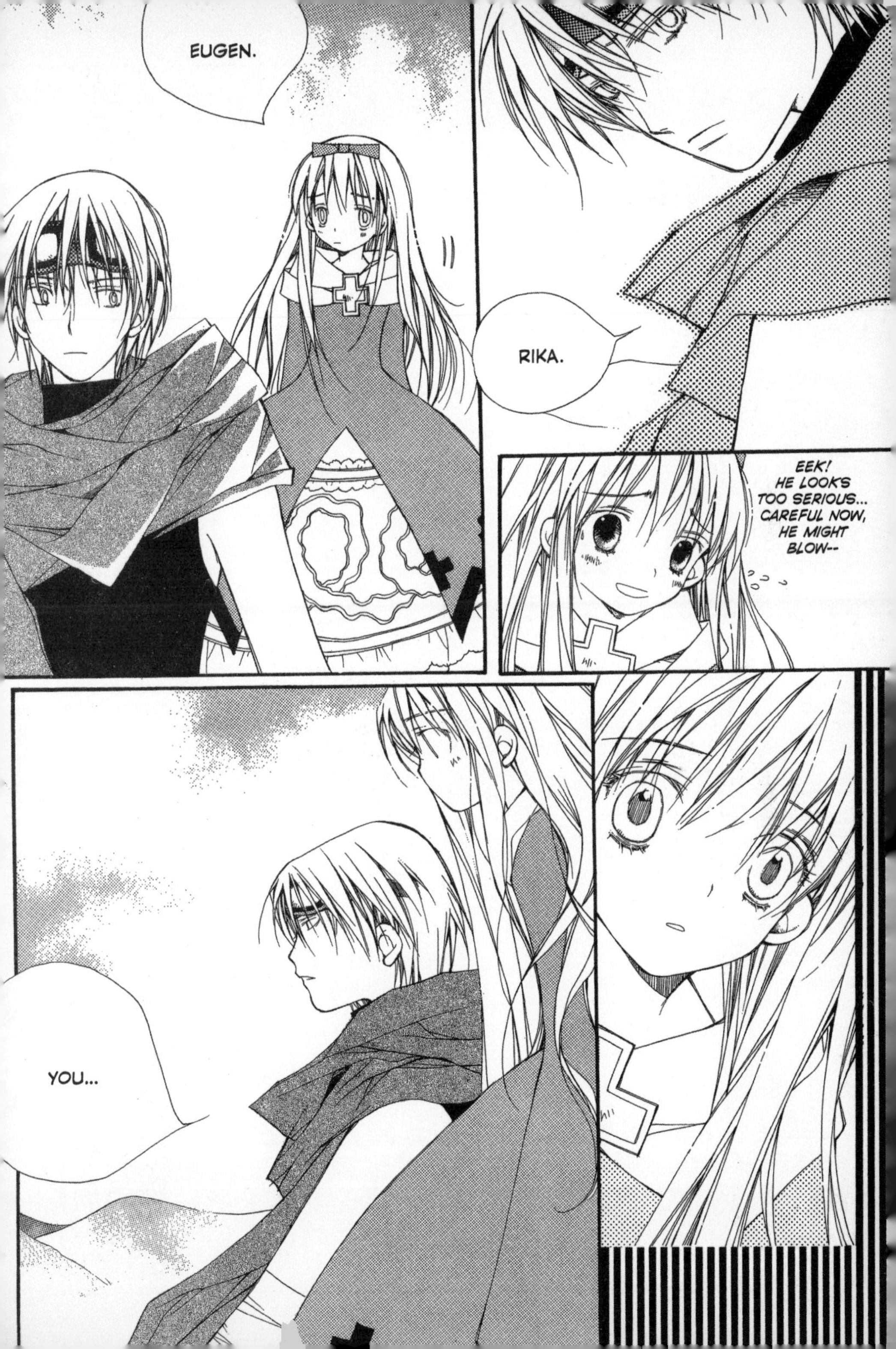
EUGEN.
RIKA.
EEK! HE LOOKS TOO SERIOUS... CAREFUL NOW, HE MIGHT BLOW--
YOU...

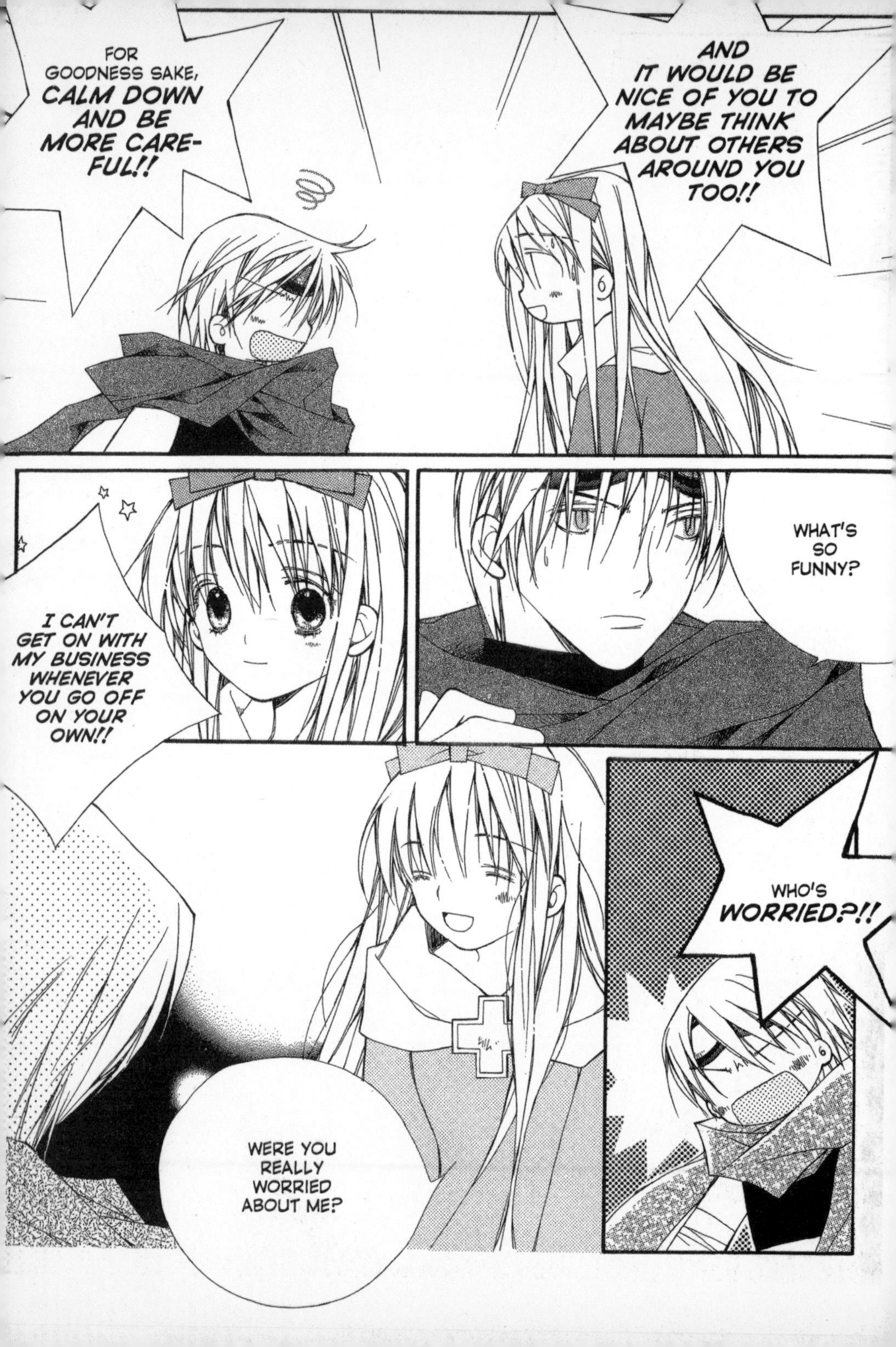
FOR GOODNESS SAKE, CALM DOWN AND BE MORE CARE-FUL!!
AND IT WOULD BE NICE OF YOU TO MAYBE THINK ABOUT OTHERS AROUND YOU TOO!!
I CAN'T GET ON WITH MY BUSINESS WHENEVER YOU GO OFF ON YOUR OWN!!
WHAT'S SO FUNNY?
WERE YOU REALLY WORRIED ABOUT ME?
WHO'S WORRIED?!!

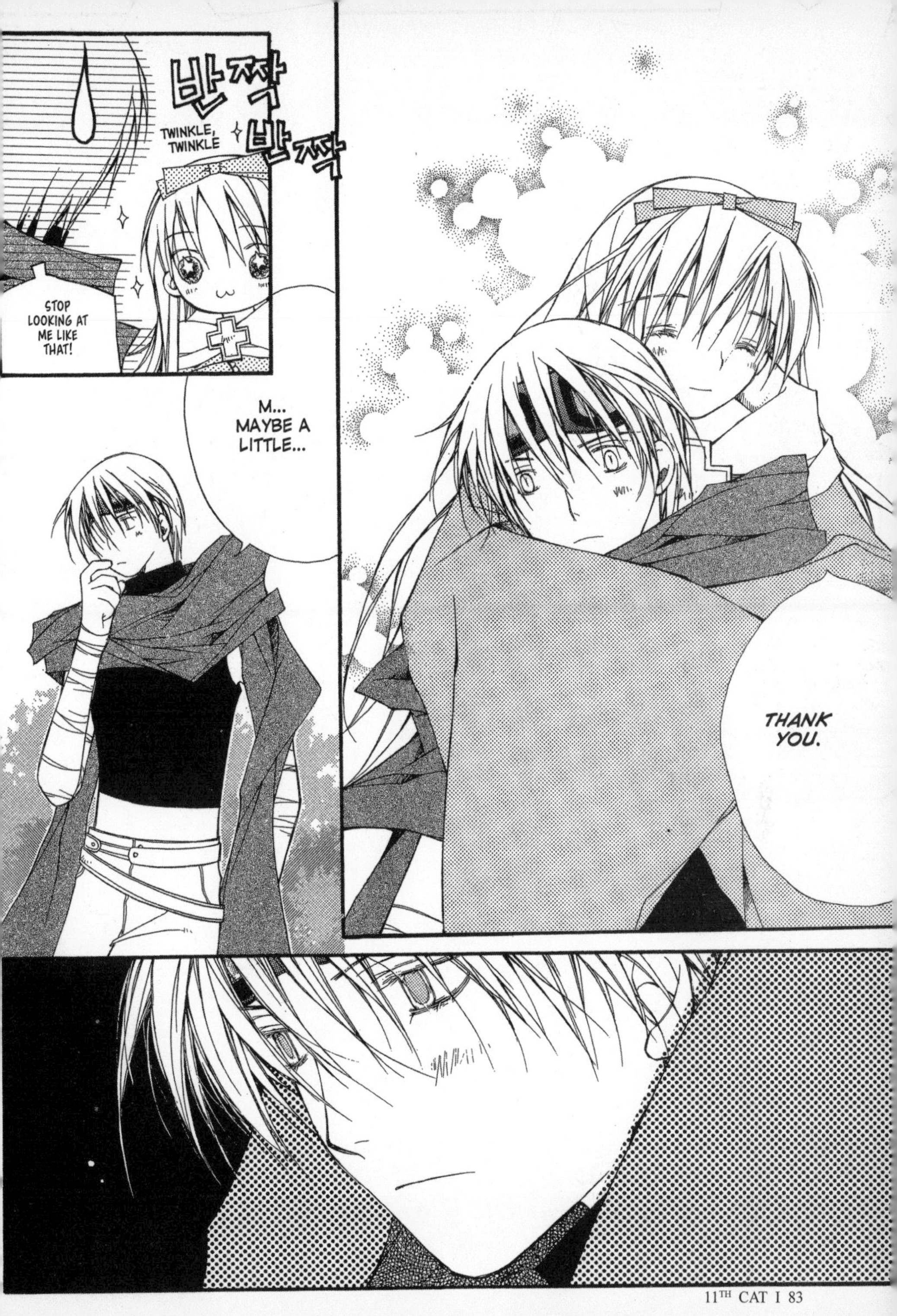
반짝 반짝
TWINKLE, TWINKLE
STOP LOOKING AT ME LIKE THAT!
M... MAYBE A LITTLE...
THANK YOU.

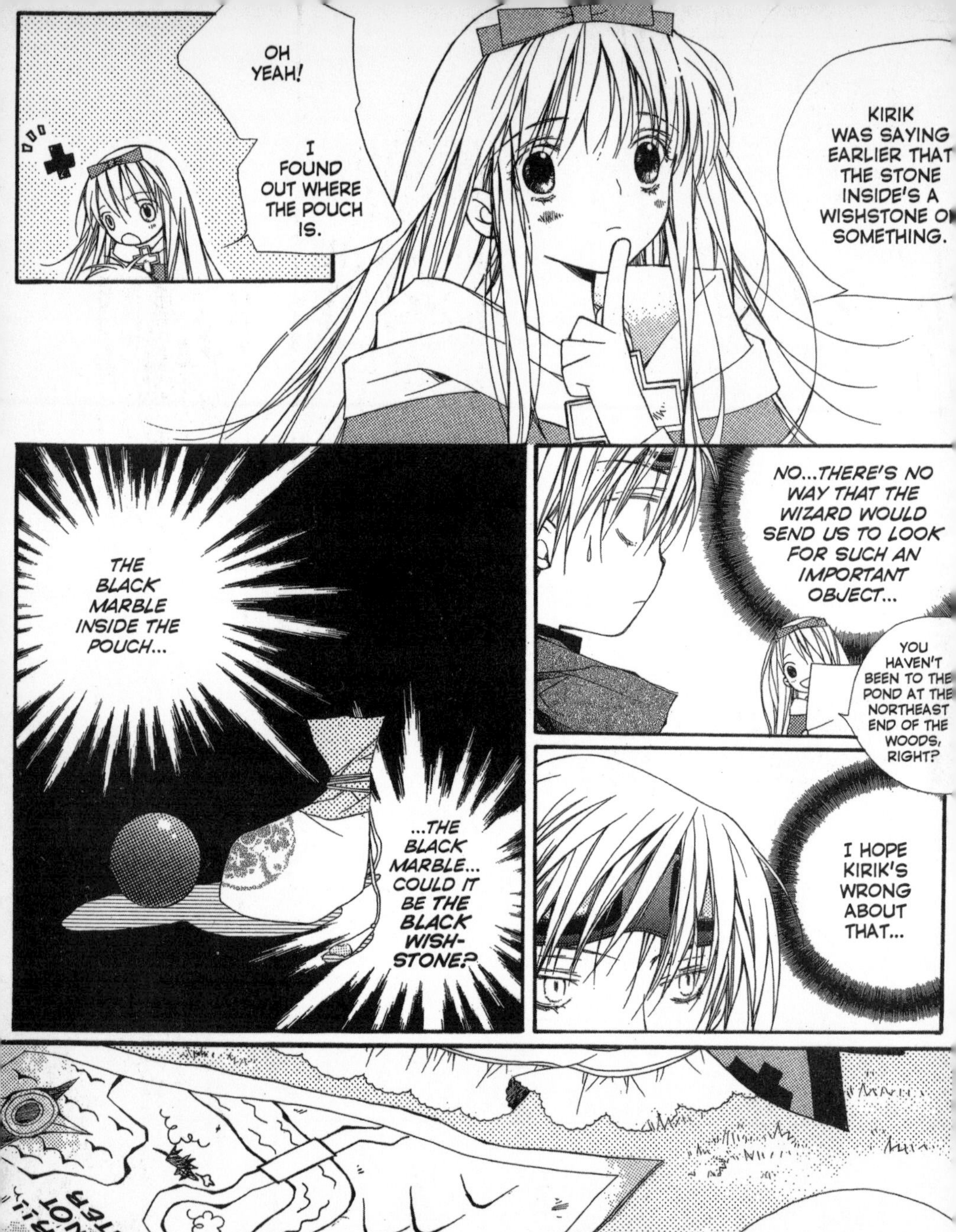
OH YEAH!
I FOUND OUT WHERE THE POUCH IS.
KIRIK WAS SAYING EARLIER THAT THE STONE INSIDE'S A WISHSTONE O SOMETHING.
THE BLACK MARBLE INSIDE THE POUCH...
...THE BLACK MARBLE... COULD IT BE THE BLACK WISH-STONE?
NO...THERE'S NO WAY THAT THE WIZARD WOULD SEND US TO LOOK FOR SUCH AN IMPORTANT OBJECT...
YOU HAVEN'T BEEN TO THE POND AT THE NORTHEAST END OF THE WOODS, RIGHT?
I HOPE KIRIK'S WRONG ABOUT THAT...
DANGER!! DO NOT ENTER
IT EVEN SAYS TO STAY AWAY FROM THAT LAKE ON THE MAP THE OLD COOT GAVE US.

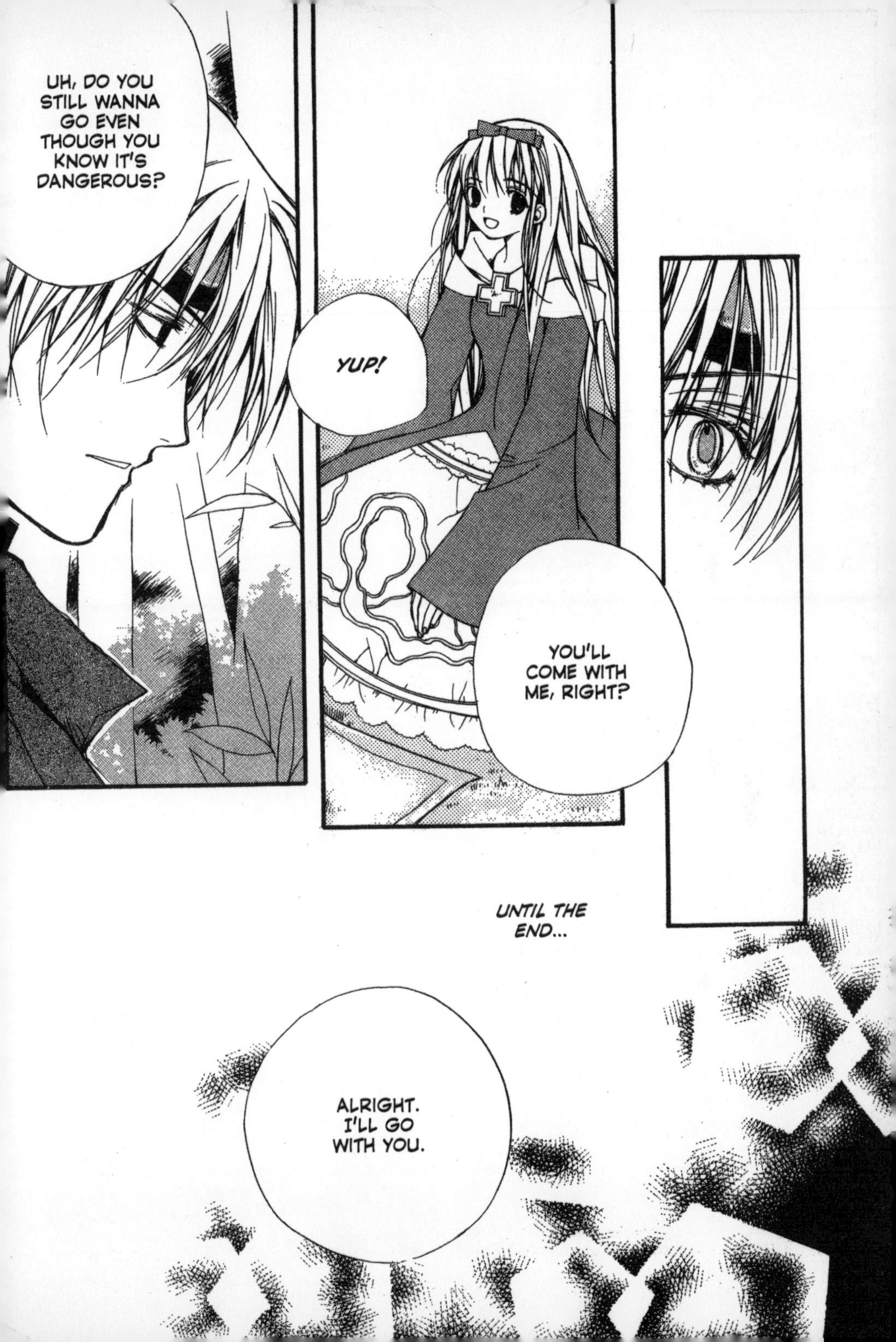
UH, DO YOU STILL WANNA GO EVEN THOUGH YOU KNOW IT'S DANGEROUS?
YUP!
YOU'LL COME WITH ME, RIGHT?
UNTIL THE END...
ALRIGHT. I'LL GO WITH YOU.

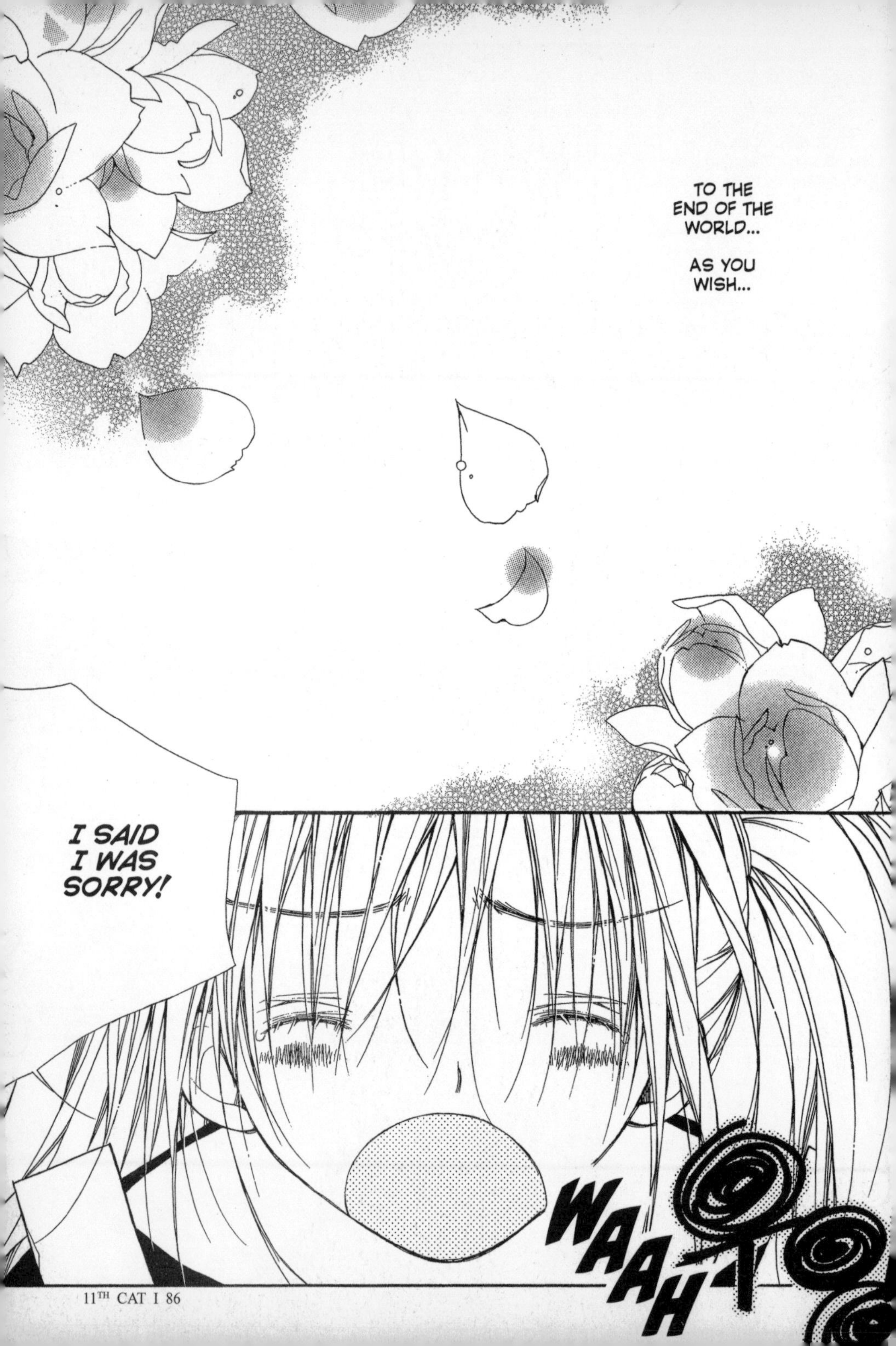
TO THE END OF THE WORLD...
AS YOU WISH...
I SAID I WAS SORRY!
WAAAH

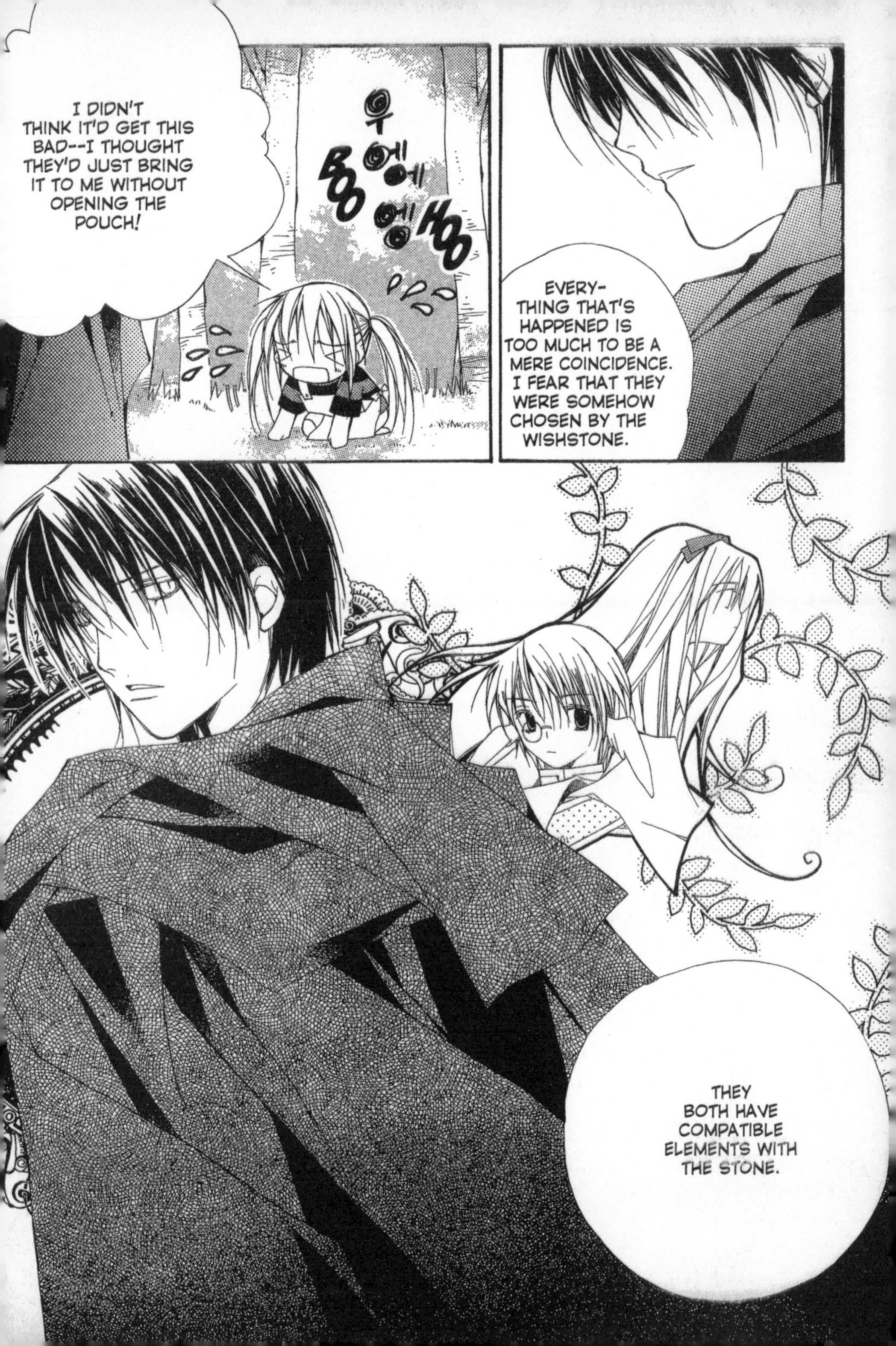
I DIDN'T THINK IT'D GET THIS BAD--I THOUGHT THEY'D JUST BRING IT TO ME WITHOUT OPENING THE POUCH!
우엥에엥
BOO HOO
EVERY-THING THAT'S HAPPENED IS TOO MUCH TO BE A MERE COINCIDENCE. I FEAR THAT THEY WERE SOMEHOW CHOSEN BY THE WISHSTONE.
THEY BOTH HAVE COMPATIBLE ELEMENTS WITH THE STONE.

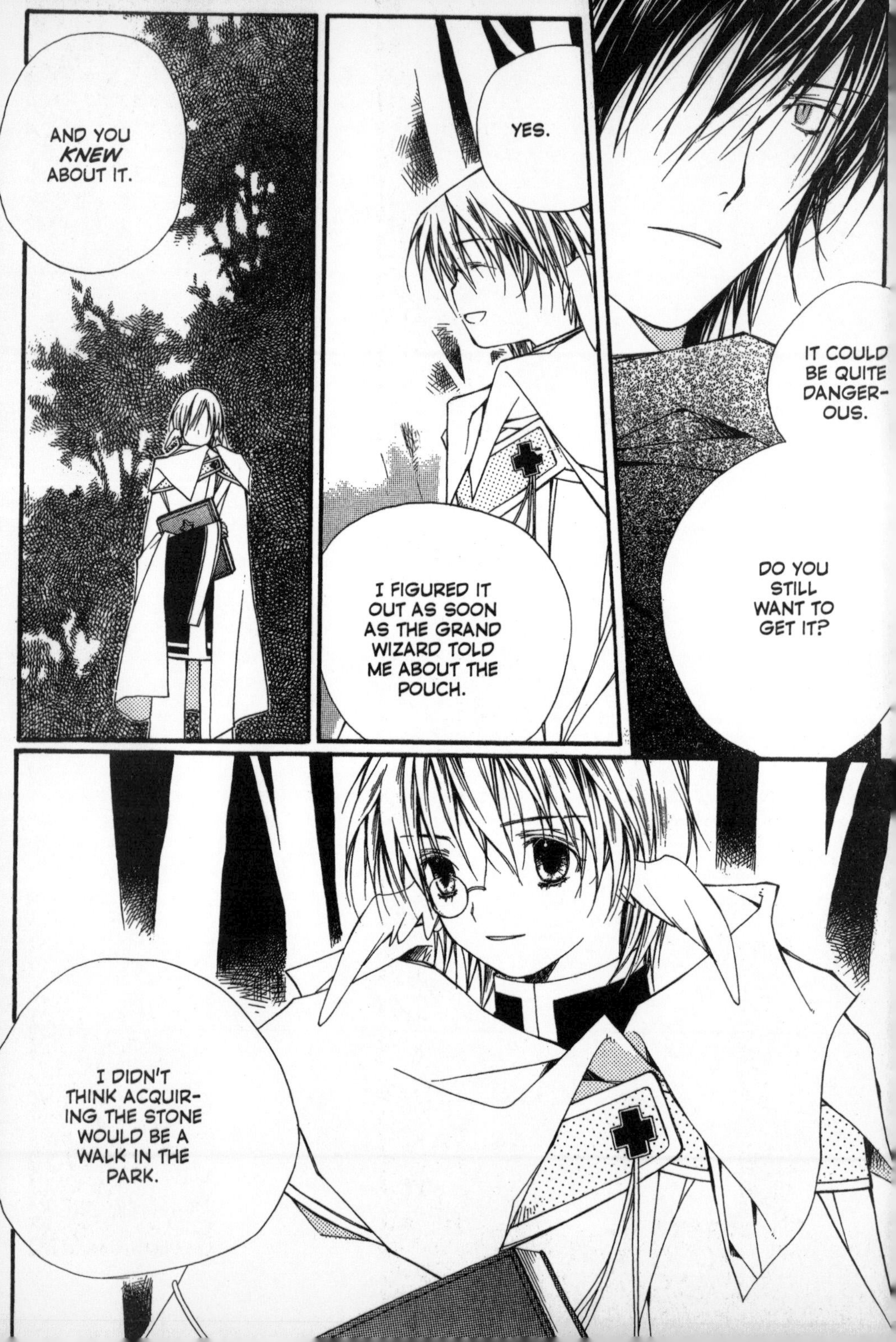
AND YOU *KNEW* ABOUT IT.
YES.
I FIGURED IT OUT AS SOON AS THE GRAND WIZARD TOLD ME ABOUT THE POUCH.
IT COULD BE QUITE DANGER-OUS.
DO YOU STILL WANT TO GET IT?
I DIDN'T THINK ACQUIR-ING THE STONE WOULD BE A WALK IN THE PARK.

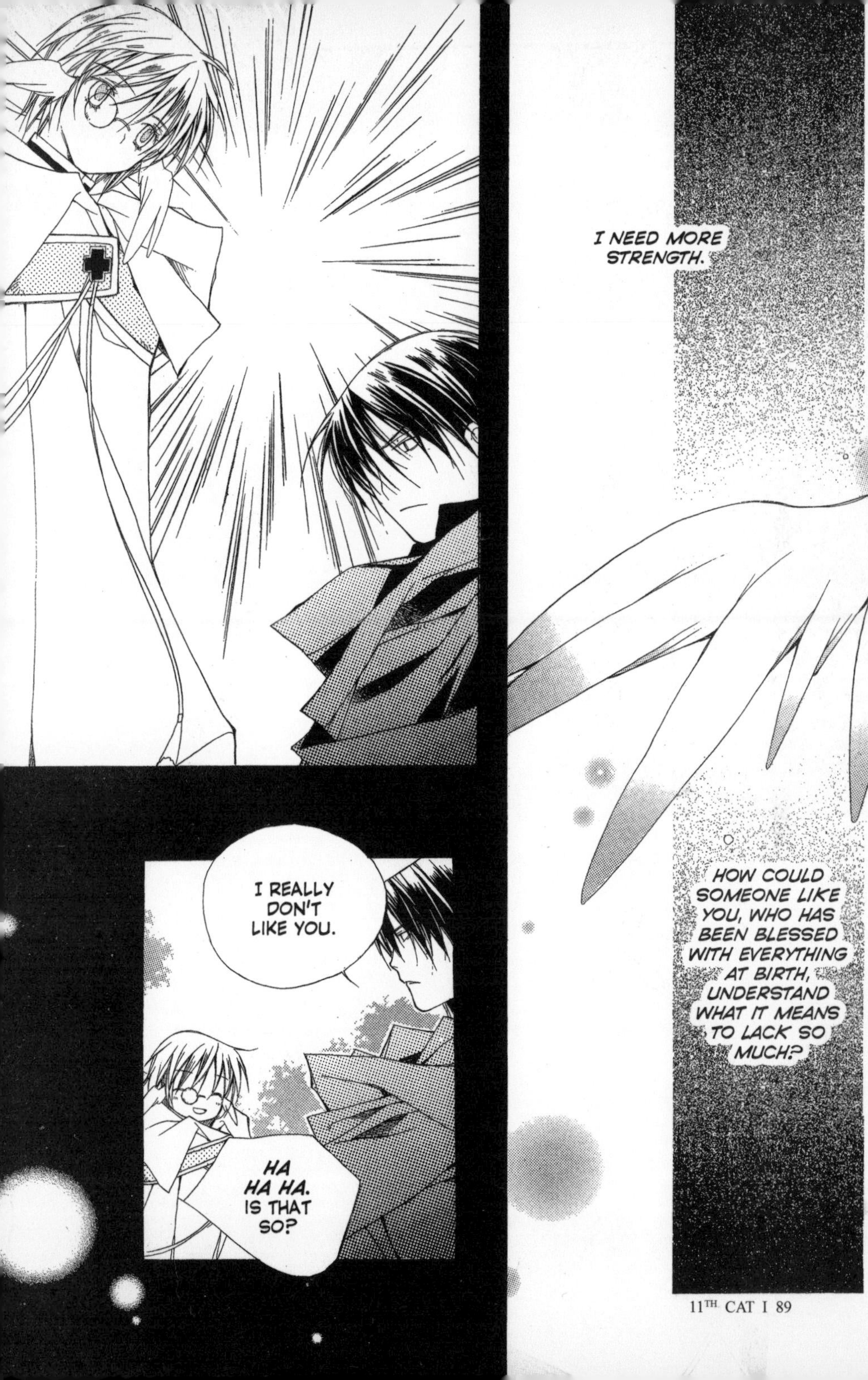
I REALLY DON'T LIKE YOU.
HA HA HA. IS THAT SO?
I NEED MORE STRENGTH.
HOW COULD SOMEONE LIKE YOU, WHO HAS BEEN BLESSED WITH EVERYTHING AT BIRTH, UNDERSTAND WHAT IT MEANS TO LACK SO MUCH?

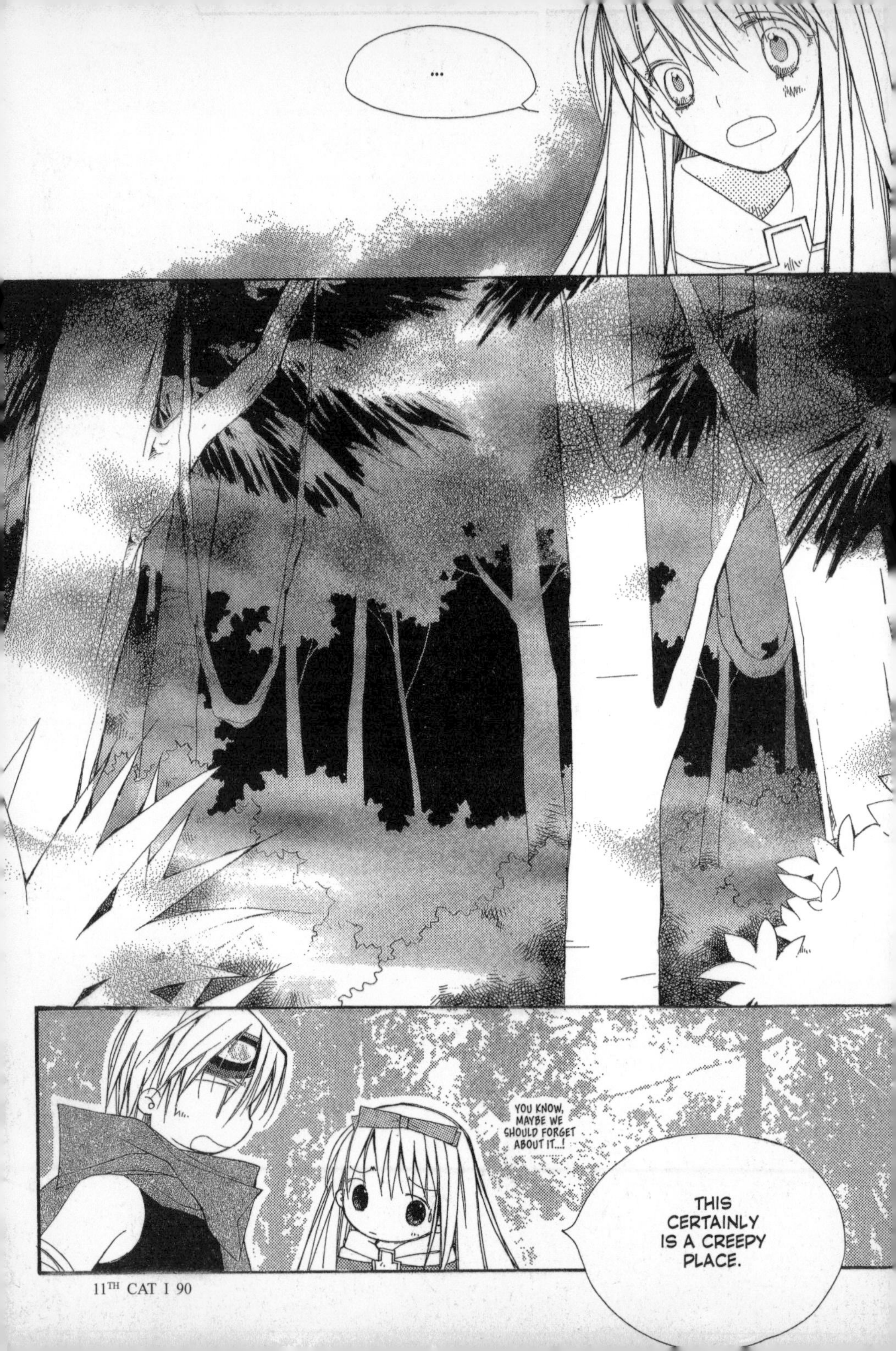
...
YOU KNOW, MAYBE WE SHOULD FORGET ABOUT IT...!
THIS CERTAINLY IS A CREEPY PLACE.

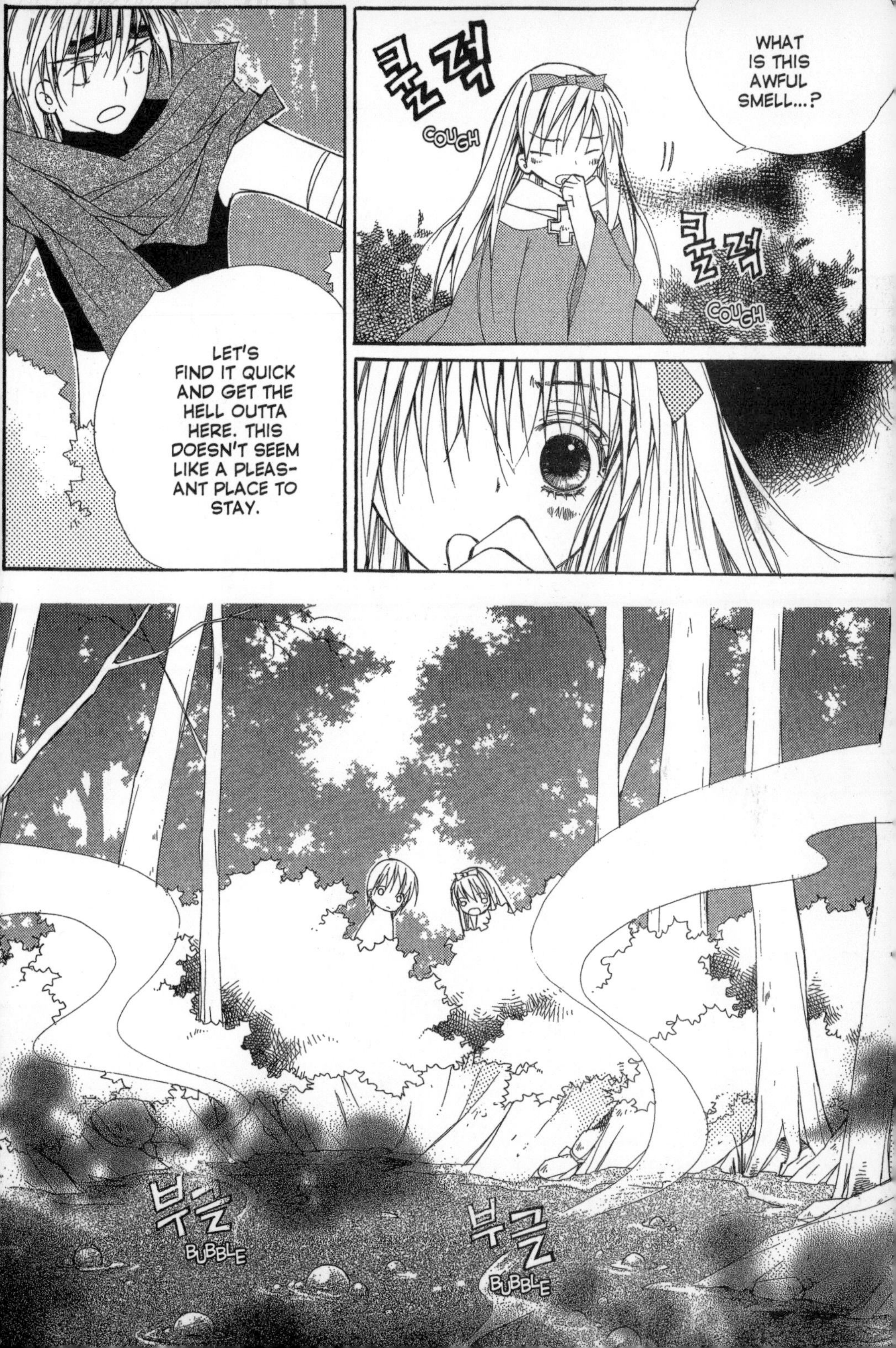
LET'S FIND IT QUICK AND GET THE HELL OUTTA HERE. THIS DOESN'T SEEM LIKE A PLEAS-ANT PLACE TO STAY.
콜럭
COUGH
WHAT IS THIS AWFUL SMELL...?
콜럭
COUGH
부글
BUBBLE
부글
BUBBLE

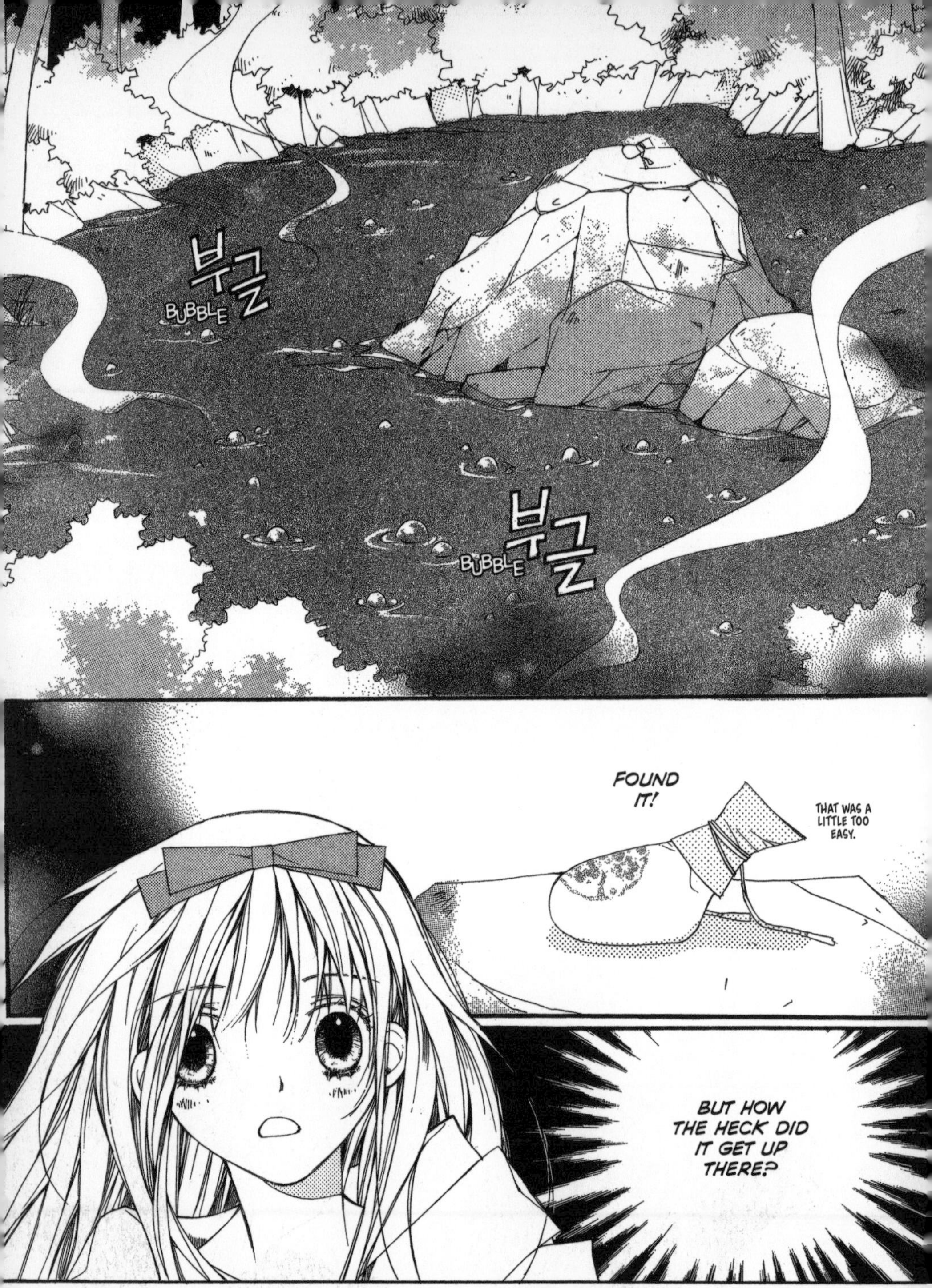
부글
BUBBLE
부글
BUBBLE
FOUND IT!
THAT WAS A LITTLE TOO EASY.
BUT HOW THE HECK DID IT GET UP THERE?

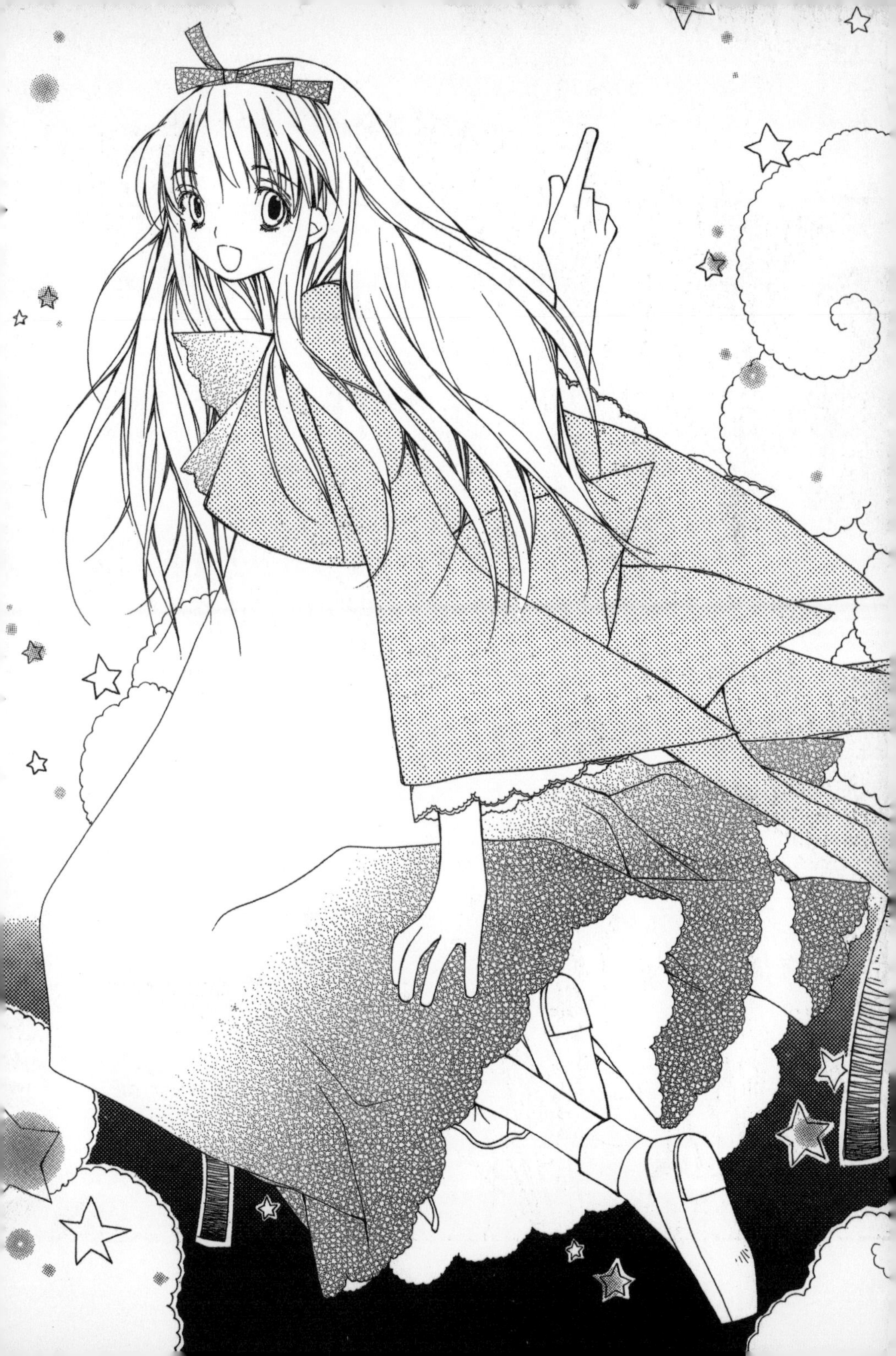

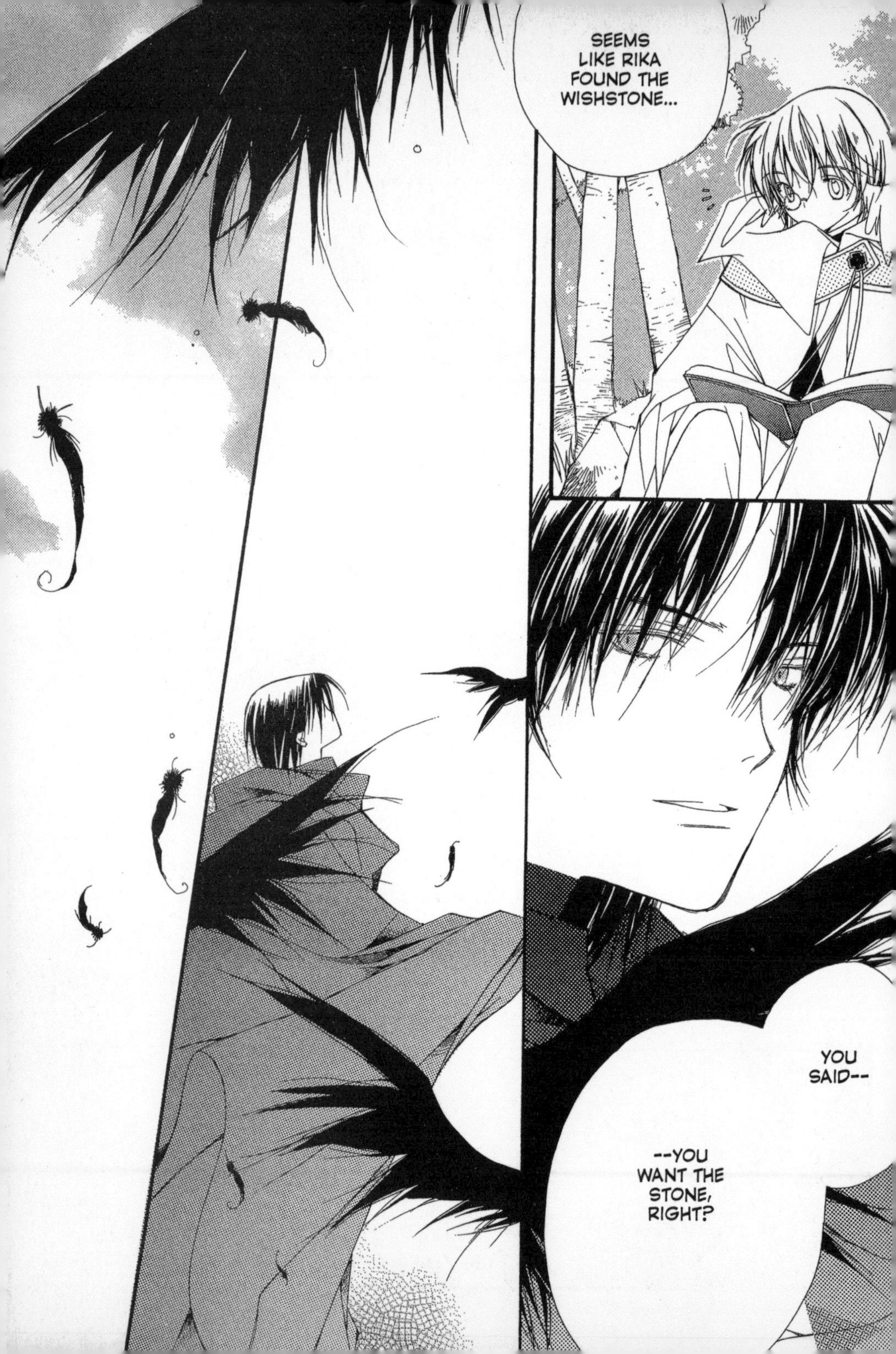
SEEMS LIKE RIKA FOUND THE WISHSTONE...
YOU SAID--
--YOU WANT THE STONE, RIGHT?

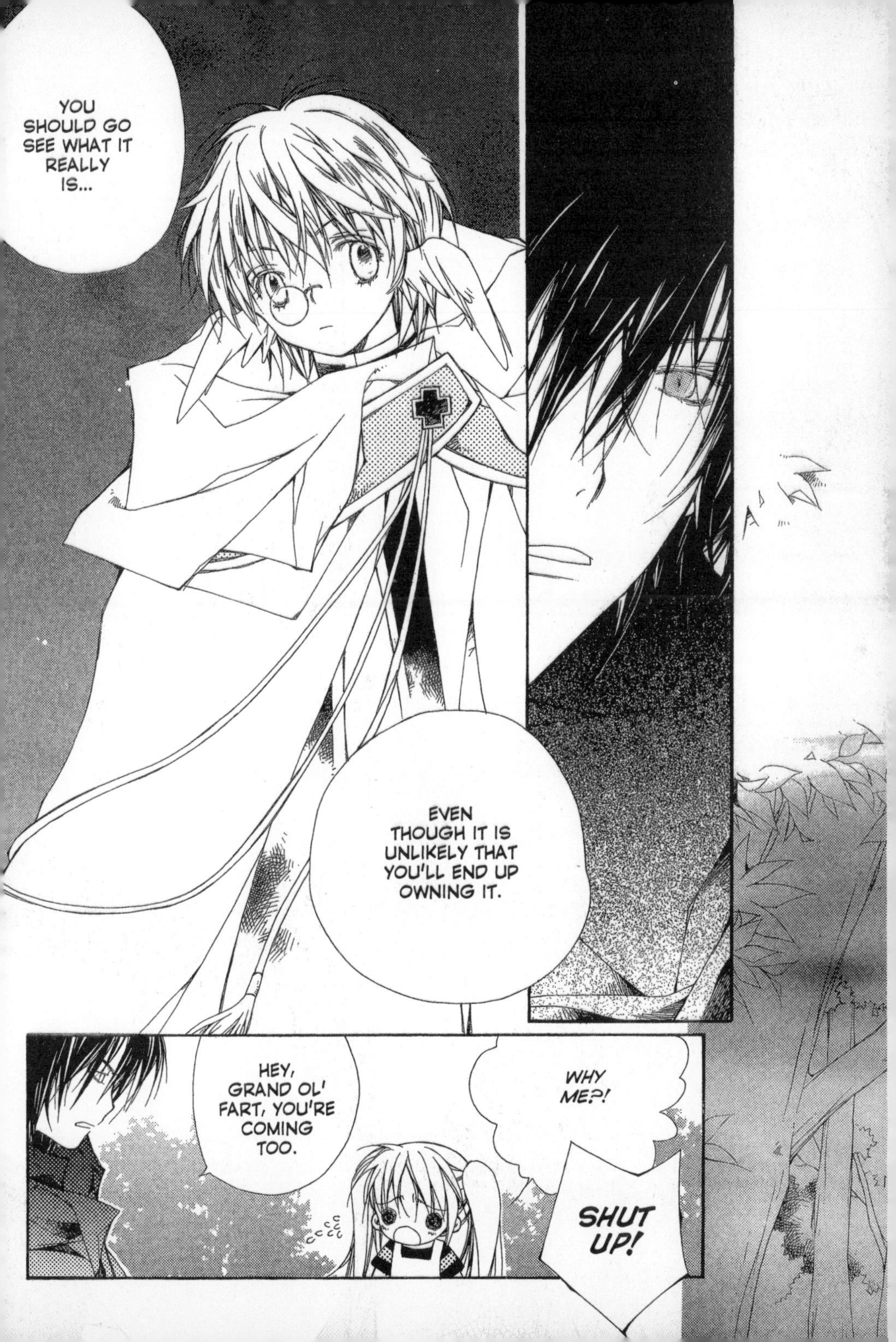
YOU SHOULD GO SEE WHAT IT REALLY IS...
EVEN THOUGH IT IS UNLIKELY THAT YOU'LL END UP OWNING IT.
HEY, GRAND OL' FART, YOU'RE COMING TOO.
WHY ME?!
SHUT UP!

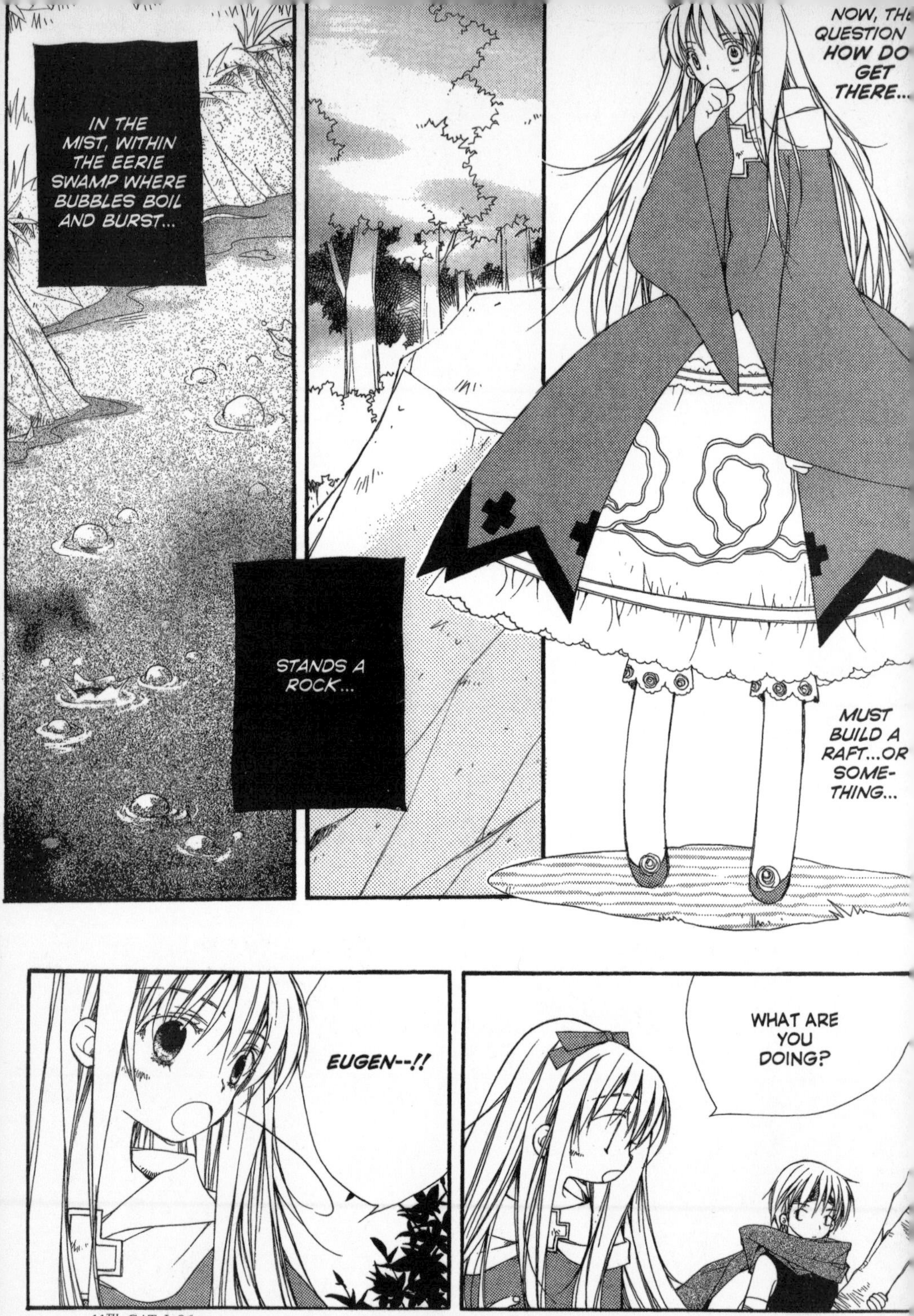
IN THE MIST, WITHIN THE EERIE SWAMP WHERE BUBBLES BOIL AND BURST...
STANDS A ROCK...
NOW, THE QUESTION HOW DO GET THERE...
MUST BUILD A RAFT...OR SOME-THING...
EUGEN--!!
WHAT ARE YOU DOING?

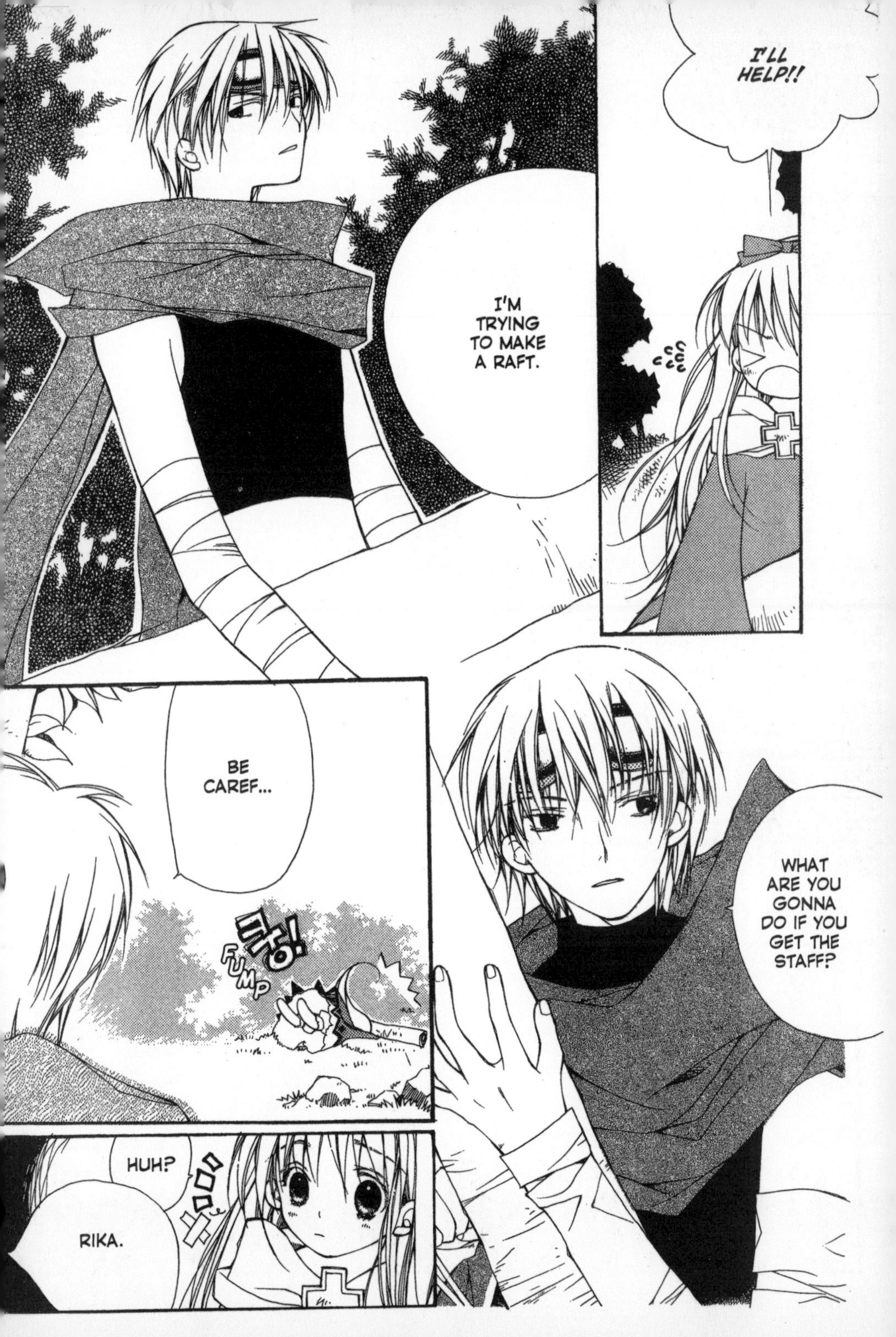
I'M TRYING TO MAKE A RAFT.
I'LL HELP!!
BE CAREF...
FUMP
WHAT ARE YOU GONNA DO IF YOU GET THE STAFF?
HUH?
RIKA.

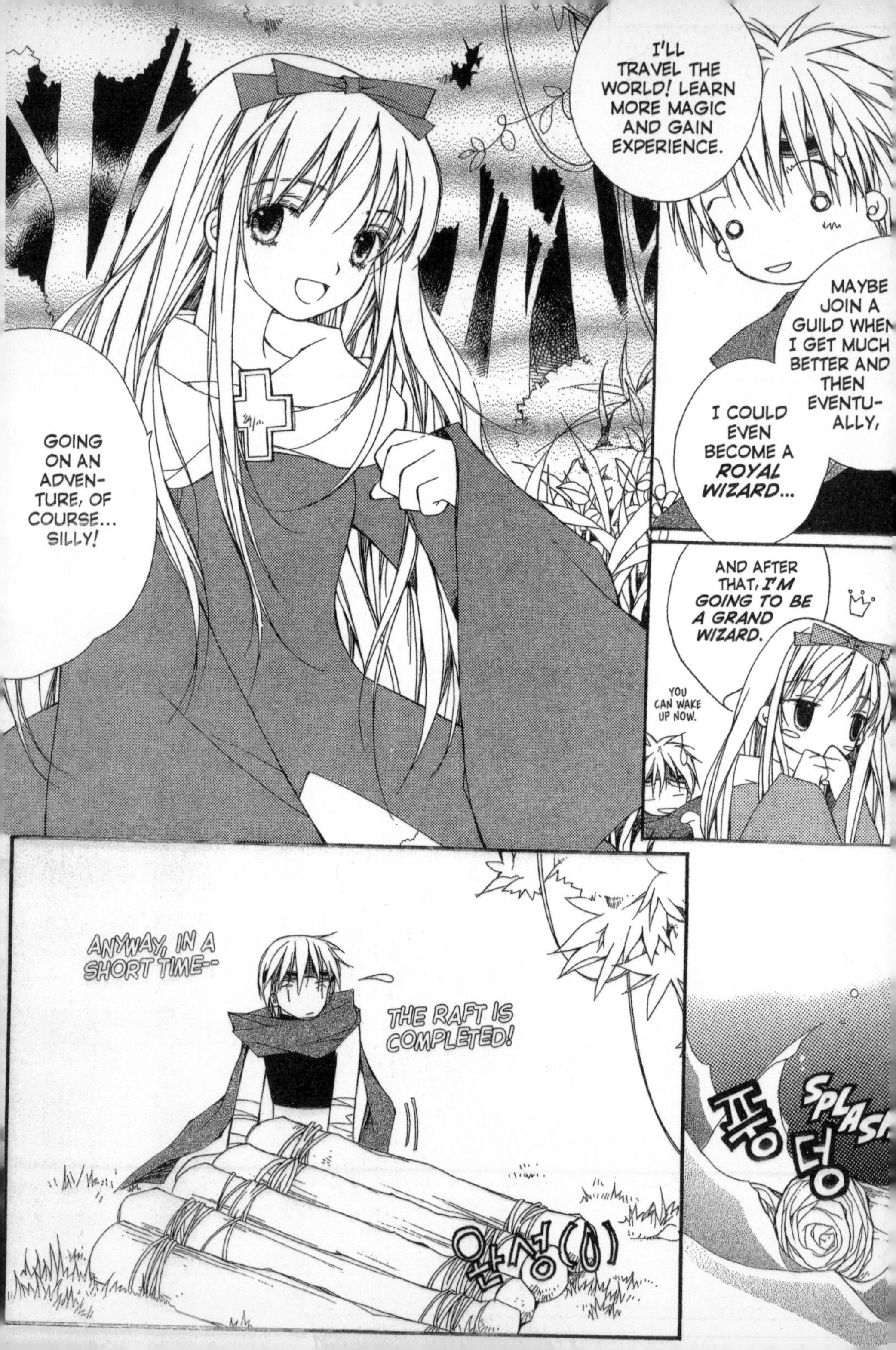
GOING ON AN ADVENTURE, OF COURSE... SILLY!
I'LL TRAVEL THE WORLD! LEARN MORE MAGIC AND GAIN EXPERIENCE.
MAYBE JOIN A GUILD WHEN I GET MUCH BETTER AND THEN EVENTUALLY,
I COULD EVEN BECOME A *ROYAL WIZARD*...
AND AFTER THAT, *I'M GOING TO BE A GRAND WIZARD.*
YOU CAN WAKE UP NOW.
ANYWAY, IN A SHORT TIME--
THE RAFT IS COMPLETED!
SPLASH

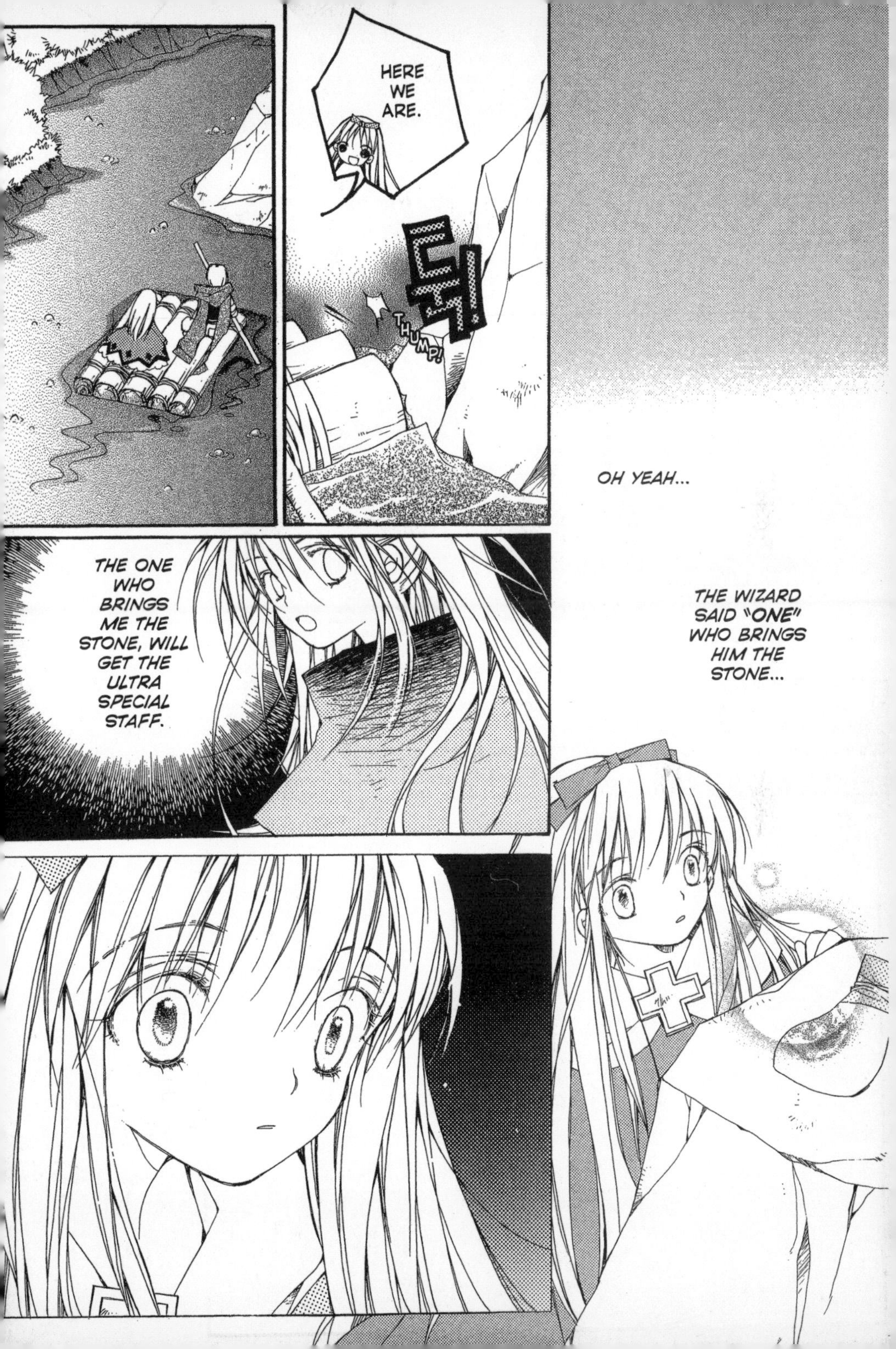
HERE WE ARE.
THUMP!
THE ONE WHO BRINGS ME THE STONE, WILL GET THE ULTRA SPECIAL STAFF.
OH YEAH...
THE WIZARD SAID "ONE" WHO BRINGS HIM THE STONE...

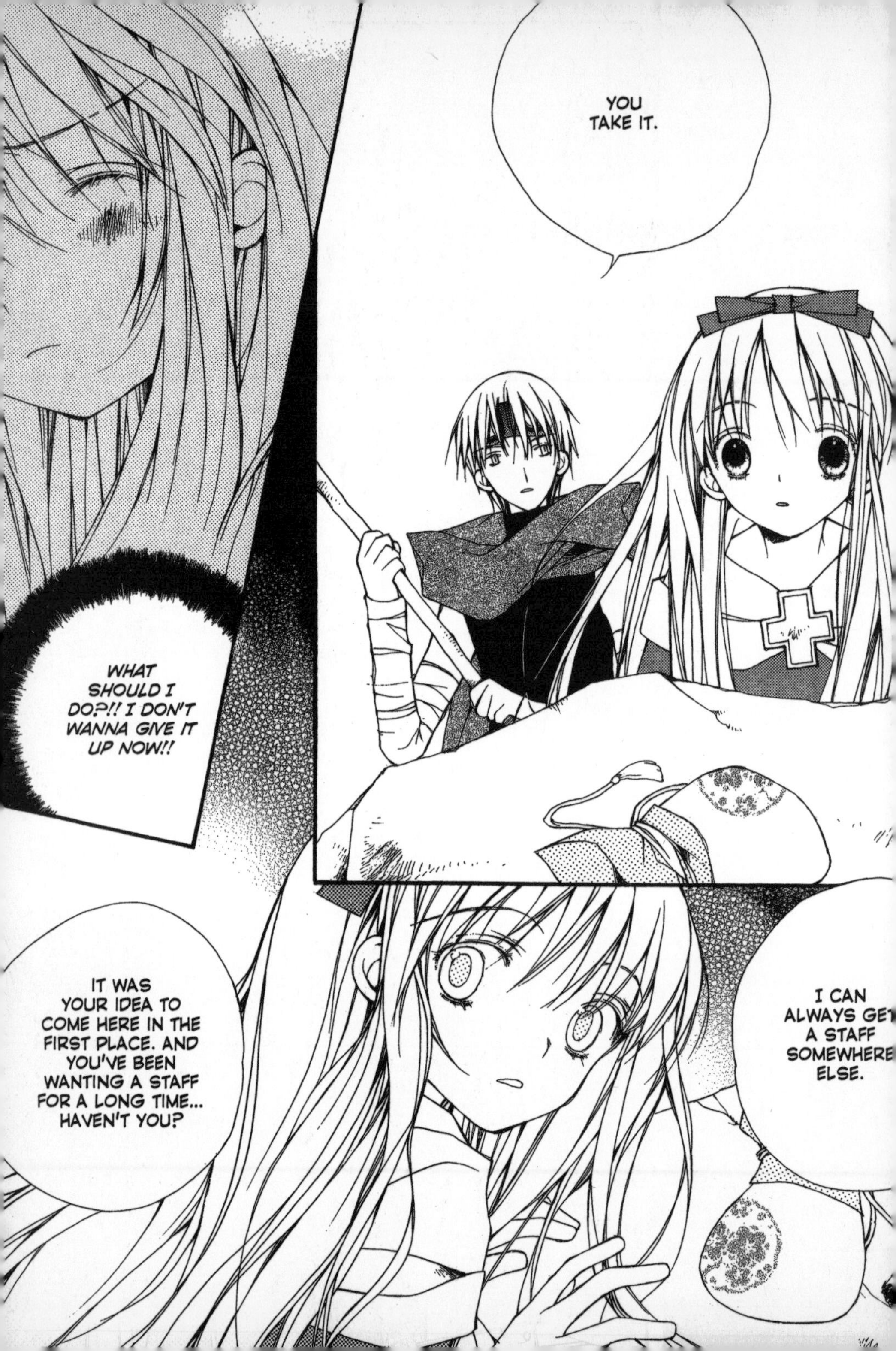
WHAT SHOULD I DO?!! I DON'T WANNA GIVE IT UP NOW!!
YOU TAKE IT.
IT WAS YOUR IDEA TO COME HERE IN THE FIRST PLACE. AND YOU'VE BEEN WANTING A STAFF FOR A LONG TIME... HAVEN'T YOU?
I CAN ALWAYS GET A STAFF SOMEWHERE ELSE.

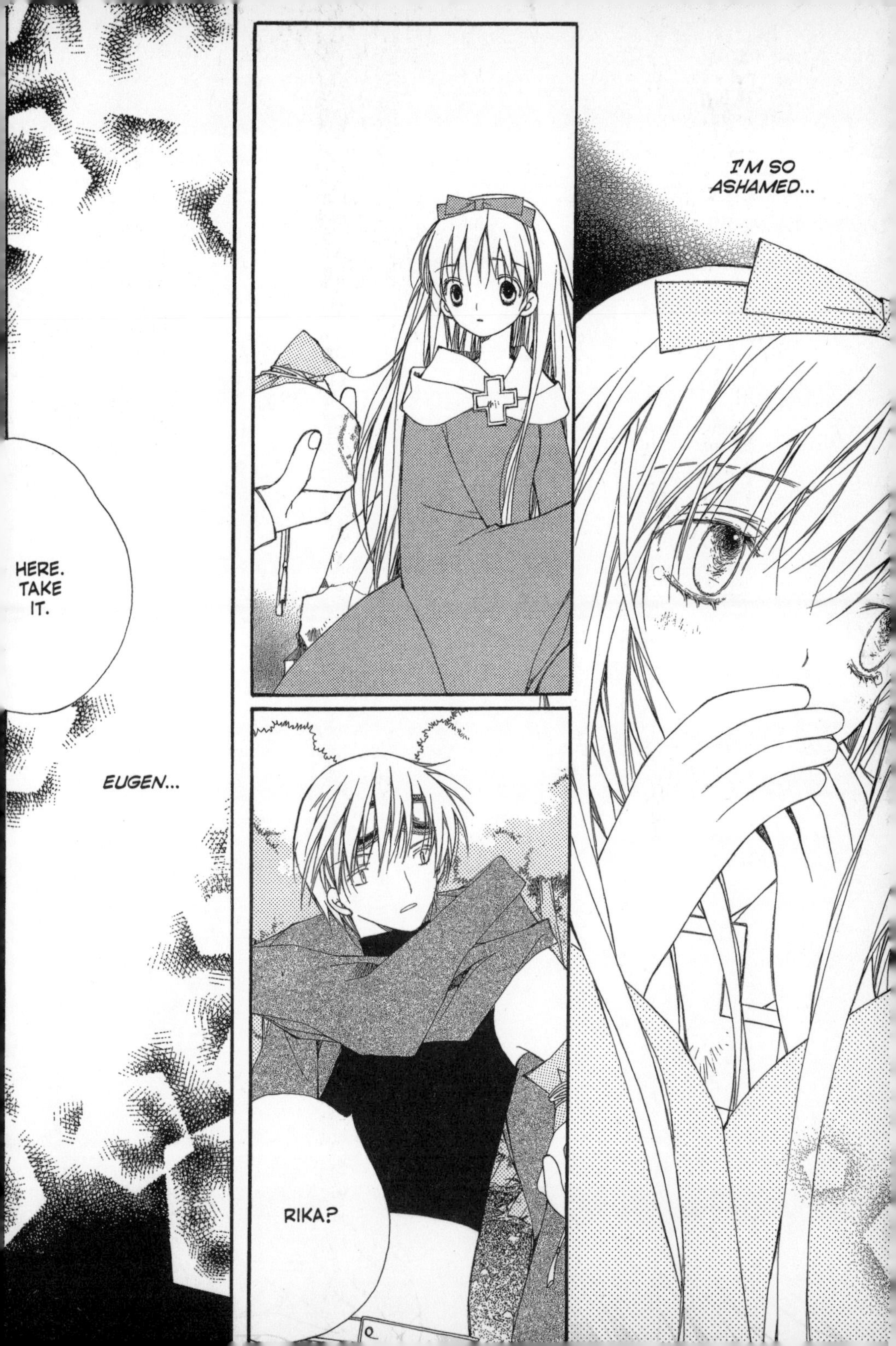
I'M SO ASHAMED...
RIKA?
HERE. TAKE IT.
EUGEN...

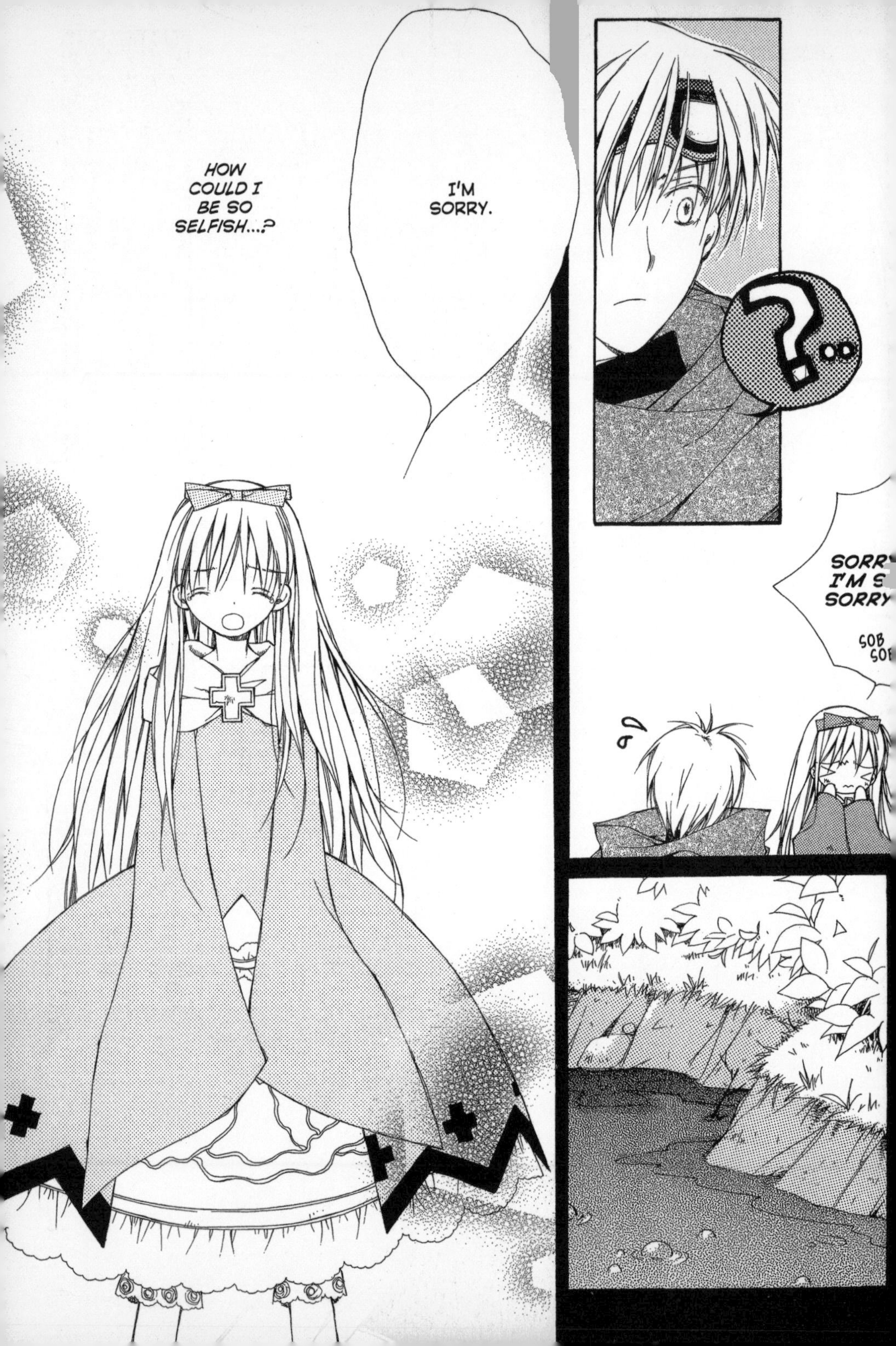
HOW COULD I BE SO SELFISH...?
I'M SORRY.
?..
SORRY I'M S SORRY
SOB SO

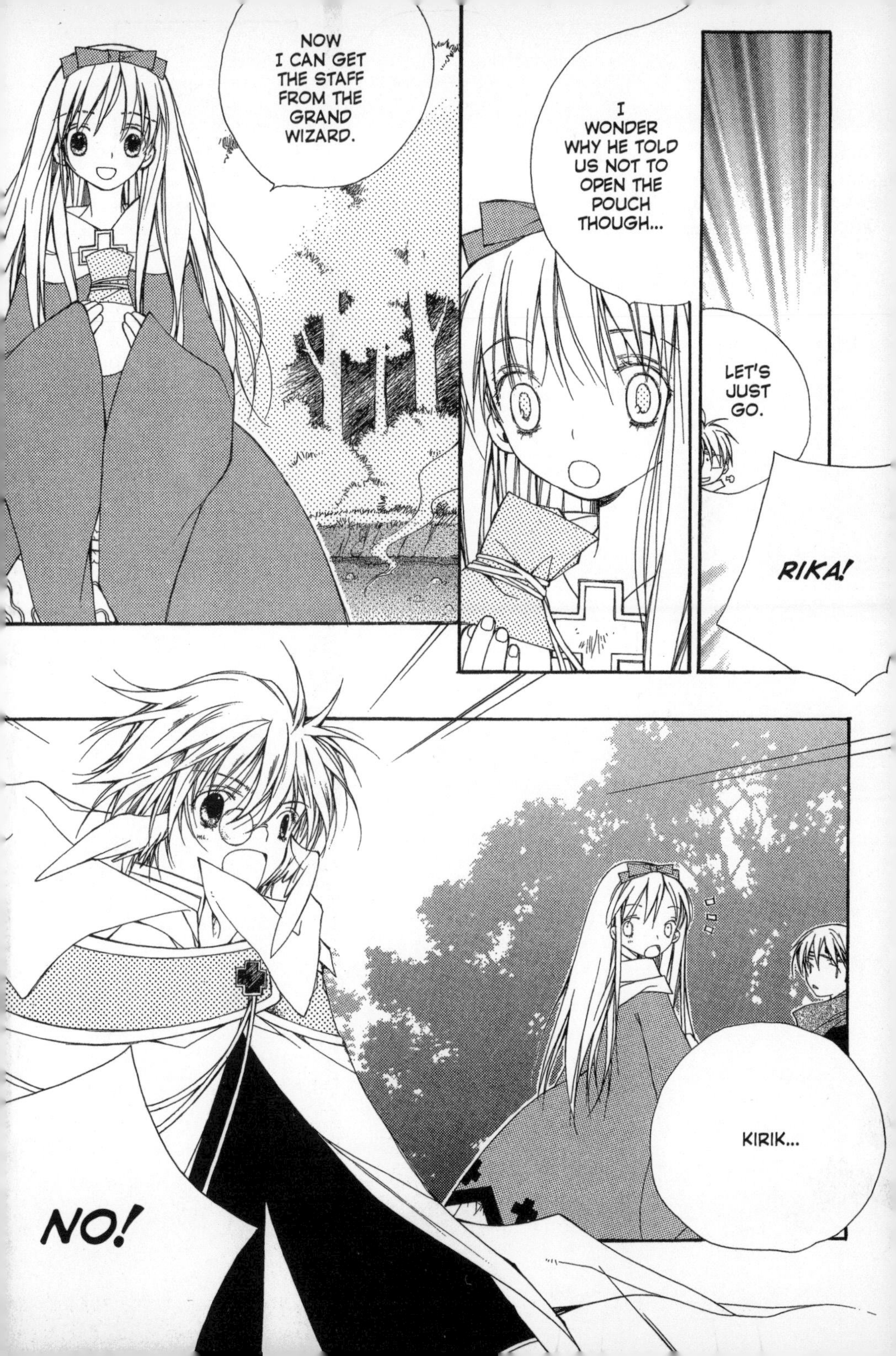
NOW I CAN GET THE STAFF FROM THE GRAND WIZARD.
I WONDER WHY HE TOLD US NOT TO OPEN THE POUCH THOUGH...
LET'S JUST GO.
RIKA!
NO!
KIRIK...

WHAT'S WRONG, KIRIK?

YOU FOUND IT AFTER ALL.

THAT ACTUALLY BELONGS TO ME. I LENT IT TO THE GRAND WIZARD BUT HE LOST IT.

YOU DIDN'T OPEN THE POUCH, DID YOU?

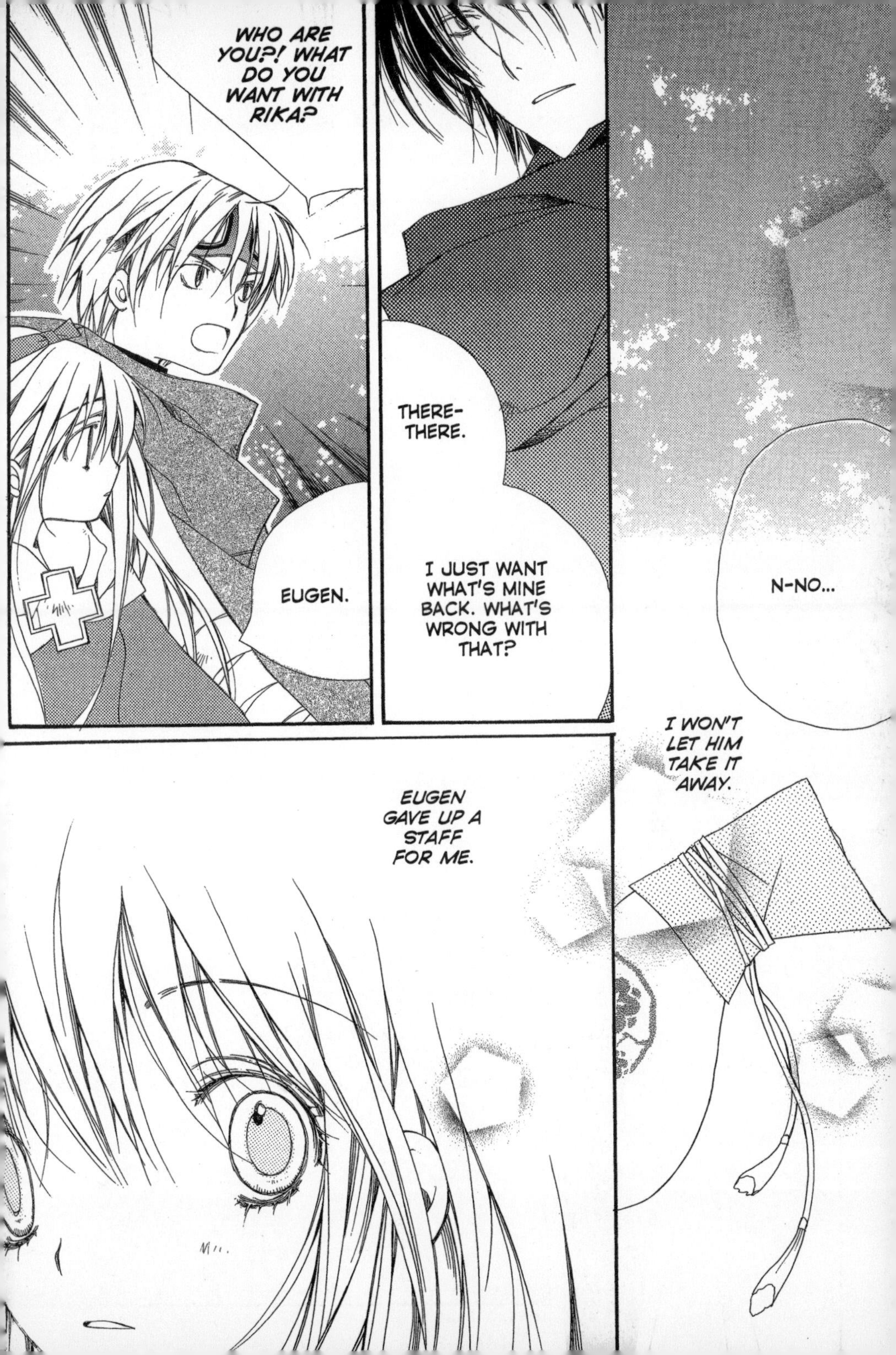
WHO ARE YOU?! WHAT DO YOU WANT WITH RIKA?
EUGEN.
THERE-THERE.
I JUST WANT WHAT'S MINE BACK. WHAT'S WRONG WITH THAT?
EUGEN GAVE UP A STAFF FOR ME.
N-NO...
I WON'T LET HIM TAKE IT AWAY.

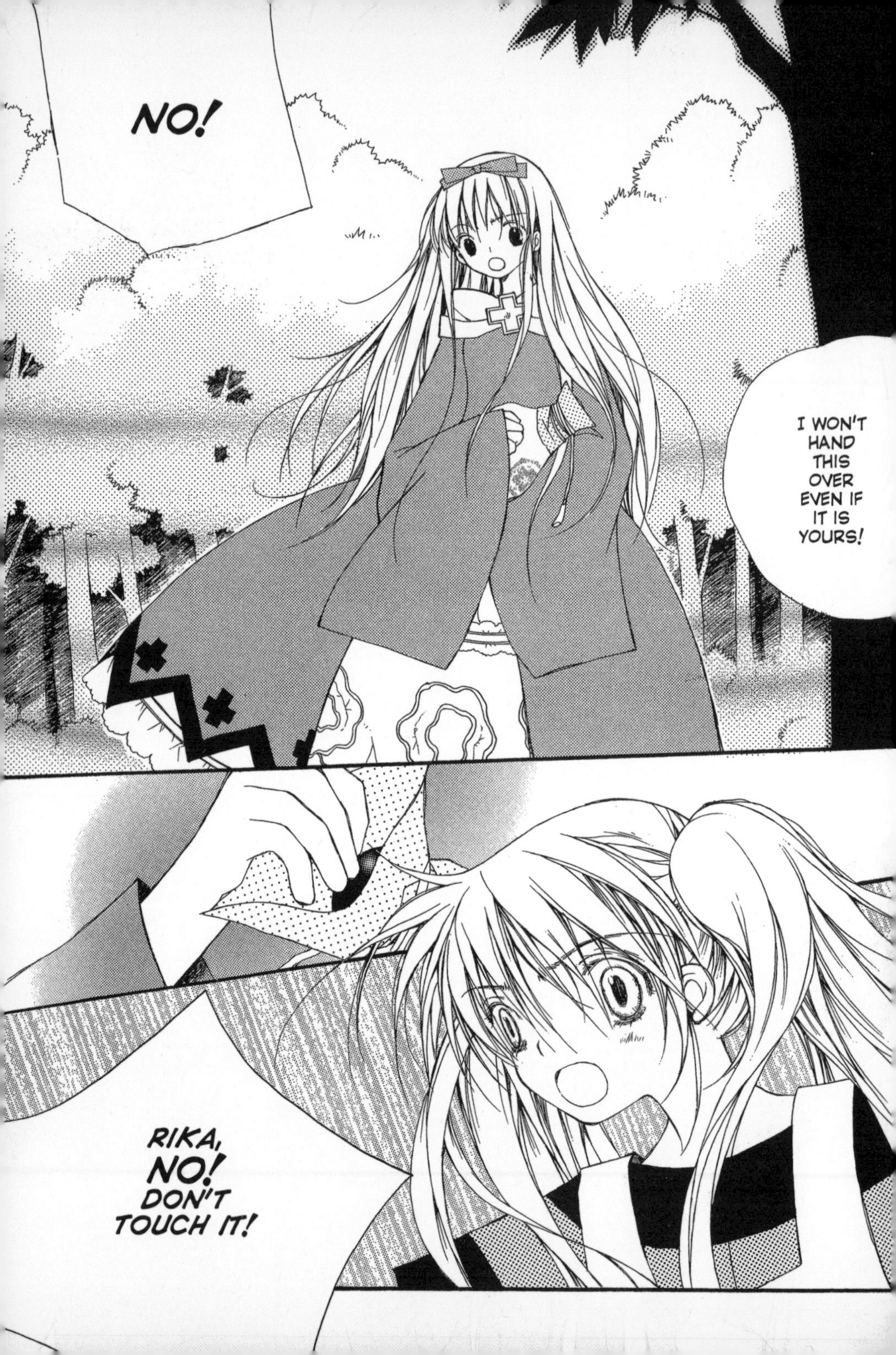
NO!
I WON'T HAND THIS OVER EVEN IF IT IS YOURS!
RIKA, NO! DON'T TOUCH IT!

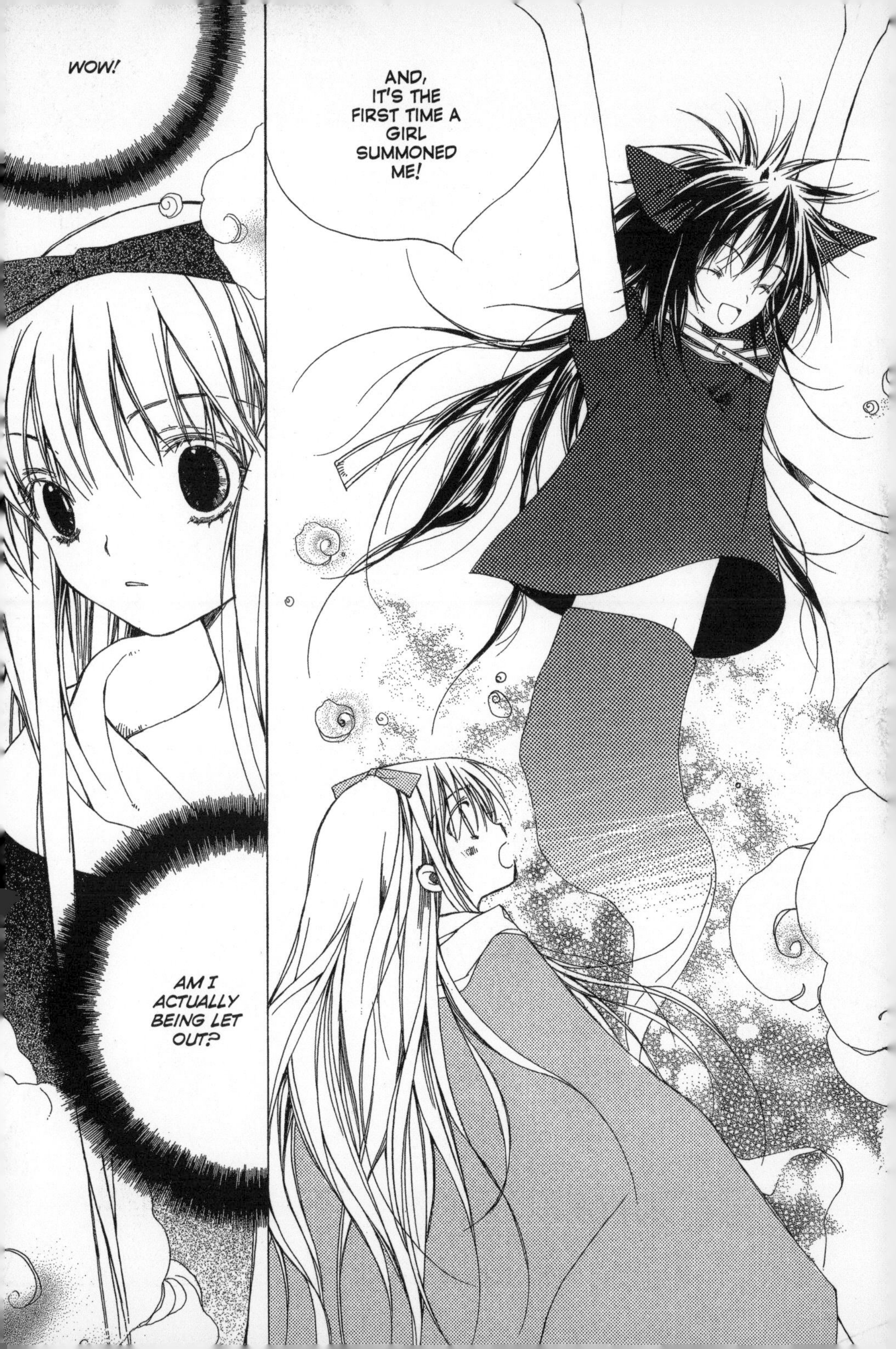
WOW!
AM I ACTUALLY BEING LET OUT?
AND, IT'S THE FIRST TIME A GIRL SUMMONED ME!

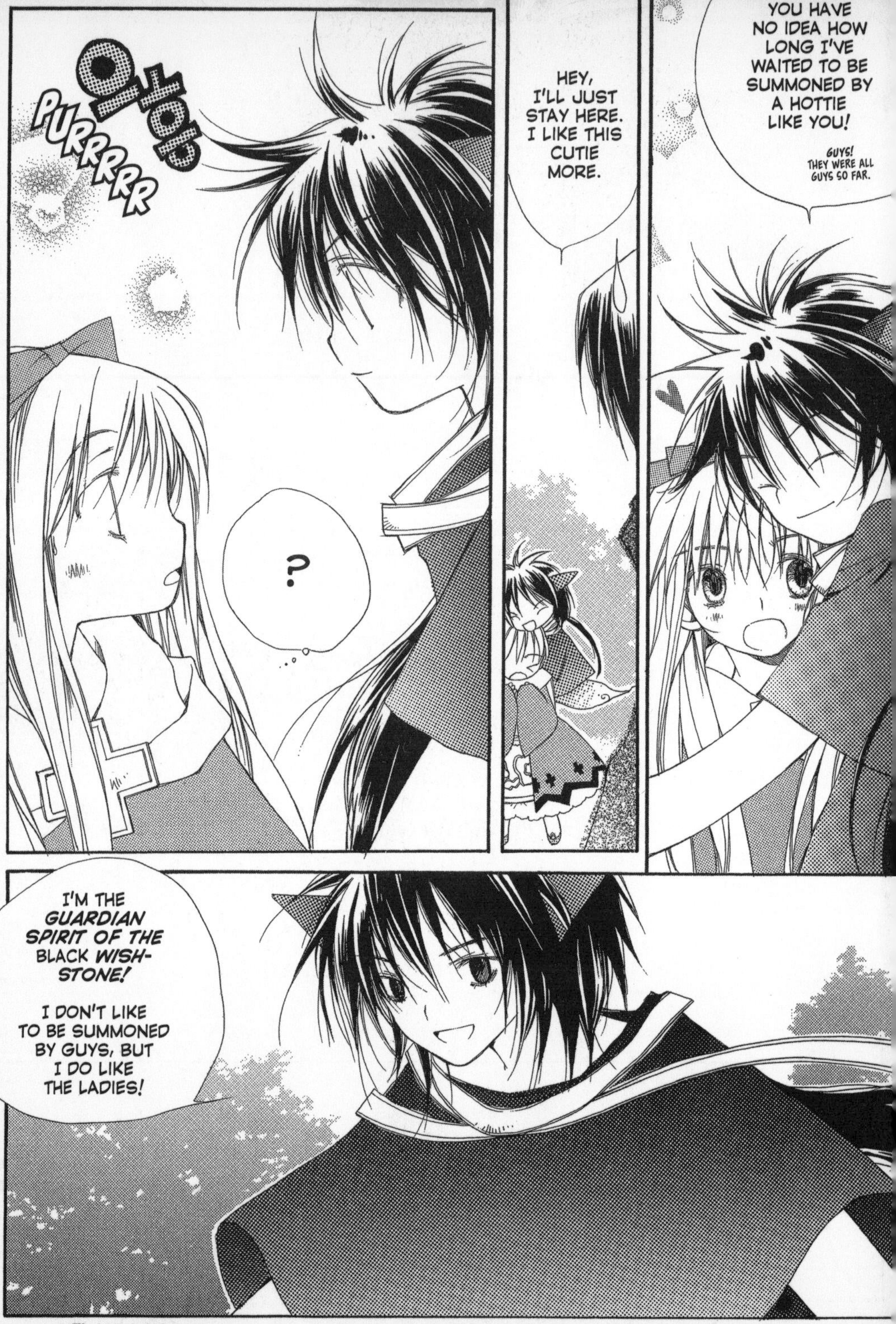
PURRRRR
?
HEY, I'LL JUST STAY HERE. I LIKE THIS CUTIE MORE.
YOU HAVE NO IDEA HOW LONG I'VE WAITED TO BE SUMMONED BY A HOTTIE LIKE YOU!
GUYS! THEY WERE ALL GUYS SO FAR.
I'M THE GUARDIAN SPIRIT OF THE BLACK WISH-STONE!
I DON'T LIKE TO BE SUMMONED BY GUYS, BUT I DO LIKE THE LADIES!

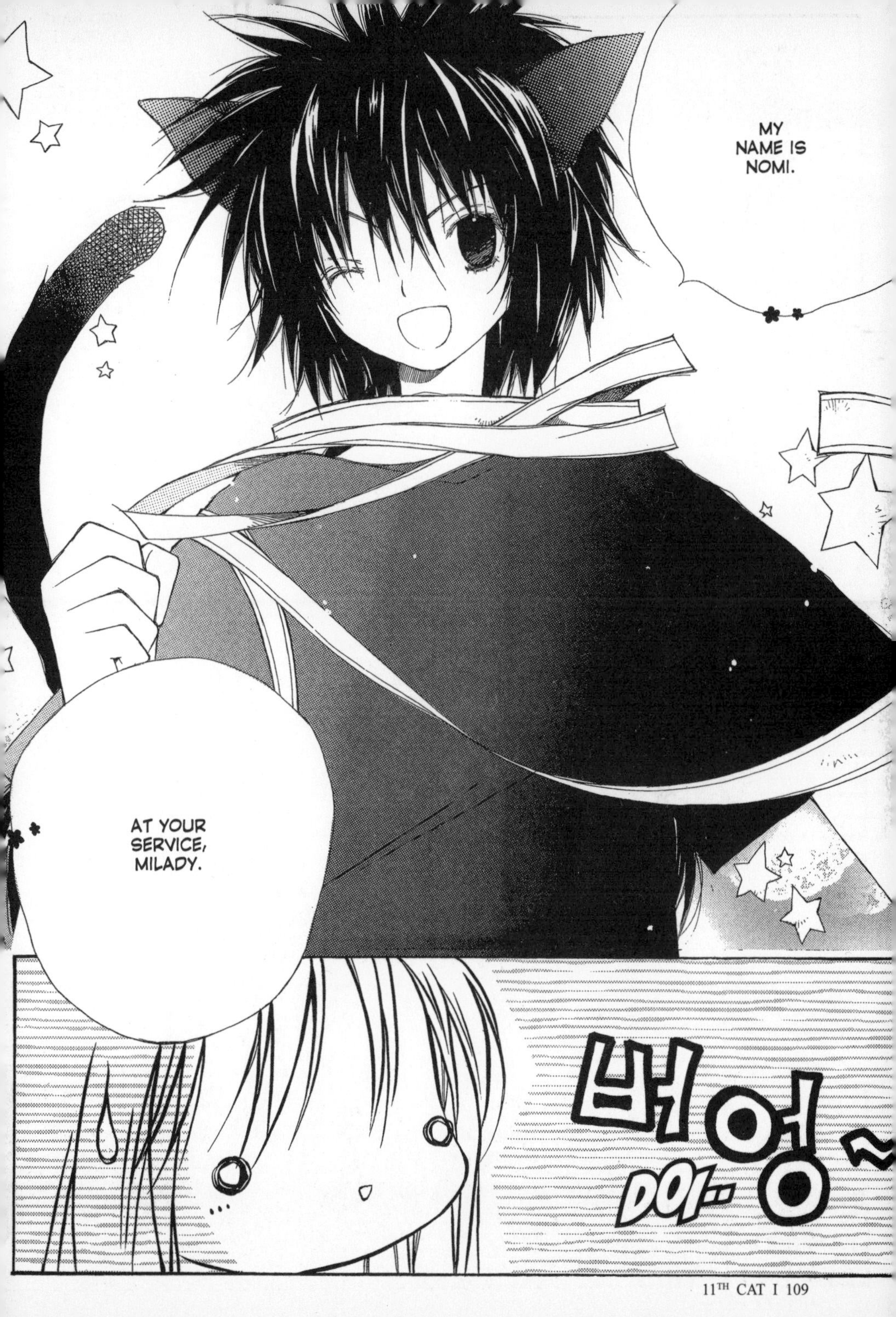
MY NAME IS NOMI.
AT YOUR SERVICE, MILADY.
벼엉~
DOI..

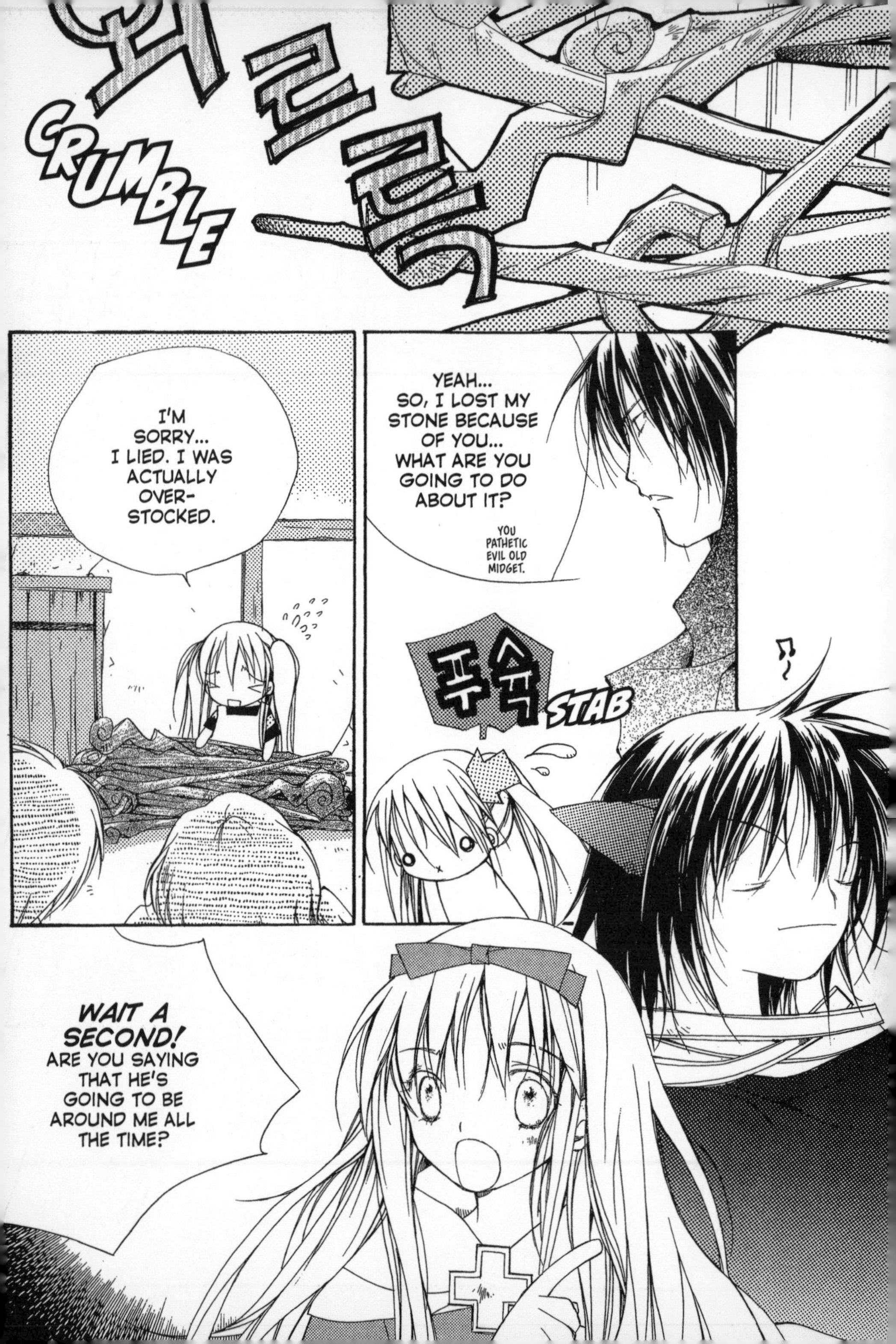

CRUMBLE
I'M SORRY... I LIED. I WAS ACTUALLY OVER-STOCKED.
YEAH... SO, I LOST MY STONE BECAUSE OF YOU... WHAT ARE YOU GOING TO DO ABOUT IT?
YOU PATHETIC EVIL OLD MIDGET.
STAB
WAIT A SECOND! ARE YOU SAYING THAT HE'S GOING TO BE AROUND ME ALL THE TIME?

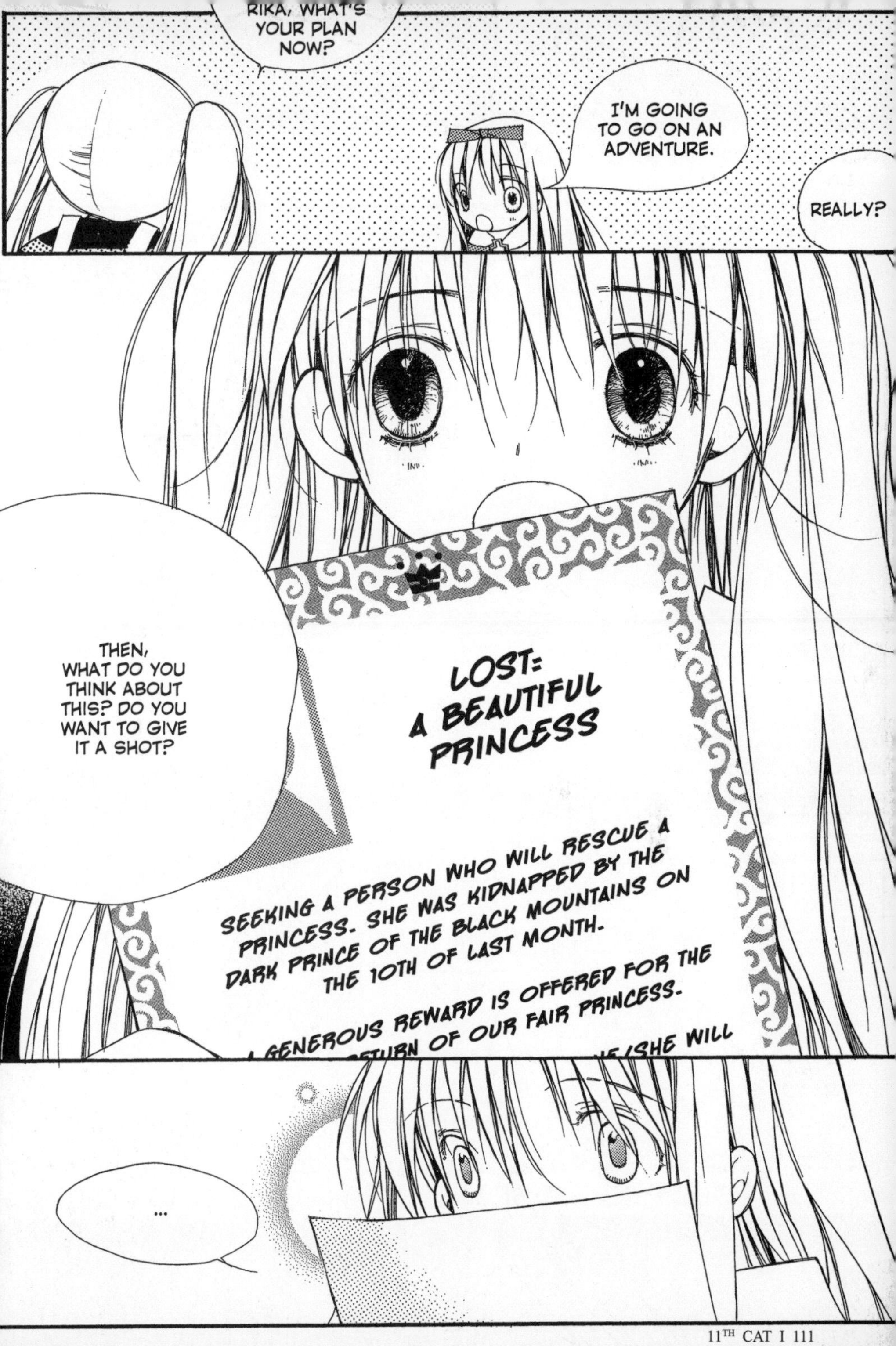
RIKA, WHAT'S YOUR PLAN NOW?
I'M GOING TO GO ON AN ADVENTURE.
REALLY?
THEN, WHAT DO YOU THINK ABOUT THIS? DO YOU WANT TO GIVE IT A SHOT?
LOST: A BEAUTIFUL PRINCESS
SEEKING A PERSON WHO WILL RESCUE A PRINCESS. SHE WAS KIDNAPPED BY THE DARK PRINCE OF THE BLACK MOUNTAINS ON THE 10TH OF LAST MONTH.
A GENEROUS REWARD IS OFFERED FOR THE
ETURN OF OUR FAIR PRINCESS.
SHE WILL
...

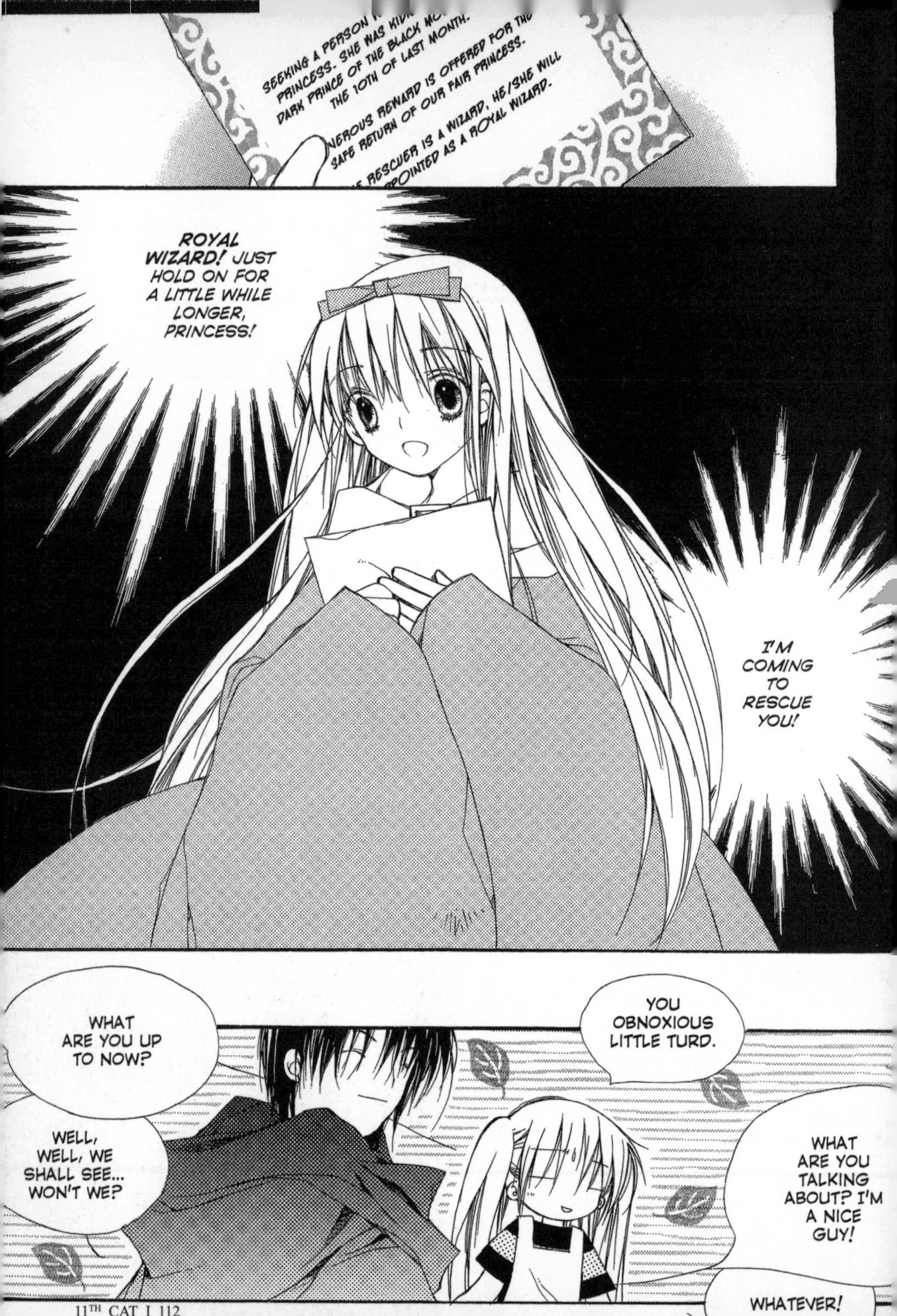
SEEKING A PERSON
PRINCESS. SHE WAS
DARK PRINCE OF THE BLACK
THE 10TH OF LAST MONTH.
REWARD IS OFFERED FOR THE
SAFE RETURN OF OUR FAIR PRINCESS.
RESCUER IS A WIZARD, HE/SHE WILL
AS A ROYAL WIZARD.
ROYAL WIZARD! JUST HOLD ON FOR A LITTLE WHILE LONGER, PRINCESS!
I'M COMING TO RESCUE YOU!
WHAT ARE YOU UP TO NOW?
WELL, WELL, WE SHALL SEE... WON'T WE?
YOU OBNOXIOUS LITTLE TURD.
WHAT ARE YOU TALKING ABOUT? I'M A NICE GUY!
WHATEVER!

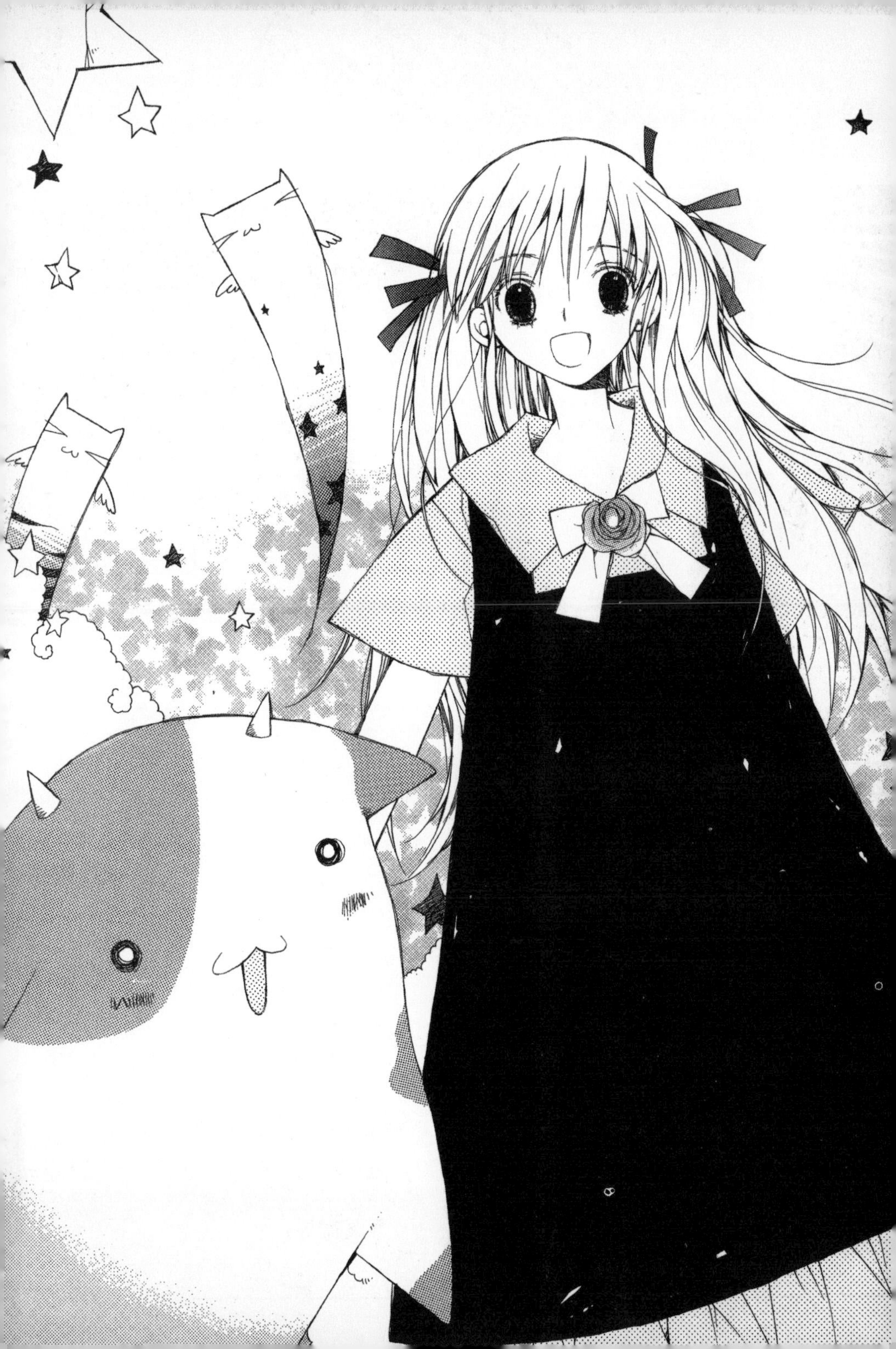

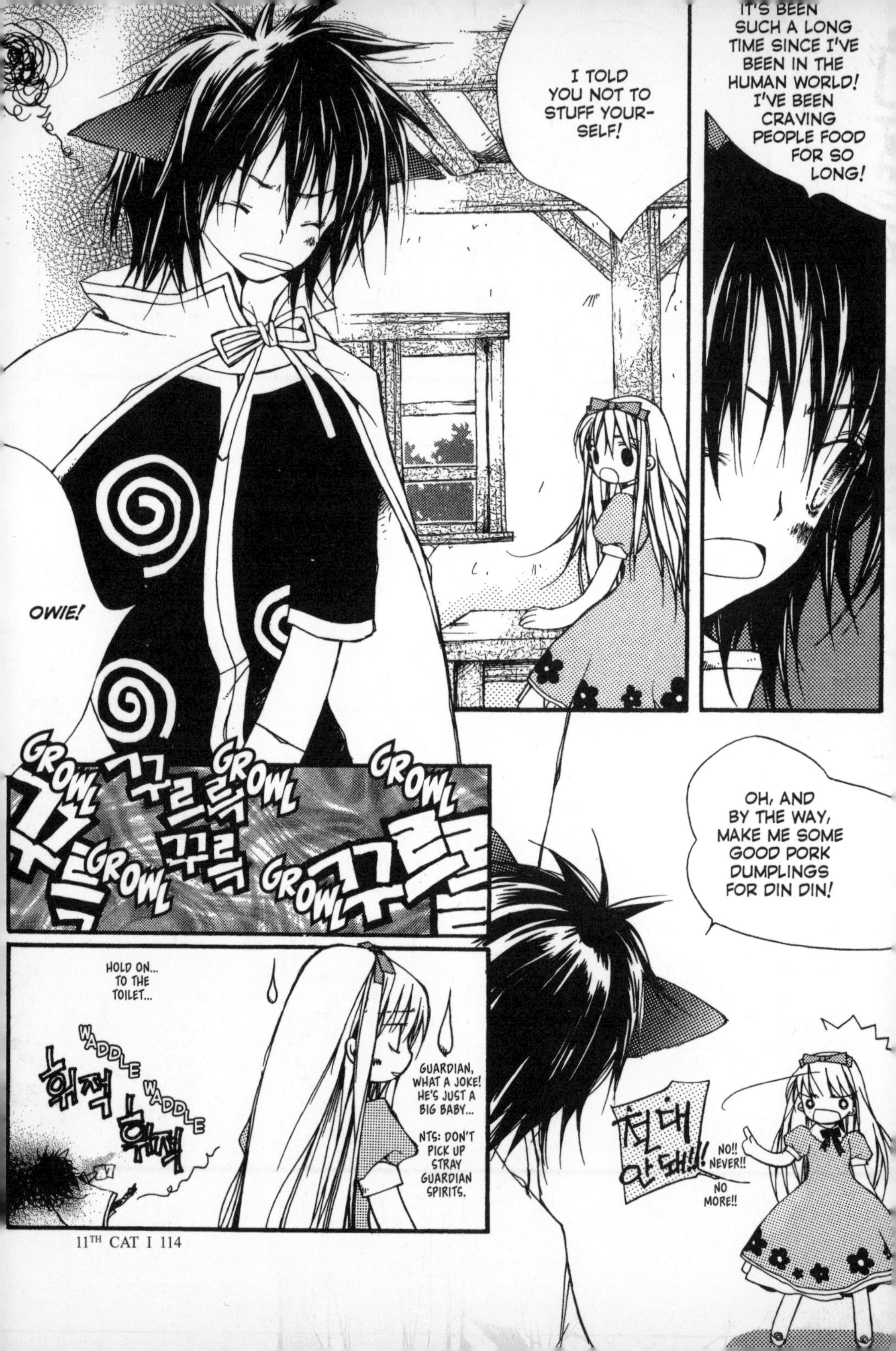

OWIE!
I TOLD YOU NOT TO STUFF YOUR-SELF!
IT'S BEEN SUCH A LONG TIME SINCE I'VE BEEN IN THE HUMAN WORLD! I'VE BEEN CRAVING PEOPLE FOOD FOR SO LONG!
GROWL GROWL GROWL GROWL GROWL
OH, AND BY THE WAY, MAKE ME SOME GOOD PORK DUMPLINGS FOR DIN DIN!
HOLD ON... TO THE TOILET...
WADDLE WADDLE
GUARDIAN, WHAT A JOKE! HE'S JUST A BIG BABY...
NTS: DON'T PICK UP STRAY GUARDIAN SPIRITS.
절대 안돼!!
NO!! NEVER!!
NO MORE!!

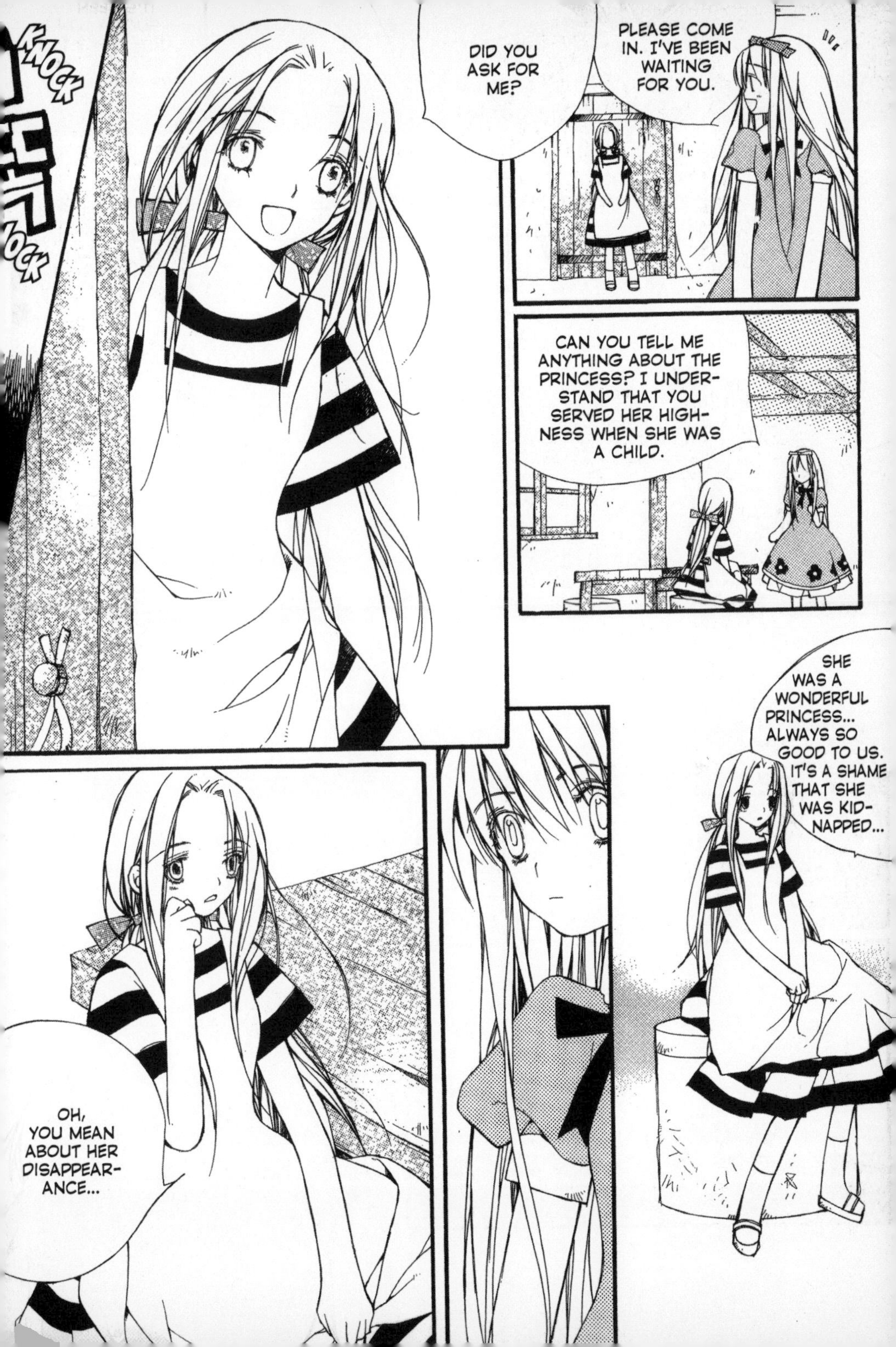
KNOCK
KNOCK
DID YOU ASK FOR ME?
PLEASE COME IN. I'VE BEEN WAITING FOR YOU.
CAN YOU TELL ME ANYTHING ABOUT THE PRINCESS? I UNDER-STAND THAT YOU SERVED HER HIGH-NESS WHEN SHE WAS A CHILD.
OH, YOU MEAN ABOUT HER DISAPPEAR-ANCE...
SHE WAS A WONDERFUL PRINCESS... ALWAYS SO GOOD TO US. IT'S A SHAME THAT SHE WAS KID-NAPPED...

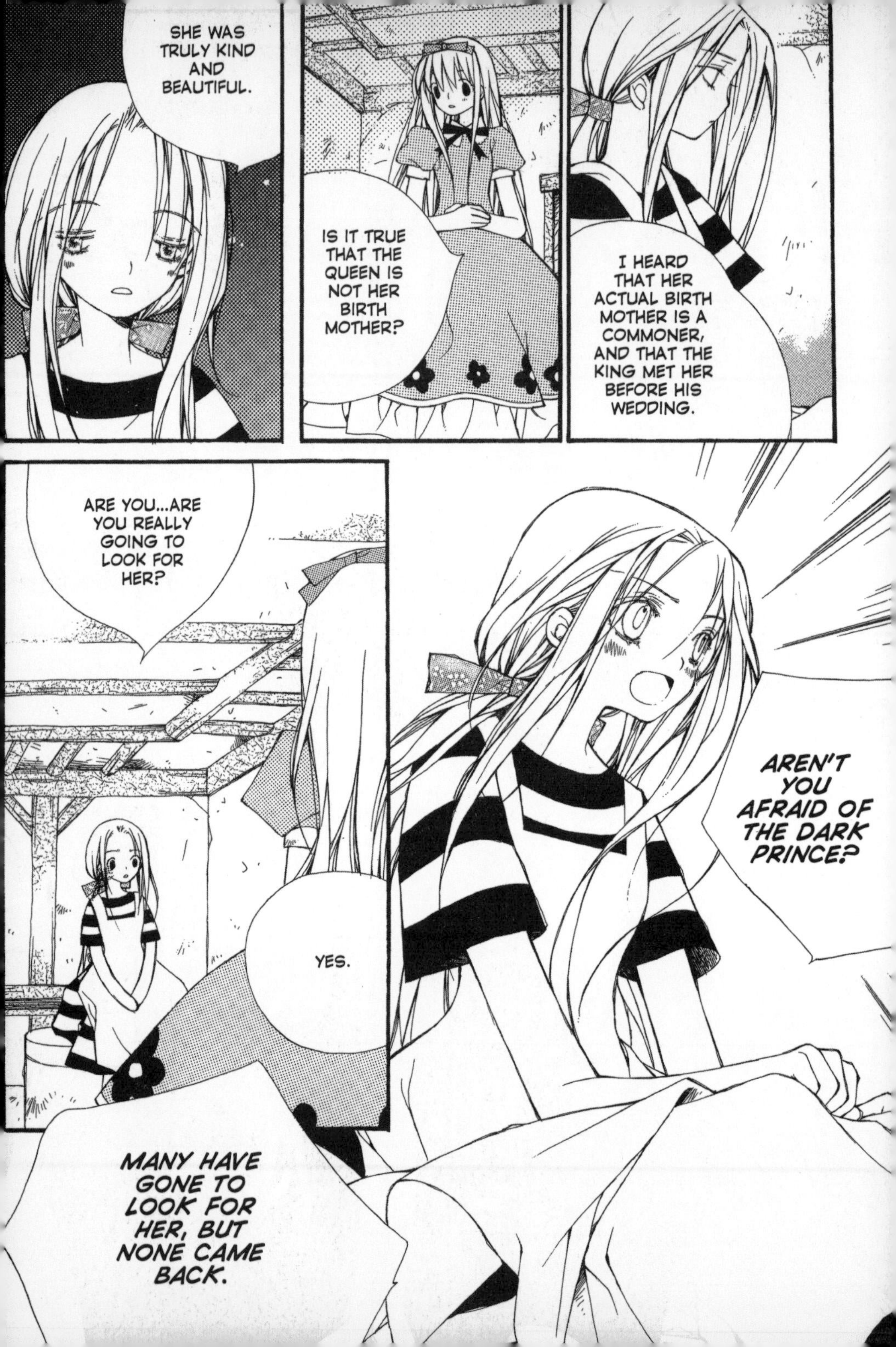
SHE WAS TRULY KIND AND BEAUTIFUL.
IS IT TRUE THAT THE QUEEN IS NOT HER BIRTH MOTHER?
I HEARD THAT HER ACTUAL BIRTH MOTHER IS A COMMONER, AND THAT THE KING MET HER BEFORE HIS WEDDING.
ARE YOU...ARE YOU REALLY GOING TO LOOK FOR HER?
YES.
AREN'T YOU AFRAID OF THE DARK PRINCE?
MANY HAVE GONE TO LOOK FOR HER, BUT NONE CAME BACK.

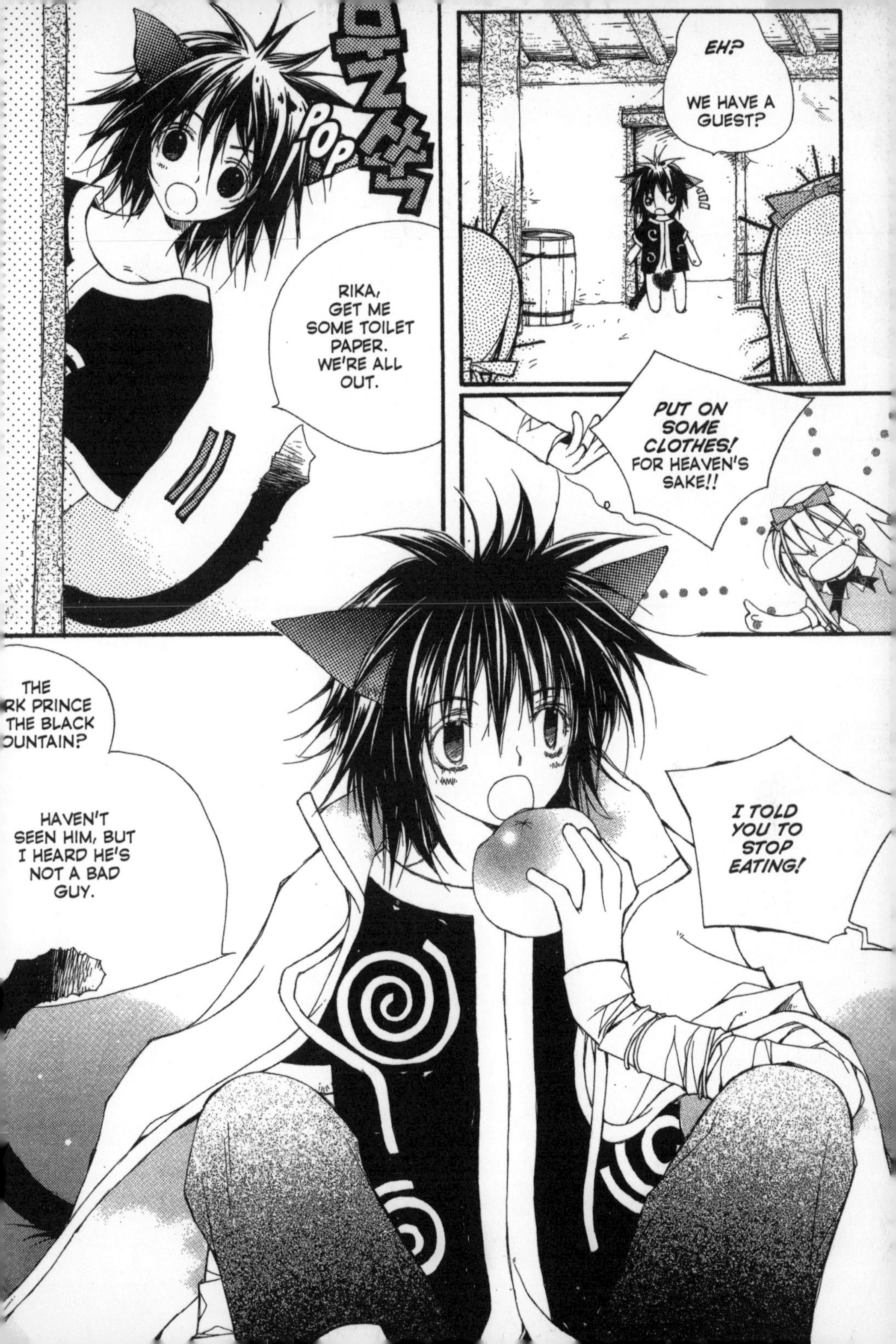
POP
RIKA, GET ME SOME TOILET PAPER. WE'RE ALL OUT.
EH?
WE HAVE A GUEST?
PUT ON SOME CLOTHES! FOR HEAVEN'S SAKE!!
THE
RK PRINCE
THE BLACK
OUNTAIN?
HAVEN'T SEEN HIM, BUT I HEARD HE'S NOT A BAD GUY.
I TOLD YOU TO STOP EATING!

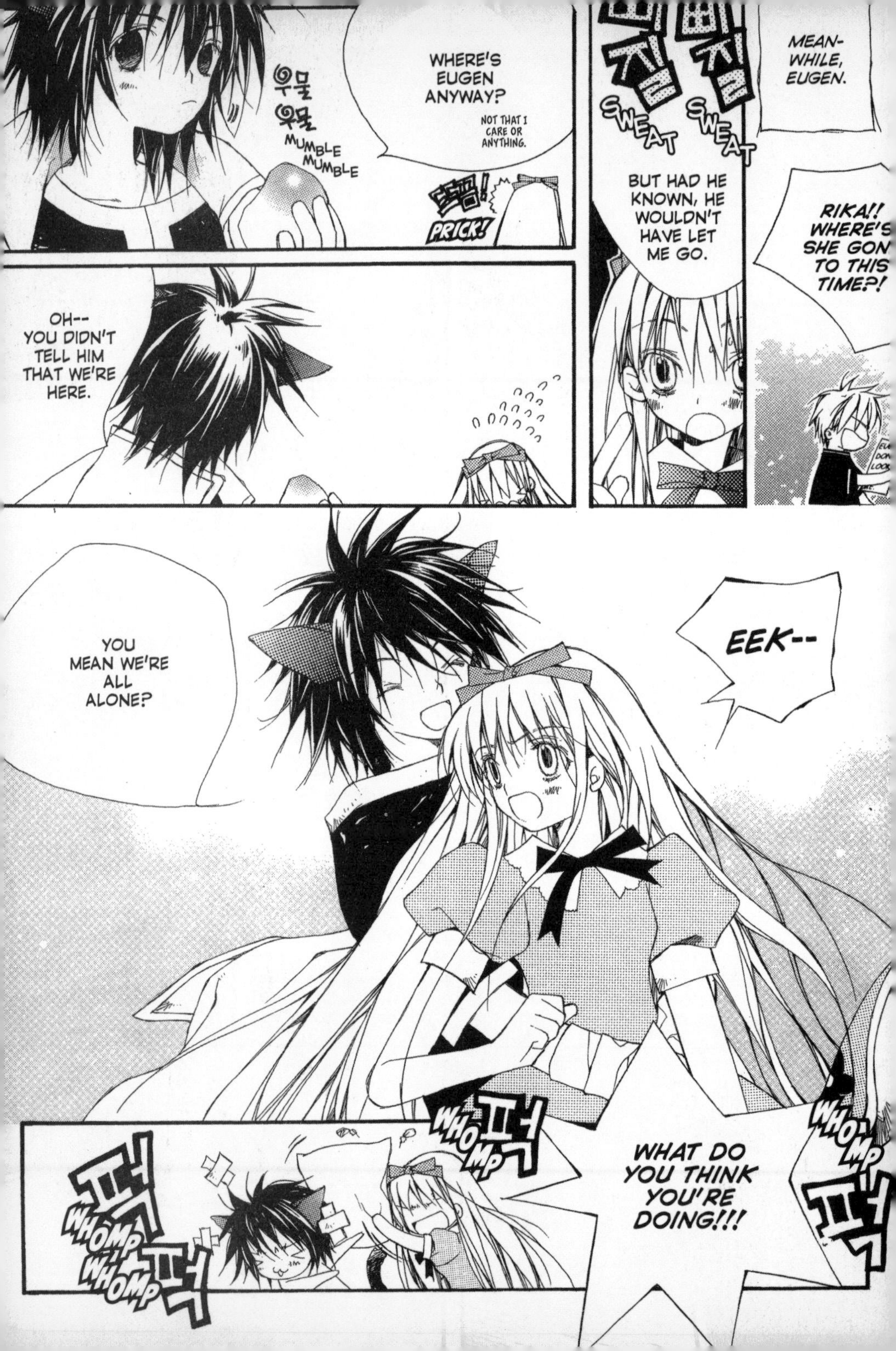

우물 우물
MUMBLE MUMBLE
WHERE'S EUGEN ANYWAY?
NOT THAT I CARE OR ANYTHING.
따끔!
PRICK!
OH-- YOU DIDN'T TELL HIM THAT WE'RE HERE.
삐질 삐질
SWEAT SWEAT
BUT HAD HE KNOWN, HE WOULDN'T HAVE LET ME GO.
MEAN-WHILE, EUGEN.
RIKA!! WHERE'S SHE GON TO THIS TIME?!
YOU MEAN WE'RE ALL ALONE?
EEK--
퍽
WHOMP
퍽
WHOMP
퍽
WHOMP
WHAT DO YOU THINK YOU'RE DOING!!!
퍽
WHOMP

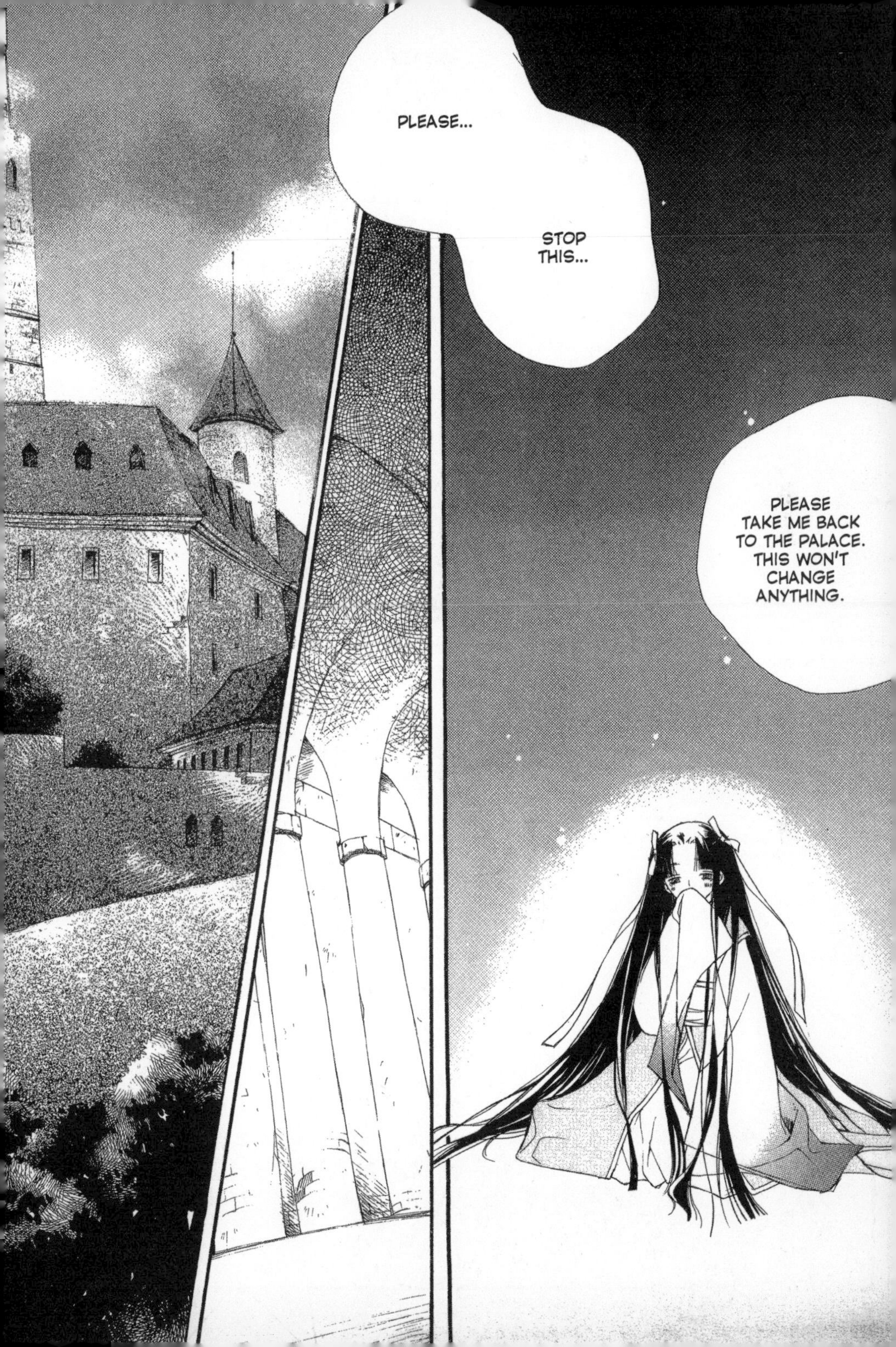
PLEASE...
STOP THIS...
PLEASE TAKE ME BACK TO THE PALACE. THIS WON'T CHANGE ANYTHING.

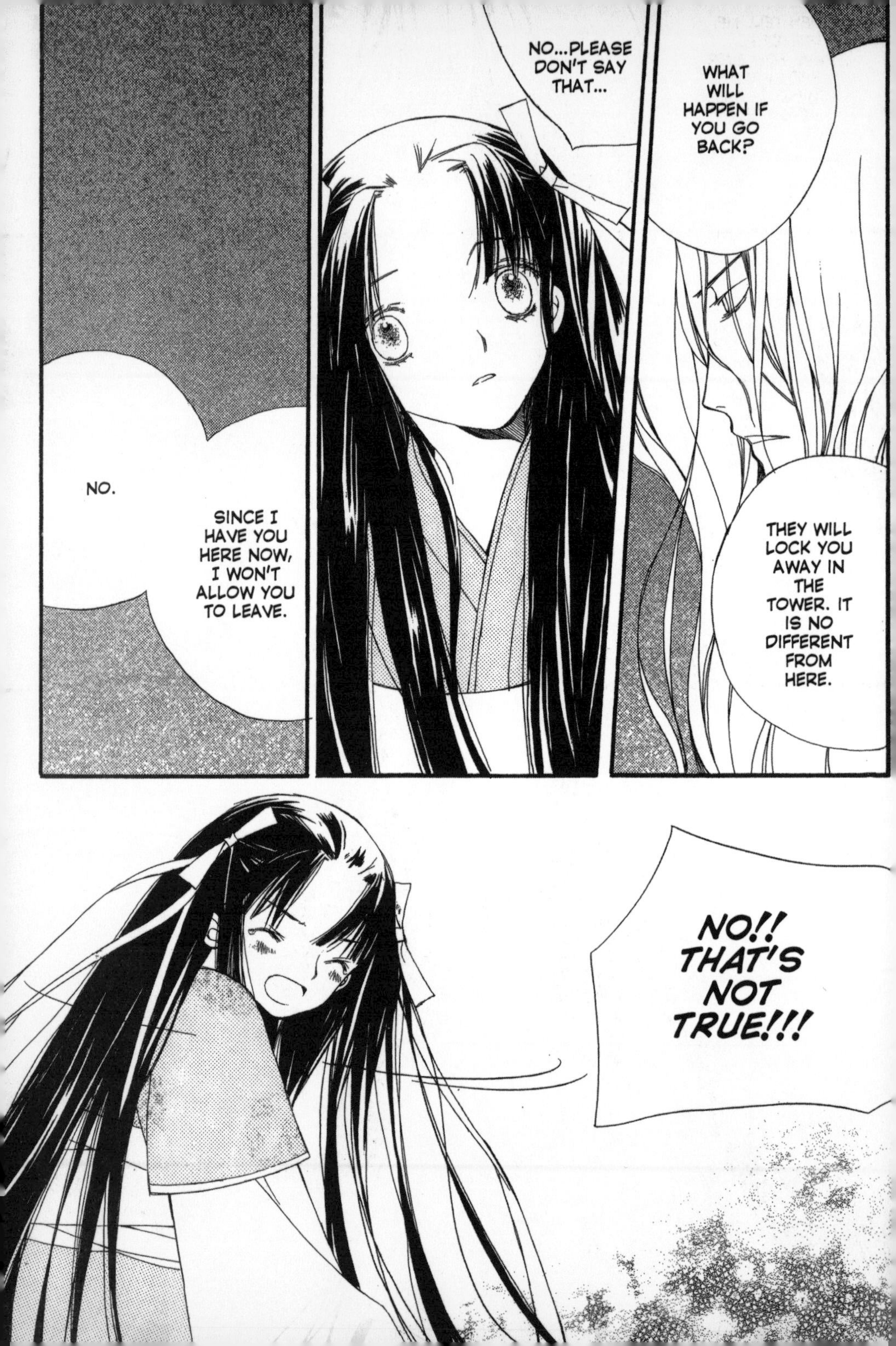
NO.
SINCE I HAVE YOU HERE NOW, I WON'T ALLOW YOU TO LEAVE.
NO...PLEASE DON'T SAY THAT...
WHAT WILL HAPPEN IF YOU GO BACK?
THEY WILL LOCK YOU AWAY IN THE TOWER. IT IS NO DIFFERENT FROM HERE.
NO!! THAT'S NOT TRUE!!!

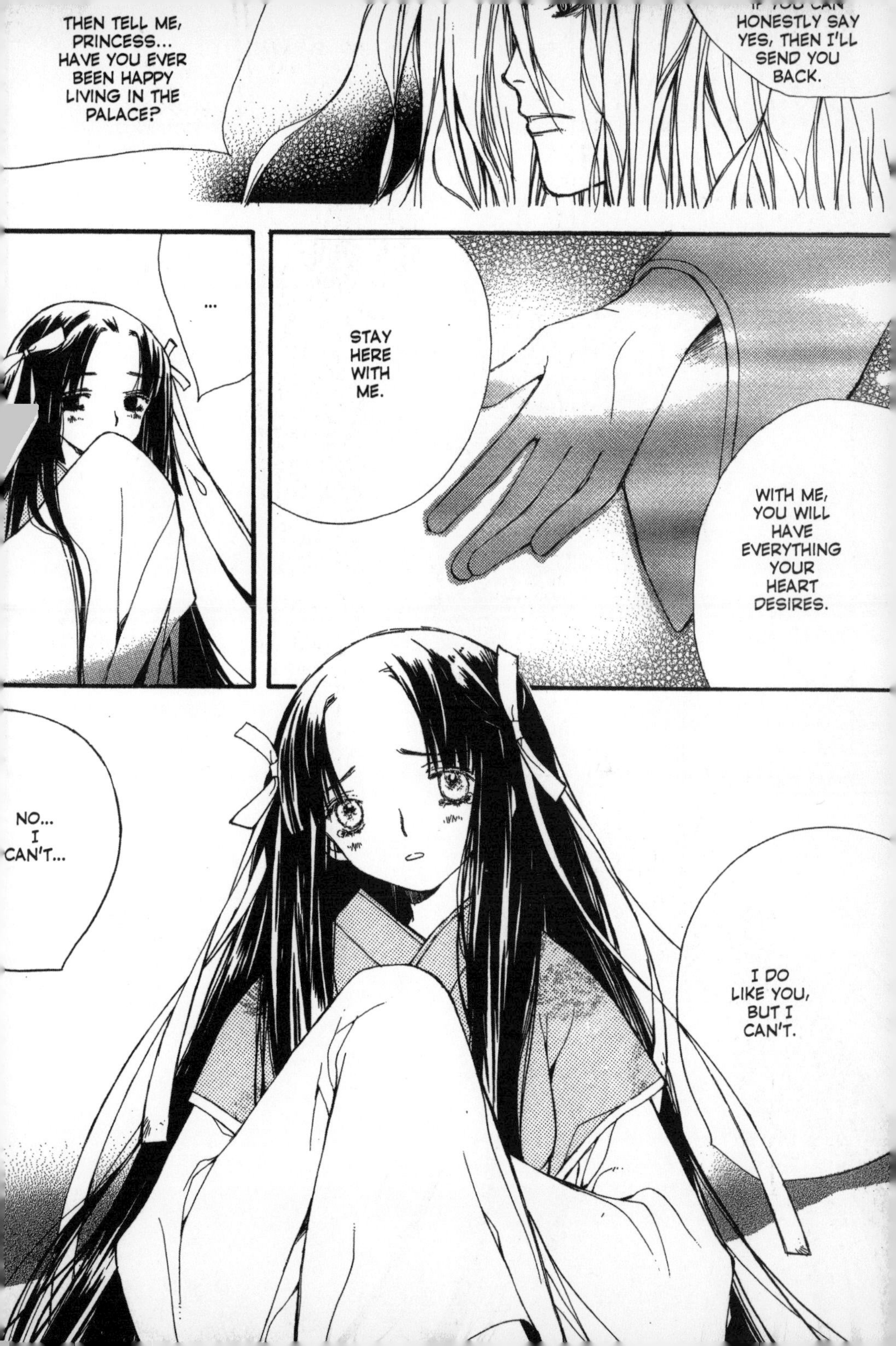
THEN TELL ME, PRINCESS... HAVE YOU EVER BEEN HAPPY LIVING IN THE PALACE?
HONESTLY SAY YES, THEN I'LL SEND YOU BACK.
...
STAY HERE WITH ME.
WITH ME, YOU WILL HAVE EVERYTHING YOUR HEART DESIRES.
NO... I CAN'T...
I DO LIKE YOU, BUT I CAN'T.

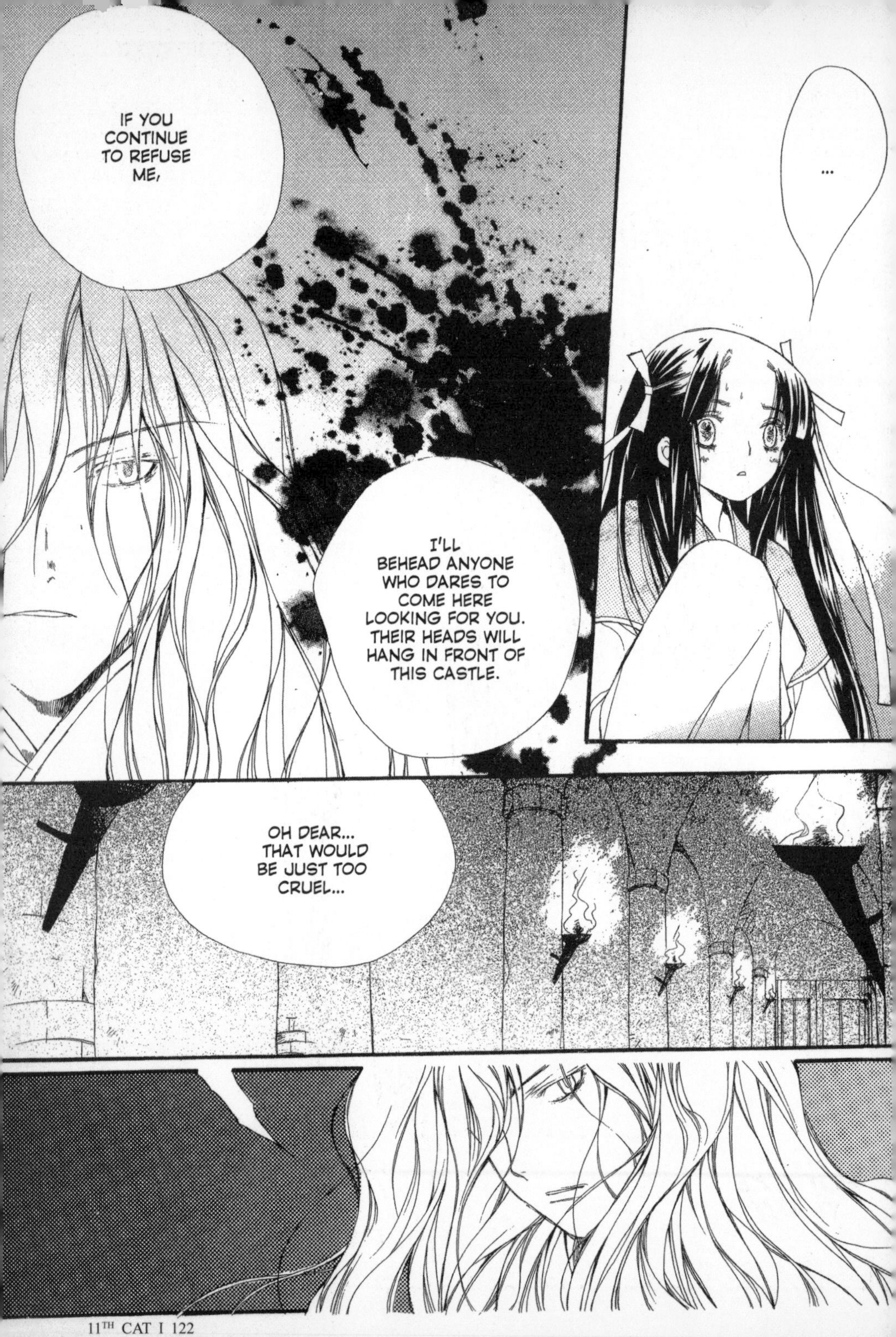
IF YOU CONTINUE TO REFUSE ME,
I'LL BEHEAD ANYONE WHO DARES TO COME HERE LOOKING FOR YOU. THEIR HEADS WILL HANG IN FRONT OF THIS CASTLE.
...
OH DEAR... THAT WOULD BE JUST TOO CRUEL...

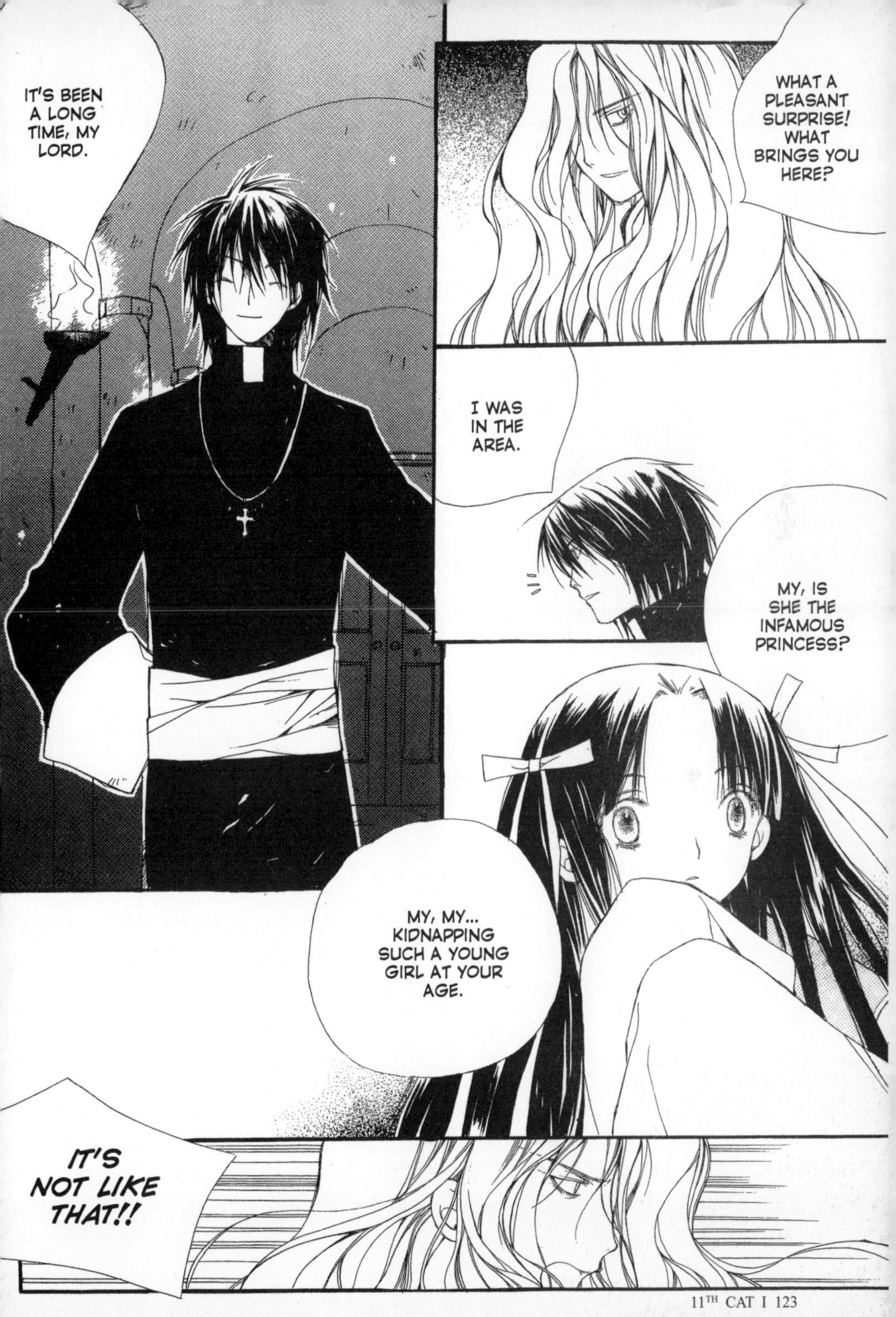
IT'S BEEN A LONG TIME, MY LORD.
WHAT A PLEASANT SURPRISE! WHAT BRINGS YOU HERE?
I WAS IN THE AREA.
MY, IS SHE THE INFAMOUS PRINCESS?
MY, MY... KIDNAPPING SUCH A YOUNG GIRL AT YOUR AGE.
IT'S NOT LIKE THAT!!

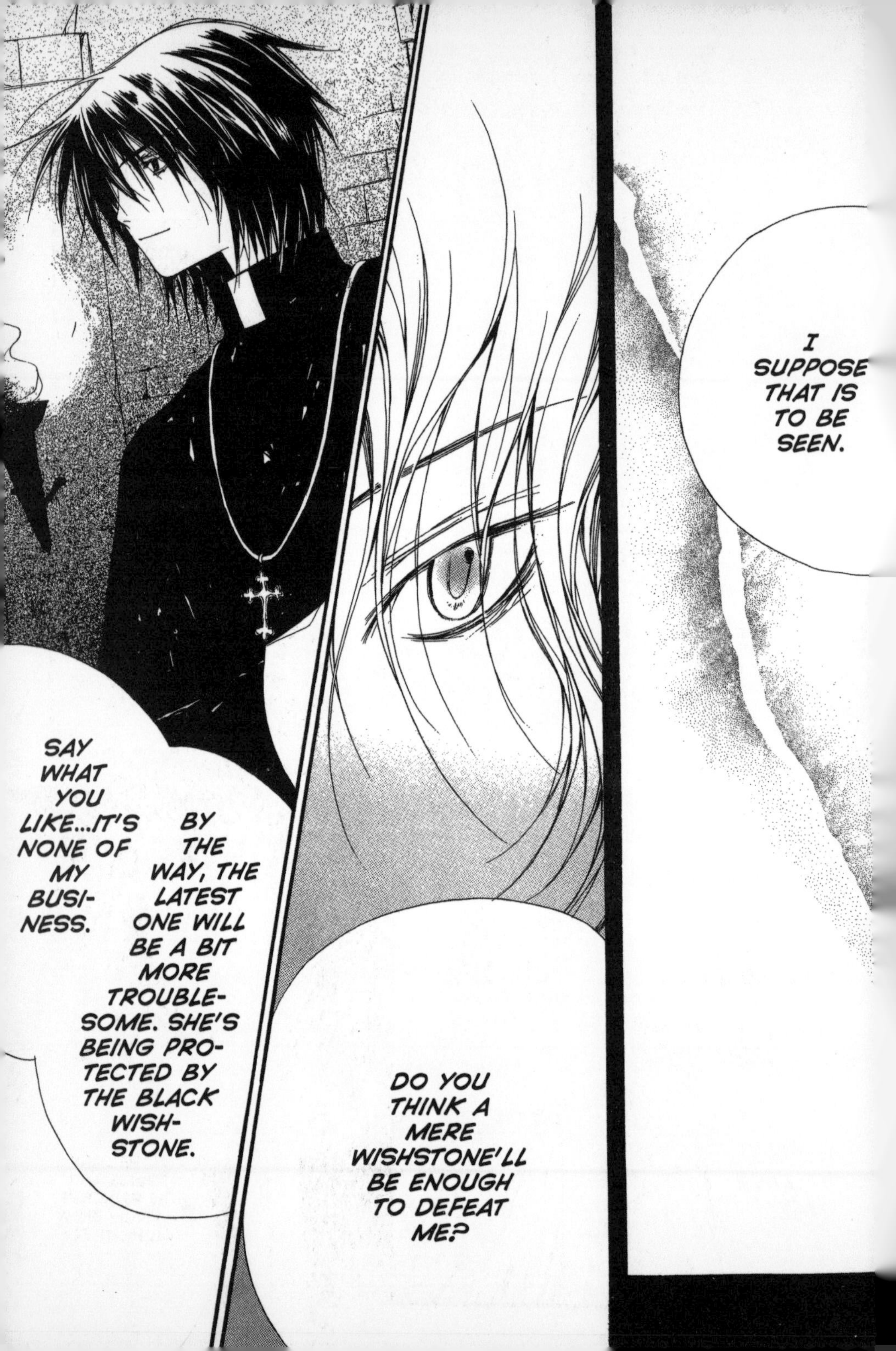
SAY WHAT YOU LIKE...IT'S NONE OF MY BUSI-NESS.
BY THE WAY, THE LATEST ONE WILL BE A BIT MORE TROUBLE-SOME. SHE'S BEING PRO-TECTED BY THE BLACK WISH-STONE.
DO YOU THINK A MERE WISHSTONE'LL BE ENOUGH TO DEFEAT ME?
I SUPPOSE THAT IS TO BE SEEN.

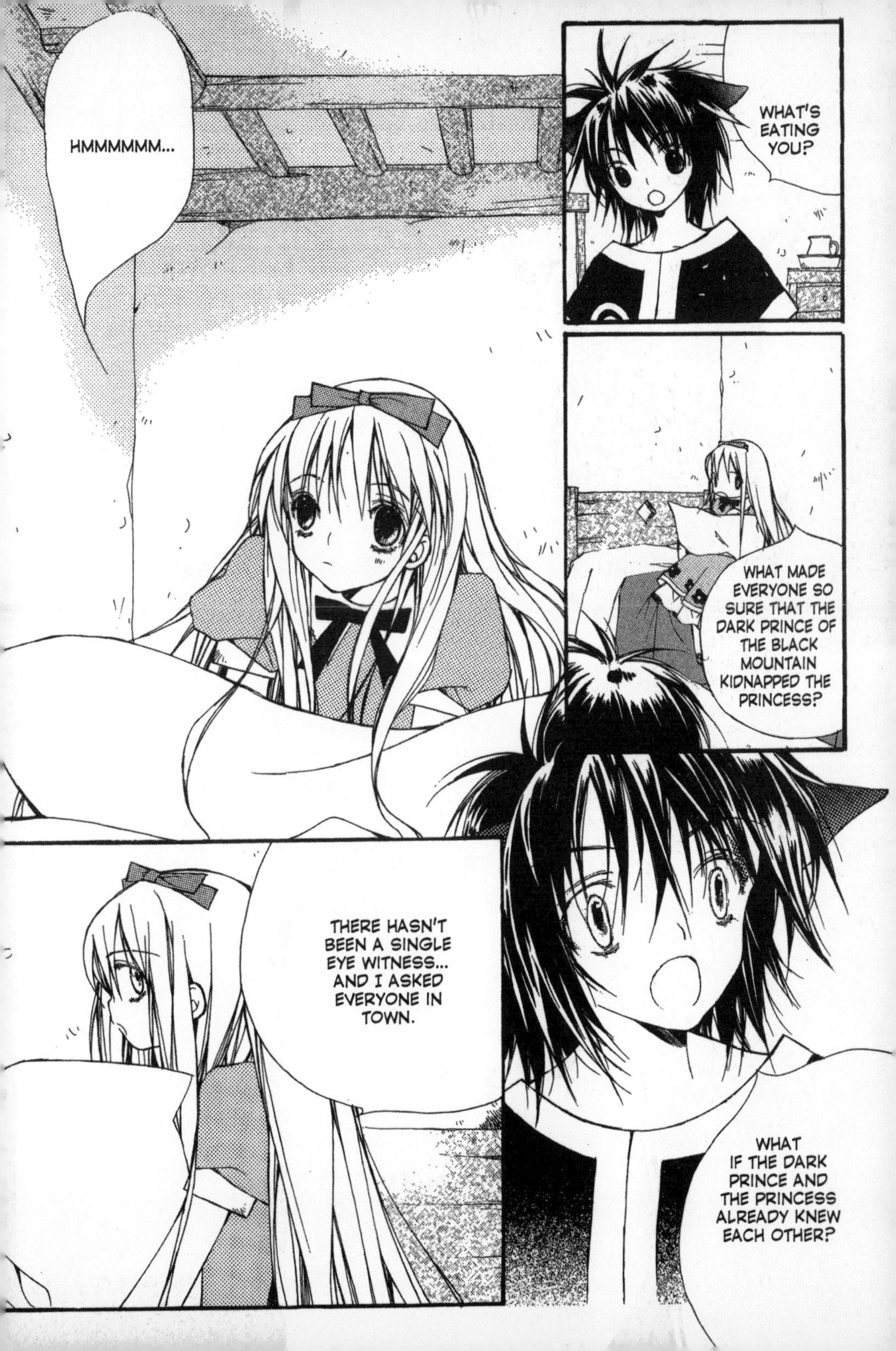
WHAT'S EATING YOU?
HMMMMMM...
WHAT MADE EVERYONE SO SURE THAT THE DARK PRINCE OF THE BLACK MOUNTAIN KIDNAPPED THE PRINCESS?
THERE HASN'T BEEN A SINGLE EYE WITNESS... AND I ASKED EVERYONE IN TOWN.
WHAT IF THE DARK PRINCE AND THE PRINCESS ALREADY KNEW EACH OTHER?

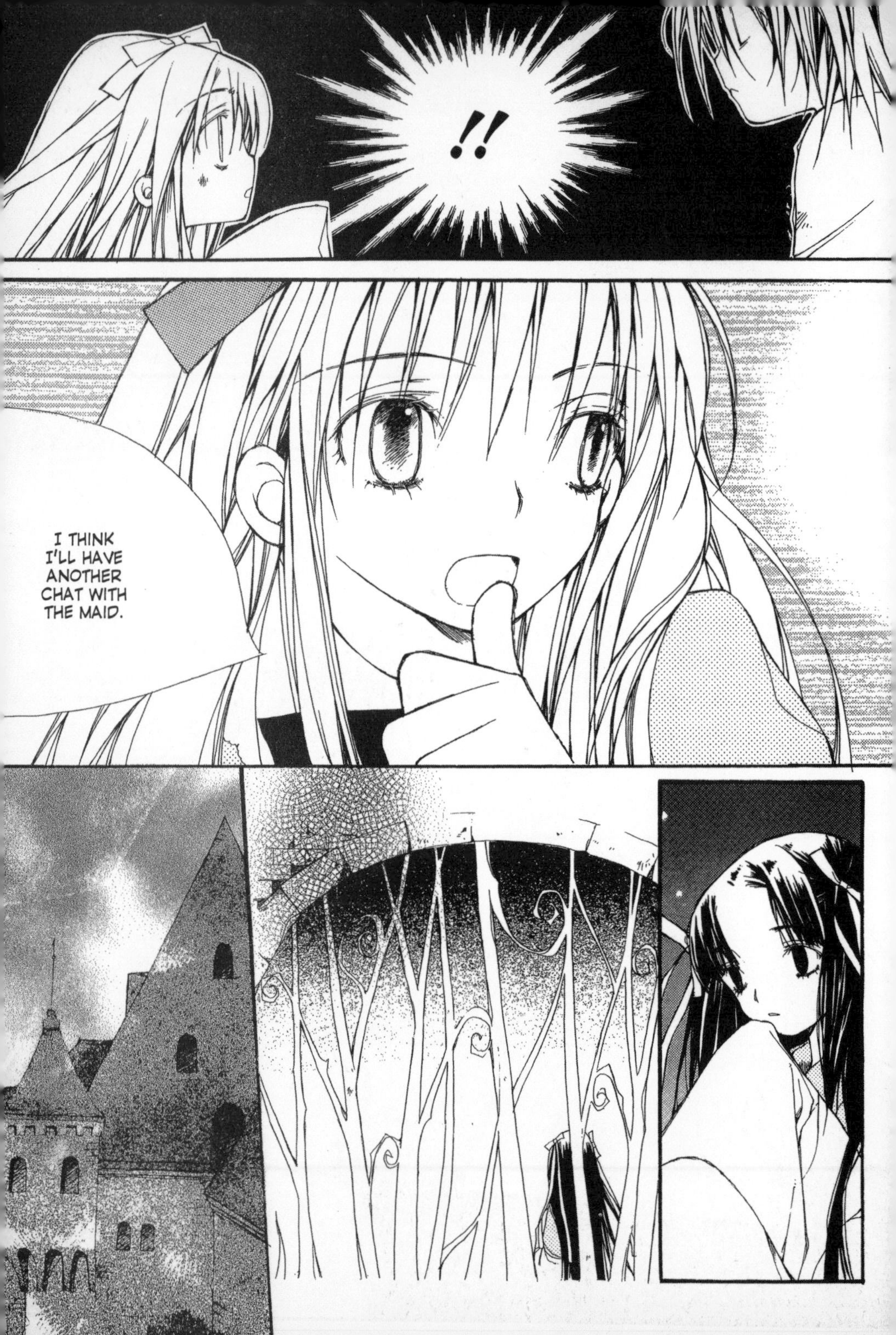
!!
I THINK I'LL HAVE ANOTHER CHAT WITH THE MAID.

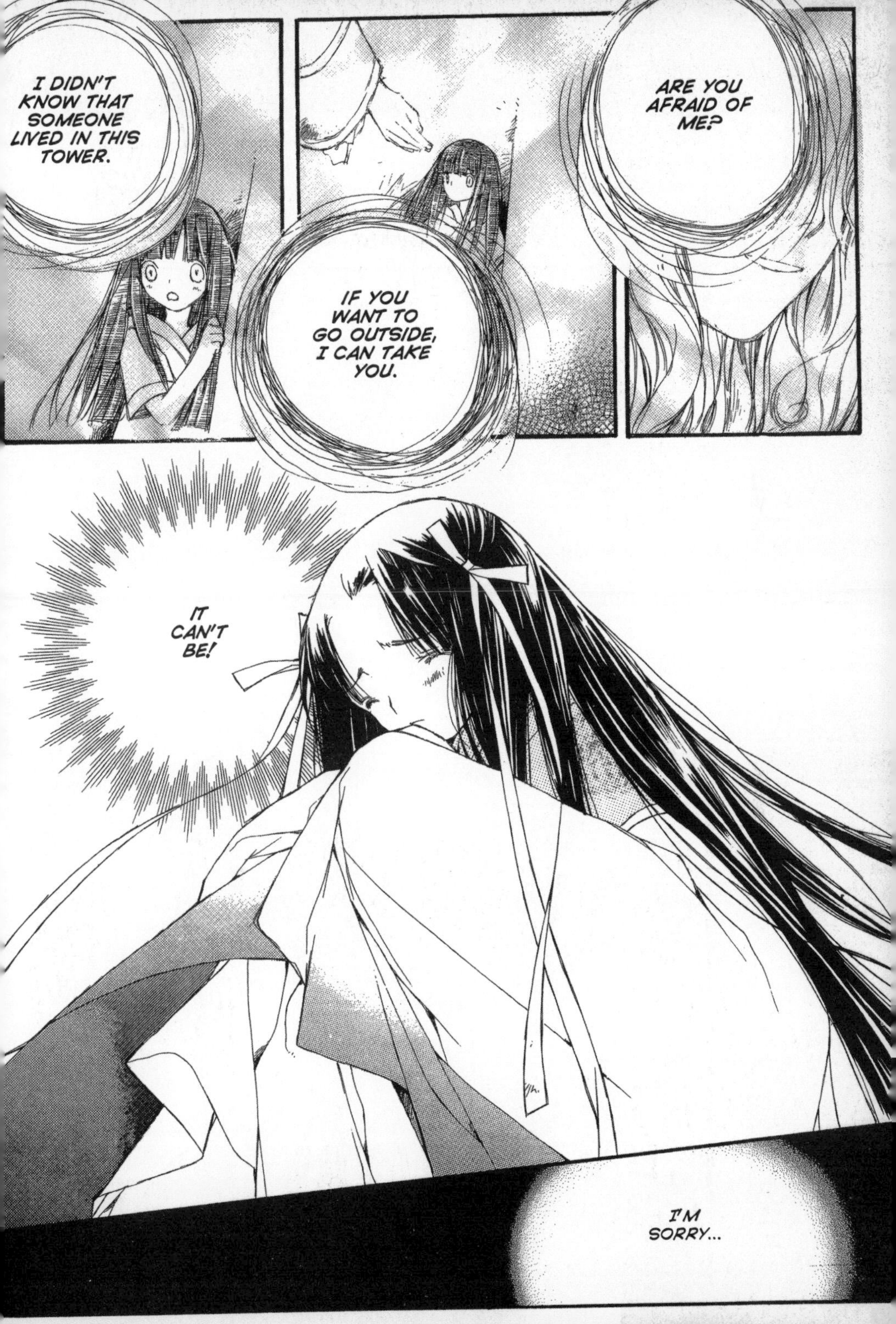
I DIDN'T KNOW THAT SOMEONE LIVED IN THIS TOWER.
IF YOU WANT TO GO OUTSIDE, I CAN TAKE YOU.
ARE YOU AFRAID OF ME?
IT CAN'T BE!
I'M SORRY...

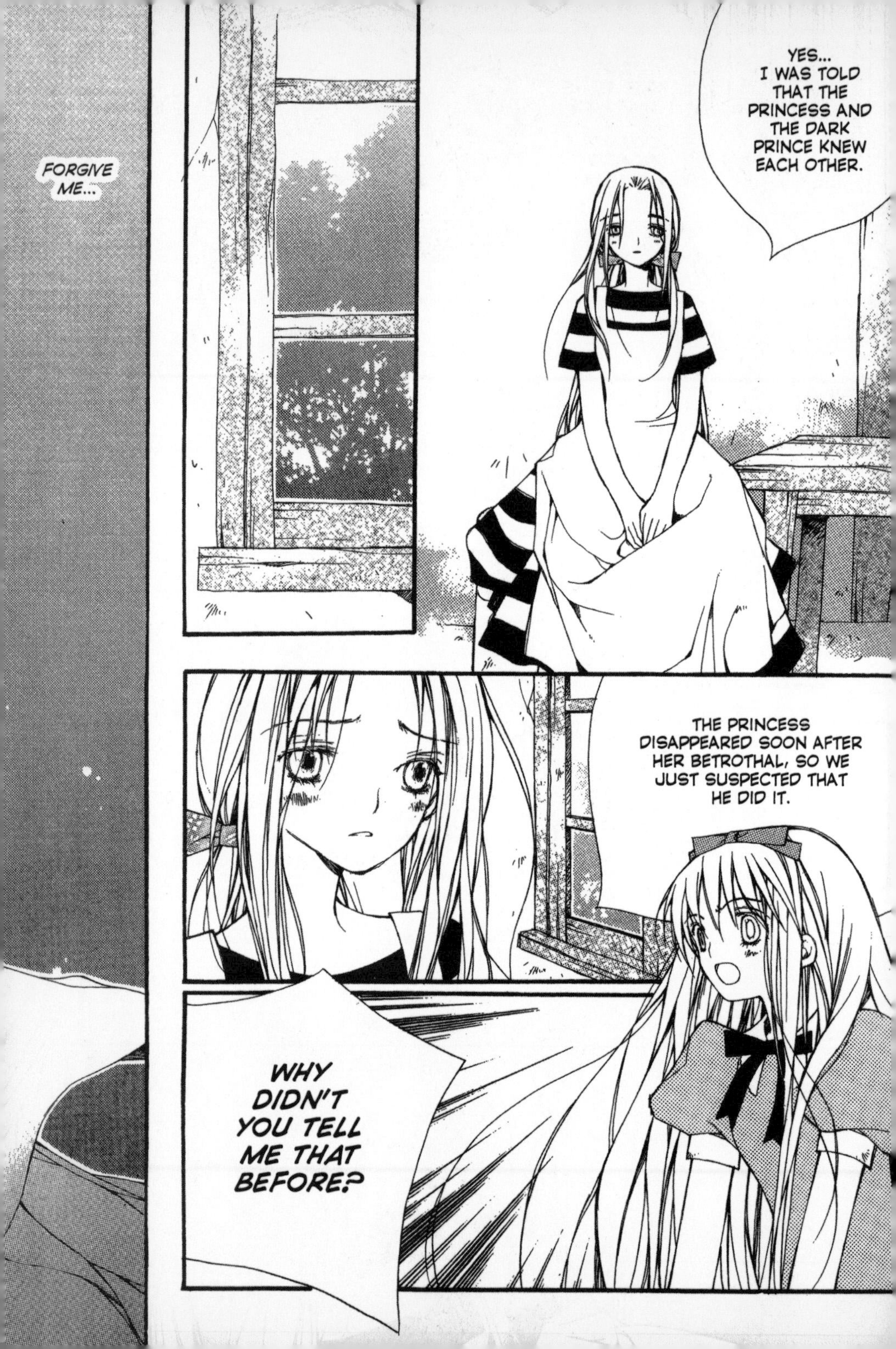
FORGIVE ME...
YES... I WAS TOLD THAT THE PRINCESS AND THE DARK PRINCE KNEW EACH OTHER.
THE PRINCESS DISAPPEARED SOON AFTER HER BETROTHAL, SO WE JUST SUSPECTED THAT HE DID IT.
WHY DIDN'T YOU TELL ME THAT BEFORE?

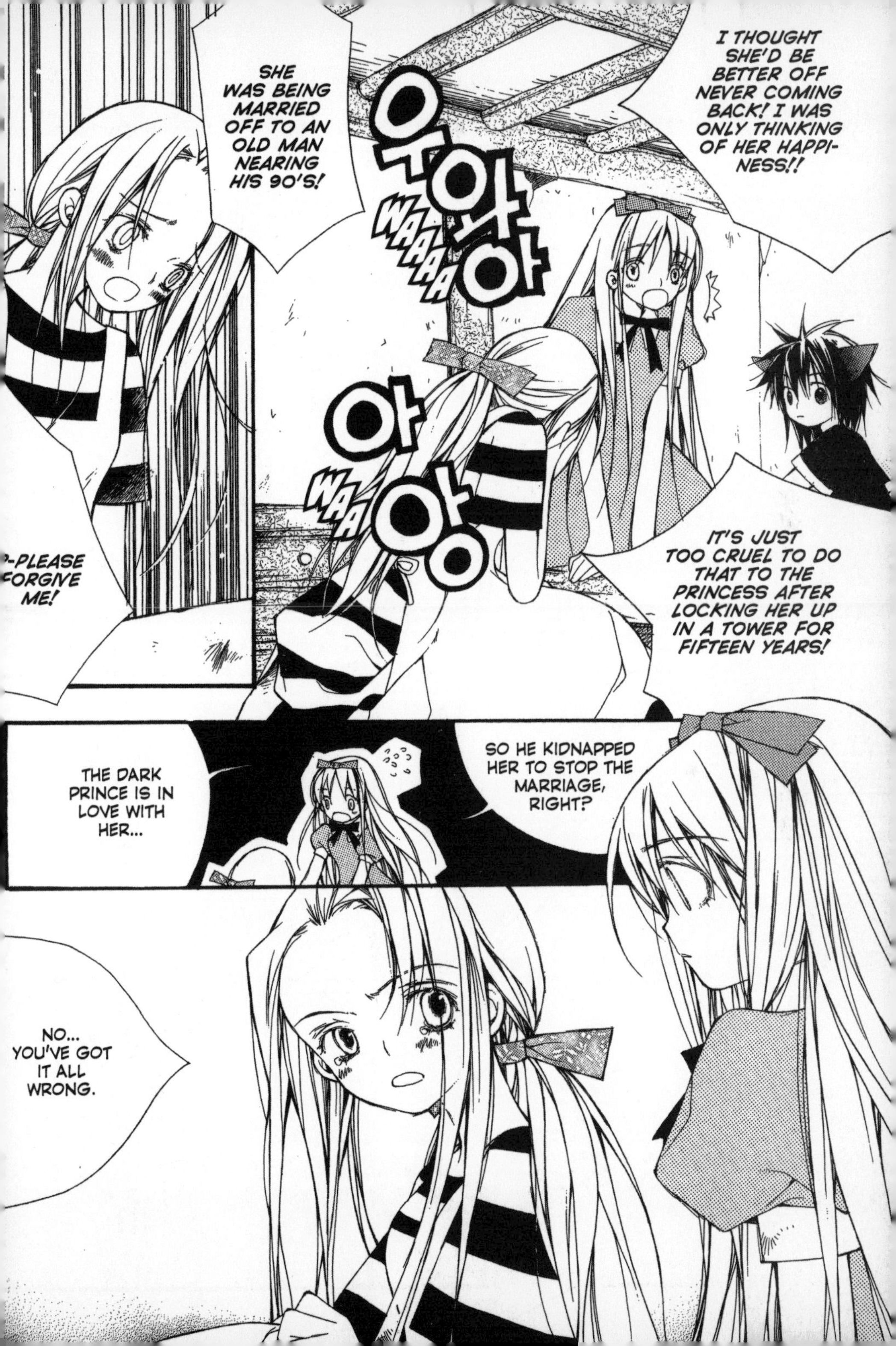
SHE WAS BEING MARRIED OFF TO AN OLD MAN NEARING HIS 90'S!
P-PLEASE FORGIVE ME!
WAAAA
WAAA
I THOUGHT SHE'D BE BETTER OFF NEVER COMING BACK! I WAS ONLY THINKING OF HER HAPPI-NESS!!
IT'S JUST TOO CRUEL TO DO THAT TO THE PRINCESS AFTER LOCKING HER UP IN A TOWER FOR FIFTEEN YEARS!
THE DARK PRINCE IS IN LOVE WITH HER...
SO HE KIDNAPPED HER TO STOP THE MARRIAGE, RIGHT?
NO... YOU'VE GOT IT ALL WRONG.

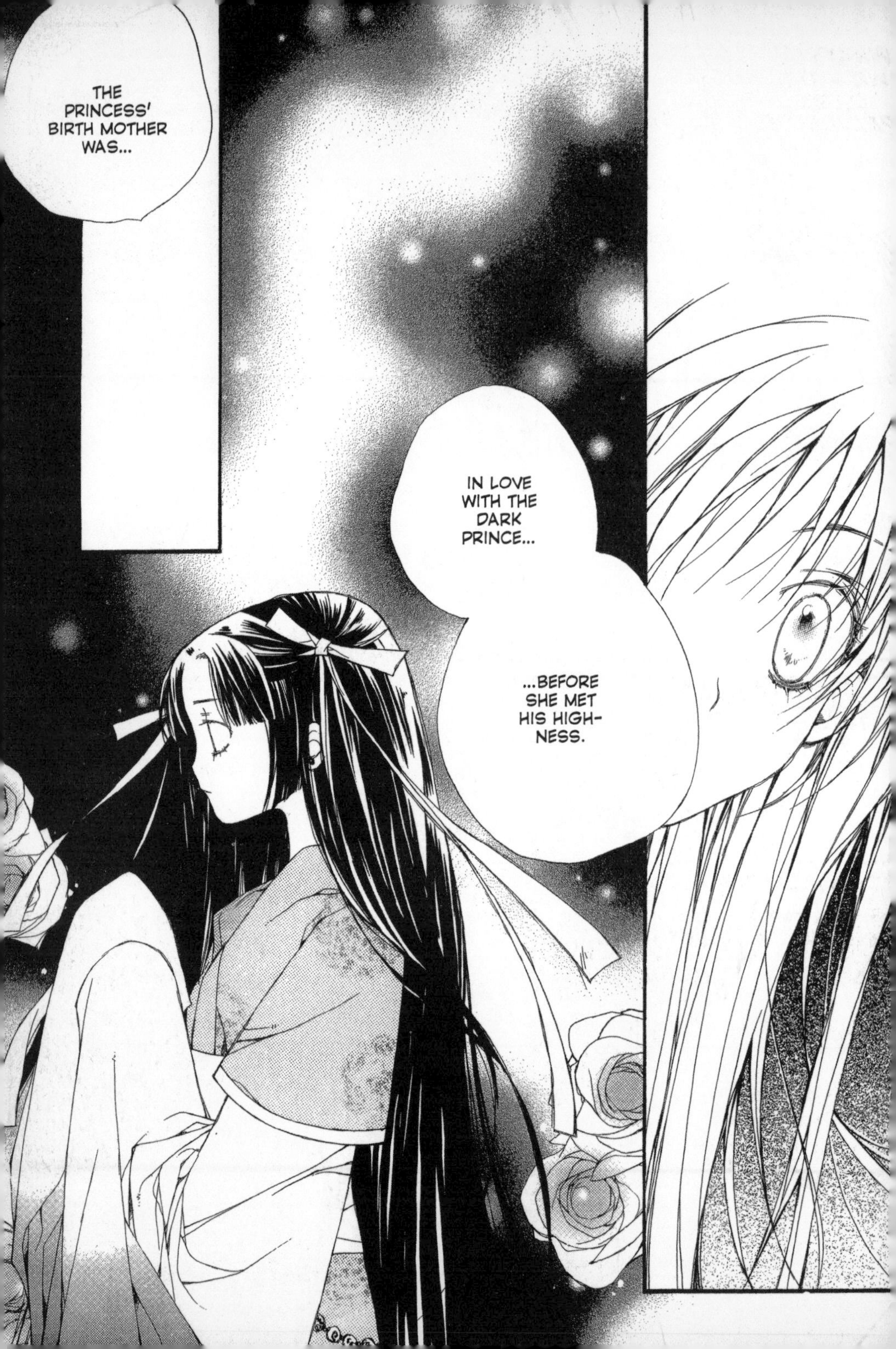
THE PRINCESS' BIRTH MOTHER WAS...
IN LOVE WITH THE DARK PRINCE...
...BEFORE SHE MET HIS HIGH-NESS.

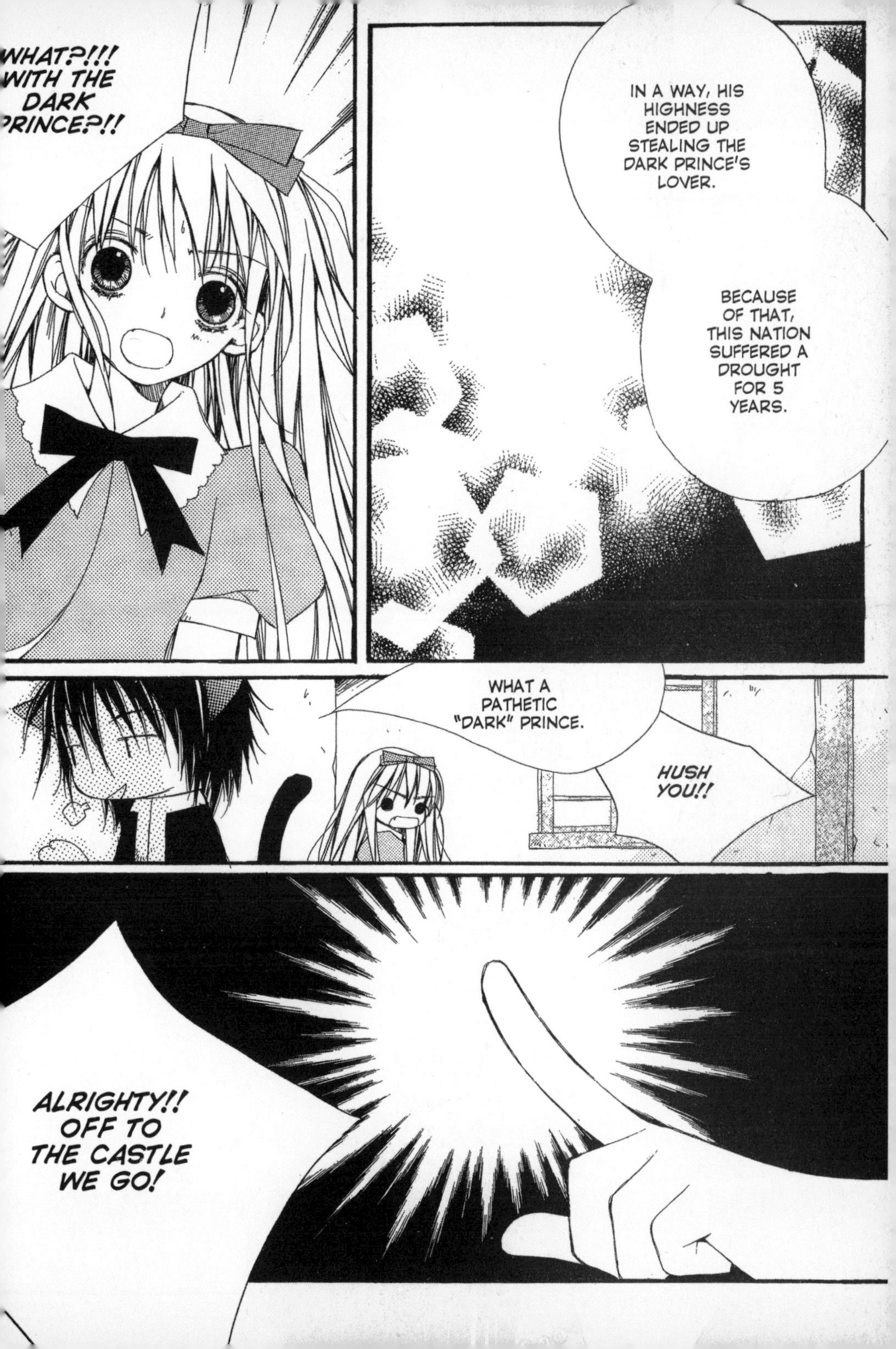
WHAT?!!! WITH THE DARK PRINCE?!!
IN A WAY, HIS HIGHNESS ENDED UP STEALING THE DARK PRINCE'S LOVER.
BECAUSE OF THAT, THIS NATION SUFFERED A DROUGHT FOR 5 YEARS.
WHAT A PATHETIC "DARK" PRINCE.
HUSH YOU!!
ALRIGHTY!! OFF TO THE CASTLE WE GO!

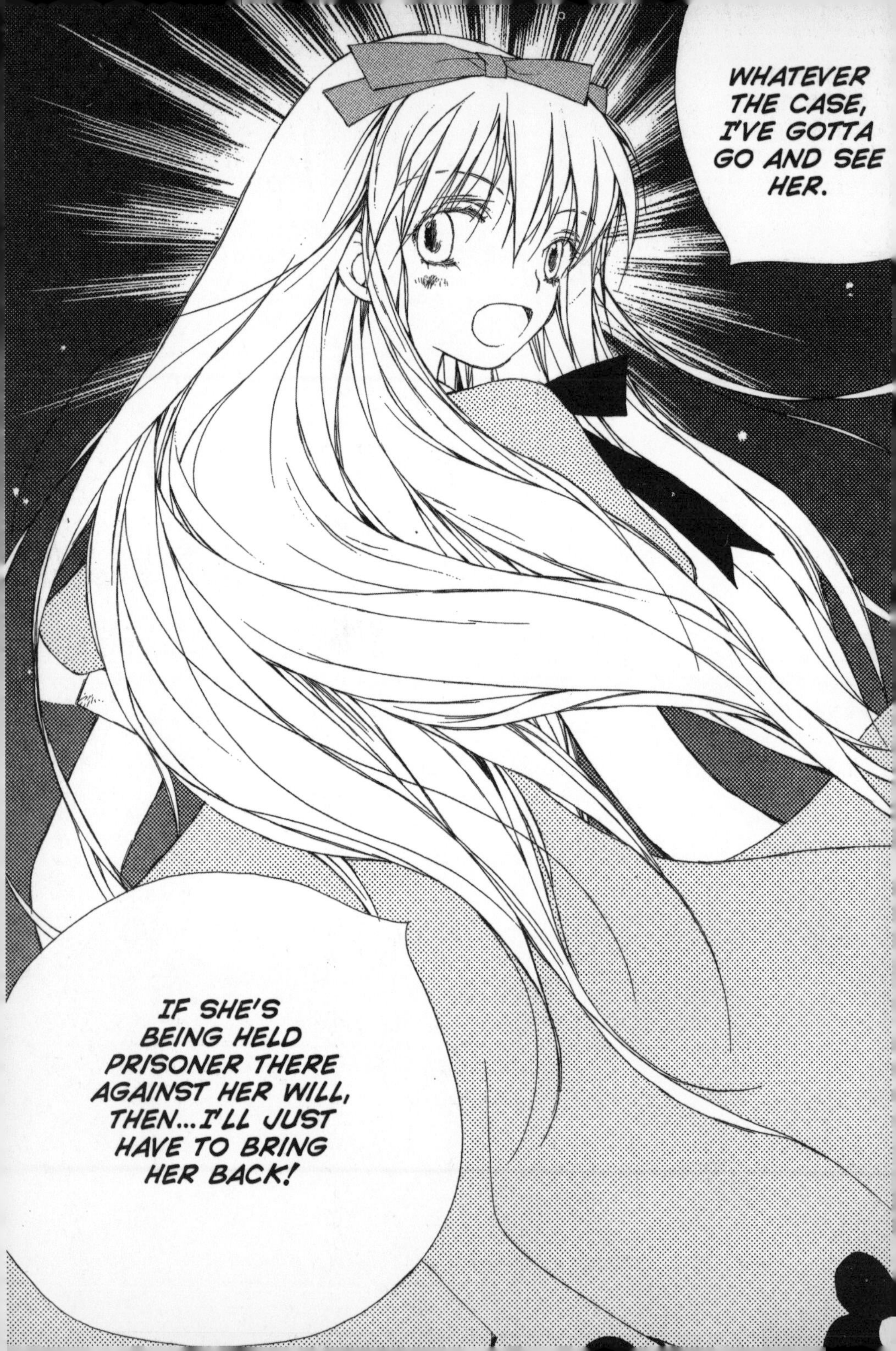
WHATEVER THE CASE, I'VE GOTTA GO AND SEE HER.
IF SHE'S BEING HELD PRISONER THERE AGAINST HER WILL, THEN...I'LL JUST HAVE TO BRING HER BACK!

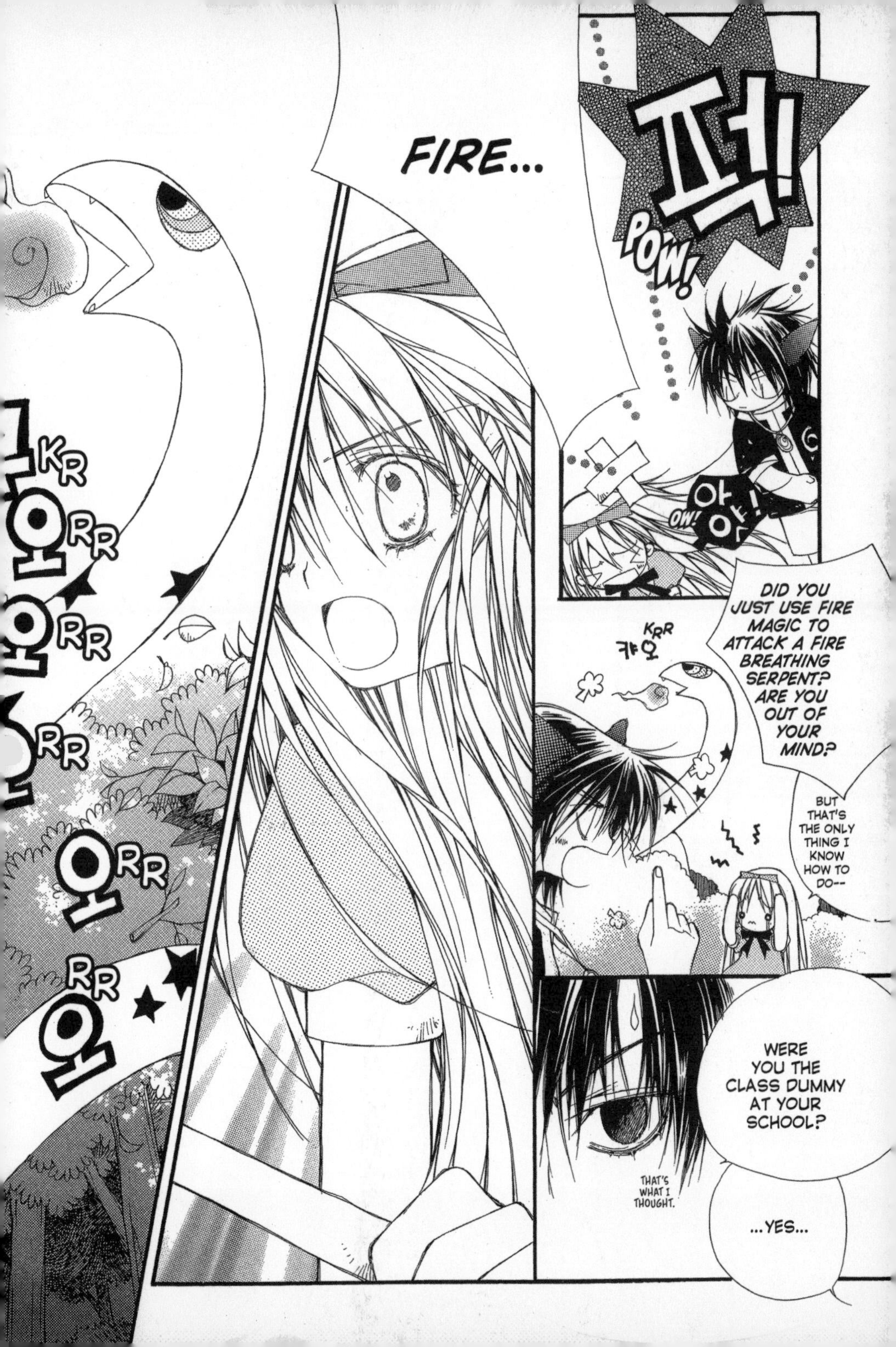
KR ORR ORR ORR ORR RR
FIRE...
퍽!
POW!
아야!
OW!
캬오
KRR
DID YOU JUST USE FIRE MAGIC TO ATTACK A FIRE BREATHING SERPENT? ARE YOU OUT OF YOUR MIND?
BUT THAT'S THE ONLY THING I KNOW HOW TO DO--
WERE YOU THE CLASS DUMMY AT YOUR SCHOOL?
...YES...
THAT'S WHAT I THOUGHT.

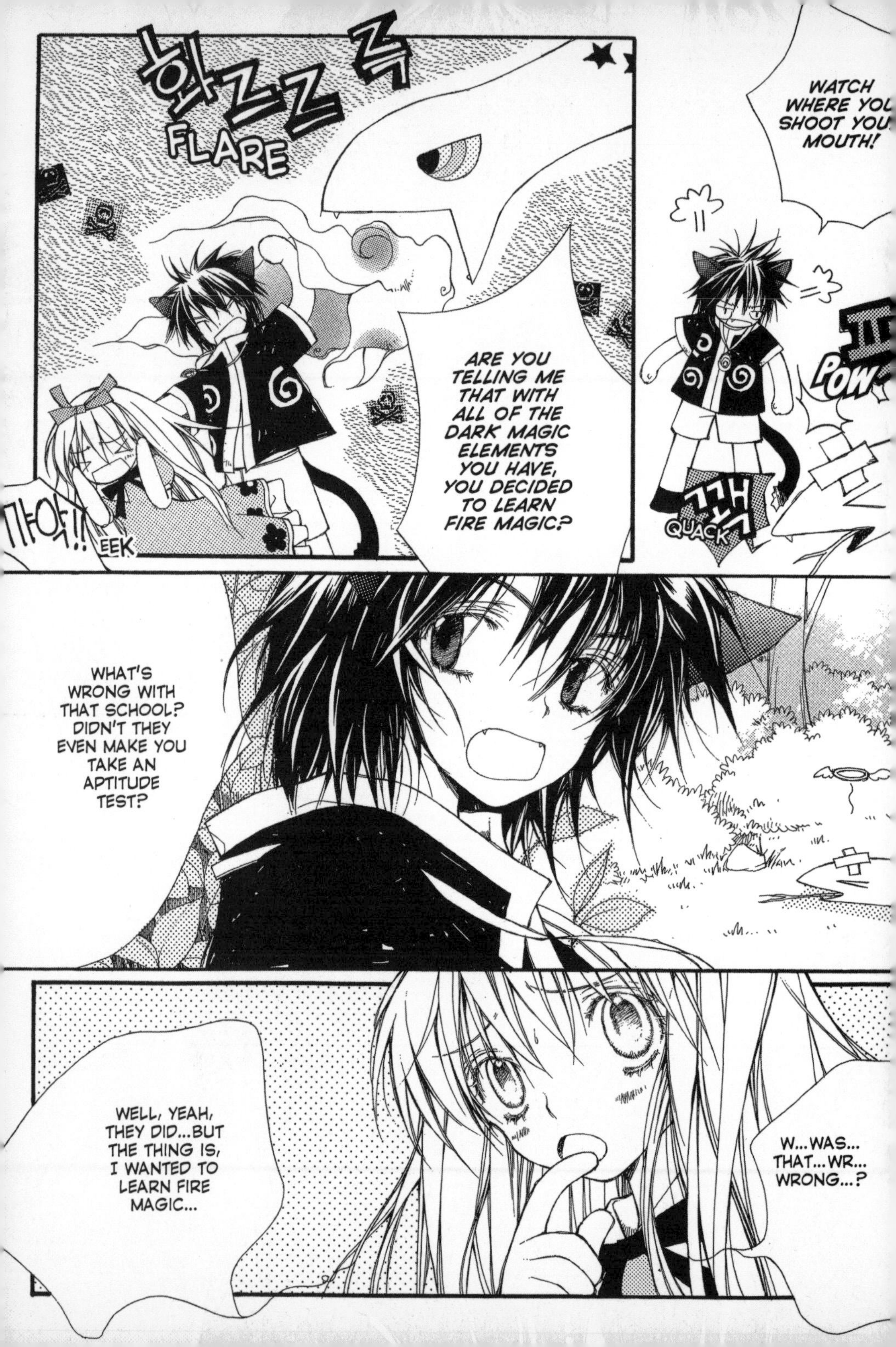
FLARE
EEK
ARE YOU TELLING ME THAT WITH ALL OF THE DARK MAGIC ELEMENTS YOU HAVE, YOU DECIDED TO LEARN FIRE MAGIC?
WATCH WHERE YOU SHOOT YOU MOUTH!
POW
QUACK
WHAT'S WRONG WITH THAT SCHOOL? DIDN'T THEY EVEN MAKE YOU TAKE AN APTITUDE TEST?
WELL, YEAH, THEY DID...BUT THE THING IS, I WANTED TO LEARN FIRE MAGIC...
W...WAS... THAT...WR... WRONG...?

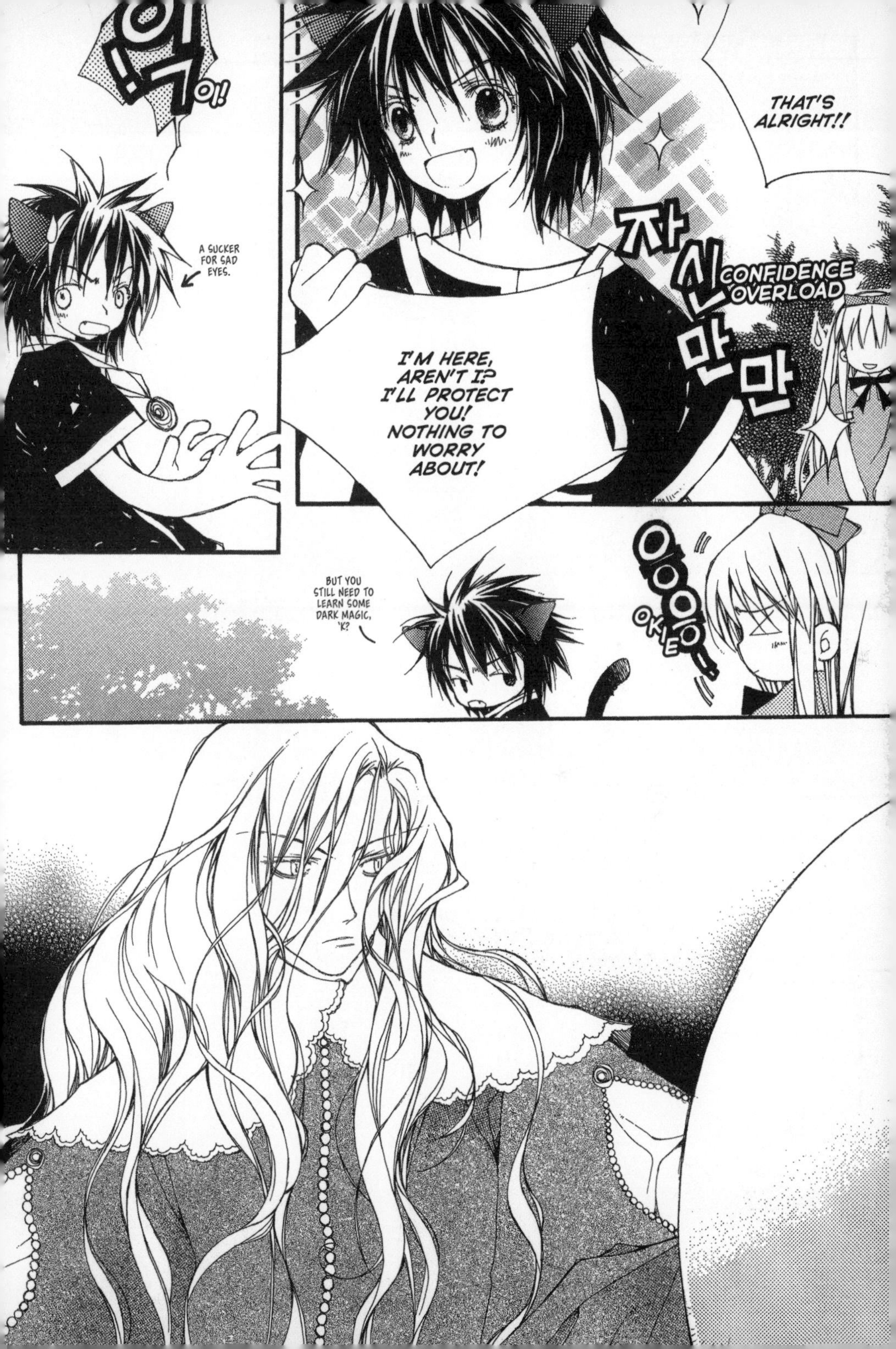
A SUCKER FOR SAD EYES.
THAT'S ALRIGHT!!
I'M HERE, AREN'T I? I'LL PROTECT YOU! NOTHING TO WORRY ABOUT!
자신만만
CONFIDENCE OVERLOAD
BUT YOU STILL NEED TO LEARN SOME DARK MAGIC, 'K?
OKIE

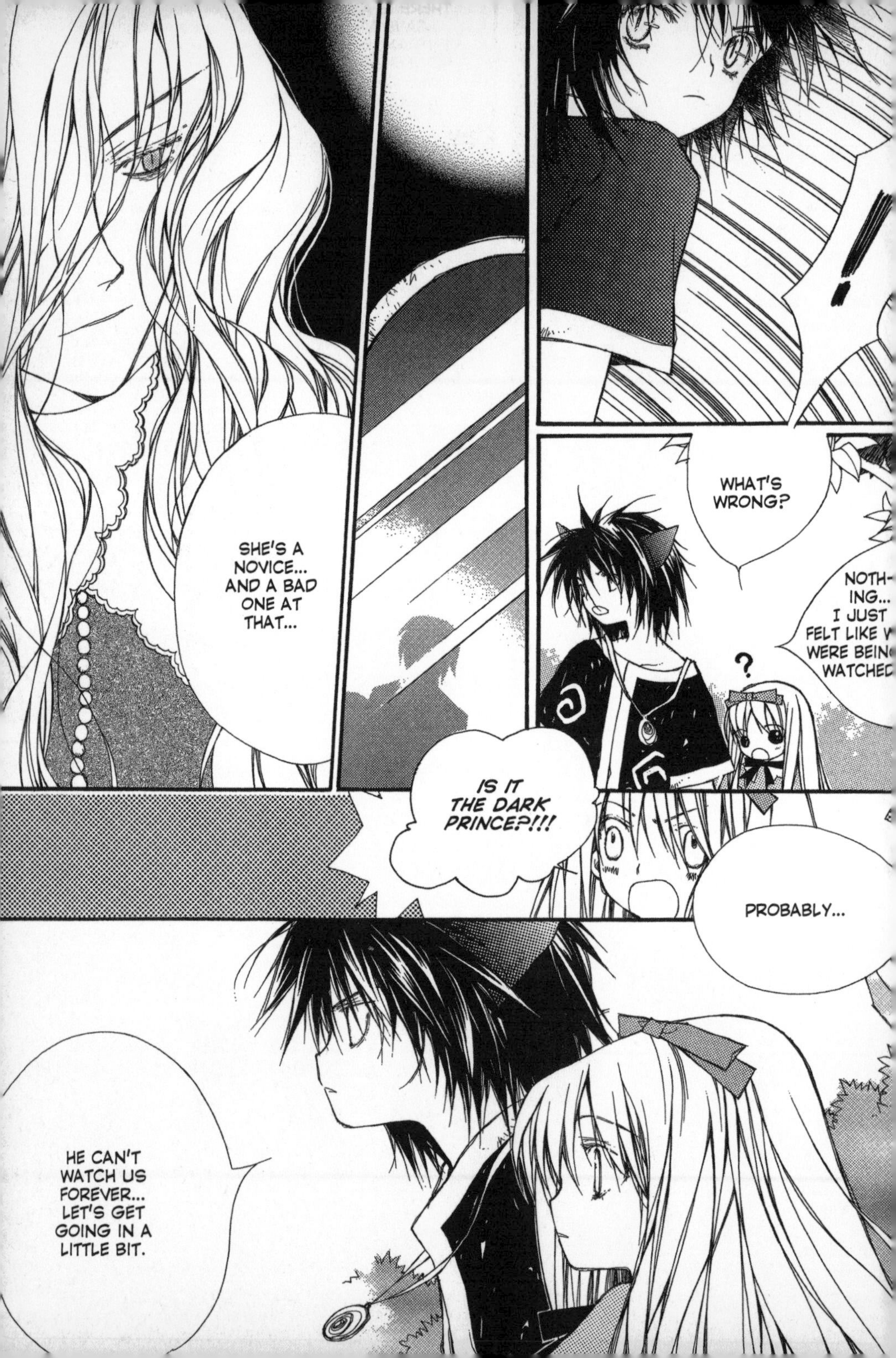
SHE'S A NOVICE... AND A BAD ONE AT THAT...
WHAT'S WRONG?
NOTH- ING... I JUST FELT LIKE W WERE BEIN WATCHED
IS IT THE DARK PRINCE?!!!
PROBABLY...
HE CAN'T WATCH US FOREVER... LET'S GET GOING IN A LITTLE BIT.

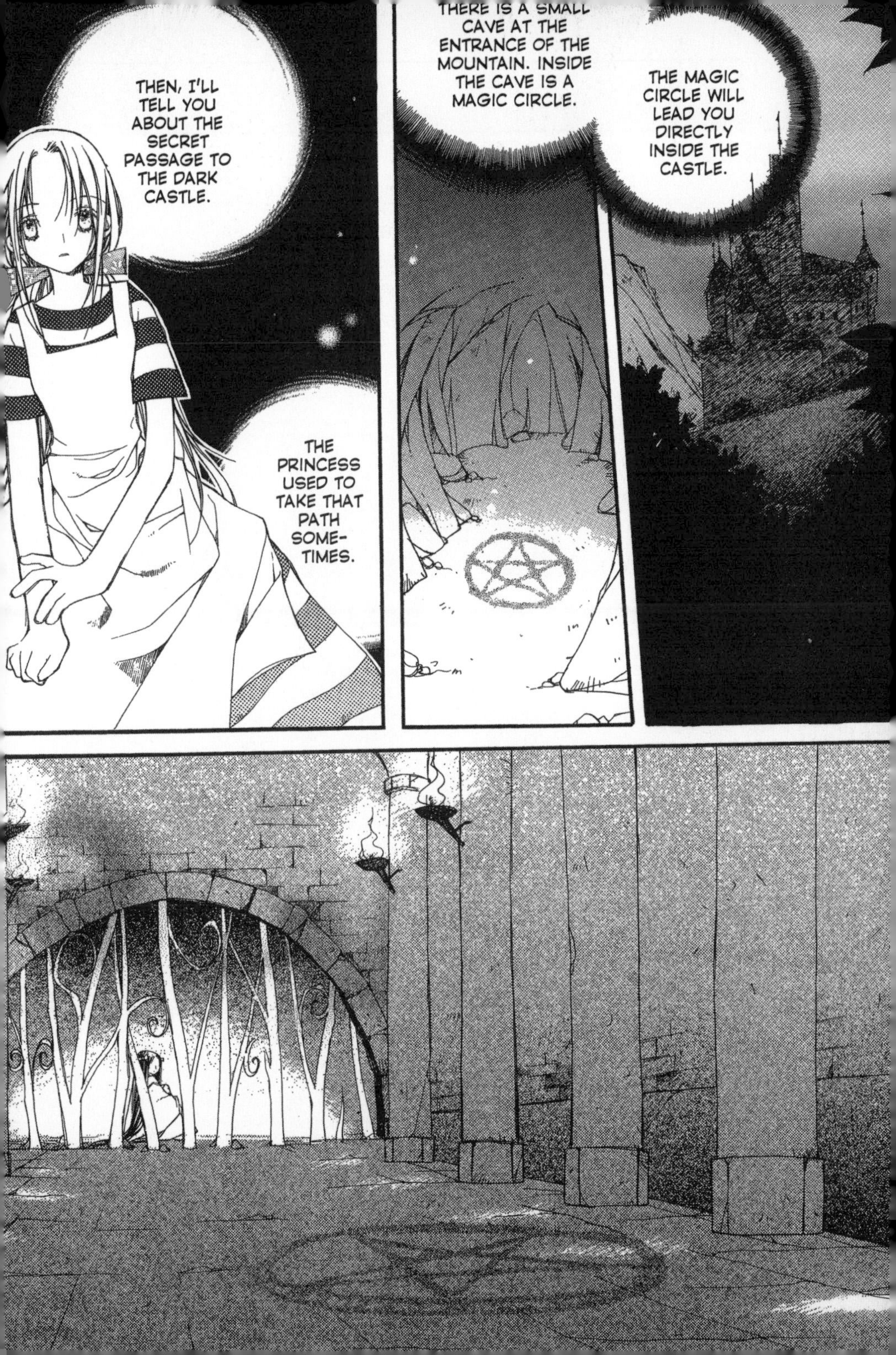
THEN, I'LL TELL YOU ABOUT THE SECRET PASSAGE TO THE DARK CASTLE.
THE PRINCESS USED TO TAKE THAT PATH SOME-TIMES.
THERE IS A SMALL CAVE AT THE ENTRANCE OF THE MOUNTAIN. INSIDE THE CAVE IS A MAGIC CIRCLE.
THE MAGIC CIRCLE WILL LEAD YOU DIRECTLY INSIDE THE CASTLE.

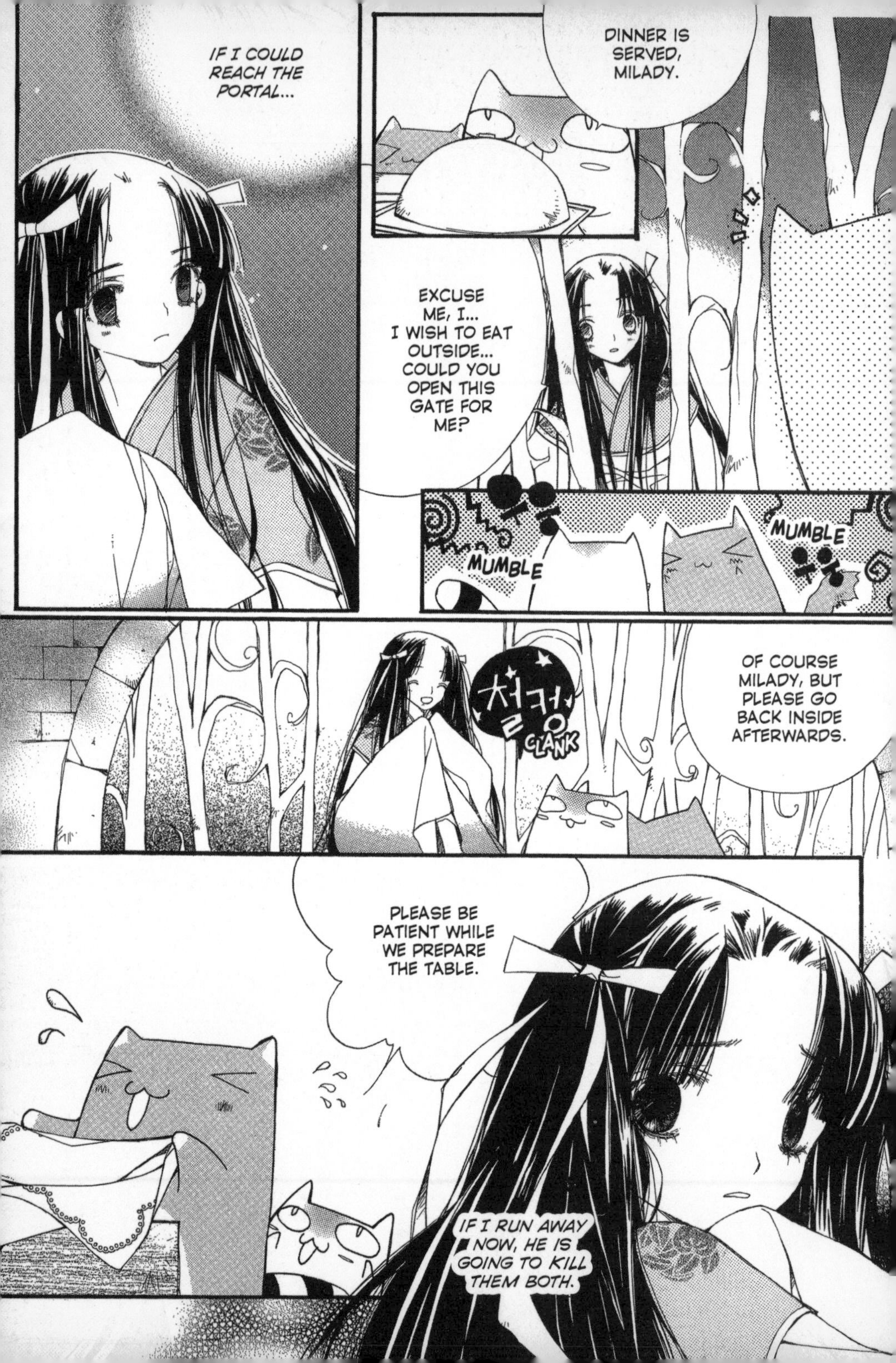
IF I COULD REACH THE PORTAL...
DINNER IS SERVED, MILADY.
EXCUSE ME, I... I WISH TO EAT OUTSIDE... COULD YOU OPEN THIS GATE FOR ME?
MUMBLE
MUMBLE
철커덩
CLANK
OF COURSE MILADY, BUT PLEASE GO BACK INSIDE AFTERWARDS.
PLEASE BE PATIENT WHILE WE PREPARE THE TABLE.
IF I RUN AWAY NOW, HE IS GOING TO KILL THEM BOTH.

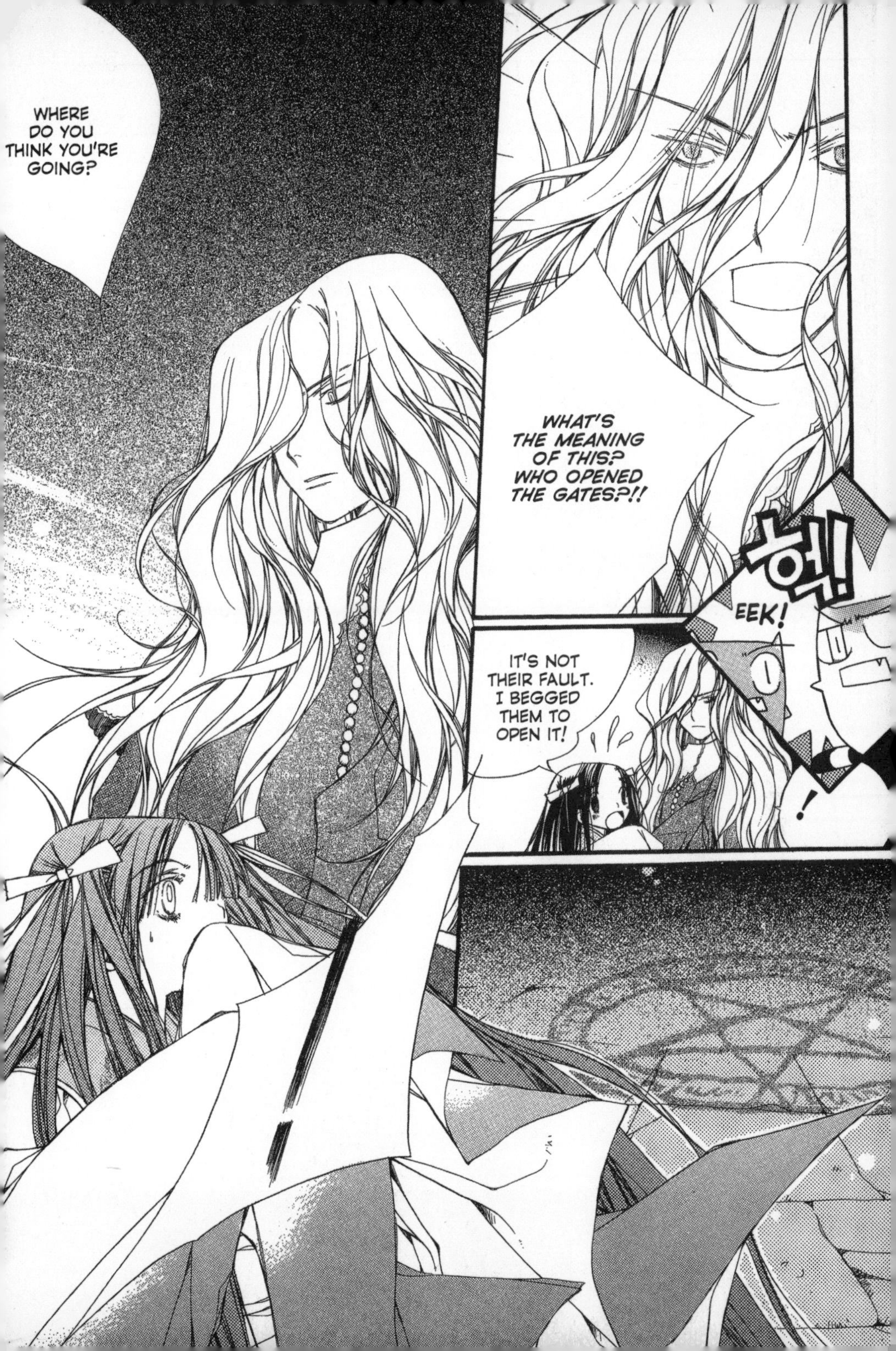
WHERE DO YOU THINK YOU'RE GOING?
WHAT'S THE MEANING OF THIS? WHO OPENED THE GATES?!!
헉!
EEK!
IT'S NOT THEIR FAULT. I BEGGED THEM TO OPEN IT!

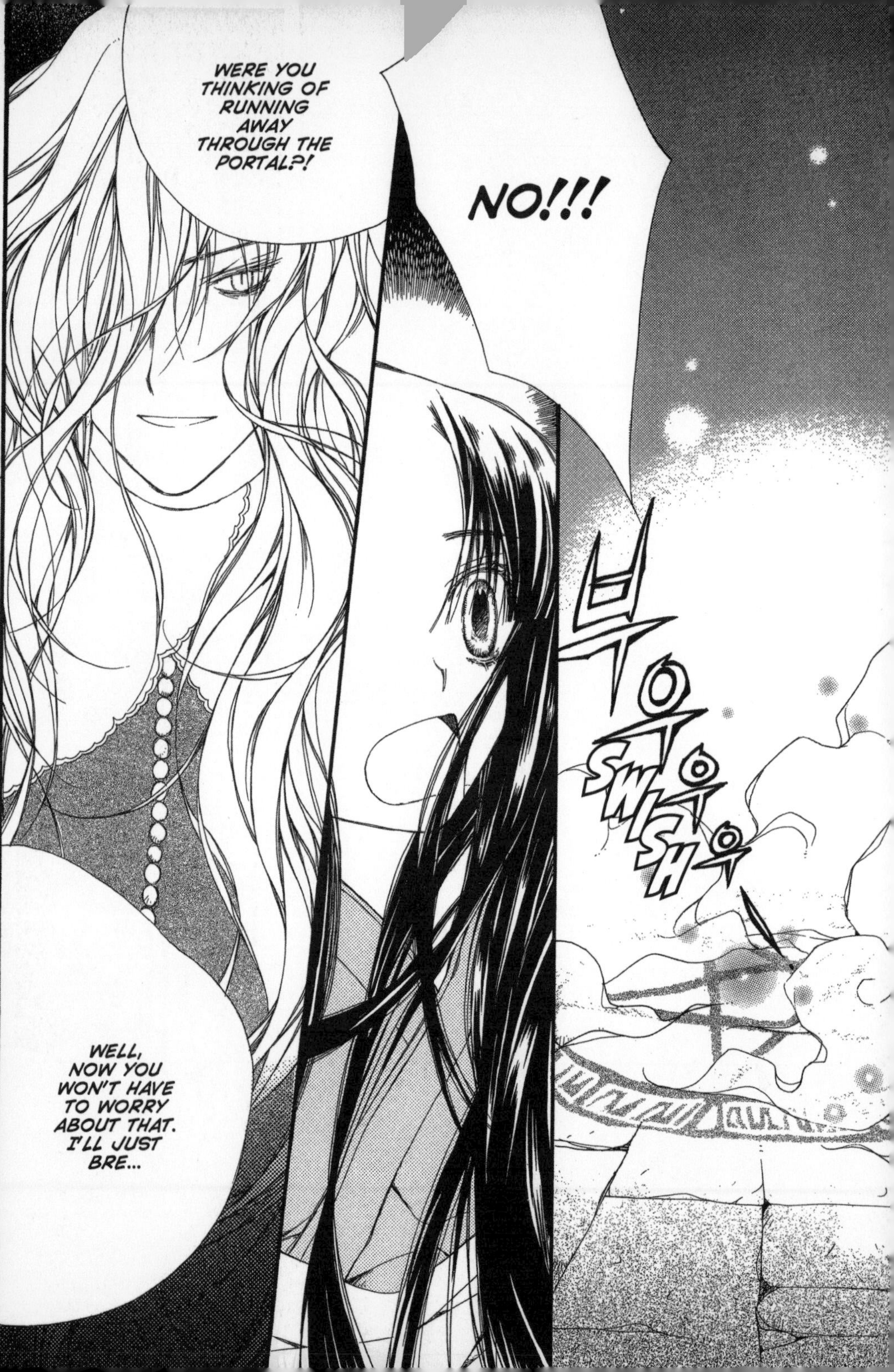
WERE YOU THINKING OF RUNNING AWAY THROUGH THE PORTAL?!
WELL, NOW YOU WON'T HAVE TO WORRY ABOUT THAT. I'LL JUST BRE...
NO!!!
SWISH

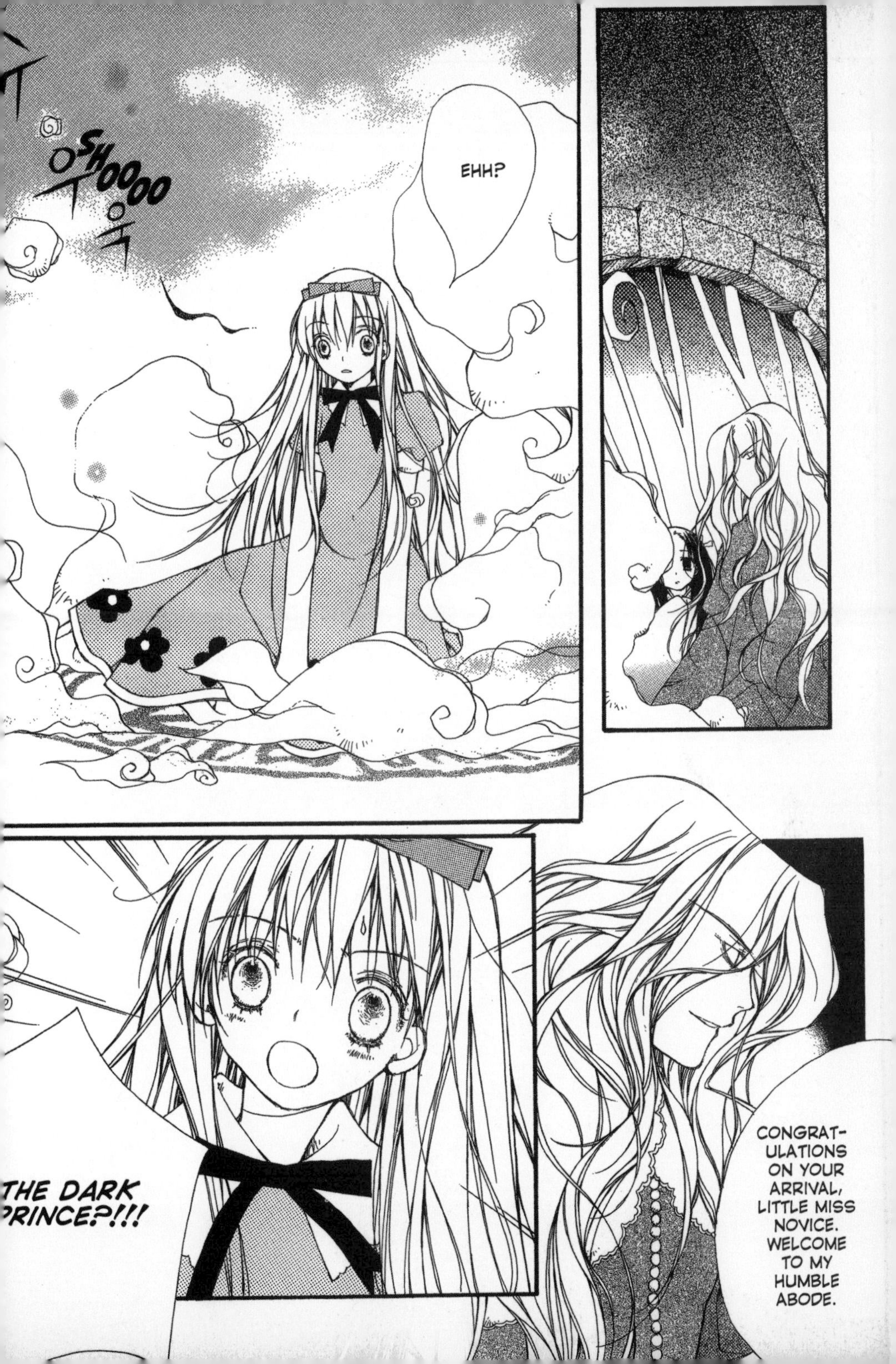
SHOOOOO
EHH?
THE DARK PRINCE?!!!
CONGRAT-ULATIONS ON YOUR ARRIVAL, LITTLE MISS NOVICE. WELCOME TO MY HUMBLE ABODE.

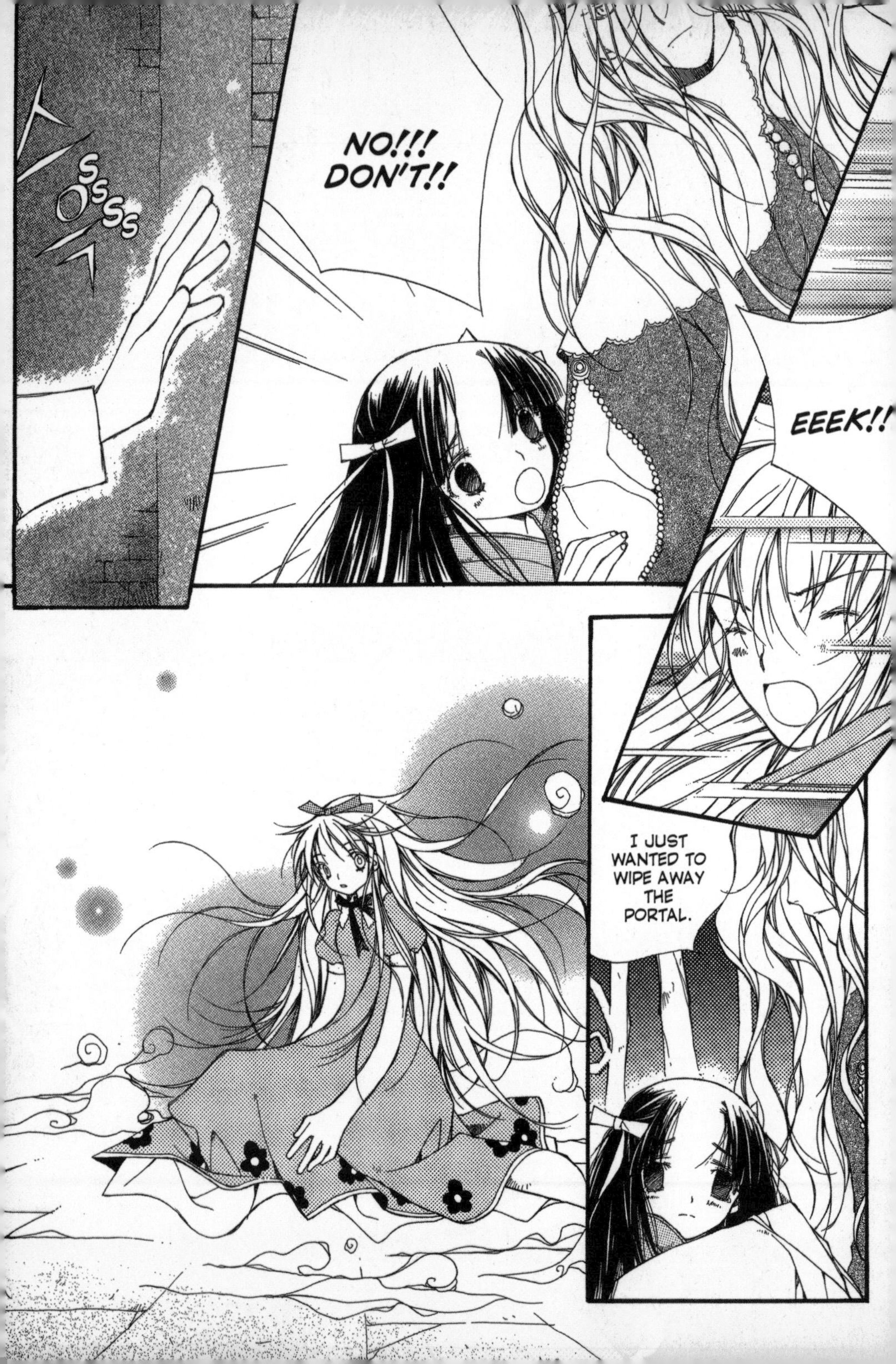
SSSS
NO!!!
DON'T!!
EEEK!!
I JUST WANTED TO WIPE AWAY THE PORTAL.

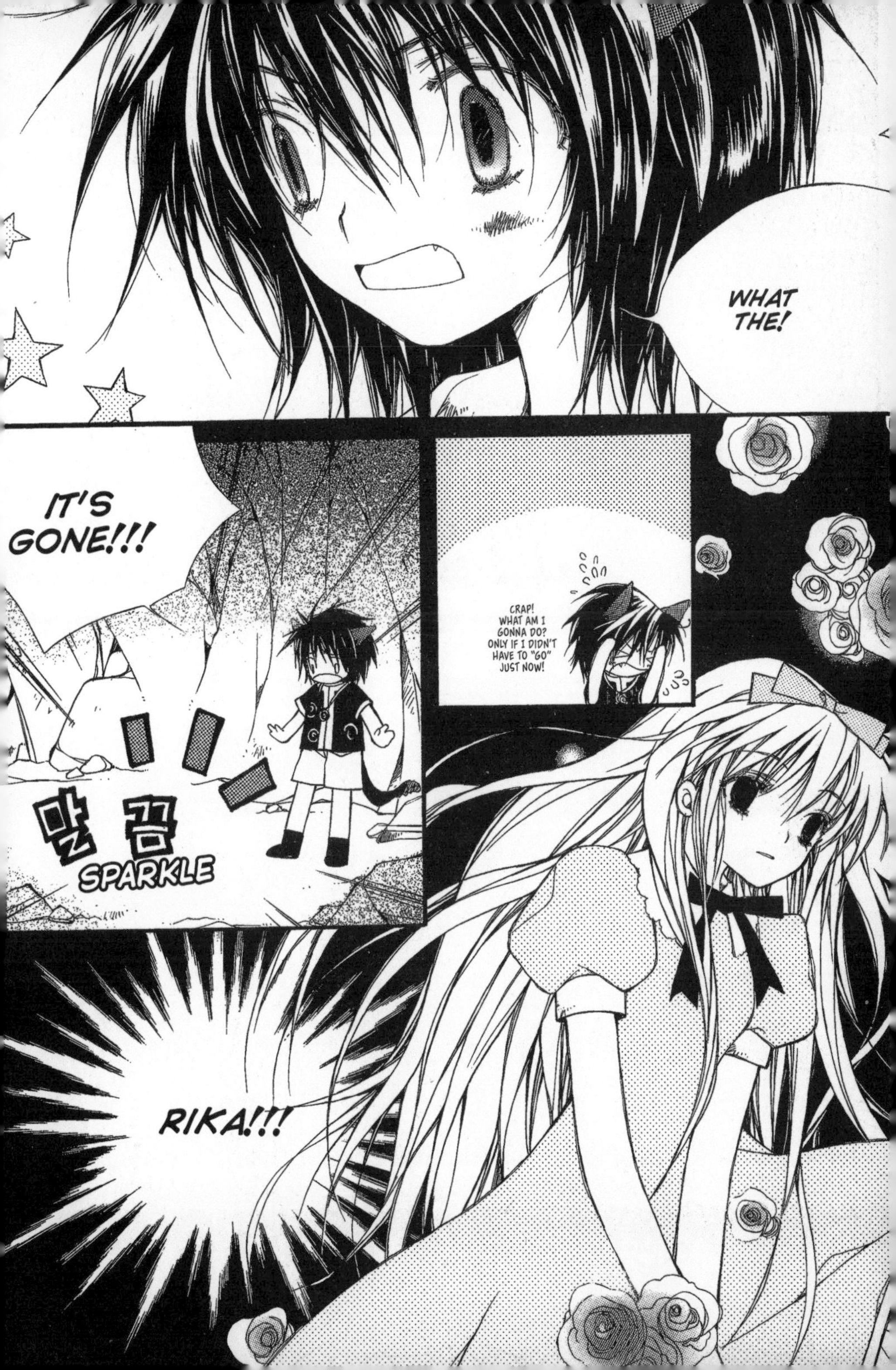
WHAT THE!
IT'S GONE!!!
말끔
SPARKLE
CRAP! WHAT AM I GONNA DO? ONLY IF I DIDN'T HAVE TO "GO" JUST NOW!
RIKA!?!

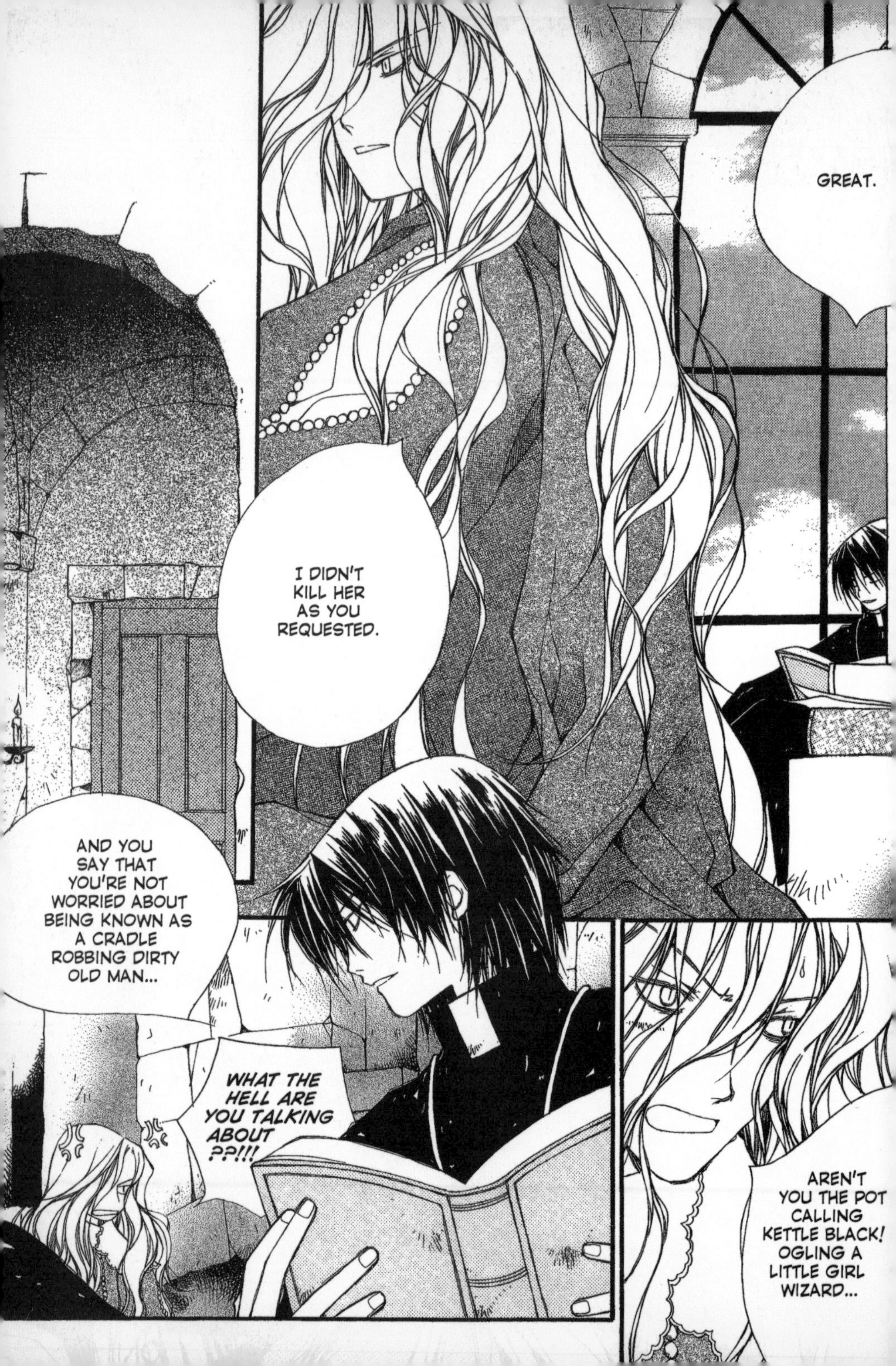
I DIDN'T KILL HER AS YOU REQUESTED.
GREAT.
AND YOU SAY THAT YOU'RE NOT WORRIED ABOUT BEING KNOWN AS A CRADLE ROBBING DIRTY OLD MAN...
WHAT THE HELL ARE YOU TALKING ABOUT ??!!!
AREN'T YOU THE POT CALLING KETTLE BLACK! OGLING A LITTLE GIRL WIZARD...

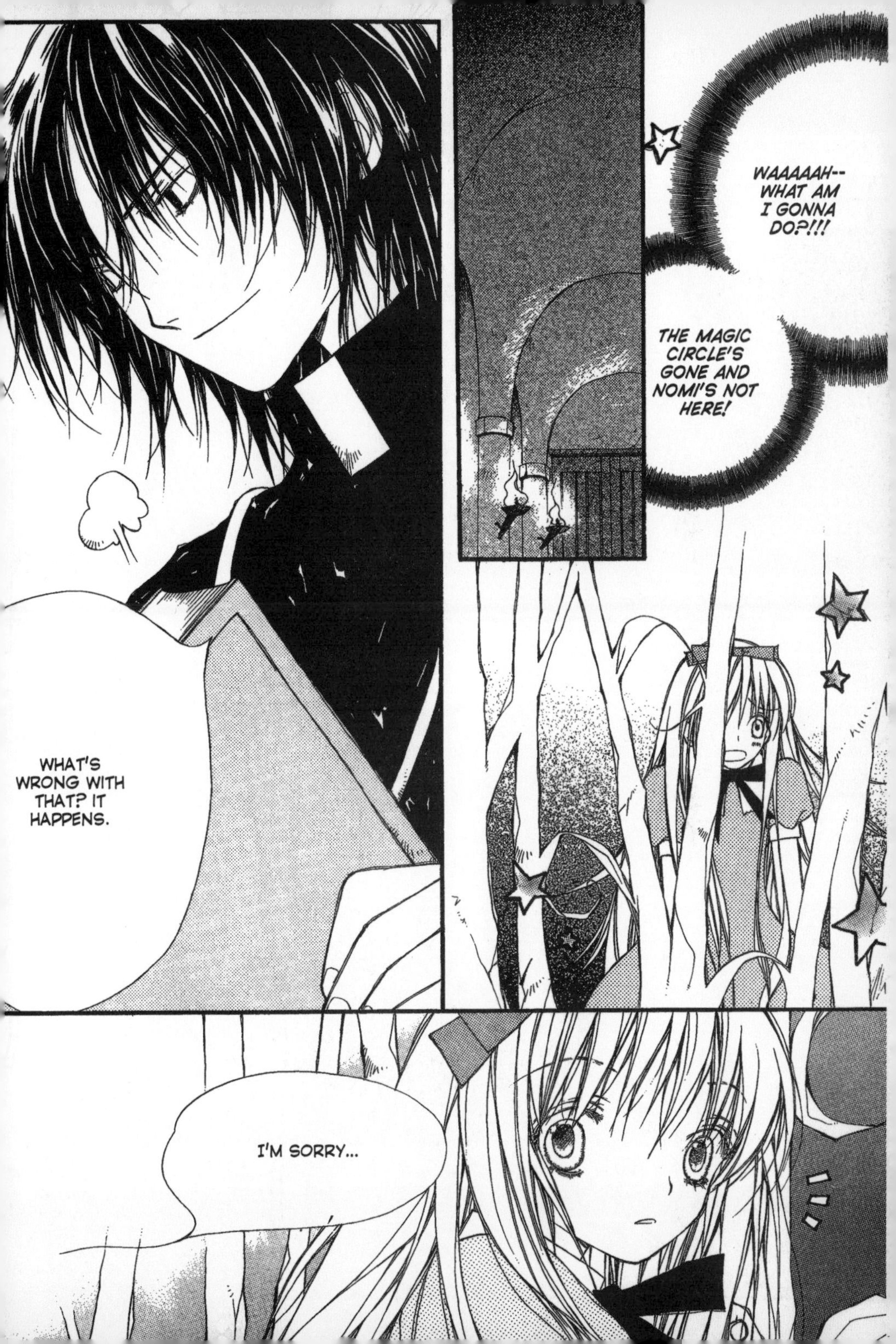
WHAT'S WRONG WITH THAT? IT HAPPENS.
WAAAAAH-- WHAT AM I GONNA DO?!!!
THE MAGIC CIRCLE'S GONE AND NOMI'S NOT HERE!
I'M SORRY...

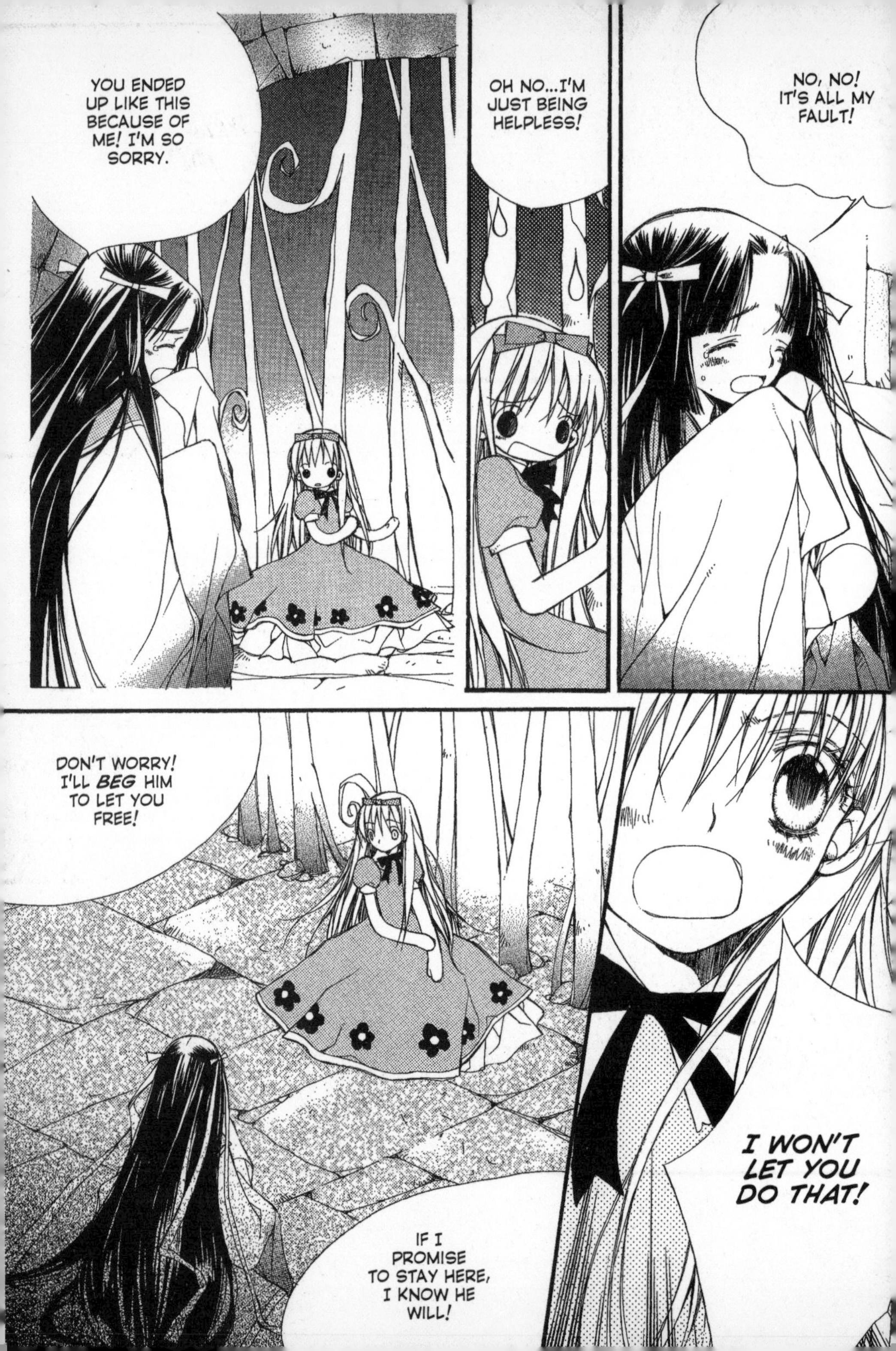
YOU ENDED UP LIKE THIS BECAUSE OF ME! I'M SO SORRY.
OH NO...I'M JUST BEING HELPLESS!
NO, NO! IT'S ALL MY FAULT!
DON'T WORRY! I'LL *BEG* HIM TO LET YOU FREE!
IF I PROMISE TO STAY HERE, I KNOW HE WILL!
I WON'T LET YOU DO THAT!

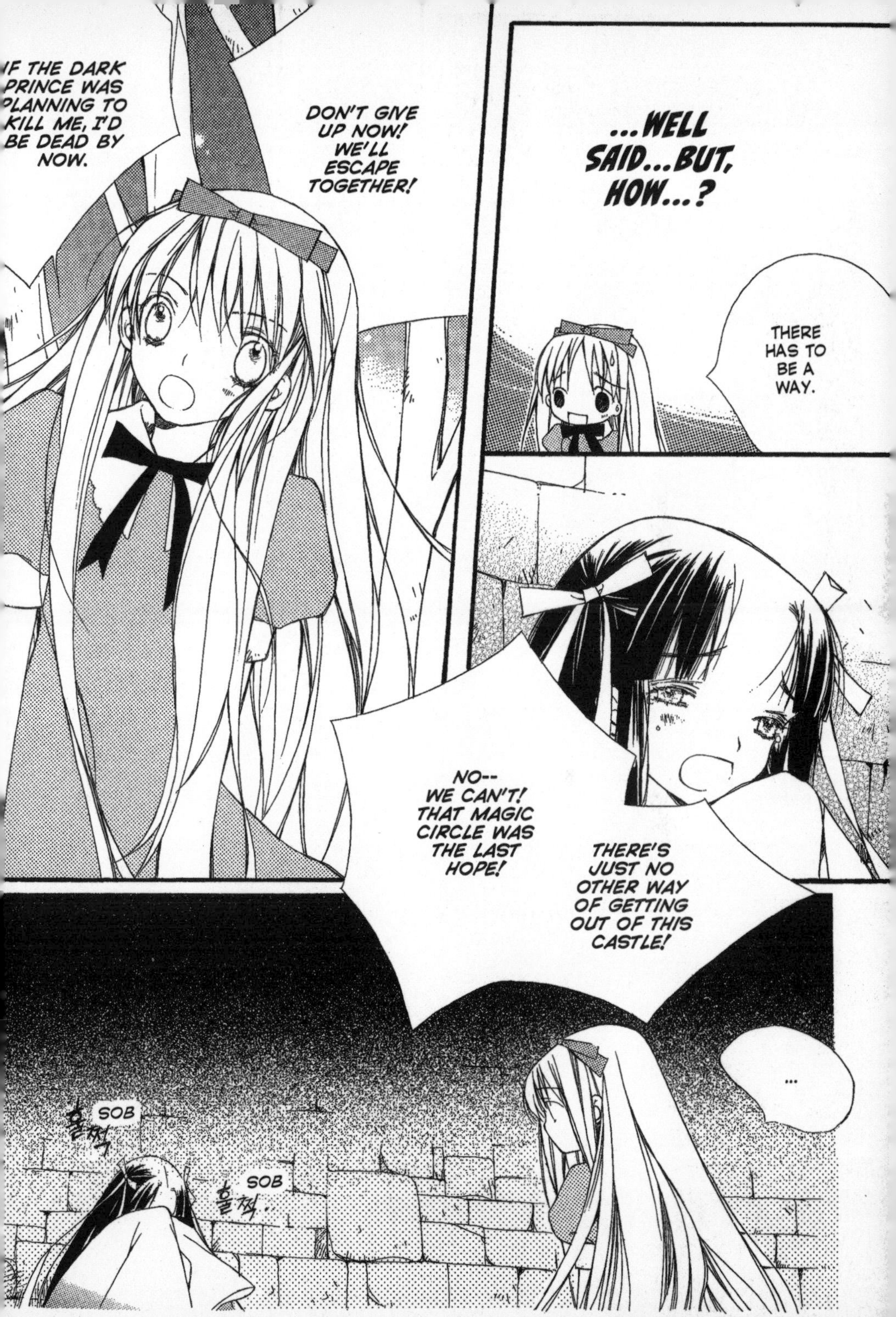

IF THE DARK PRINCE WAS PLANNING TO KILL ME, I'D BE DEAD BY NOW.
DON'T GIVE UP NOW! WE'LL ESCAPE TOGETHER!
...WELL SAID...BUT, HOW...?
THERE HAS TO BE A WAY.
NO-- WE CAN'T! THAT MAGIC CIRCLE WAS THE LAST HOPE!
THERE'S JUST NO OTHER WAY OF GETTING OUT OF THIS CASTLE!
SOB
훌쩍
SOB
훌쩍
...

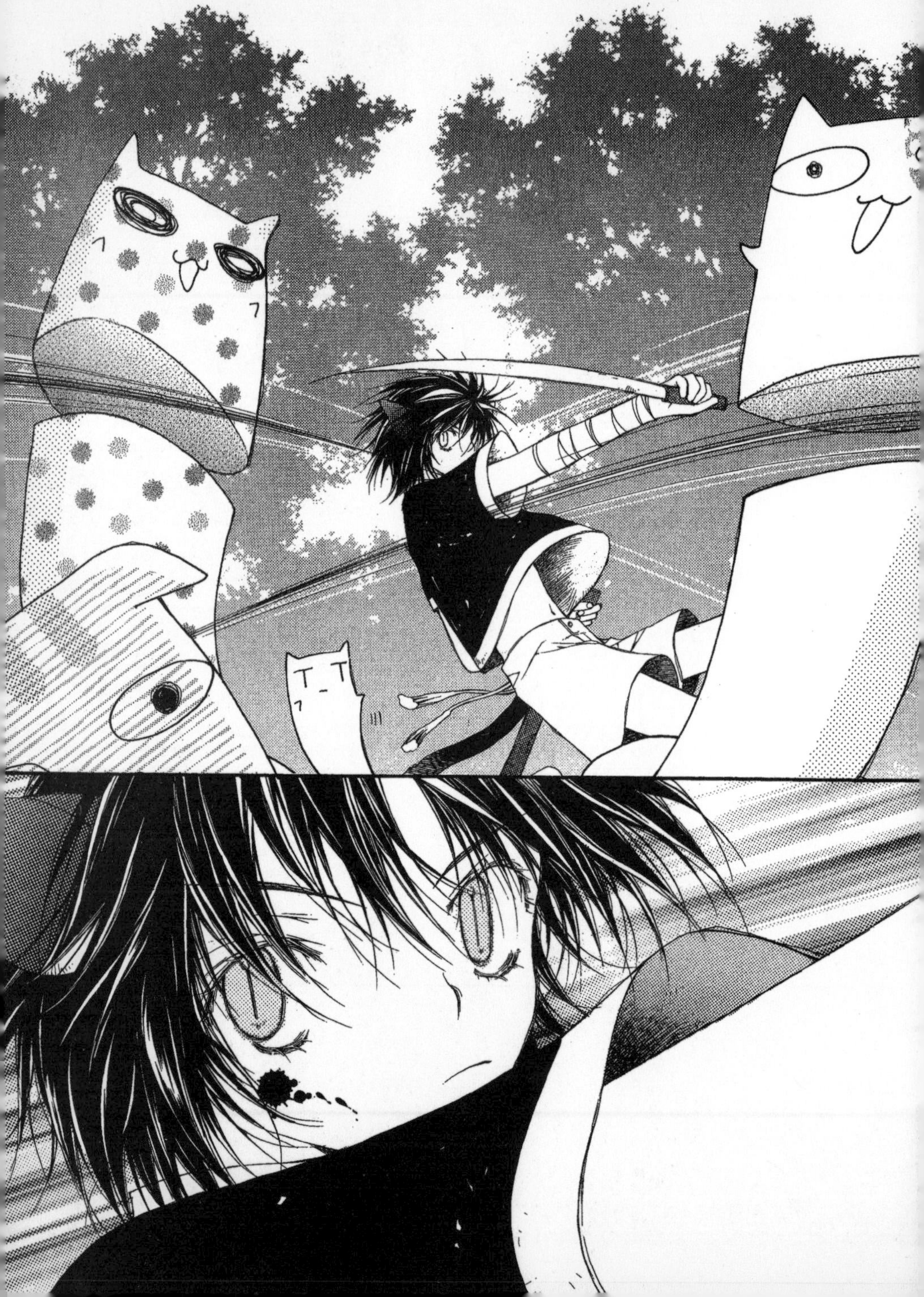

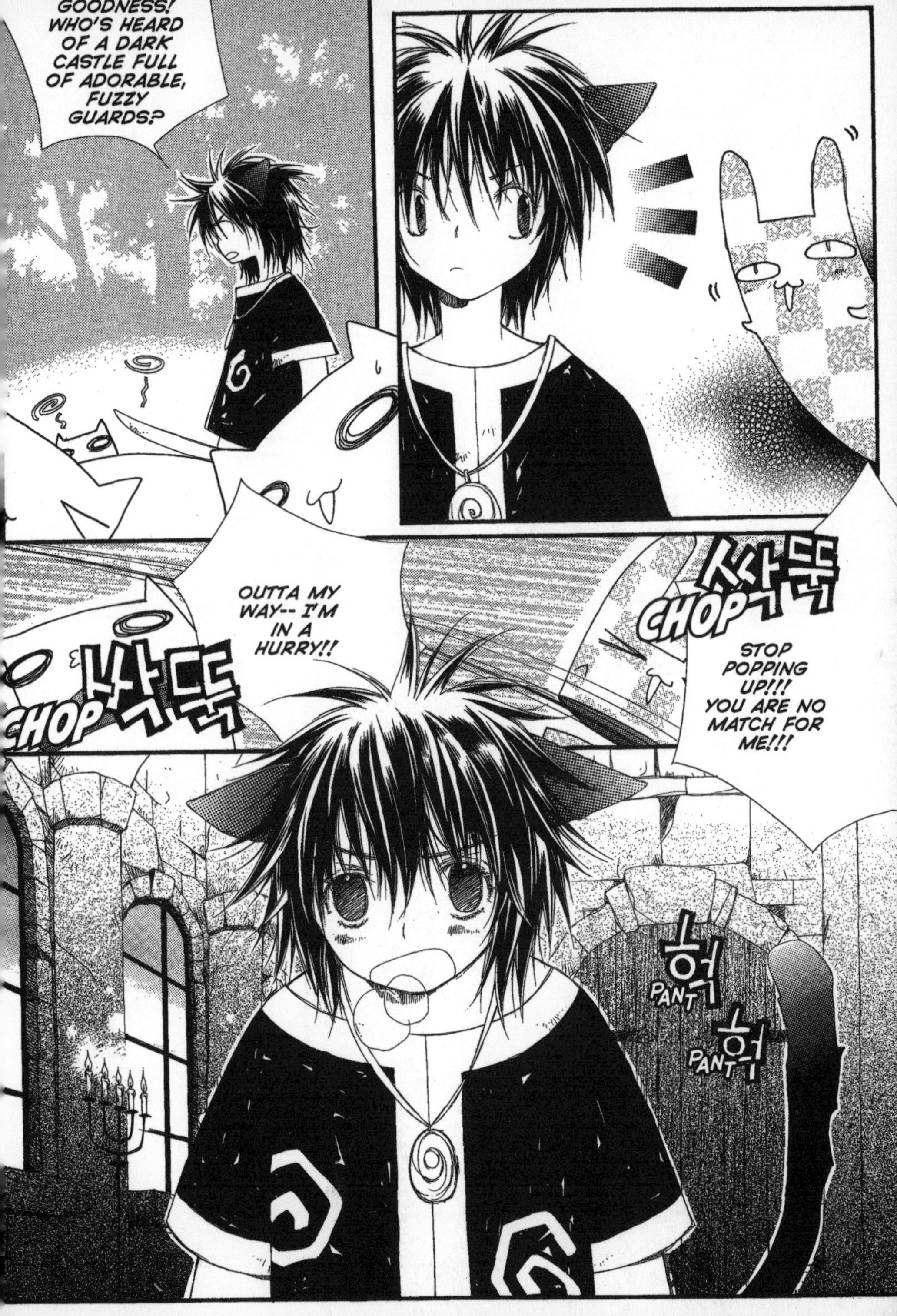
GOODNESS! WHO'S HEARD OF A DARK CASTLE FULL OF ADORABLE, FUZZY GUARDS?
OUTTA MY WAY-- I'M IN A HURRY!!
CHOP
CHOP
STOP POPPING UP!!! YOU ARE NO MATCH FOR ME!!!
헉 PANT
헉 PANT

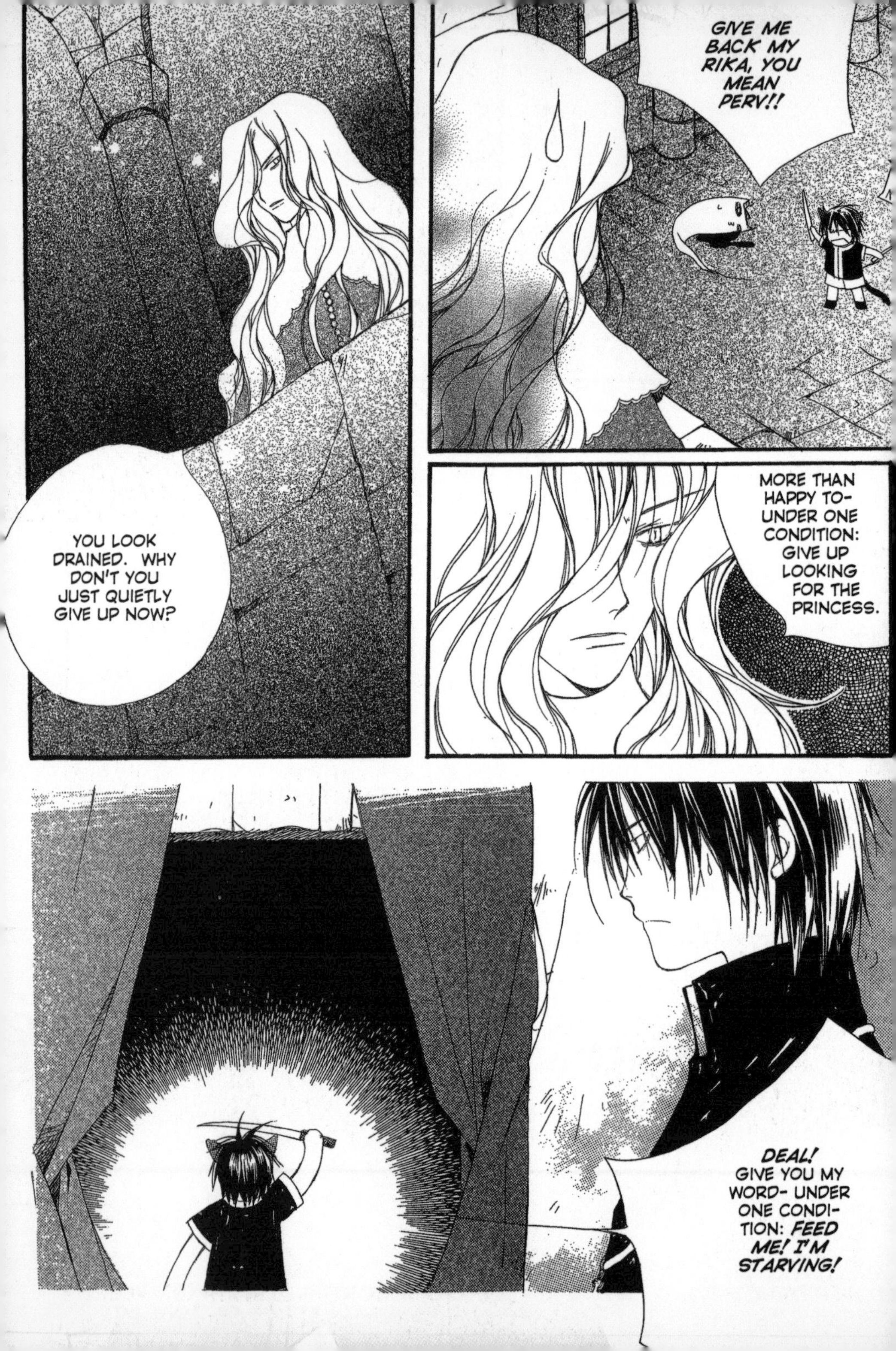
YOU LOOK DRAINED. WHY DON'T YOU JUST QUIETLY GIVE UP NOW?
GIVE ME BACK MY RIKA, YOU MEAN PERV!!
MORE THAN HAPPY TO- UNDER ONE CONDITION: GIVE UP LOOKING FOR THE PRINCESS.
DEAL! GIVE YOU MY WORD- UNDER ONE CONDI-TION: FEED ME! I'M STARVING!

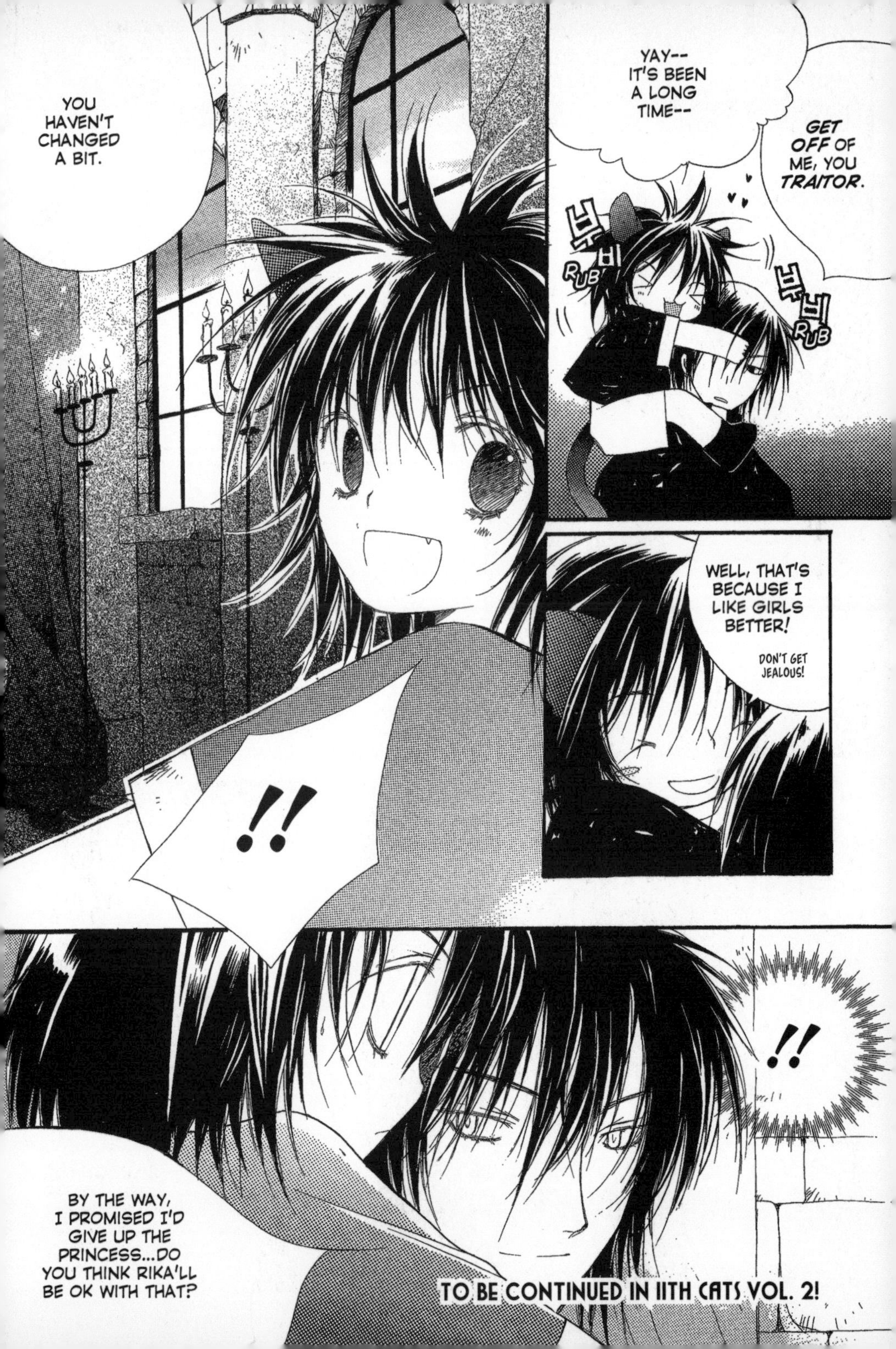
YOU HAVEN'T CHANGED A BIT.
!!
YAY-- IT'S BEEN A LONG TIME--
GET OFF OF ME, YOU TRAITOR.
부비 RUB
부비 RUB
WELL, THAT'S BECAUSE I LIKE GIRLS BETTER!
DON'T GET JEALOUS!
!!
BY THE WAY, I PROMISED I'D GIVE UP THE PRINCESS...DO YOU THINK RIKA'LL BE OK WITH THAT?
TO BE CONTINUED IN 11TH CATS VOL. 2!

APPENDIX

About the creator

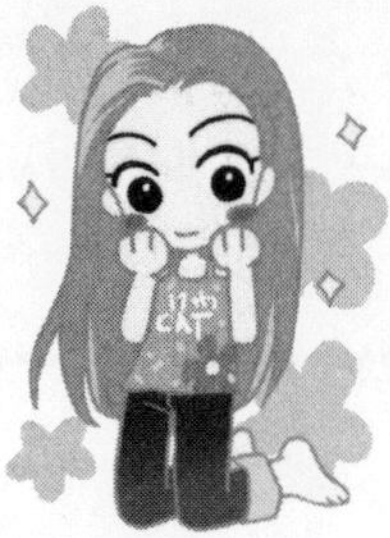
11th CAT

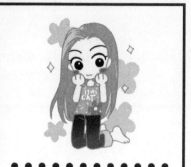

11th Cat
Mi-Kyung Kim
Brithday : February 29th(Pisces)
Blood type : O

Catmates : Nene, Mitz, Pico, and the youngest is yet to be named(stay tuned).

Nickname : Gone in five seconds. (I sleep whenever my head touches a surface. Am I a narcoleptic?)

Hobbies : Falling asleep cuddling my cats.

Three wishes : Winning the lottery, my cats living long and healthy lives, and marring the son of a billionaire.

Happiness is : Living a content life...

Quick Chat with the Creator

A tough bishounen trainer
Mi-Kyung Kim

Mi-Kyung Kim is most well known for her incredibly cute art style in Korea.
From her works, people might expect her to be a quiet and homebody type, but she's quite the opposite - extremely outgoing and active.

How did you come up with the title "11th Cat?"
I just wanted to have a very cute title. (lol) Also it means there are total of 11 bishounens in the story.

You must like cats a lot.
Of course. I used to be a dog person, but I've slowly started liking cats more (My family doesn't know it yet though). I have one cat right now that I picked up on the street, and my housemate has two. So we have 3 cats at our place.

You draw such cute characters. What do you think is the cutest thing about yourself?
Everything about me is cute of cour.. (PUNCH!!!)

What's the most difficult part of the whole comic-making process?
Probably paneling and rough drawings. Once I'm stuck on one scene, it's very difficult to progress onto the next scenes. (It's like a school exam that you can not finish because you are stuck on one question and can not move on to the next question.)

What do you do if you mess up an illustration at the very end?
I usually like to ask for more time and start fresh again... (Although in a lot of cases, because of time constrains, I try to fix it using computer CG) One time, I spilled ink on an illustration while cleaning up the lines after everything was done. I instantly lost my mind. o_o

Describe your dream man.
Etsushi Toyokawa (Japanese Movie star from <Night Head>) and Yosuke Kubotsuka (from movie <GO>)

What is happiness to you?
To live a comfortable and content life... (sorry for the boring answer -_-;)

Don't draw yourself too cute!

why not ?!??!

It's already too late.

Character Introduction

11th Cat

Mi-Kyung Kim

Come along on the sweet adventure with the cutest wizard ever, Rika!

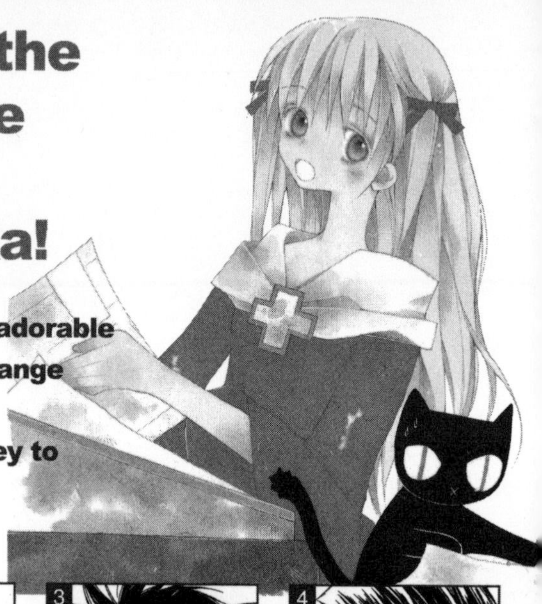

A cute fantasy adventure of an adorable novice wizard, Rika, and her strange companion, Nomi.
Let's follow their exciting journey to become a true wizard.

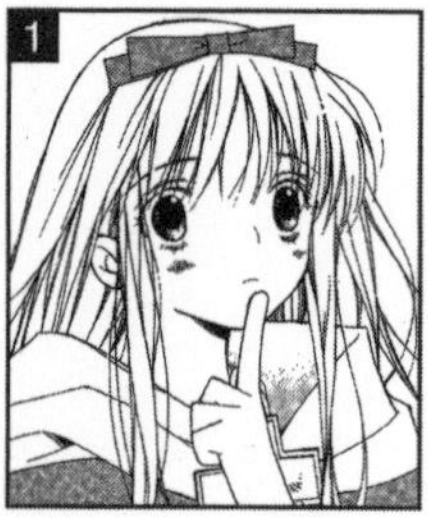
1
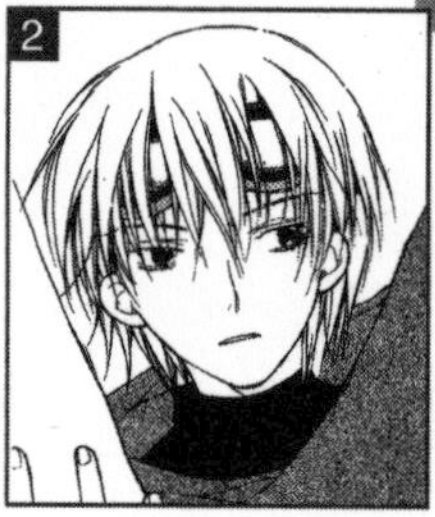
2
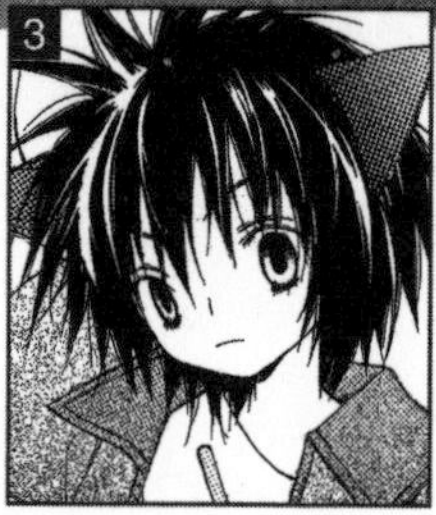
3
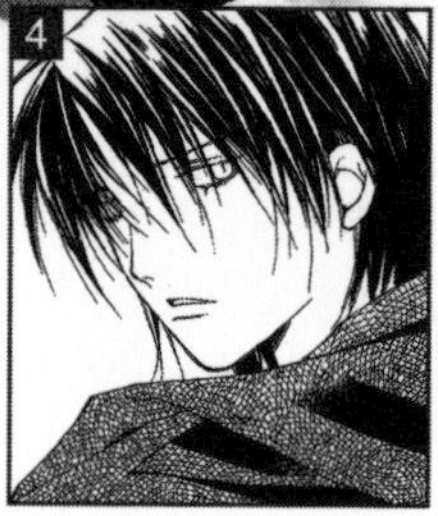
4

1. Rika : A novice wizard-in-training who causes a lot of drama because of her clumsiness. She comes across a guardian spirit, Nomi, and travels together to become a true wizard.

2. Eugen : Childhood friend of Rika. He ends up saving her from trouble all the time. He is very protective of her, but also nags on her a lot which causes Rika to get upset at him often.

3. Nomi (Guardian Spirit of Black Wishstone) : A cute guardian spirit that came out of the Black Wishstone. He likes Rika since she's the first female owner of the wishstone, and travels alongside her. He's loud and obnoxious, but has quite powerful powers despite his appearance.

4. Sword Master of Black Iron : A mysterious character who seems to be in the middle of everything that's going on with Rika. He saved Rika once, but his intention is unclear.

The Cutest Characters from the Cutest Creator!

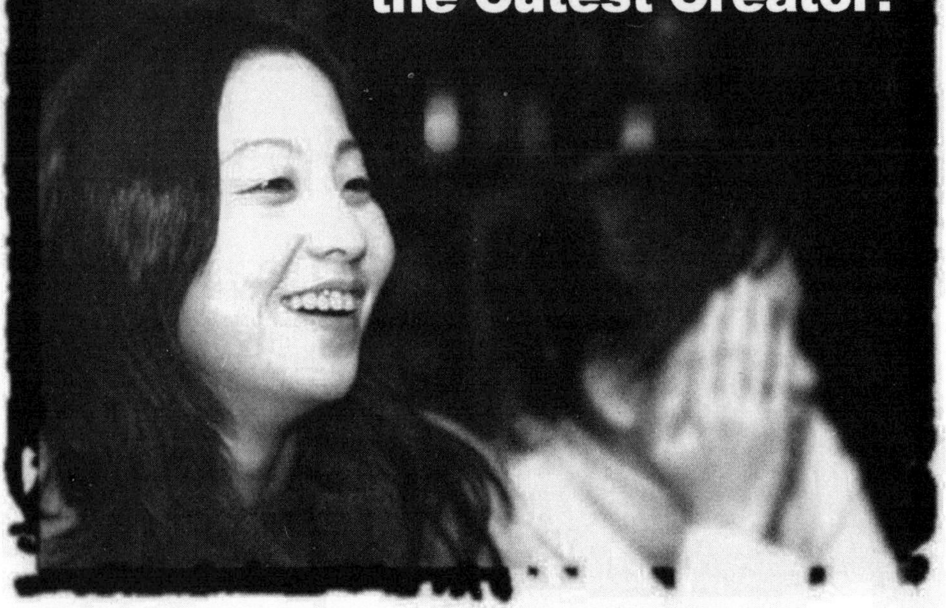

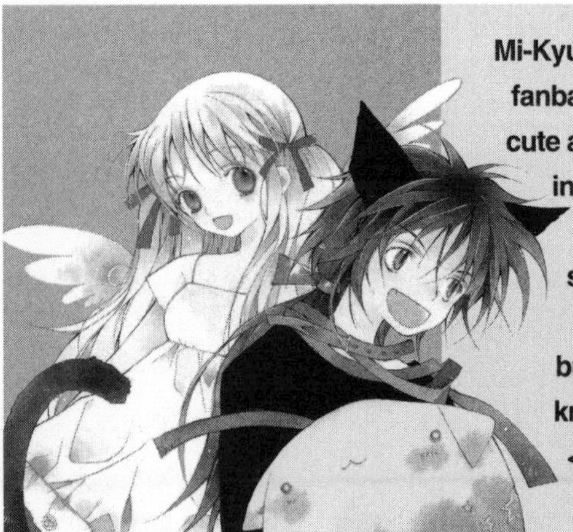

Mi-Kyung Kim has captured a huge fanbase and raging popularity for her cute artwork ever since her initial debut in 1997. However, an even more amazing achievement can be seen in the Doujinshi market where her name alone will bring fans to buy the books without even knowing what the book is about. <11th Cat> is her first ongoing series in Manhwa anthology.

Q. How would you describe this series?
K. Hm... That's quite a difficult question. Usually when I point out one element about a series, readers tend to focus on that element only, and don't see anything else that I am doing in the story. So I'd prefer readers to find out about my manhwa rather than listening to me describe it.

Q. Tell us about your experience with your first ongoing series.
K. It is nice to be in a bigger and longer running project. I feel like I am accomplishing a lot and not wasting any time (... although I did slack off here and there...). However I am more grateful for all the new colleagues and fans I meet from working on this project. I even had an assistant for the first time in my life for a while.

Q. What is this photo?
K. It's me holding my cat, Mitz. Ever since this photo was taken, I started liking film cameras. (Digital cameras are great, but with film cameras, it feels more like you are really taking pictures.) Sorry for the weird pose of Mitz. (lol)

Q. Who are your favorite and least favorite characters in your manhwa?
K. Well, I hated the Sword Master and Nomi, and my favorite is of course the Dark Prince~. The Sword Master and Nomi both wear too much black, that's why I am not too fond of them. But if they don't appear, then the pages look too light, so they balance the black and white value of the pages.

Q. Did you have a model for any of your characters?

K. Model... Our cats. Although they don't look the same because it was too hard to draw them like how they really look. So I drew them a little simpler and rounder and rounder...

Q. Can you share any interesting story that happened while working on this project?

K. hehe... I usually hang out in this one online community. I never mentioned anything about manhwa in there, but one day, somehow people found out. So I was pummeled with comments and questions. (I was stupid. I mean, my photo is printed right on the book, and I thought people wouldn't recognize me ... -.-;;;)

Q. Does the Doujinshi world have any special meaning to you? I wonder why you are still more active in Doujinshi market even after your professional debut.

K. It's not because Doujinshi has any special meaning. It's just the freedom that I enjoy. You can create anything you want in Doujinshi, including parodies of other properties. Even when working on original material, you have more freedom than if it were a commercial manhwa. I'm not saying that commercial manhwa is not fun, but I just think there is more variety and freedom in the Doujinshi market.

Q . Any last words?

K. I'm sorry for being late on e-mail replies. I'm not good at that. I think I'm going to reply today... then today becomes a week... and then that becomes a month... and then it feels awkward to reply that late, so I run away from them... -.-;;;;;
I would like to thank everyone who read my first ongoing manhwa. And special thanks to all the colleagues and publishing staffs who have been putting up with me and helping me to make a better manhwa. Thank you so much. >o<

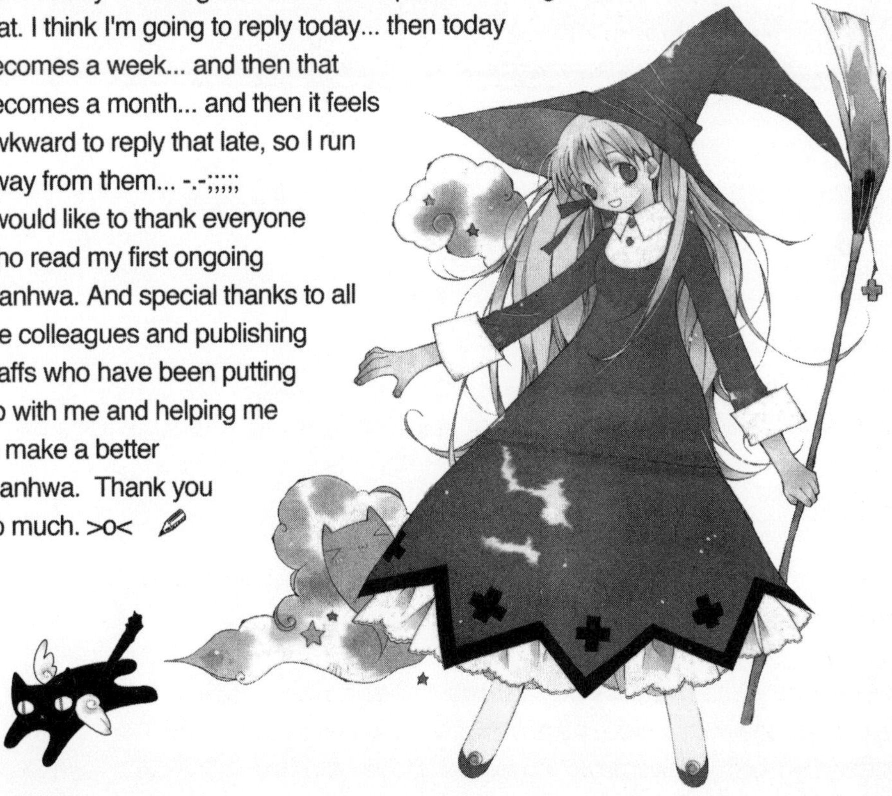

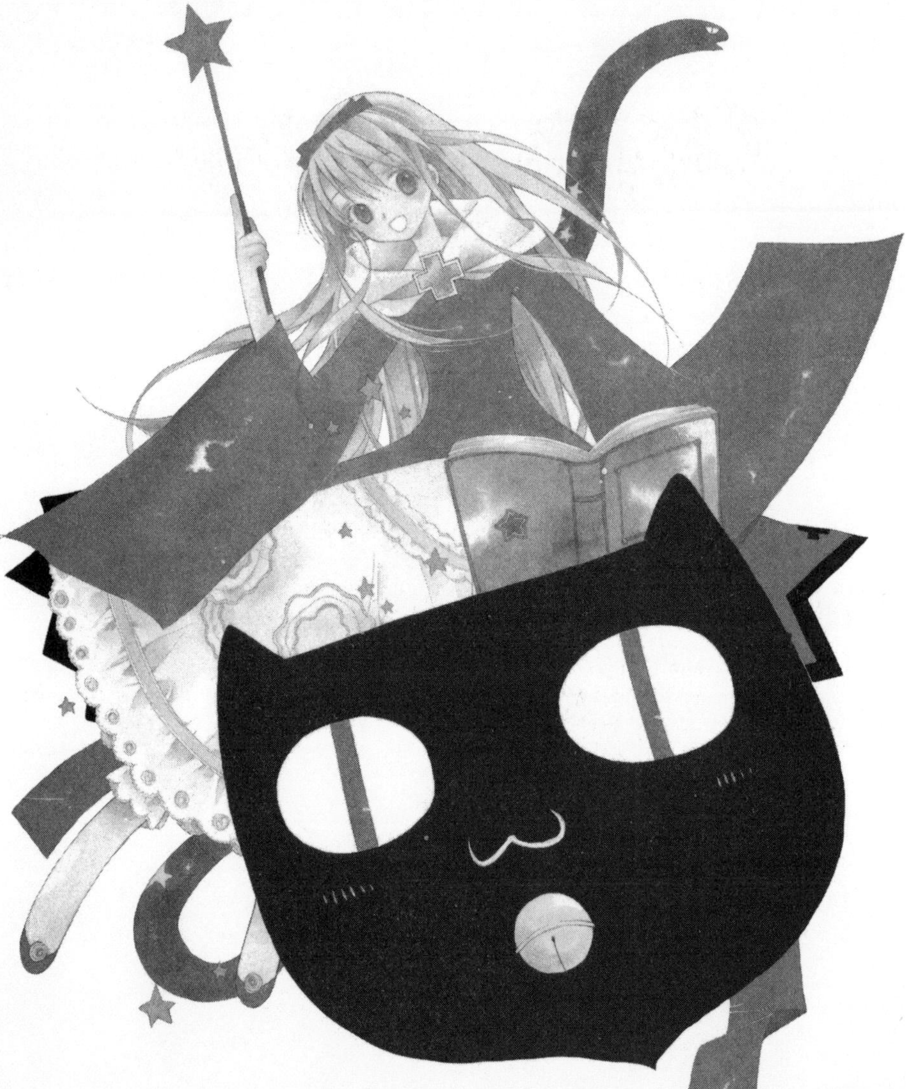

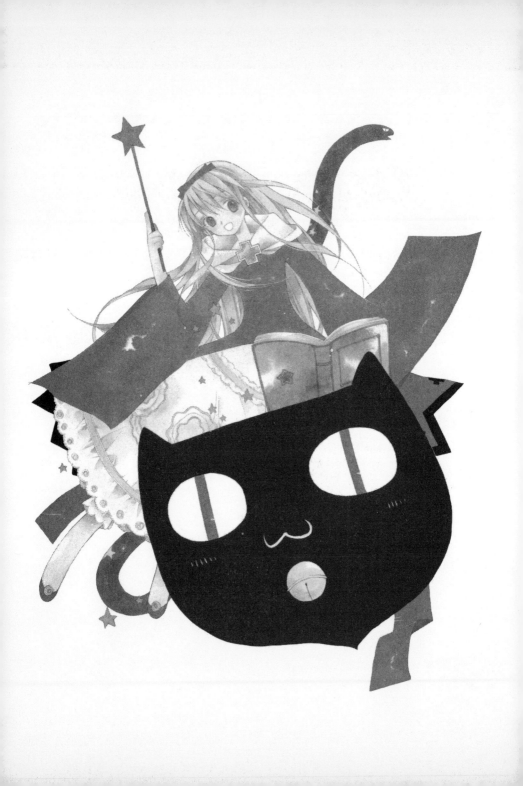

CHOCOLAT

vol.1

Shin JiSang ·Geo

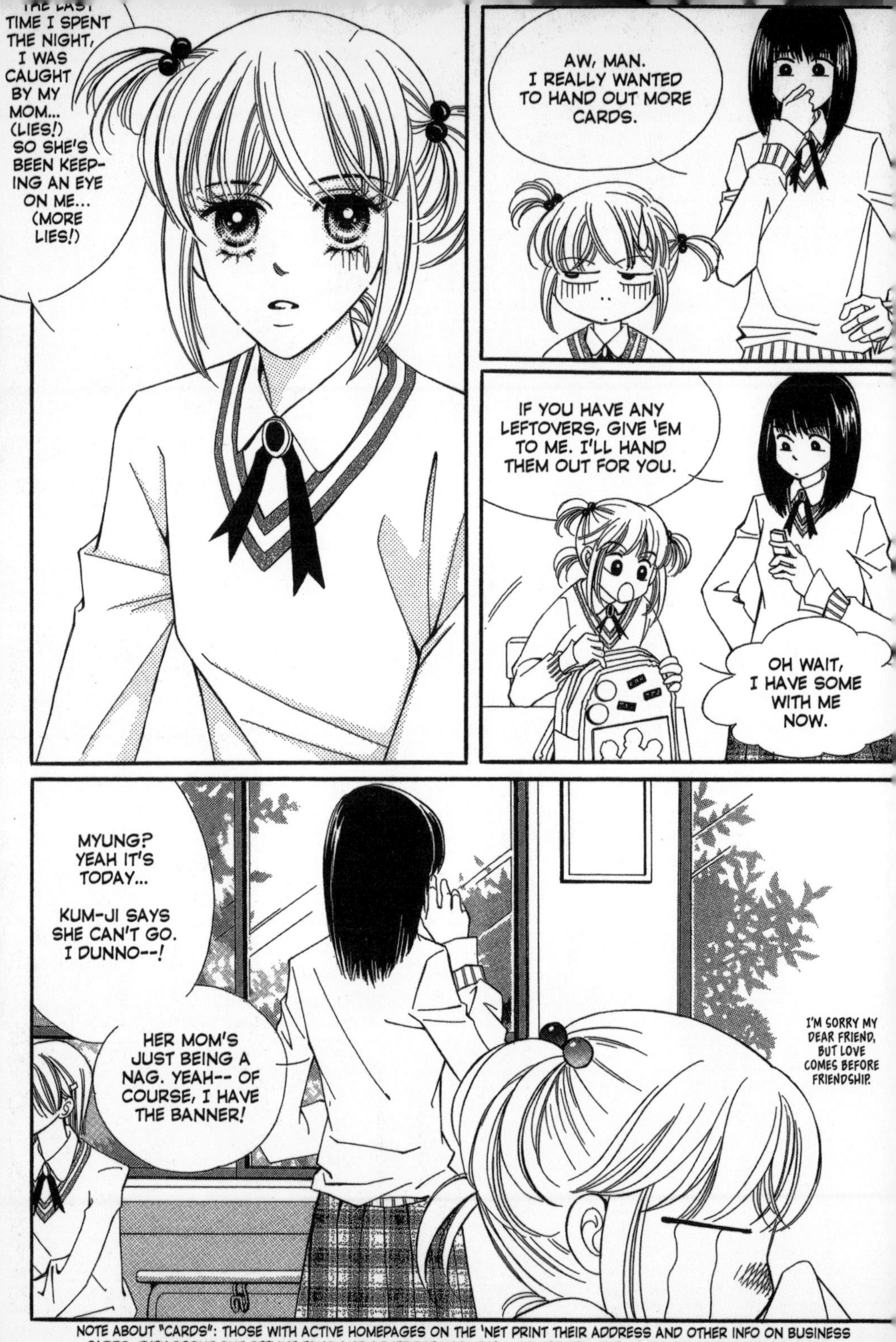
THE LAST TIME I SPENT THE NIGHT, I WAS CAUGHT BY MY MOM... (LIES!) SO SHE'S BEEN KEEP-ING AN EYE ON ME... (MORE LIES!)
AW, MAN. I REALLY WANTED TO HAND OUT MORE CARDS.
IF YOU HAVE ANY LEFTOVERS, GIVE 'EM TO ME. I'LL HAND THEM OUT FOR YOU.
OH WAIT, I HAVE SOME WITH ME NOW.
MYUNG? YEAH IT'S TODAY...
KUM-JI SAYS SHE CAN'T GO. I DUNNO--!
HER MOM'S JUST BEING A NAG. YEAH-- OF COURSE, I HAVE THE BANNER!
I'M SORRY MY DEAR FRIEND, BUT LOVE COMES BEFORE FRIENDSHIP.

NOTE ABOUT "CARDS": THOSE WITH ACTIVE HOMEPAGES ON THE 'NET PRINT THEIR ADDRESS AND OTHER INFO ON BUSINESS CARDS. THEY SCOUT OUT OFFLINE FANS AND ADVERTISE WITH THEM. SOMETIMES, THEY JUST TRADE AND COLLECT THEM.

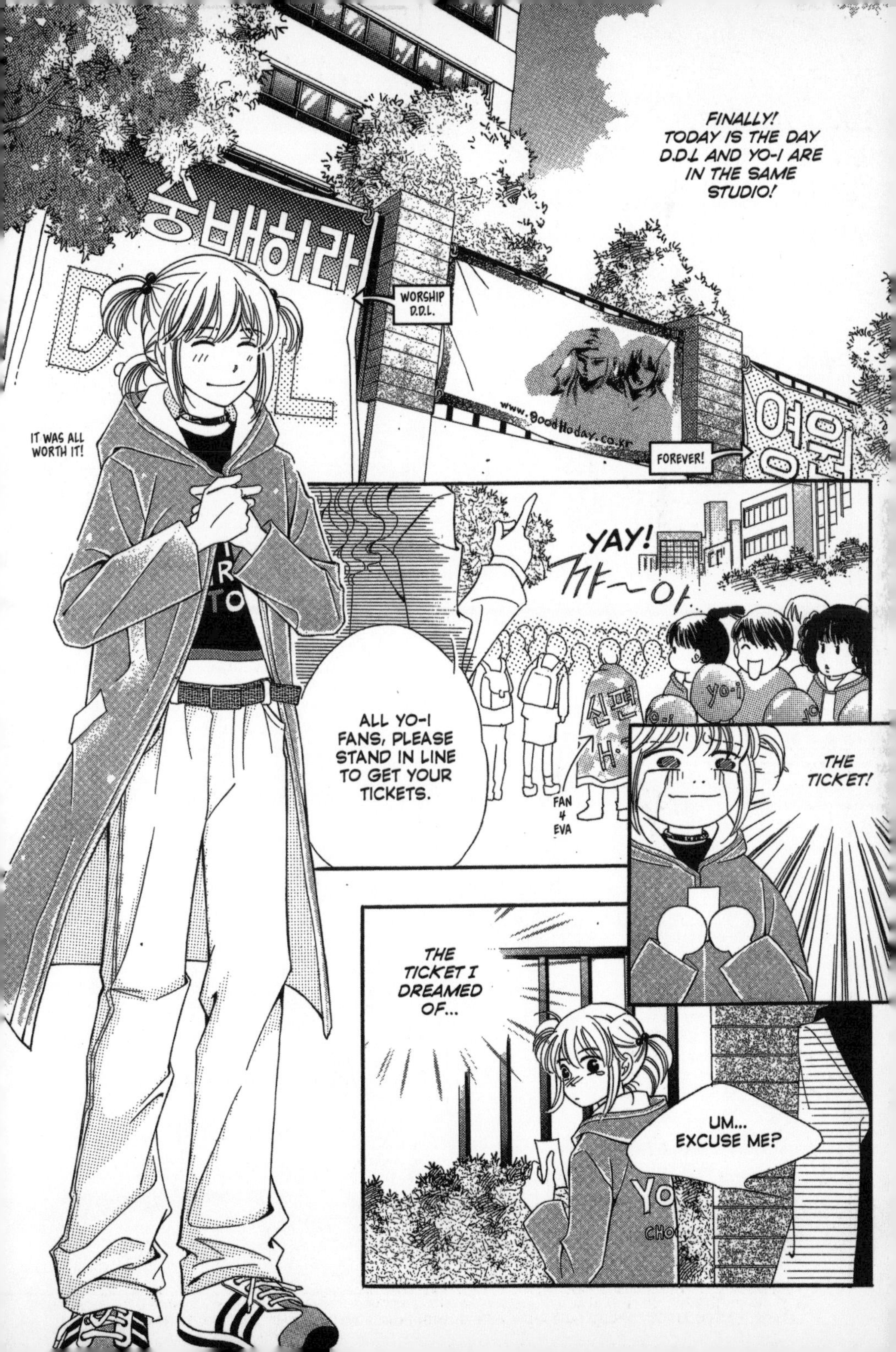
숭배하라
D.D.L.
WORSHIP D.D.L.
FINALLY! TODAY IS THE DAY D.D.L AND YO-I ARE IN THE SAME STUDIO!
www.goodtoday.co.kr
FOREVER!
IT WAS ALL WORTH IT!
YAY!
꺄~아
ALL YO-I FANS, PLEASE STAND IN LINE TO GET YOUR TICKETS.
FAN 4 EVA
THE TICKET!
THE TICKET I DREAMED OF...
UM... EXCUSE ME?

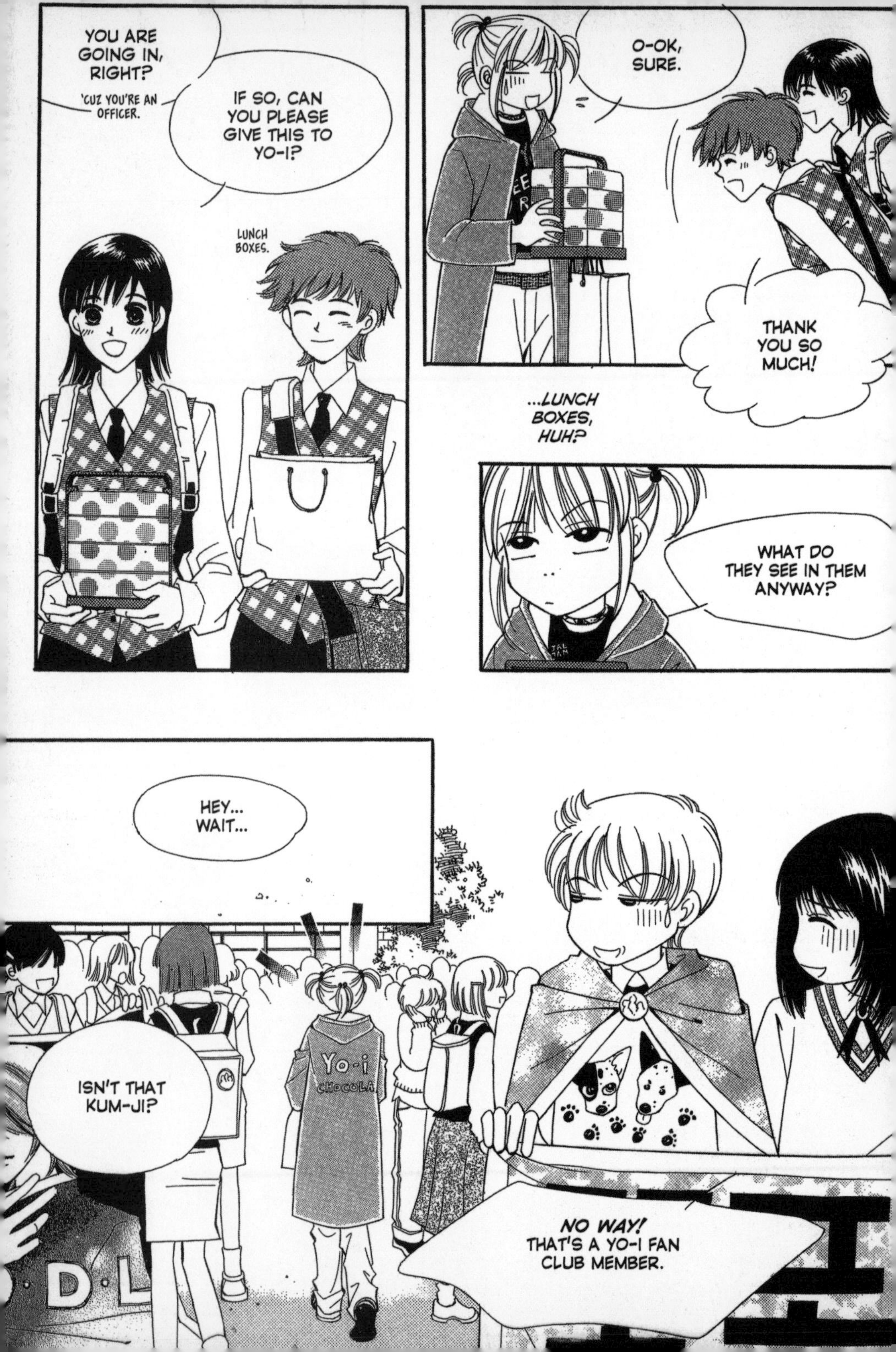
YOU ARE GOING IN, RIGHT?
'CUZ YOU'RE AN OFFICER.
IF SO, CAN YOU PLEASE GIVE THIS TO YO-I?
LUNCH BOXES.
O-OK, SURE.
THANK YOU SO MUCH!
...LUNCH BOXES, HUH?
WHAT DO THEY SEE IN THEM ANYWAY?
HEY... WAIT...
ISN'T THAT KUM-JI?
Yo-i
CHOCOLA
NO WAY! THAT'S A YO-I FAN CLUB MEMBER.

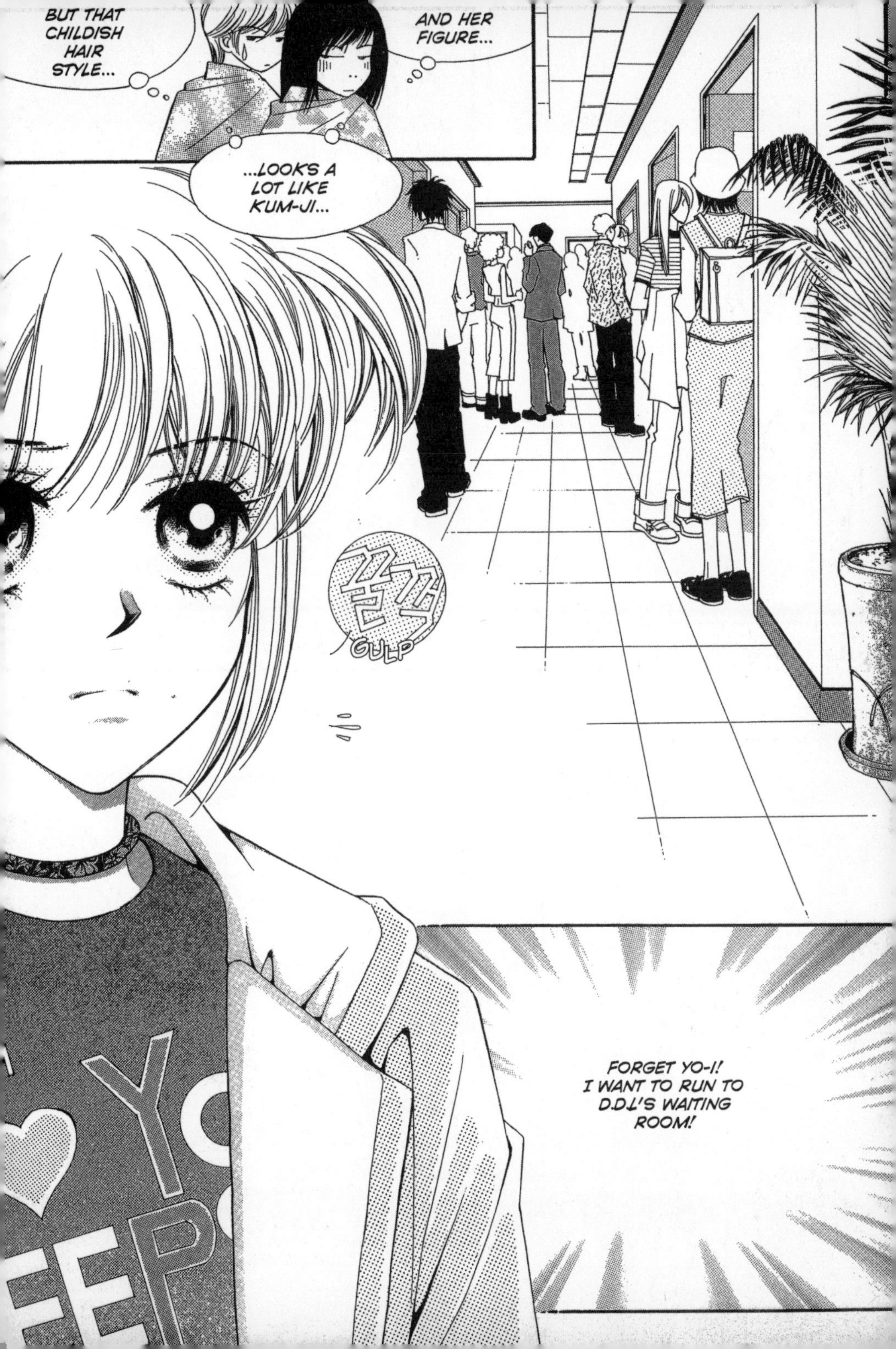
BUT THAT CHILDISH HAIR STYLE...
AND HER FIGURE...
...LOOKS A LOT LIKE KUM-JI...
꿀꺽
GULP
FORGET YO-I! I WANT TO RUN TO D.D.L'S WAITING ROOM!

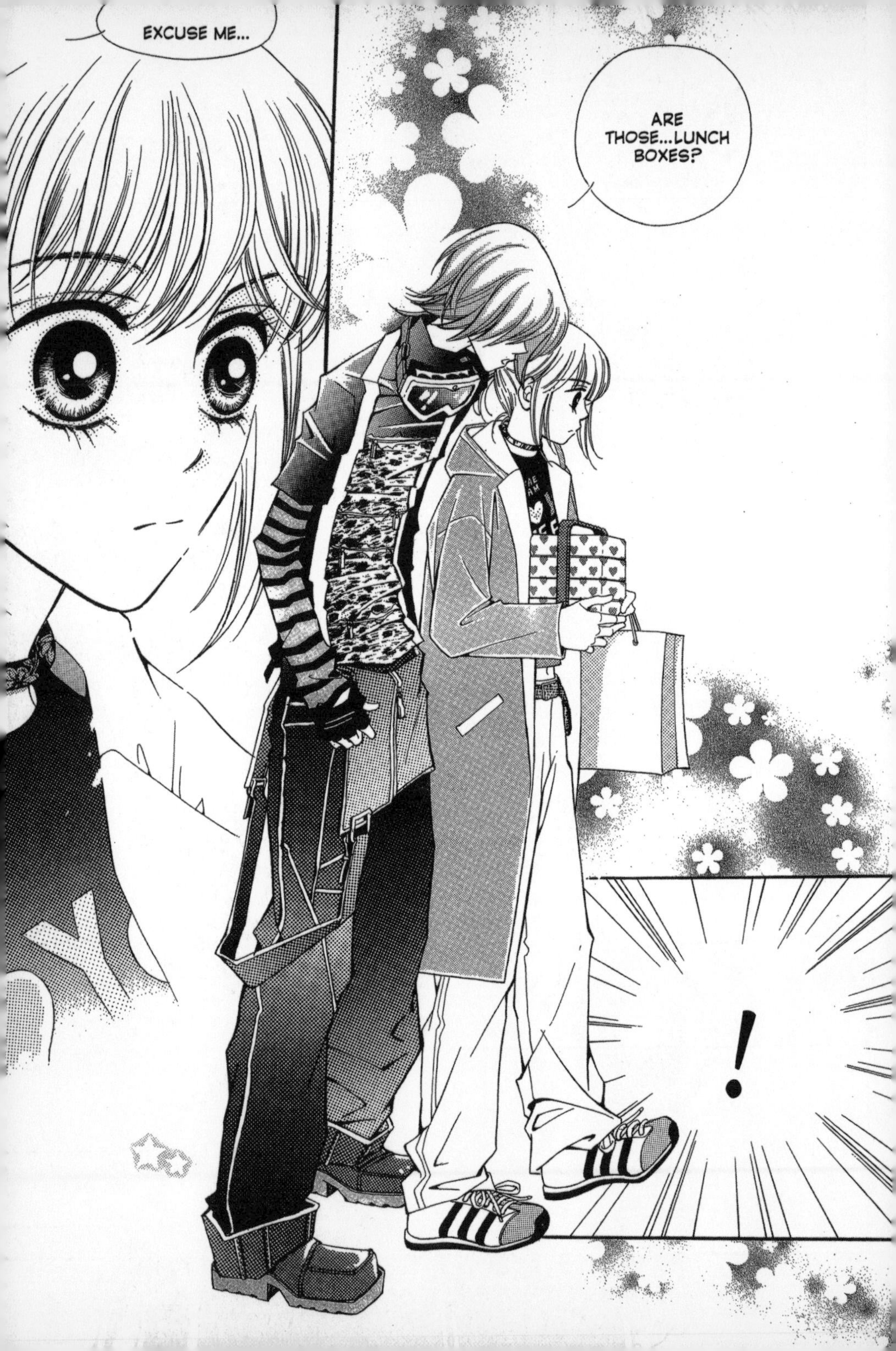
EXCUSE ME...
ARE THOSE...LUNCH BOXES?
!

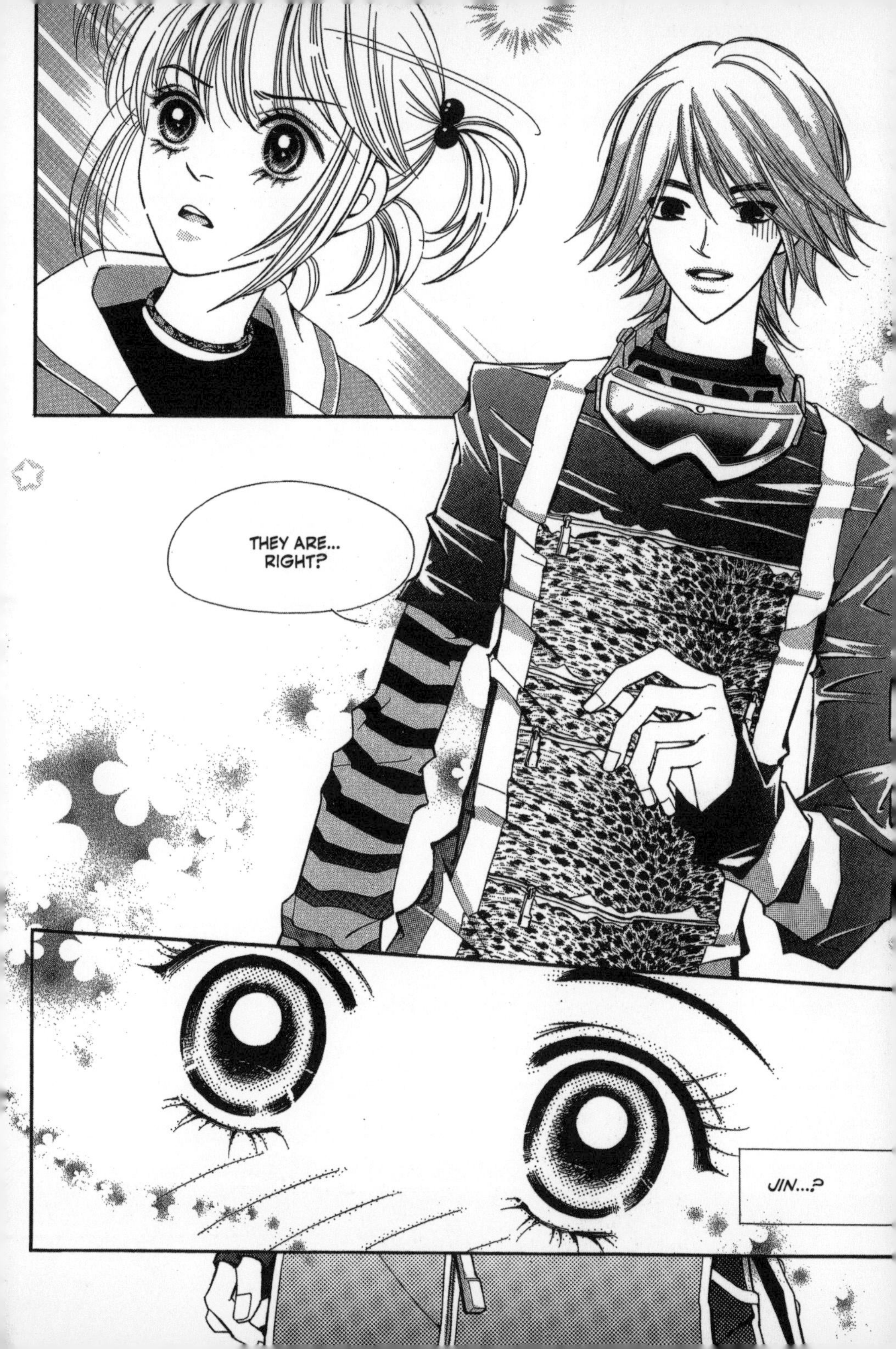
THEY ARE... RIGHT?
JIN...?

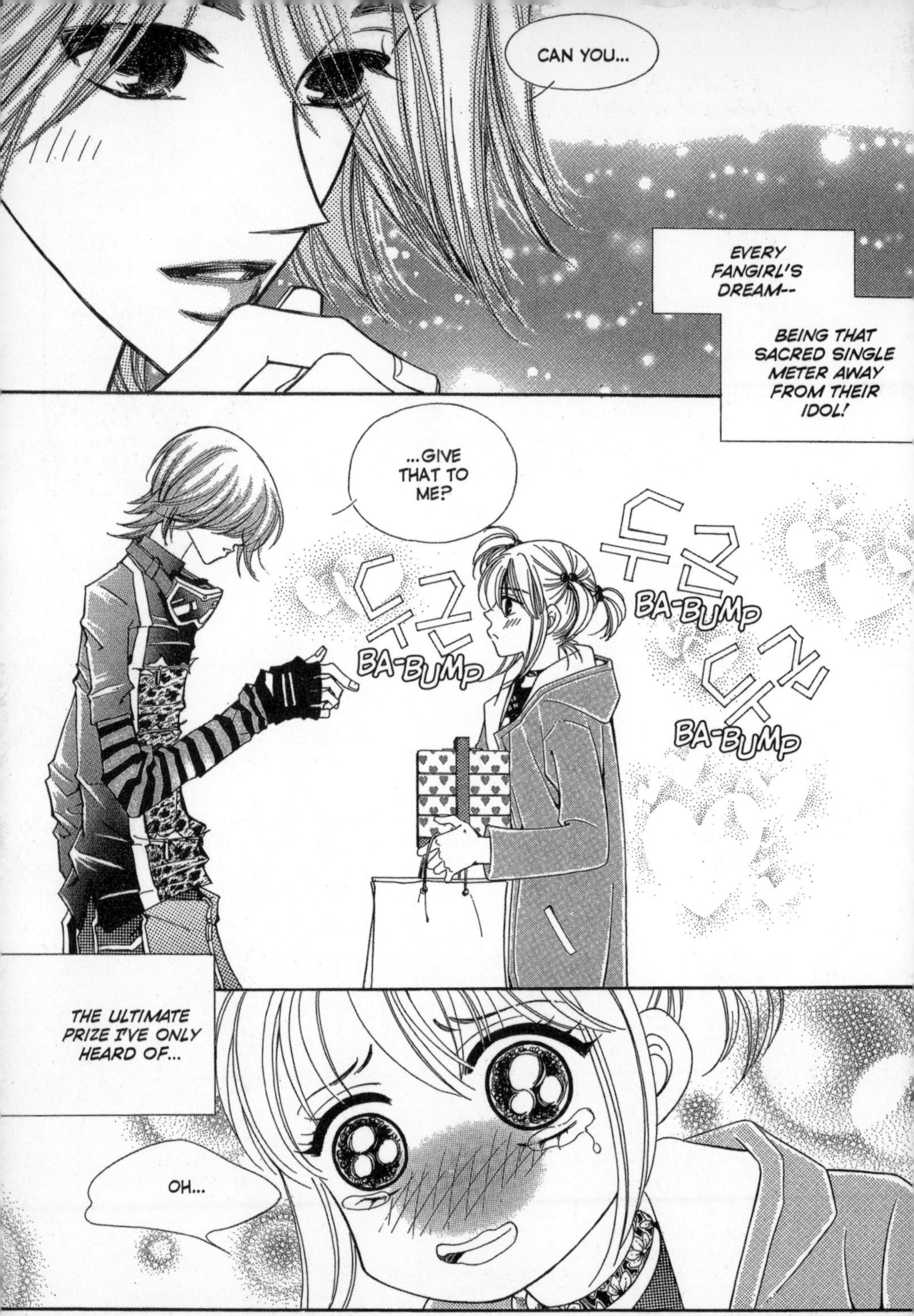
CAN YOU...
EVERY FANGIRL'S DREAM--
BEING THAT SACRED SINGLE METER AWAY FROM THEIR IDOL!
...GIVE THAT TO ME?
두근
BA-BUMP
두근
BA-BUMP
두근
BA-BUMP
THE ULTIMATE PRIZE I'VE ONLY HEARD OF...
OH...

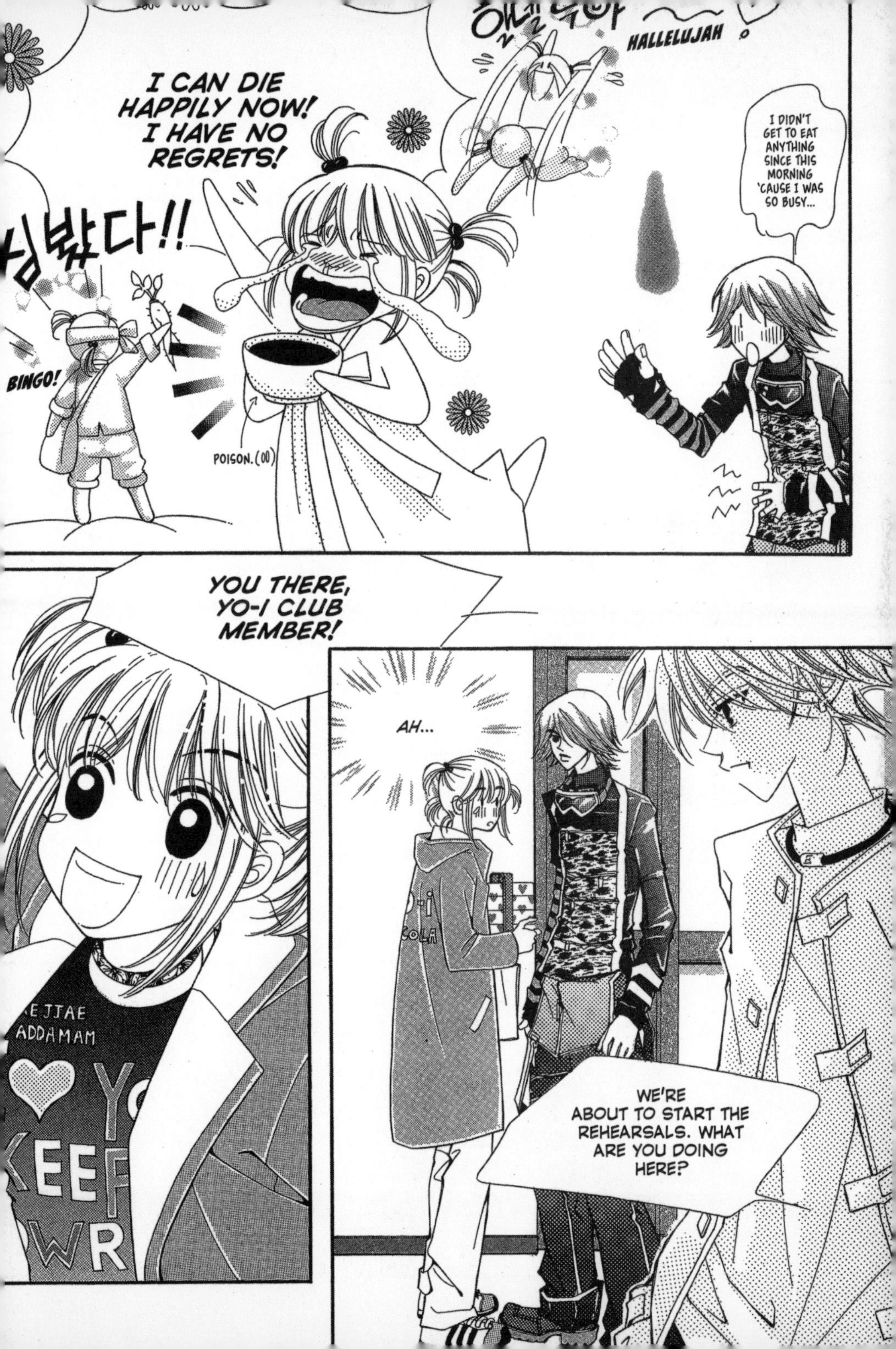
I CAN DIE HAPPILY NOW! I HAVE NO REGRETS!
심봤다!!
BINGO!
POISON.(00)
HALLELUJAH
I DIDN'T GET TO EAT ANYTHING SINCE THIS MORNING 'CAUSE I WAS SO BUSY...
YOU THERE, YO-I CLUB MEMBER!
AH...
WE'RE ABOUT TO START THE REHEARSALS. WHAT ARE YOU DOING HERE?

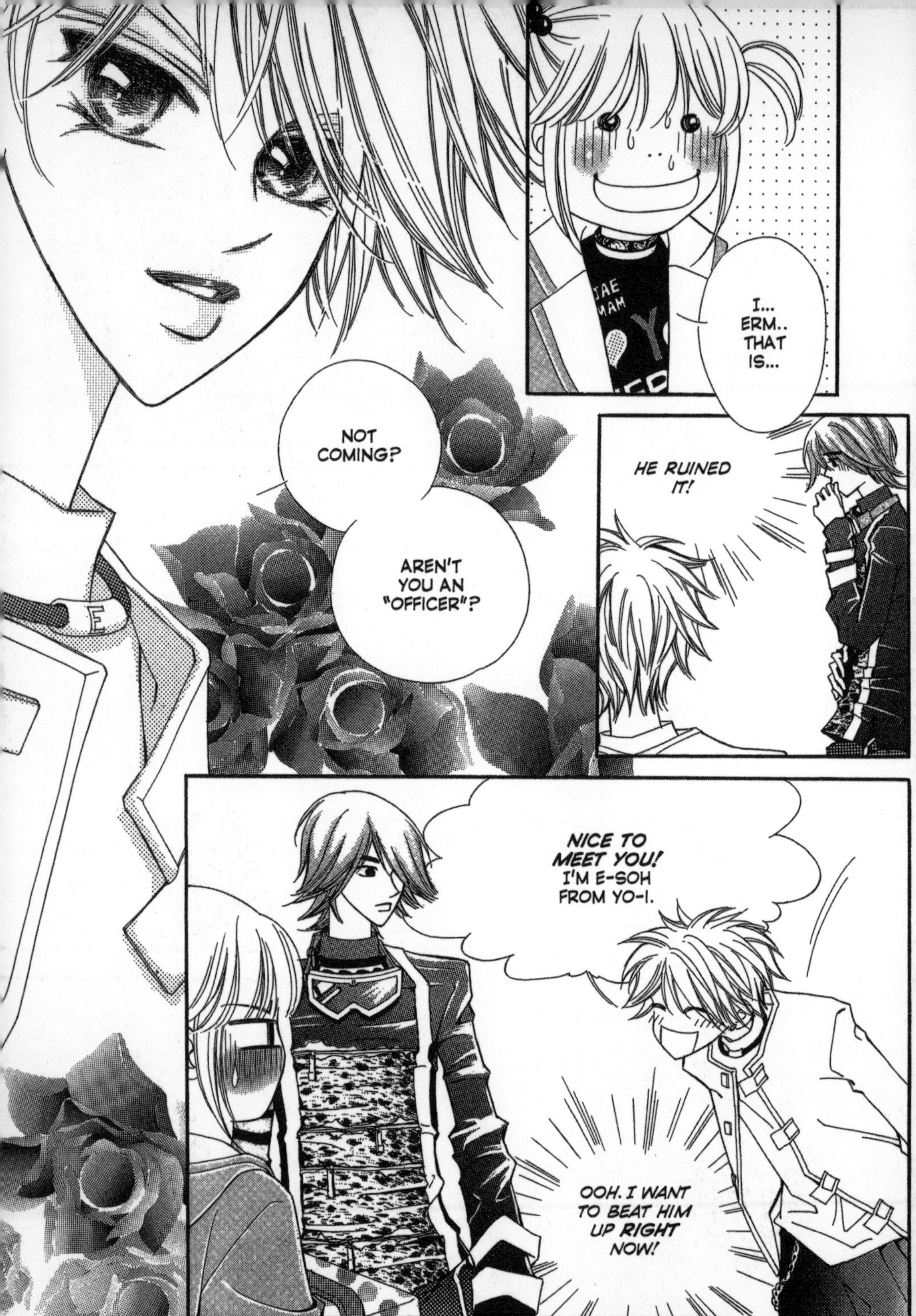
NOT COMING?
AREN'T YOU AN "OFFICER"?
I... ERM.. THAT IS...
HE RUINED IT!
NICE TO MEET YOU! I'M E-SOH FROM YO-I.
OOH. I WANT TO BEAT HIM UP RIGHT NOW!

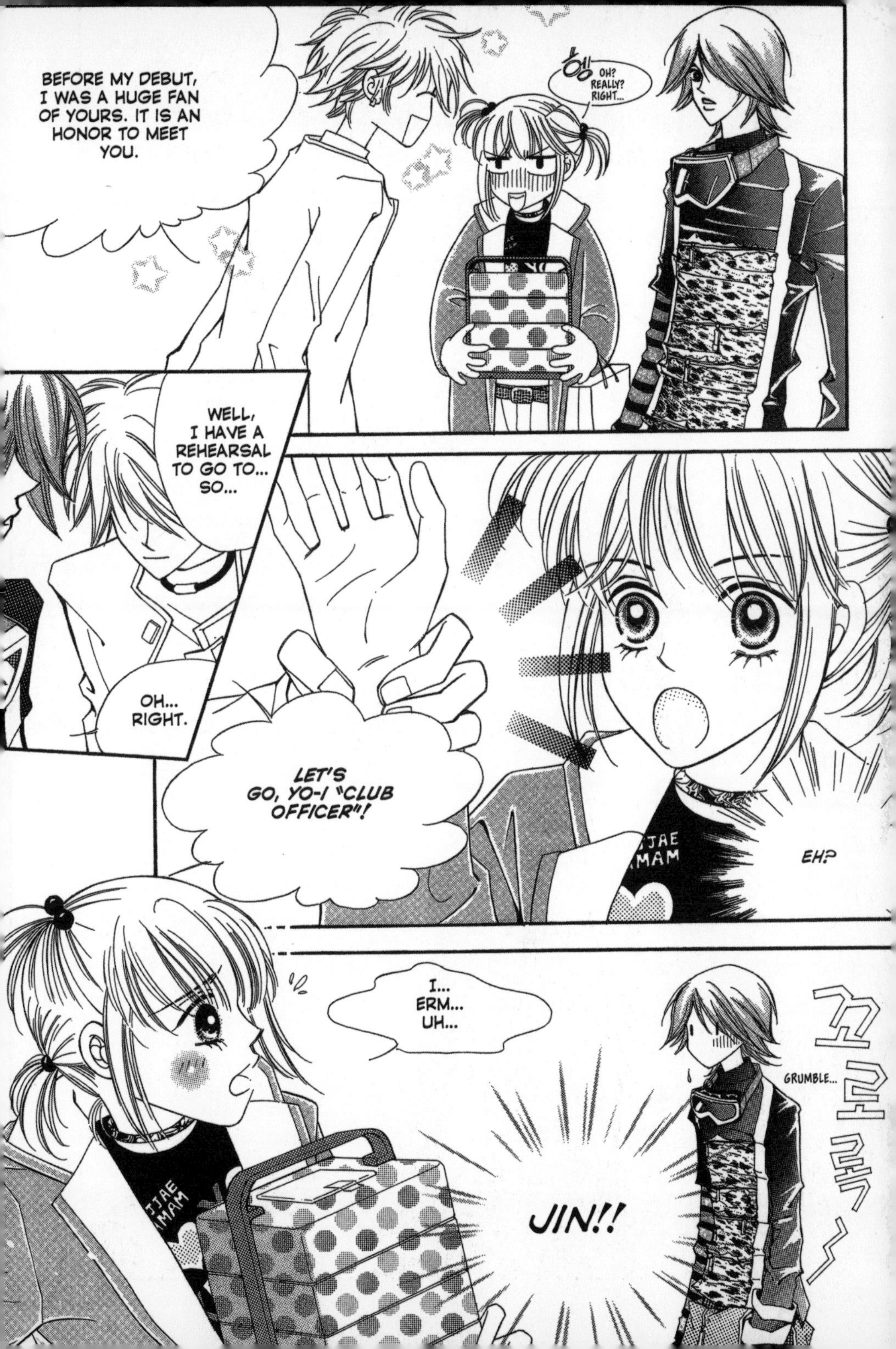
BEFORE MY DEBUT, I WAS A HUGE FAN OF YOURS. IT IS AN HONOR TO MEET YOU.
OH? REALLY? RIGHT...
WELL, I HAVE A REHEARSAL TO GO TO... SO...
OH... RIGHT.
LET'S GO, YO-I "CLUB OFFICER"!
EH?
I... ERM... UH...
JIN!!
GRUMBLE...

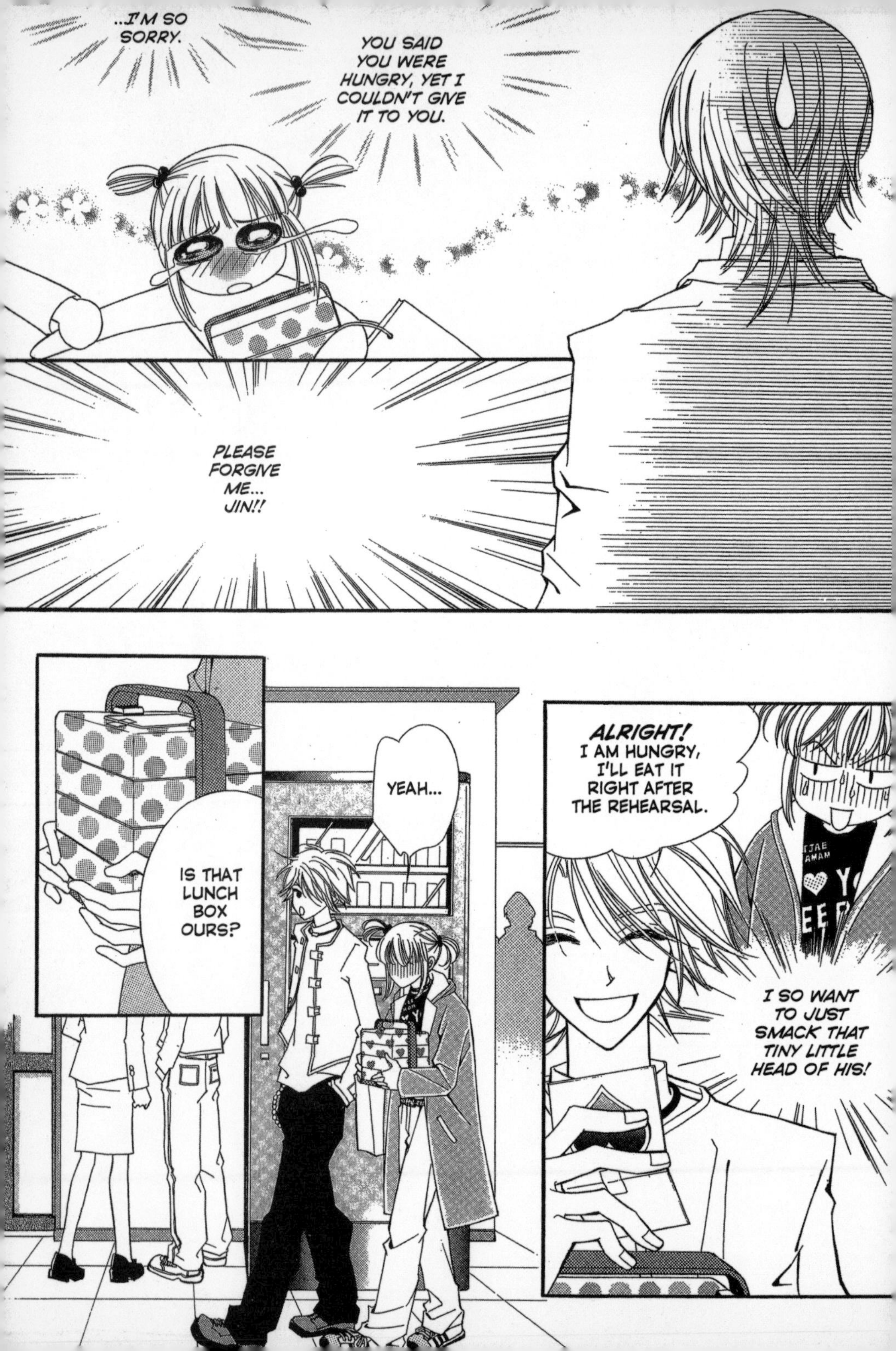
...I'M SO SORRY.
YOU SAID YOU WERE HUNGRY, YET I COULDN'T GIVE IT TO YOU.
PLEASE FORGIVE ME... JIN!!
IS THAT LUNCH BOX OURS?
YEAH...
ALRIGHT! I AM HUNGRY, I'LL EAT IT RIGHT AFTER THE REHEARSAL.
I SO WANT TO JUST SMACK THAT TINY LITTLE HEAD OF HIS!

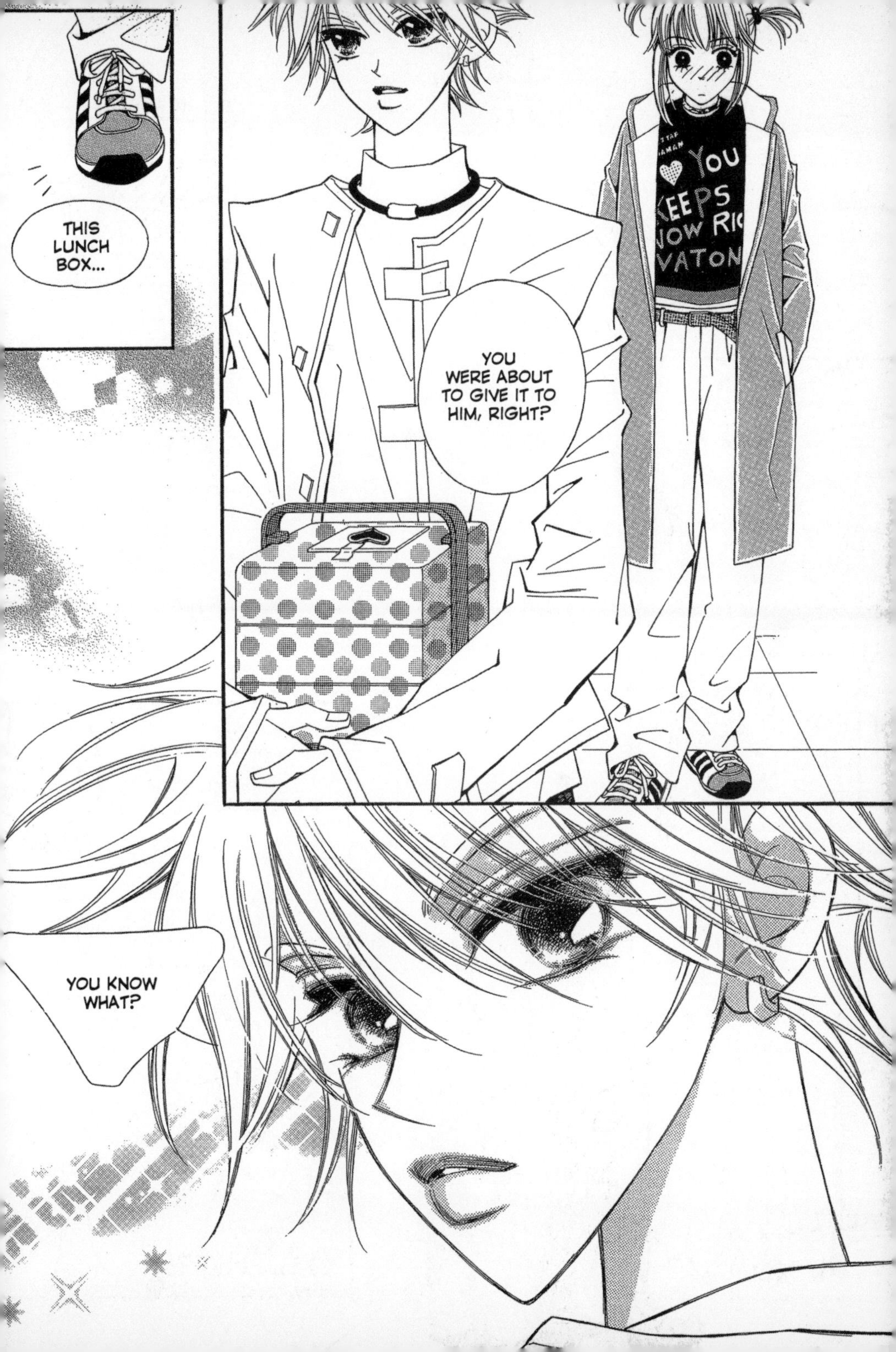
THIS LUNCH BOX...
YOU WERE ABOUT TO GIVE IT TO HIM, RIGHT?
YOU KNOW WHAT?

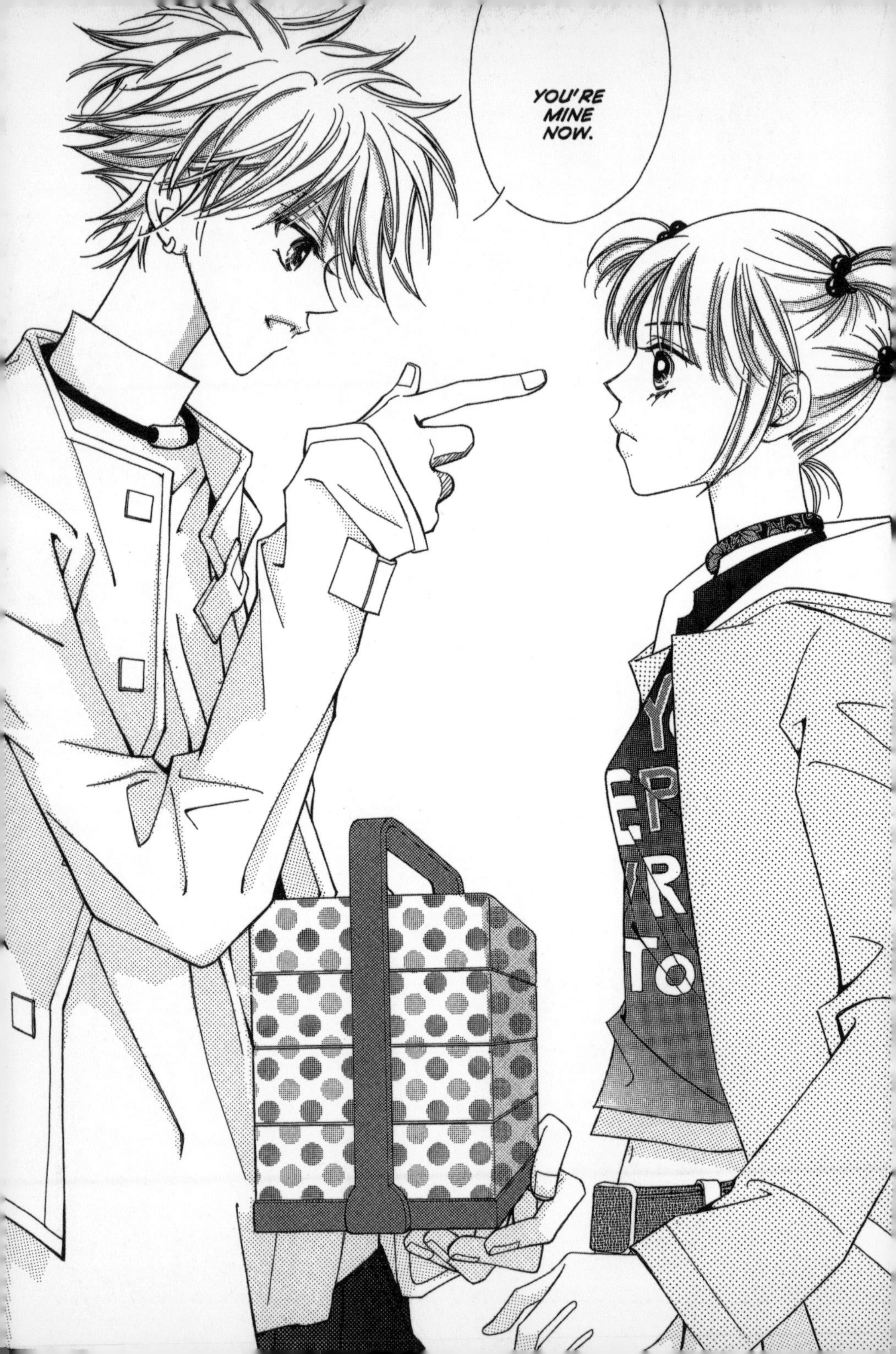
YOU'RE MINE NOW.

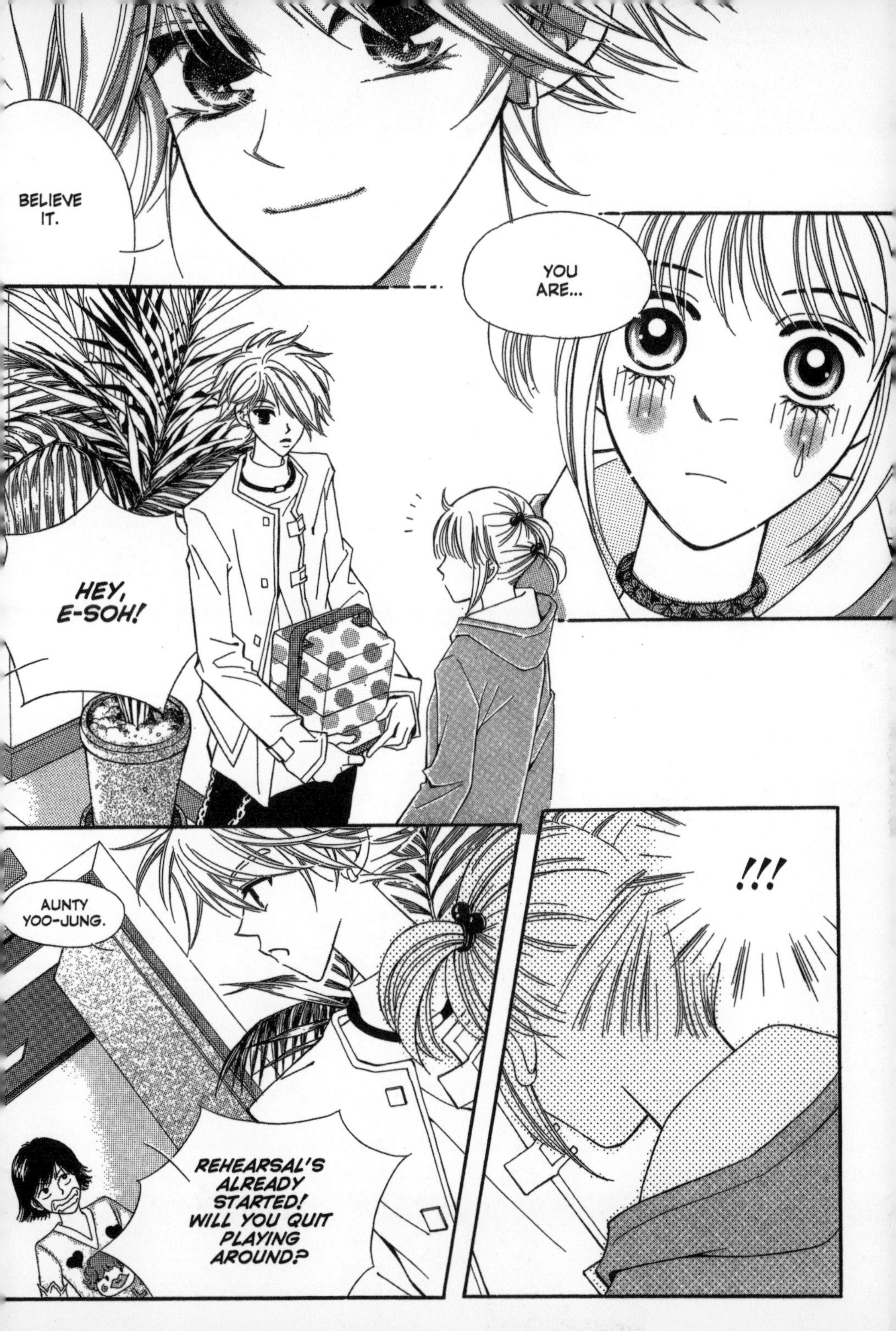
BELIEVE IT.
YOU ARE...
HEY, E-SOH!
AUNTY YOO-JUNG.
!!!
REHEARSAL'S ALREADY STARTED! WILL YOU QUIT PLAYING AROUND?

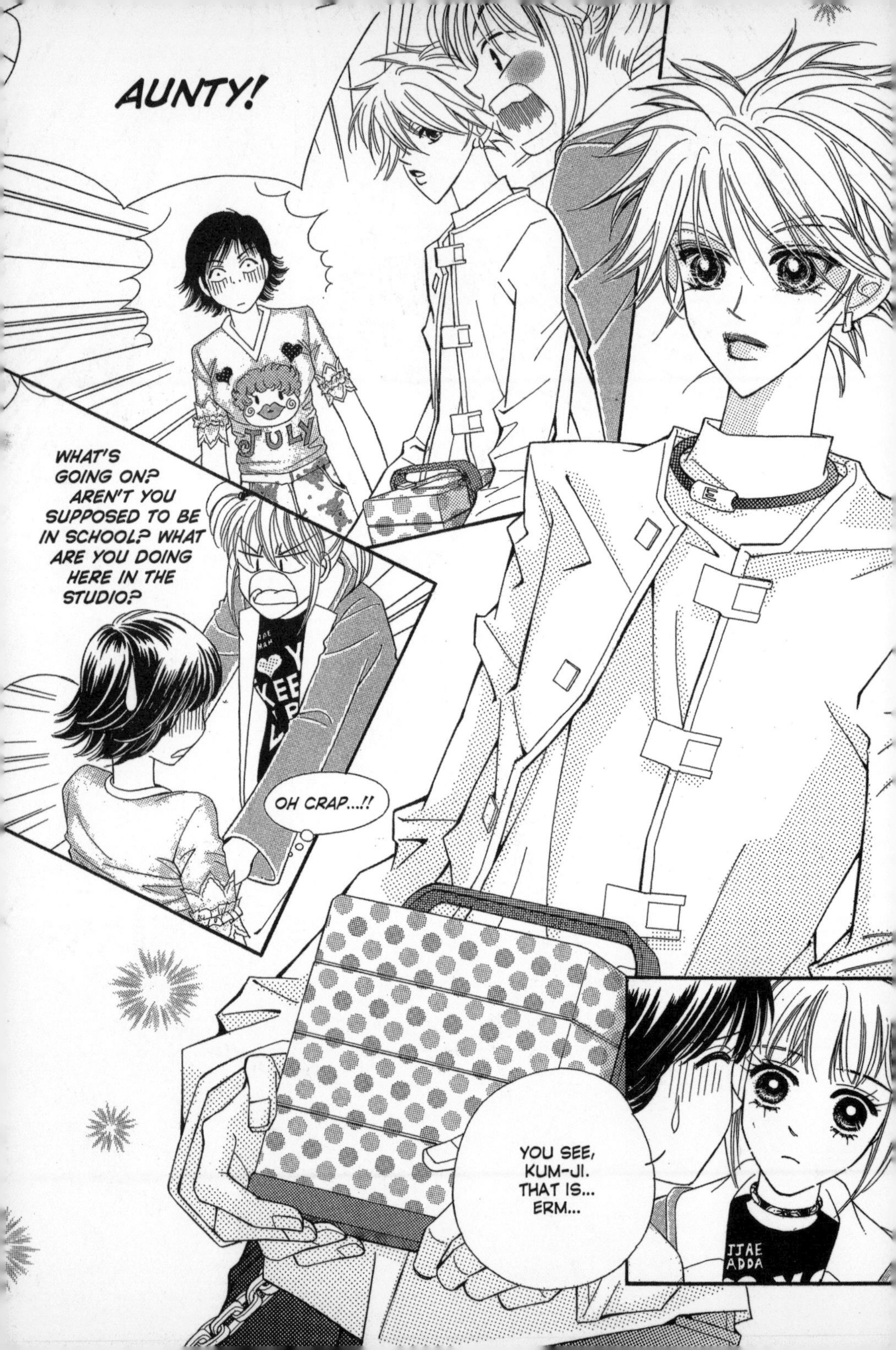
AUNTY!
WHAT'S GOING ON? AREN'T YOU SUPPOSED TO BE IN SCHOOL? WHAT ARE YOU DOING HERE IN THE STUDIO?
OH CRAP...!!
YOU SEE, KUM-JI. THAT IS... ERM...

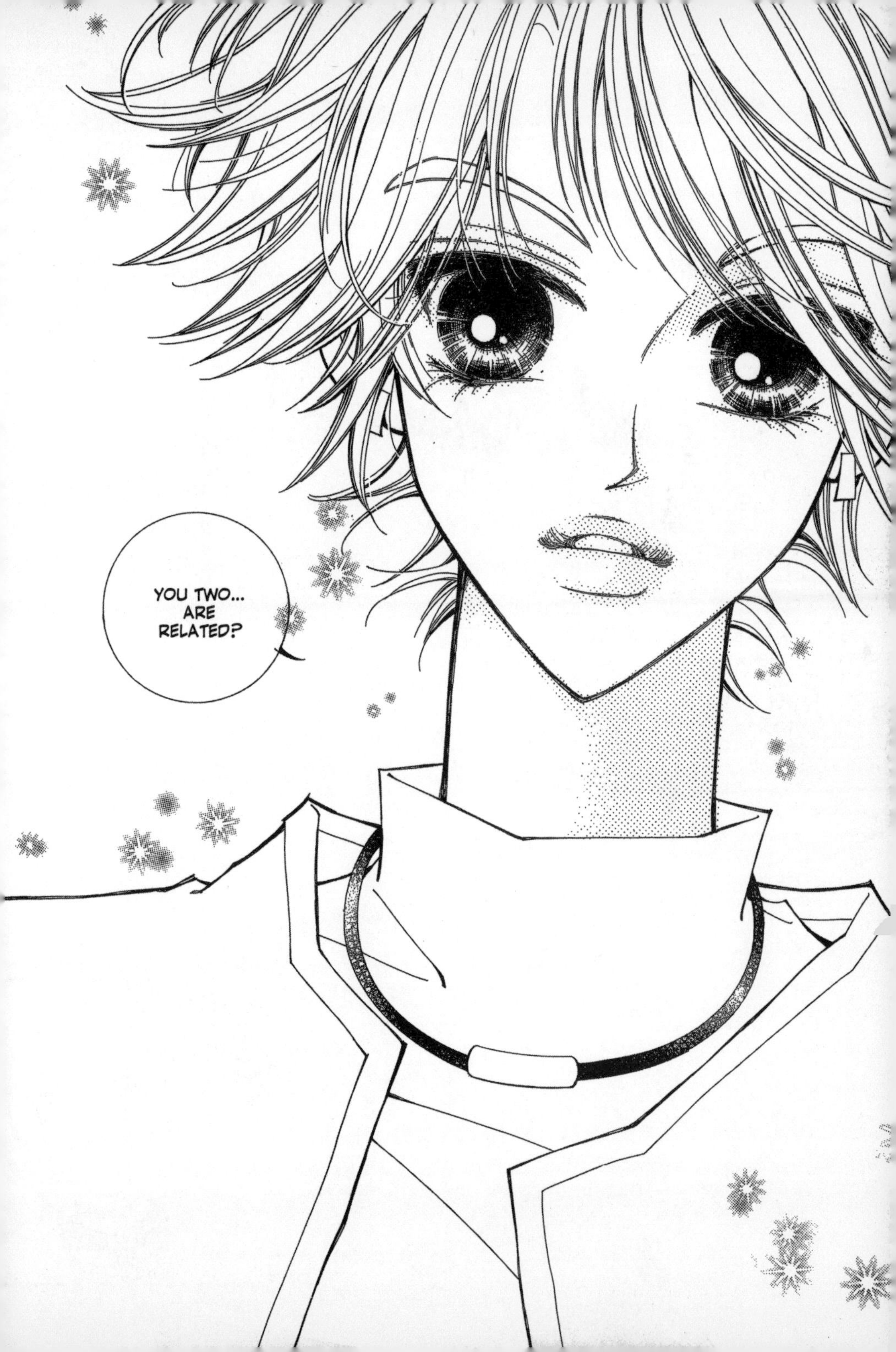
YOU TWO... ARE RELATED?

Danbi Original

11th cat vol.1

Story and art by MiKyung Kim

Translation JiMin Gong · Michelle Lee
English Adaptation Michelle Lee
Touch-up and Lettering Marshall Dillon
Graphic Design EunKyung Kim · YoungAh Cho
Assistant Editor Audra Furuichi
Editor JuYoun Lee

ICE Kunion

Project Manager Chan Park
Marketing Manager Erik Ko
Editor in Chief Eddie Yu
Publishing Director JeongHyun Chin
Publisher and C.E.O. JaeKook Chun

11th cat © 2005 MiKyung Kim
First published in Korea in 2002 by SIGONGSA Co., Ltd.
English text translation rights arranged by SIGONGSA Co., Ltd.
English text © 2005 ICE KUNION

Published by ICE Kunion
SIGONGSA 2F Yeil Bldg. 1619-4, Seocho-dong, Seocho-gu, Seoul, 137-878, Korea

ISBN : 89-527-4461-6

First printing, October 2005
10 9 8 7 6 5 4 3 2 1
Printed in Canada

www.ICEkunion.com/www.koreanmanhwa.com